# English-Tagalog
# Tagalog-English

Word to Word®
Bilingual Dictionary

Compiled by:
C. Sesma M.A.

Translated by:
Norma Smith

**Bilingual Dictionaries, Inc.**

**Tagalog Word to Word® Bilingual Dictionary**



Published in the United States by:

**Bilingual Dictionaries, Inc.**
PO Box 1154
Murrieta, CA 92562
T: (951) 461-6893 • F: (951) 461-3092
www.BilingualDictionaries.com

**ISBN13: 978-0-933146-37-2**
**ISBN: 0-933146-37-X**
**Printed in India**

# Preface

Bilingual Dictionaries, Inc. is committed to providing schools, libraries and educators with a great selection of bilingual materials for students. Along with bilingual dictionaries we also provide ESL materials, children's bilingual stories and children's bilingual picture dictionaries.

Sesma's Tagalog Word to Word® Bilingual Dictionary was created specifically with students in mind to be used for reference and testing. This dictionary contains approximately 17,500 entries targeting common words used in the English language.

# List of Irregular Verbs

**present - past - past participle**

**arise** - arose - arisen
**awake** - awoke - awoken, awaked
**be** - was - been
**bear** - bore - borne
**beat** - beat - beaten
**become** - became - become
**begin** - began - begun
**behold** - beheld - beheld
**bend** - bent - bent
**beseech** - besought - besought
**bet** - bet - betted
**bid** - bade (bid) - bidden (bid)
**bind** - bound - bound
**bite** - bit - bitten
**bleed** - bled - bled
**blow** - blew - blown
**break** - broke - broken
**breed** - bred - bred
**bring** - brought - brought
**build** - built - built
**burn** - burnt - burnt *
**burst** - burst - burst
**buy** - bought - bought
**cast** - cast - cast
**catch** - caught - caught
**choose** - chose - chosen
**cling** - clung - clung
**come** - came - come
**cost** - cost - cost
**creep** - crept - crept
**cut** - cut - cut
**deal** - dealt - dealt
**dig** - dug - dug
**do** - did - done
**draw** - drew - drawn
**dream** - dreamt - dreamed
**drink** - drank - drunk
**drive** - drove - driven
**dwell** - dwelt - dwelt
**eat** - ate - eaten
**fall** - fell - fallen
**feed** - fed - fed
**feel** - felt - felt
**fight** - fought - fought
**find** - found - found
**flee** - fled - fled
**fling** - flung - flung
**fly** - flew - flown
**forebear** - forbore - forborne
**forbid** - forbade - forbidden
**forecast** - forecast - forecast
**forget** - forgot - forgotten
**forgive** - forgave - forgiven
**forego** - forewent - foregone
**foresee** - foresaw - foreseen
**foretell** - foretold - foretold
**forget** - forgot - forgotten
**forsake** - forsook - forsaken
**freeze** - froze - frozen
**get** - got - gotten
**give** - gave - given
**go** - went - gone
**grind** - ground - ground
**grow** - grew - grown
**hang** - hung * - hung *
**have** - had - had

**hear -** heard - heard
**hide -** hid - hidden
**hit -** hit - hit
**hold -** held - held
**hurt -** hurt - hurt
**hit -** hit - hit
**hold -** held - held
**keep -** kept - kept
**kneel -** knelt * - knelt *
**know -** knew - known
**lay -** laid - laid
**lead -** led - led
**lean -** leant * - leant *
**leap -** lept * - lept *
**learn -** learnt * - learnt *
**leave -** left - left
**lend -** lent - lent
**let -** let - let
**lie -** lay - lain
**light -** lit * - lit *
**lose -** lost - lost
**make -** made - made
**mean -** meant - meant
**meet -** met - met
**mistake -** mistook - mistaken
**must -** had to - had to
**pay -** paid - paid
**plead -** pleaded - pled
**prove -** proved - proven
**put -** put - put
**quit -** quit * - quit *
**read -** read - read
**rid -** rid - rid
**ride -** rode - ridden
**ring -** rang - rung
**rise -** rose - risen
**run -** ran - run
**saw -** sawed - sawn
**say -** said - said
**see -** saw - seen
**seek -** sought - sought
**sell -** sold - sold
**send -** sent - sent
**set -** set - set
**sew -** sewed - sewn
**shake -** shook - shaken
**shear -** sheared - shorn
**shed -** shed - shed
**shine -** shone - shone
**shoot -** shot - shot
**show -** showed - shown
**shrink -** shrank - shrunk
**shut -** shut - shut
**sing -** sang - sung
**sink -** sank - sunk
**sit -** sat - sat
**slay -** slew - slain
**sleep -** sleep - slept
**slide -** slid - slid
**sling -** slung - slung
**smell -** smelt * - smelt *
**sow -** sowed - sown *
**speak -** spoke - spoken
**speed -** sped * - sped *
**spell -** spelt * - spelt *
**spend -** spent - spent
**spill -** spilt * - spilt *
**spin -** spun - spun

**spit** - spat - spat
**split** - split - split
**spread** - spread - spread
**spring** - sprang - sprung
**stand** - stood - stood
**steal** - stole - stolen
**stick** - stuck - stuck
**sting** - stung - stung
**stink** - stank - stunk
**stride** - strode - stridden
**strike** - struck - struck (stricken)
**strive** - strove - striven
**swear** - swore - sworn
**sweep** - swept - swept
**swell** - swelled - swollen *
**swim** - swam - swum
**take** - took - taken
**teach** - taught - taught
**tear** - tore - torn
**tell** - told - told
**think** - thought - thought
**throw** - threw - thrown
**thrust** - thrust - thrust
**tread** - trod - trodden
**wake** - woke - woken
**wear** - wore - worn
**weave** - wove * - woven *
**wed** - wed * - wed *
**weep** - wept - wept
**win** - won - won
**wind** - wound - wound
**wring** - wrung - wrung
**write** - wrote - written

**Those tenses with an * also have regular forms.**

# English-Tagalog

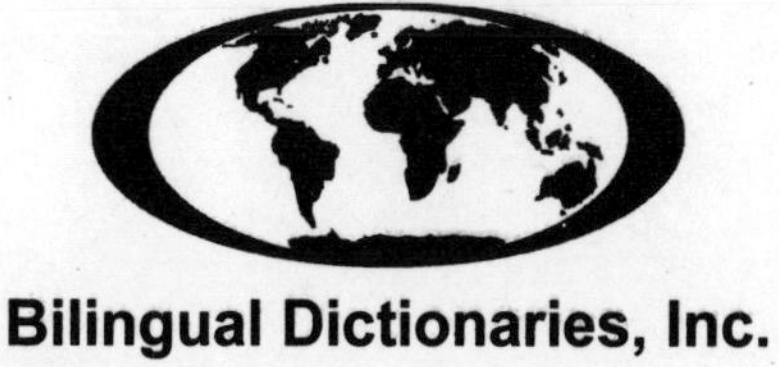

Bilingual Dictionaries, Inc.

# Abbreviations

**a** - article

**n** - noun

**e** - exclamation

**pro** - pronoun

**adj** - adjective

**adv** - adverb

**v** - verb

**iv** - irregular verb

**pre** - preposition

**c** - conjunction

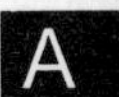

**a** *a* ang
**abandon** *v* iwanan
**abandonment** *n* pabayaan
**abbey** *n* kumbento
**abbot** *n* kura paroko
**abbreviate** *v* isatitik
**abbreviation** *n* panitik
**abdicate** *v* isuko
**abdication** *n* pag-suko
**abdomen** *n* tiyan
**abduct** *v* agawin
**abduction** *n* pag-sagw
**aberration** *n* sira
**abhor** *v* namumuhi
**abide by** *v* sundin
**ability** *n* kakayanan
**ablaze** *adj* pag-apoy
**able** *adj* kakayanan
**abnormal** *adj* hindi normal
**abnormality** *n* abnormalidad
**aboard** *adv* nakalulan
**abolish** *v* burahin
**abort** *v* tanggalin
**abortion** *n* pagtanggal
**abound** *v* pasaganain
**about** *pre* ukol sa
**about** *adv* ayon sa
**above** *pre* sa itaas
**abreast** *adv* inaalam
**abridge** *v* paikliin; pinaikli
**abroad** *adv* sa ibang bayan
**abrogate** *v* alisin; kanselahin
**abruptly** *adv* kaagad
**absence** *n* pagliban
**absent** *adj* maliban
**absolute** *adj* kabuuan
**absolution** *n* kapatawaran
**absolve** *v* pawalang sala
**absorb** *v* sipsipin
**absorbent** *adj* masipsip
**abstain** *v* mangiling
**abstinence** *n* pangiling
**absurd** *adj* walang katuturan
**abundance** *n* kasaganaan
**abundant** *adj* masagana
**abuse** *v* nilapastangan
**abuse** *n* lapastangan
**abysmal** *adj* karumaldumal
**academic** *adj* karunungan
**academy** *n* akademya
**accelerate** *v* itaas
**accent** *n* aksento
**accept** *v* tanggapin
**acceptance** *n* pagtanggap
**access** *n* daan; daanan
**accessible** *adj* dinadaanan
**accident** *n* aksidente
**accidental** *adj* di-sinasadya
**acclaim** *v* kilala
**acclimatize** *v* masanay
**accommodate** *v* patuluyin

**accompany** *v* samahan
**accomplice** *n* kasapakat
**accomplish** *v* ginawa
**accomplishment** *n* nagawa
**accord** *n* pagkakasundo
**according to** *pre* ayon sa
**accordion** *n* akordyon
**account** *n* pananagutan
**account for** *v* panagutan
**accountable** *adj* mananagot
**accountant** *n* taga-tuos
**accumulate** *v* naipon
**accuracy** *n* ganap
**accurate** *adj* tamang-tama
**accusation** *n* akusasyon
**accuse** *v* inakusahan
**accustom** *v* magsanay
**ace** *n* alas
**ache** *n* sakit
**achieve** *v* gawin
**achievement** *n* nagawa
**acid** *n* asim
**acidity** *n* kaasiman
**acknowledge** *v* kilalanin
**acorn** *n* bunga
**acoustic** *adj* akustika
**acquaint** *v* kilalanin
**acquaintance** *n* kakilala
**acquire** *v* magkamit
**acquisition** *n* nakamit
**acquit** *v* patawarin
**acquittal** *n* kapatawaran
**acre** *n* eyker
**acrobat** *n* payaso
**across** *pre* katapat
**act** *v* gumanap
**action** *n* aksyon
**activate** *v* paganahin
**activation** *n* pinagana
**active** *adj* magalaw
**activity** *n* kaganapan
**actor** *n* artistang lalaki
**actress** *n* artistang babae
**actual** *adj* tunay
**actually** *adv* sa katotohanan
**acute** *adj* matindi
**adamant** *adj* urong-sulong
**adapt** *v* umayon
**adaptable** *adj* mapag-ayon
**adaptation** *n* pag-aayon
**adapter** *n* pagsamahin
**add** *v* pagsamahin
**addicted** *adj* pagkasugapa
**addiction** *n* sugapa
**addictive** *adj* nakakasugapa
**addition** *n* pagdaragdag
**additional** *adj* karagdagan
**address** *n* adres
**address** *v* tirahan; talumpati
**addressee** *n* pinatungkulan
**adequate** *adj* sapat
**adhere** *v* idikit
**adhesive** *adj* madikit
**adjacent** *adj* katabi

**adjective** *n* pang-uri
**adjoin** *v* sumunod
**adjoining** *adj* kasunod
**adjourn** *v* itinigil
**adjust** *v* iayos; ayusin
**adjustable** *adj* maaayos
**adjustment** *n* pag-ayos
**administer** *v* mangasiwa
**admirable** *adj* kahanga-hanga
**admiral** *n* almirante
**admiration** *n* paghanga
**admire** *v* humanga
**admirer** *n* taagahanga
**admission** *n* tanggapan
**admit** *v* tanggapin
**admittance** *n* taga-tanggap
**admonish** *v* pagsabihan
**admonition** *n* paalala
**adolescence** *n* pabibinata
**adolescent** *n* pagbibinata
**adopt** *v* mag-ampon
**adoption** *n* ampon
**adorable** *adj* kahanga-hanga
**adoration** *n* pagsamba
**adore** *v* sambahin
**adorn** *v* palamutian
**adrift** *adv* naligaw
**adulation** *n* pagsamba
**adult** *n* matanda
**adulterate** *v* haluan
**adultery** *n* pangangalunya
**advance** *v* iuna; isulong
**advance** *n* pauna
**advantage** *n* pakinabang
**Advent** *n* Pagdating
**adverb** *n* panag-uri
**adversary** *n* kalaban
**adverse** *adj* di -sang-ayon
**adversity** *n* kamalasan
**advertise** *v* ipamalita
**advertising** *n* balita; anunsyo
**advice** *n* turo; payo
**advisable** *adj* maipapayo
**advise** *v* turuan
**adviser** *n* tagapayo
**advocate** *v* mag-apila
**aeroplane** *n* salipawpaw
**aesthetic** *adj* kagandahan
**afar** *adv* malayo
**affable** *adj* palakaibigan
**affair** *n* gawain
**affect** *v* naim
**affection** *n* pagmamahal
**affectionate** *adj* mapagmahal
**affiliate** *v* sumali
**affiliation** *n* pagsali
**affinity** *n* pagka-gusto
**affirm** *v* patunayan
**affirmative** *adj* katunayan
**affix** *v* isama
**afflict** *v* nagkasakit
**affliction** *n* sakit
**affluence** *n* kasaganaan
**affluent** *adj* marangya

**afford** *v* kaya
**affordable** *adj* kakayanan
**affront** *v* bastusin
**affront** *n* nakalutang
**afloat** *adv* lumutang
**afraid** *adj* takot
**afresh** *adv* na naman
**after** *pre* bago
**afternoon** *n* hapon
**afterwards** *adv* pagkatapos
**again** *adv* ulitin
**against** *pre* di ayon
**age** *n* gulang
**agency** *n* ahensya
**agent** *n* ahente
**agglomerate** *v* palalain
**aggravate** *v* palalain
**aggravation** *n* malala
**aggregate** *v* pagsamahin
**aggression** *n* pagsugod
**aggressive** *adj* nanunugod
**aggressor** *n* manunugod
**aghast** *adj* nagulantang
**agile** *adj* maliksi
**agitator** *n* kapural
**agnostic** *n* walang paniwala
**agonize** *v* nagdurusa
**agonizing** *adj* nakapag-durusa
**agony** *n* paghihirap
**agree** *v* sumang-ayon
**agreeable** *adj* naaayon
**agreement** *n* kasunduan
**agricultural** *adj* kabukiran
**agriculture** *n* pag-bubukid
**ahead** *pre* nauna
**aid** *n* tulong
**aid** *v* tinulungan
**aide** *n* katulong
**ailing** *adj* may sakit
**ailment** *n* sakit
**aim** *v* balakin
**aimless** *adj* walang pakay
**air** *n* hangin
**air** *v* hanginan
**airfare** *n* pamasahe
**airfield** *n* paliparan
**airplane** *n* salipawpaw
**airport** *n* paliparan
**airspace** *n* hangin
**aisle** *n* pasilyo
**ajar** *adj* katapat
**akin** *adj* ukol sa
**alarm** *n* alarma
**alarming** *adj* nagbabadya
**alcoholic** *adj* sugapa sa alak
**alert** *adj* listo
**algebra** *n* palatuusan
**alien** *n* banyaga; dayuhan
**alight** *adv* bumaba
**align** *v* itapat
**alignment** *n* pagtapat
**alike** *adj* katulad
**alive** *adj* pagkabuhay
**all** *adj* lahat

**allegation** *n* bintang
**allege** *v* nagbibintang
**allegedly** *adv* di umano
**allegiance** *n* katapatan
**allergic** *adj* alerhiya
**allergy** *n* alerhiya
**alleviate** *v* ibsan
**alley** *n* iskinita
**alliance** *n* pagkaka-isa
**allied** *adj* kakampi
**alligator** *n* buwaya
**allot** *v* hatiin
**allotment** *n* pondo
**allow** *v* payagan
**allowance** *n* pondo
**alloy** *n* aloy
**allure** *n* bighani
**alluring** *adj* kabigha-bighani
**allusion** *n* patungkol
**ally** *n* kakampi
**ally** *v* kampihan
**almanac** *n* almanak
**almighty** *adj* kamahal-mahalan
**almond** *n* almon
**almost** *adv* halos
**alms** *n* abuloy
**alone** *adj* nag-iisa
**along** *pre* katabi
**alongside** *pre* katabi
**aloof** *adj* mailap
**aloud** *adv* malakas
**alphabet** *n* alpabeto
**already** *adv* dati
**alright** *adv* sagayon
**also** *adv* din
**altar** *n* altar
**alter** *v* ibahin
**alteration** *n* kaibahan
**altercation** *n* sagutan
**alternate** *v* palitan
**alternate** *adj* kapalit
**alternative** *n* kapalit
**although** *c* subalit
**altitude** *n* kaitaasan
**altogether** *adj* lahat-lahat
**aluminum** *n* aluminyo
**always** *adv* palagi
**amass** *v* isalansan
**amateur** *adj* bagito; bago
**amaze** *v* nagulat
**amazement** *n* kagulat-gulat
**amazing** *adj* nakakapagtaka
**ambassador** *n* embahador
**ambiguous** *adj* malabo
**ambition** *n* pangarap
**ambitious** *adj* ambisyoso
**ambivalent** *adj* di tiyak
**ambulance** *n* ambulansya
**ambush** *v* tambangan
**amenable** *adj* sang-ayon
**amend** *v* baguhin
**amendment** *n* pagbabago
**amenities** *n* kasaganaan
**American** *adj* amerikano

**amiable** *adj* kaibig-ibig
**amicable** *adj* mapayapa
**amid** *pre* sa kabila ng
**ammonia** *n* amonya
**ammunition** *n* bala
**amnesia** *n* pagkalimot
**amnesty** *n* kapatawaran
**among** *pre* sa, sa gitna ng
**amoral** *adj* walang moralidad
**amorphous** *adj* walang hugis
**amortize** *v* hatiin
**amount** *n* halaga
**amount to** *v* nagkahalaga
**amphitheater** *n* sinehan
**ample** *adj* sapat
**amplify** *v* palakihin
**amputate** *v* putulin
**amputation** *n* pagputol
**amuse** *v* aliwin
**amusement** *n* aliwan
**amusing** *adj* nakaaaliw
**an** *a* ang
**analogy** *n* analohiya
**analysis** *n* pagsusuri
**analyze** *v* suriin
**anarchist** *n* anarkista
**anarchy** *n* anarkiya
**anatomy** *n* anatomya
**ancestor** *n* ninuno
**ancestry** *n* pinagmulan
**anchor** *n* pag daong
**anchovy** *n* dilis
**ancient** *adj* luma
**and** *c* at
**anemia** *n* anemya
**anemic** *adj* kulang sa dugo
**anesthesia** *n* anestisya
**anew** *adv* ulit
**angel** *n* anghel
**angelic** *adj* mala anghel
**anger** *v* nagalit
**anger** *n* galit
**angina** *n* ukol sa puso
**angle** *n* anggulo
**Anglican** *adj* angliko
**angry** *adj* galit
**anguish** *n* paghihirap
**animal** *n* hayop
**animate** *v* buhayin
**animation** *n* bigyan buhay
**animosity** *n* galit
**ankle** *n* bukong-bukong
**annex** *n* karugtong
**annexation** *n* pag dugtong
**annihilate** *v* sugpuin
**annihilation** *n* pag sugpo
**anniversary** *n* anibersaryo
**annotate** *v* ipaliwanag
**annotation** *n* paliwanag
**announce** *v* italastas
**announcement** *n* patalastas
**announcer** *n* tagapamalita
**annoy** *v* inisin
**annoying** *adj* nakakainis

**annual** *adj* taon-taon
**annul** *v* ipawalang-bisa
**annulment** *n* walang-bisa
**anoint** *v* kumpilan
**anonymity** *n* di kilala
**anonymous** *adj* di kilala
**another** *adj* kaibahan
**answer** *v* sagutin
**answer** *n* sagot
**ant** *n* langgam
**antagonize** *v* awayin
**antecedent** *n* kasunod
**antecedents** *n* mga kasunod
**antelope** *n* usa
**antenna** *n* antena
**anthem** *n* pambansang awit
**antibiotic** *n* gamot
**anticipate** *v* hulaan
**anticipation** *n* hulaan
**antidote** *n* pamatay-bisa
**antipathy** *n* kontra
**antiquated** *adj* niluma
**antiquity** *n* kalumaam
**anvil** *n* pako
**anxiety** *n* pagkabalisa
**anxious** *adj* balisa
**any** *adj* kahit ano
**anybody** *pro* kahit sino
**anyhow** *pro* kahit papano
**anyone** *pro* sinuman
**anything** *pro* alinman
**apart** *adv* magkahiwalay
**apartment** *n* aprtamento
**apathy** *n* walang pakiramdam
**ape** *n* unggoy
**aperitif** *n* pampagana
**apex** *n* dulo
**apiece** *adv* bawat isa
**apocalypse** *n* pagpapahayag
**apologize** *v* magpaumanhin
**apology** *n* pagpapaumnahin
**apostle** *n* alagad
**apostrophe** *n* kudlit
**appall** *v* natakot
**appalling** *adj* nakakatakot
**apparel** *n* kasuotan
**apparent** *adj* maliwanag
**apparently** *adv* sa malas
**apparition** *n* malik-mata
**appeal** *n* apila
**appeal** *v* umapila
**appealing** *adj* ka-akit-akit
**appear** *v* nagpakita
**appearance** *n* itsura; anyo
**appease** *v* payapain
**appeasement** *n* pagpapahupa
**appendicitis** *n* apendisitis
**appendix** *n* apendiks
**appetite** *n* gana
**appetizer** *n* pampagana
**applaud** *v* palakpakan
**applause** *n* palakpakan
**apple** *n* mansanas
**applicable** *adj* maaaring gamitin

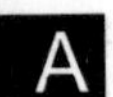



**applicant** *n* aplikante
**application** *n* paglalagay
**apply** *v* ilagay; magsikap
**appoint** *v* hirangin; piliin
**appointment** *n* paghirang; tipunin
**appraisal** *n* tantya
**appreciate** *v* pahalagahan
**appreciation** *n* pagpapahalaga
**apprehend** *v* hulihin
**apprehensive** *adj* urong-sulong
**apprentice** *n* baguhan
**approach** *v* lapitan
**approach** *n* paglapit
**approachable** *adj* madaling lapitan
**approbation** *n* pagsang-ayon
**appropriate** *adj* nararapat
**approval** *n* pag-sang-ayon
**approve** *v* payagan
**approximate** *adj* estima
**apricot** *n* aprikot
**April** *n* Abril
**apron** *n* epron
**aptitude** *n* kakayanan
**aquarium** *n* akwaryum
**aquatic** *adj* ukol sa tubig
**aqueduct** *n* daluyan ng tubig
**Arabic** *adj* Arabo
**arable** *adj* matabang lupa
**arbiter** *n* taga - awat
**arbitrary** *adj* nag-awat
**arbitrate** *v* inawat
**arbitration** *n* pag-awat
**arc** *n* arko
**archaeology** *n* arkeyolohiya
**archaic** *adj* pinaka mataas
**archbishop** *n* arsobispo
**architect** *n* arkitekto
**architecture** *n* arkitektura
**arctic** *adj* malamig
**ardent** *adj* marubdob
**ardor** *n* sigla
**arduous** *adj* mahirap gawin
**area** *n* lunan
**arena** *n* teatro
**argue** *v* nagtalo
**argument** *n* pagtalunan
**arid** *adj* tuyot; tigang
**arise** *iv* tumindig; tumayo
**aristocracy** *n* aristokrasya
**aristocrat** *n* aristokrata
**arithmetic** *n* matematika
**ark** *n* arko
**arm** *n* braso
**arm** *v* abraso
**armaments** *n* sandata
**armchair** *n* silyon
**armed** *adj* armado
**armor** *n* pang sangga
**armpit** *n* kilikili
**army** *n* hukbo
**aromatic** *adj* mabango
**around** *pre* sa paligid

**arouse** *v* pukawin
**arrange** *v* ayusin
**arrangement** *n* pag-ayos
**array** *n* pulutong
**arrest** *v* hulihin
**arrest** *n* pag-huli
**arrival** *n* pag dating
**arrive** *v* dumating
**arrogant** *adj* mayabang
**arrow** *n* sibat
**arsenal** *n* bodega ng armas
**arsenic** *n* arsenik
**arsonist** *n* manununog
**art** *n* sining
**artery** *n* ugat
**arthritis** *n* artritis
**artichoke** *n* gulay
**article** *n* artikulo
**articulate** *v* sabihin
**articulation** *n* pagsabi
**artificial** *adj* di totoo
**artillery** *n* sandata
**artisan** *n* ukol sa tubig
**artist** *n* artista
**artistic** *adj* masining na gawa
**artwork** *n* sining
**as** *c* tulad ng
**as** *adv* tulad ng
**ascend** *v* itaas; umakyat
**ascendancy** *n* pag-taas
**ascertain** *v* tiyakin; alamin
**ascetic** *adj* banal
**ash** *n* abo
**ashamed** *adj* nahiya
**ashore** *adv* baybay
**ashtray** *n* lalagyan ng abo
**aside** *adv* bukod
**aside from** *adv* bukod tangi
**ask** *v* tanungin
**asleep** *adj* tulog
**asparagus** *n* asparagus
**aspect** *n* aspeto
**asphalt** *n* aspalto
**asphyxiate** *v* mawalan ng hininga
**aspiration** *n* pangarap
**aspire** *v* mangarap
**aspirin** *n* aspirin
**assail** *v* sugurin
**assailant** *n* manunugod
**assassin** *n* mamamatay-tao
**assassinate** *v* patayin
**assassination** *n* pagpatay
**assault** *n* pag-sugod
**assault** *v* sinugod; inatake
**assemble** *v* tipunin
**assembly** *n* pagtitipon
**assent** *v* itaas
**assert** *v* magpatotoo
**assertion** *n* palagay
**assess** *v* sukatin; bilangin
**assessment** *n* pagbilang
**asset** *n* kakayanan; talino
**assets** *n* kayamanan
**assign** *v* itakda; ipagawa

**assignment** *n* gawain
**assimilate** *v* ipagsama
**assimilation** *n* pagsasama-sama
**assist** *v* tulungan
**assistance** *n* tulong
**associate** *v* kasamahan
**association** *n* samahan
**assorted** *adj* iba-iba
**assortment** *n* pagkaka-iba
**assume** *v* gampanan
**assumption** *n* palagay
**assurance** *n* katiyakan
**assure** *v* tiyakin
**asterisk** *n* asterisko
**asteroid** *n* maliit na planeta
**asthma** *n* hika
**asthmatic** *adj* hikain
**astonish** *v* gulatin
**astonishing** *adj* nakakagulat
**astound** *v* gimbalin
**astounding** *adj* kagimba-gimbal
**astray** *v* naligaw
**astrology** *n* astrolohiya
**astronaut** *n* astronot
**astronomy** *n* astronomiya
**astute** *adj* matalino
**asunder** *adv* pira-piraso
**asylum** *n* asilo; ampunan
**at** *pre* sa
**atheist** *n* hindi naniniwala
**athlete** *n* manlalaro
**athletic** *adj* mahilig sa laro
**atmosphere** *n* kapaligiran
**atmospheric** *adj* nauukol sa paligid
**atone** *v* nagsisi
**atonement** *n* pagsisisi
**atrocious** *adj* kagimba-gimbal
**atrocity** *n* kalupitan
**atrophy** *v* walang silbi
**attach** *v* ikabit
**attached** *adj* nakakabit
**attachment** *n* nakakabit
**attack** *n* pagsugod
**attack** *v* sugurin
**attacker** *n* manunugod
**attain** *v* nakamit
**attainable** *adj* makakamit
**attainment** *n* nagawa; nakamit
**attempt** *v* nagtangka
**attempt** *n* tangkain
**attend** *v* dumalo
**attendance** *n* pagdalo
**attendant** *n* nagdalo
**attention** *n* pansin
**attentive** *adj* nakikinig
**attenuate** *v* bawasan
**attenuating** *adj* binawasan
**attest** *v* magtagumpay
**attic** *n* maliit na silid
**attitude** *n* pag-uugali
**attorney** *n* abogado
**attract** *v* akitin
**attraction** *n* pagka-akit

**attractive** *adj* ka-akit-akit
**attribute** *v* katangian
**auction** *n* subasta
**auction** *v* sinubasta
**auctioneer** *n* nanunubasta
**audacious** *adj* malakas ang loob
**audacity** *n* lakas ng loob
**audible** *adj* naririnig
**audience** *n* manonood
**auditorium** *n* bahay tanghalan
**augment** *v* tulungan
**August** *n* Agosto
**aunt** *n* tiya
**austere** *adj* katipiran
**austerity** *n* pagtitipid
**authentic** *adj* kakaiba
**authenticity** *n* tunay
**author** *n* may akda
**authority** *n* awtoridad
**authorization** *n* pahintulot
**authorize** *v* payagan
**auto** *n* awto
**autograph** *n* sulat kamay
**automatic** *adj* awtomatik
**automobile** *n* kotse
**autonomous** *adj* nagsasarili
**autonomy** *n* nagsarili
**autumn** *n* otonyo
**auxiliary** *adj* dagdag tulong
**avail** *v* samantalahin
**availability** *n* nakalaan
**available** *adj* handang gamitin
**avarice** *n* kagahaman
**avaricious** *adj* gahaman
**avenge** *v* gumanti
**avenue** *n* kalye
**average** *n* katamtaman
**averse** *adj* kabaliktaran
**aversion** *n* iba
**avert** *v* iniba
**aviator** *n* piloto
**avid** *adj* masugid
**avoid** *v* iwasan
**avoidable** *adj* maiiwasan
**avoidance** *n* pag-iwas
**avowed** *adj* nangako
**await** *v* gisingin
**awake** *iv* ginising
**awake** *adj* gising
**awakening** *n* pag-gising
**award** *v* bigyan pabuya
**award** *n* pabuya
**aware** *adj* may alam
**awareness** *n* kaalaman
**away** *adv* malayo
**awe** *n* mangha
**awesome** *adj* nakamamangha
**awful** *adj* masagwa
**awkward** *adj* saliwa
**awning** *n* lona
**ax** *n* palakol
**axis** *n* gitna
**axle** *n* palakol

# B

**babble** *v* nagsalita
**baby** *n* sanggol
**babysitter** *n* yaya
**bachelor** *n* binata
**back** *n* likod
**back** *adv* pagtalikod
**back** *v* italikod
**back down** *v* sumuko
**back up** *v* isunod
**backbone** *n* buto
**backdoor** *n* pinto sa likod
**backfire** *v* bumalik
**background** *n* kapaligiran
**backing** *n* pangsuporta
**backlash** *n* siwang
**backlog** *n* tambakna trabaho
**backpack** *n* bag
**backup** *n* suporta
**backward** *adj* paatras
**backwards** *adv* iatras
**backyard** *n* paligid
**bacon** *n* bekon
**bacteria** *n* mikrobyo
**bad** *adj* masama
**badge** *n* pagkakakilanlan
**badly** *adv* masama
**baffle** *v* nilito
**bag** *n* bag
**baggage** *n* bagahe
**baggy** *adj* naluwag
**baguette** *n* baget
**bail** *n* pyansa
**bail out** *v* pyansahan
**bait** *n* pain
**bake** *v* hurno
**baker** *n* panadero
**bakery** *n* panaderia
**balance** *v* ipantay
**balance** *n* pantay
**balcony** *n* balkonahe
**bald** *adj* kalbo
**bale** *n* bagahe
**ball** *n* bola
**balloon** *n* lobo
**ballot** *n* balota
**ballroom** *n* bulwagan
**balm** *n* bam
**bamboo** *n* kawayan
**ban** *n* bawal
**ban** *v* ipagbawal
**banality** *n* kabanalan
**banana** *n* saging
**band** *n* banda
**bandage** *n* benda
**bandage** *v* bendahan
**bang** *v* bang
**bandit** *n* bandido
**banish** *v* nawala
**banishment** *n* pagkawala
**bank** *n* bangko
**bankrupt** *v* nabangkarote

**bankrupt** *adj* nalugi
**bankruptcy** *n* bangkarote
**banner** *n* bandera
**banquet** *n* hapag
**baptism** *n* binyag
**baptize** *v* binyagan
**bar** *n* bar
**bar** *v* pagbawalan
**barbarian** *n* barbaro
**barbaric** *adj* makahayop
**barbarism** *n* asal barbaro
**barbecue** *n* barbikyu
**barber** *n* barbero
**bare** *adj* hubad
**barefoot** *adj* nakapaa
**barely** *adv* lantad
**bargain** *n* baratilyo
**bargain** *v* baratin
**bargaining** *n* baratilyo
**barge** *n* balsa
**bark** *v* tumahol
**bark** *n* tahol
**barley** *n* halaman
**barmaid** *n* serbedora
**barman** *n* tapag silbi
**barn** *n* bukid
**barracks** *n* tirahan
**barrage** *n* harang
**barrel** *n* barilis
**barren** *adj* tigang
**barricade** *n* harang
**barrier** *n* harang
**barring** *pre* harangan
**barter** *v* palitan
**base** *n* hanggahan
**base** *v* hamak; imbi
**baseball** *n* beysbol
**baseless** *adj* walang basehan
**basement** *n* ilalim; silong
**bashful** *adj* mahiyain
**basic** *adj* basiko
**basics** *n* basiko
**basin** *n* planggana
**basis** *n* basehan
**bask** *v* ibilad
**basket** *n* basket
**basketball** *n* basketbol
**bastard** *n* bastarda
**bat** *n* bat
**batch** *n* pangkat; bungkos
**bath** *n* paligo
**bathe** *v* maligo
**bathrobe** *n* bata de banyo
**bathroom** *n* palikuran
**bathtub** *n* paliguan
**baton** *n* baton
**battalion** *n* batalyon
**batter** *v* bugbugin
**battery** *n* baterya
**battle** *n* gera
**battle** *v* gerahin
**bay** *n* dagat
**bayonet** *n* bayoneta
**bazaar** *n* tindahan

**be** *iv* ay
**be born** *v* ipanganak
**beach** *n* dalampasigan
**beacon** *n* parola
**beak** *n* tuka
**beam** *n* ilaw
**bean** *n* patani
**bear** *n* oso
**bear** *iv* balikatin
**bearable** *adj* matitiis
**beard** *n* balbas
**bearded** *adj* may balbas
**bearer** *n* tagapagdala
**beast** *n* hayop
**beat** *iv* talunin
**beat** *n* talunan
**beaten** *adj* natalo
**beating** *n* talunin
**beautiful** *adj* maganda
**beautify** *v* pagandahin
**beauty** *n* ganda
**because** *c* sapagkat
**because of** *pre* dahil sa
**beckon** *v* senyasan
**become** *iv* maging
**bed** *n* kama
**bedding** *n* gamit pangkama
**bedroom** *n* silid tulugan
**bedspread** *n* kumot
**bee** *n* bubuyog
**beef** *n* karneng baka
**beef up** *v* magpalakas
**beehive** *n* bahay-pukyutan
**beer** *n* serbesa
**beet** *n* gulay
**beetle** *n* salagubang
**before** *adv* bago
**before** *pre* bago
**beforehand** *adv* antimano
**befriend** *v* kaibiganin
**beg** *v* mamalimos
**beggar** *n* pulubi
**begin** *iv* simulan
**beginner** *n* baguhan
**beginning** *n* simulan
**beguile** *v* iligaw
**behalf (on)** *adv* sa ngalan
**behave** *v* umayos
**behavior** *n* pag-uugali
**behead** *v* pinugutan
**behind** *pre* sa kabila
**behold** *iv* pagmasdan
**being** *n* katauhan
**belated** *adj* nahuli
**belch** *v* dumighay
**belch** *n* dighay
**belfry** *n* kampana
**Belgium** *n* Belgium
**belief** *n* paniniwala
**believe** *v* maniwala
**belittle** *v* minaliit
**bell** *n* kampana
**bell pepper** *n* sili
**belligerent** *adj* palaaway

**belly** *n* tiyan
**belly button** *n* pusod
**belong** *v* nauukol
**belongings** *n* kagamitan
**beloved** *adj* mahal
**below** *adv* ilalim
**below** *pre* kailaliman
**belt** *n* sinturon
**bench** *n* bangko
**bend** *iv* namaluktot
**bend down** *v* hutukin
**beneath** *pre* paligid
**benediction** *n* bendisyon
**beneficial** *adj* may pakininabang
**benefit** *n* benepisyo
**benefit** *v* benepisyo
**benevolence** *n* kagandahang-loob
**benevolent** *adj* magandang-loob
**bequeath** *v* ipamana
**bereaved** *adj* na-ulila
**bereavement** *n* pagdadalamhati
**beret** *n* berey
**berserk** *adv* huramentado
**berth** *n* teheras
**beseech** *iv* pahingi
**beset** *iv* paligiran
**beside** *pre* katabi
**besides** *pre* bukod
**besiege** *iv* kubkubin; kulungin
**best** *adj* pinakamahusay
**best man** *n* abay
**bestial** *adj* makahayop
**bestiality** *n* kapurihan
**bestow** *v* ibigay; ipagkaloob
**bet** *iv* pumusta
**bet** *n* pusta
**betray** *v* ipagkanulo
**betrayal** *n* daya
**better** *adj* higit
**between** *pre* sa pagitan
**beverage** *n* inumin
**beware** *v* mag-ingat
**bewilder** *v* nalito
**bewitch** *v* nabighani
**beyond** *adv* sa kabilang ibayo
**bias** *n* bayas
**bible** *n* bibliya
**biblical** *adj* ayin sa bibliya
**bicycle** *n* bisikleta
**bid** *n* tawad
**bid** *iv* tawaran
**big** *adj* malaki
**bigamy** *n* bigamya
**bigot** *adj* hindi sang-ayon
**bigotry** *n* di pag-sang-ayon
**bike** *n* bisikleta
**bile** *n* apdo
**bilingual** *adj* baylinggwal
**bill** *n* tuka; kwenta
**billion** *n* bilyon
**billionaire** *n* mayaman
**billiards** *n* bilyar
**bin** *n* basurahan
**bind** *iv* bigkisin; talian

B

**binding** *adj* makompromiso
**binoculars** *n* larga bista
**biography** *n* talambuhay
**biology** *n* biyolohiya
**bird** *n* ibon
**birth** *n* ipanganak
**birthday** *n* kapanganakan
**biscuit** *n* biskwit
**bishop** *n* obispo
**bison** *n* kalabaw
**bit** *n* kagatin
**bite** *iv* kinagat
**bite** *n* kagatin
**bitter** *adj* mapait
**bitterly** *adv* kapaitan
**bitterness** *n* kapaitan
**black** *adj* maitim
**blackberry** *n* duhat
**blackboard** *n* pisara
**blackmail** *n* pangongotong
**blackmail** *v* kotongan
**blackness** *n* kaitiman
**blackout** *n* walang koryente
**blacksmith** *n* panday
**bladder** *n* apdo
**blade** *n* panghiwa
**blame** *n* sisi
**blame** *v* sisihin
**blameless** *adj* walang pagsisisi
**bland** *adj* naaayon
**blank** *adj* blangko
**blanket** *n* kumot
**blaspheme** *v* alipustahin
**blasphemy** *n* alipusta
**blast** *n* pagsabog
**blaze** *v* ningas
**bleach** *v* ikula
**bleach** *n* kula
**bleak** *adj* kalabuan
**bleed** *iv* dumugo
**bleeding** *n* duguan
**blemish** *n* may bahid
**blemish** *v* bahiran
**blend** *n* halo
**blend** *v* ihalo
**blender** *n* pang halo
**bless** *v* bendisyunan
**blessed** *adj* banal
**blessing** *n* bendisyon
**blind** *v* bulagin
**blind** *adj* bulagin
**blindfold** *n* piring
**blindfold** *v* piringan
**blindly** *adv* bulagan
**blindness** *n* bulag
**blink** *v* kindat
**bliss** *n* kasaganaan
**blissful** *adj* masagana
**blister** *n* paltos
**bloat** *v* lumaki; lumobo
**bloated** *adj* malaki, maga
**block** *n* bloke; tipak
**block** *v* hadlangan
**blockade** *v* hinarangan

**blockade** *n* harang
**blockage** *n* bara
**blond** *adj* olandes
**blood** *n* dugo
**bloodthirsty** *adj* bayolente
**bloody** *adj* duguan
**bloom** *v* sumibol
**blossom** *v* bulaklak
**blot** *n* mantsa
**blot** *v* namantsahan
**blouse** *n* blusa
**blow** *n* ihip
**blow** *iv* hipan
**blow out** *iv* magpakain
**blow up** *iv* nag-sagutan
**blowout** *n* pagputok
**bludgeon** *v* tinaga; pinukpok
**blue** *adj* bughaw; asul
**blueprint** *n* kopya
**bluff** *v* magkunwari
**blunt** *adj* mapurol
**bluntness** *n* kapurulan
**blur** *v* lumabo
**blurred** *adj* malabo
**blush** *v* namula
**blush** *n* hiya
**boar** *n* baboy ramo
**board** *n* tabla
**board** *v* nakasakay
**boast** *v* nagyabang
**boat** *n* barko
**bodily** *adj* pangkatawan
**body** *n* katawan
**bog** *n* putikan; lusak
**bog down** *v* nasira
**boil** *v* kumulo
**boil down to** *v* samakatuwid
**boil over** *v* umapaw
**boiler** *n* kaldero
**boisterous** *adj* garapal
**bold** *adj* matapang
**boldness** *n* katapangan
**bolster** *v* kalangan ng unan
**bolt** *n* kandado
**bolt** *v* ikandado
**bomb** *n* bomba
**bomb** *v* bombahin
**bombing** *n* bombahan
**bond** *n* tali; bigkis
**bondage** *n* pagka tali
**bone** *n* buto
**bone marrow** *n* utak sa buto
**bonfire** *n* paapoy
**bonus** *n* bonus
**book** *n* aklat
**bookcase** *n* lalagyan ng aklat
**bookkeeping** *n* kwenta
**booklet** *n* maliit na aklat
**bookseller** *n* nagtitinda ng aklat
**bookstore** *n* tindahan ng aklat
**boom** *n* malakas na putok
**boost** *v* itaas ang antas
**boost** *n* pagtaas ng antas
**boot** *n* bota

**booth** *n* pwesto
**booty** *n* puwet
**booze** *n* alak
**border** *n* gilid
**border on** *v* nakapagilid
**borderline** *adj* gilid
**bore** *v* nagbutas
**bored** *adj* na-inip
**boredom** *n* pagka - inip
**boring** *adj* nakaka-inip
**born** *adj* pinanganak
**borough** *n* barangay
**borrow** *v* hiniram
**bosom** *n* dibdib
**boss** *n* amo
**boss around** *v* mamuno
**bossy** *adj* pala-utos
**botany** *n* botanya
**botch** *v* madaliang pag-ayos
**both** *adj* pareho
**bother** *v* abalahin
**bothersome** *adj* nakaka-abala
**bottle** *n* bote
**bottle** *v* ibote
**bottleneck** *n* masikip na daan
**bottom** *n* ibaba
**bottomless** *adj* kalaliman
**bough** *n* sanga
**boulder** *n* baton
**boulevard** *n* lansangan
**bounce** *v* tumalbog
**bounce** *n* talbog
**bound** *adj* patungo
**bound for** *adj* patungo
**boundary** *n* hangganan
**boundless** *adj* walang hanggan
**bounty** *n* mapagbigay
**bourgeois** *adj* negosyante
**bow** *n* pana; arkong biyolin
**bow** *v* magpugay
**bow out** *v* umalis
**bowels** *n* lagusan
**bowl** *n* mangkok
**box** *n* kahon
**boxer** *n* boksingero
**boxing** *n* boksing
**box office** *n* takilya
**boy** *n* batang lalaki
**boycott** *v* boykot
**boyfriend** *n* kasintahan
**boyhood** *n* kabataan
**bra** *n* bra
**brace for** *v* kumapit
**bracelet** *n* pulsera
**bracket** *n* suporta
**brag** *v* magyabang
**braid** *n* tirintas
**brain** *n* utak
**brainwash** *v* lasunin ang isip
**brake** *n* preno
**brake** *v* i-preno
**branch** *n* sanga
**branch office** *n* opisina
**branch out** *v* mag-sanga

**brand** *n* tatak; marka
**brand-new** *adj* bago
**brandy** *n* alak
**brat** *n* walang galang
**brave** *adj* matapang
**bravely** *adv* katapangan
**bravery** *n* katapangan
**brawl** *n* away
**breach** *n* nasirang pangako
**bread** *n* tinapay
**breadth** *n* kalaliman
**break** *n* sira
**break** *iv* sirain
**break away** *v* tumiwalag
**break down** *v* nasira
**break free** *v* tumakas
**break in** *v* pilit na pumasok
**break off** *v* winakasan
**break open** *v* buksan
**break up** *v* magkasira
**break out** *v* dumating
**breakable** *adj* babasagin
**breakdown** *n* sira
**breakfast** *n* almusal
**breakthrough** *n* pauna
**breast** *n* dibdib
**breath** *n* hininga
**breathe** *v* huminga
**breathing** *n* hininga
**breathtaking** *adj* makapigil-hininga
**breed** *iv* mag-alaga
**breed** *n* lahi
**breeze** *n* simoy ng hangin
**brethren** *n* kapatid
**brevity** *n* maiksi
**bribe** *v* suhulan
**bribe** *n* suhol
**bribery** *n* pagsuhol
**brick** *n* ladrilyo
**bricklayer** *n* ladrilyador
**bridal** *adj* pangkasal
**bride** *n* nobya
**bridegroom** *n* nobyo
**bridesmaid** *n* abay
**bridge** *n* tulay
**bridle** *n* renda
**brief** *adj* maiksi
**brief** *v* iniksian
**briefcase** *n* tampipi
**briefing** *n* pulong
**briefly** *adv* iklian
**briefs** *n* maikling salita
**brigade** *n* brigada
**bright** *adj* maliwanag
**brighten** *v* liwanagin
**brightness** *n* maliwanag
**brilliant** *adj* makinang
**brim** *n* gilid
**bring** *iv* dalahin
**bring back** *v* ibalik
**bring down** *v* ibaba
**bring up** *v* palakihin
**brink** *n* bingid
**brisk** *adj* mabilis

B

**Britain** *n* Britanya
**British** *adj* taga-Britanya
**brittle** *adj* malutong
**broad** *adj* malawak
**broadcast** *v* italastas
**broadcast** *n* talastas
**broadcaster** *n* mananalastas
**broaden** *v* palawakin
**broadly** *adv* kalaparan
**broadminded** *adj* maunawain
**brochure** *n* papelito
**broil** *v* ihawin
**broiler** *n* pang-ihaw
**broke** *adj* salat
**broken** *adj* nasira
**bronchitis** *n* brongkitis
**bronze** *n* tanso
**broom** *n* walis
**broth** *n* sabaw
**brother** *n* kapatid na lalaki
**brotherhood** *n* kapatiran
**brother-in-law** *n* bayaw
**brotherly** *adj* kapatiran
**brow** *n* kilay
**brown** *adj* kulay kape
**browse** *v* hanapin
**browser** *n* pang hanap
**bruise** *n* pasa
**bruise** *v* napasa
**brunette** *adj* mapula ang buhok
**brush** *n* sepilyo, eskoba
**brush** *v* linisin
**brush aside** *v* isa-isan tabi
**brush up** *v* maghilamos
**brusque** *adj* brusko
**brutal** *adj* brutal
**brutality** *n* kalupitan
**brutalize** *v* pagmalupitan
**brute** *adj* malupit
**bubble** *n* bula
**bubble gum** *n* babolgam
**buck** *n* isang lalaki
**bucket** *n* timba
**buckle** *n* tali
**buckle up** *v* itali
**bud** *n* ubod
**buddy** *n* kaibigan
**budge** *v* lana
**budget** *n* pondo
**buffalo** *n* kalabaw
**bug** *n* insekto
**build** *iv* gawin
**builder** *n* maggagawa
**building** *n* gusali
**buildup** *n* na-ipon
**built-in** *adj* sadyang ginawa
**bulb** *n* bumbilya
**bulge** *n* maga
**bulk** *n* dami; kapal; laki
**bulky** *adj* makapal
**bull** *n* lalaking baka
**bulldoze** *v* bantaan; takutin
**bullet** *n* bala
**bulletin** *n* patalastas

**bull fight** *n* away ng kalabaw
**bull fighter** *n* torero
**bully** *adj* siga
**bulwark** *n* portalesa
**bum** *n* palaboy
**bump** *n* banggaan
**bump into** *v* nakasalubong
**bumper** *n* harapan
**bumpy** *adj* bako-bako
**bun** *n* tianpay
**bunch** *n* bungkos
**bundle** *n* bungkos
**bundle** *v* i-bungkos
**bunk bed** *n* papag
**bunker** *n* pang salo
**buoy** *n* panglutang
**burden** *n* pasan
**burden** *v* pinasan
**burdensome** *adj* pasanin
**bureau** *n* ahensya
**bureaucrat** *n* tao sa kawanihan
**burger** *n* giniling na karne
**burglar** *n* magnanakaw
**burglarize** *v* nakawan
**burglary** *n* pananakaw
**burial** *n* libing
**burly** *adj* matipuno
**burn** *iv* nasunog
**burn** *n* sunog
**burp** *v* dumighay
**burp** *n* dighay
**burrow** *n* hukay
**burst** *iv* isabog
**burst into** *v* sumabog
**bury** *v* ilibing
**bus** *n* bus
**bus** *v* mag-bus
**bush** *n* halamanan
**busily** *adv* abala
**business** *n* kabuhayan
**bust** *n* dibdib
**bustling** *adj* sagana
**busy** *adj* abala
**but** *c* subalit
**butcher** *n* matadero
**butchery** *n* taga tadtad
**butler** *n* tagapangisiwa
**butt** *n* puwet
**butter** *n* mantekilya
**butterfly** *n* paru-paro
**button** *n* botones
**buy** *iv* bumili
**buy off** *v* bilihin
**buyer** *n* mamimili
**buzz** *n* ugong; hinging
**buzz** *v* umugong
**buzzard** *n* pang ugong
**buzzer** *n* pang hinging
**by** *pre* ng
**bye** *e* paalam
**bypass** *n* lampas
**bypass** *v* lampasan
**by-product** *n* produkto
**bystander** *n* istambay

# C

**cab** *n* sasakyan
**cabbage** *n* repolyo
**cabin** *n* silid sa barko
**cabinet** *n* kabinete
**cable** *n* kable
**cafeteria** *n* kapihan
**caffeine** *n* kapeyn
**cage** *n* hawla
**cake** *n* keyk
**calamity** *n* kalamidad
**calculate** *v* estimahin
**calculation** *n* estima
**calendar** *n* kalendaryo
**calf** *n* bisiro; bulo
**caliber** *n* kalibre
**calibrate** *v* sukatin
**call** *n* tawag
**call** *v* tawagin
**call off** *v* ipagpaliban
**call on** *v* dalawin
**call out** *v* tawagin
**calling** *n* tumatawag
**callous** *adj* kalyo
**calm** *adj* tahimik
**calm** *n* katahimikan
**calm down** *v* tumahimik
**calorie** *n* kaloriya
**calumny** *n* paninirang - puri
**camel** *n* kamelyo
**camera** *n* kamera
**camouflage** *v* nagbalat-kayo
**camouflage** *n* balat-kayo
**camp** *n* pahingahan
**camp** *v* magpahinga
**campaign** *v* mangampanya
**campaign** *n* kampanya
**campfire** *n* paapuyan
**can** *iv* maaari
**can** *v* i-de lata
**can** *n* lata
**canal** *n* kanal
**canary** *n* kanaryo
**cancel** *v* kanselahin
**cancellation** *n* pagkansela
**cancer** *n* kanser
**cancerous** *adj* nakakakanser
**candid** *adj* prangka; tapat
**candidacy** *n* pagkanditato
**candidate** *n* kandidato
**candle** *n* kandila
**candor** *n* prangka
**candy** *n* kendi
**cane** *n* tungkod
**canister** *n* lalagyan
**canned** *adj* de- lata
**cannibal** *n* kanibal
**cannon** *n* kanyon
**canoe** *n* bangka
**canonize** *v* gawint banal
**cantaloupe** *n* melon
**canteen** *n* kantina

**canvas** *n* lona
**canvas** *v* lonahan
**canyon** *n* dalawang bundok
**cap** *n* gora; takip; tapon
**capability** *n* kakayanan
**capable** *adj* kaya
**capacity** *n* tungkulin
**capital** *n* puhunan
**capital letter** *n* malalaking titik
**capitalism** *n* kapitalismo
**capitalize** *v* mamuhunan
**capitulate** *v* sumuko
**capsize** *v* tumaob
**capsule** *n* kapsula
**captain** *n* kapitan
**captivate** *v* nahuli
**captive** *n* bilanggo; bihag
**captivity** *n* nabihag
**capture** *v* bihagin
**capture** *n* bihag
**car** *n* kotse
**carat** *n* karat
**caravan** *n* parada
**carburetor** *n* karburador
**carcass** *n* bangkay
**card** *n* baraha; tarheta
**cardboard** *n* karton
**cardiac** *adj* ukol sa puso
**cardiac arrest** *n* atake sa puso
**cardiology** *n* kardiyolohiya
**care** *n* pag tingin
**care** *v* ingatan
**care about** *v* alagaan
**care for** *v* tingnan
**career** *n* karera
**carefree** *adj* pabaya
**careful** *adj* maingat
**careless** *adj* walang ingat
**carelessness** *n* walang bahala
**caress** *n* paghaplos
**caress** *v* haplusin; himasin
**caretaker** *n* tagapag-alaga
**cargo** *n* kargamento
**caricature** *n* dibuho
**caring** *adj* maalaga
**carnage** *n* kalamanan
**carnal** *adj* nauukol sa laman
**carnation** *n* karneysyon
**carol** *n* Carolina
**carpenter** *n* panday
**carpentry** *n* pamamanday
**carpet** *n* tapete
**carriage** *n* sasakyan
**carrot** *n* karot
**carry** *v* kargahin
**carry on** *v* baon
**carry out** *v* iuwi
**cart** *n* kariton
**cart** *v* ikariton
**cartoon** *n* karton
**cartridge** *n* kartrids
**carve** *v* inukit
**cascade** *n* pag-agos
**case** *n* kaha

**cash** *n* salapi; kuwarta
**cashier** *n* kahera
**casino** *n* kasino
**casket** *n* kabaong; ataul
**casserole** *n* kaserola
**cassock** *n* damit ng pari
**cast** *iv* ihugis; ihagis
**castaway** *n* patapon
**caste** *n* kauri
**castle** *n* kastilyo
**casual** *adj* pangkaraniwan
**casualty** *n* biktima
**cat** *n* pusa
**cataclysm** *n* pag-aklas
**catacomb** *n* nitso
**catalog** *n* katalogo
**catalog** *v* katalogo
**cataract** *n* katarata
**catastrophe** *n* kamalasan
**catch** *iv* hinuli
**catch up** *v* hahabol
**catching** *adj* humahabol
**catchword** *n* kasabihan
**catechism** *n* katekismo
**category** *n* antas
**cater to** *v* pagbigyan
**caterpillar** *n* higad
**cathedral** *n* katedral
**catholic** *adj* katoliko
**Catholicism** *n* Katolisismo
**cattle** *n* baka
**cause** *n* dahilan
**cause** *v* magdahilan
**caution** *n* pag-iingat
**cautious** *adj* maingat
**cavalry** *n* maginoo
**cave** *n* kweba
**cave in** *v* nagiba
**cavern** *n* malaking kuweba
**cavity** *n* butas
**cease** *v* itigil
**cease-fire** *n* pag-tigil
**ceaselessly** *adv* walang humpay
**ceiling** *n* kisame
**celebrate** *v* ipagdiwang
**celebration** *n* pagdiriwang
**celebrity** *n* kilala
**celery** *n* kintsay
**celestial** *adj* mala anghel
**cellar** *n* silid para sa alak
**cellphone** *n* telepono
**cement** *n* semento
**cemetery** *n* libingan
**censorship** *n* tagasuri
**censure** *v* ipagbawal
**census** *n* sensus
**cent** *n* sentimo
**centenary** *n* daang taon
**center** *n* gitna
**center** *v* i-gitna
**centimeter** *n* sentimetro
**central** *adj* kalagitnaan
**centralize** *v* ipagitna
**century** *n* daang taon

**ceramic** *n* seramika
**cereal** *n* bungang butil
**cerebral** *adj* ukol sa utak
**ceremony** *n* pagdiriwang
**certain** *adj* tiyak
**certainty** *n* katiyakan
**certificate** *n* sertipiko
**certify** *v* magpatunay
**chagrin** *n* kabiguan
**chain** *n* kadena; tanikala
**chain** *v* ikadena
**chair** *n* silya; upuan
**chair** *v* paupuan
**chairman** *n* pangulo; pinuno
**chalet** *n* bahay sa bukid
**chalice** *n* kalis
**chalk** *n* tisa
**chalkboard** *n* pisara
**challenge** *v* hamunin
**challenge** *n* pahamon
**challenging** *adj* nanghahamon
**chamber** *n* kapulungan
**champ** *n* kampeon
**champion** *n* panalo
**champion** *v* nanalo
**chance** *n* pagkakataon
**chancellor** *n* kataas-taasan
**chandelier** *n* aranya
**change** *v* palitan
**change** *n* ipalit
**channel** *n* daan
**chant** *n* awir
**chaos** *n* kaguluhan
**chaotic** *adj* magulo
**chapel** *n* kapilya
**chaplain** *n* pari
**chapter** *n* yugto
**char** *v* nag-uling
**character** *n* ugali
**characteristic** *adj* pag-uugali
**charade** *n* sareyd
**charbroil** *adj* mala-uling
**charcoal** *n* uling
**charge** *v* paratangan
**charge** *n* bayad
**charisma** *n* karisma
**charismatic** *adj* magiliw
**charitable** *adj* mapagbigay
**charity** *n* pag alay
**charm** *v* halina; pang-akit
**charm** *n* halina; akit
**charming** *adj* mahalina
**chart** *n* tsart; kasulatan
**charter** *n* pagkakatatag
**charter** *v* isulat; itatag
**chase** *n* habol
**chase** *v* habulin
**chase away** *v* palayasin
**chasm** *n* bangin
**chaste** *adj* disente; malinis
**chastise** *v* parusahan
**chastisement** *n* parusa
**chastity** *n* puri
**chat** *v* magdaldal

**chauffeur** *n* tsuper
**cheap** *adj* mura
**cheat** *v* magdaya; dayain
**cheater** *n* madaya
**check** *n* tsek
**check** *v* pigilin; suriin
**check in** *v* pagpatala
**check up** *n* eksamen
**checkbook** *n* libreta
**cheek** *n* pisngi
**cheekbone** *n* pisngi
**cheeky** *adj* tamad
**cheer** *v* pasayahin; aliwin
**cheer up** *v* aliwin
**cheerful** *adj* masayahin
**cheers** *n* saya; aliw; tuwa
**cheese** *n* keso
**chef** *n* puno ng kusinero
**chemical** *adj* kemikal
**chemist** *n* kimiko
**chemistry** *n* kemistri
**cherish** *v* pinahalagahan
**cherry** *n* seresa
**chess** *n* ahedres
**chest** *n* dibdib
**chestnut** *n* kastanyas
**chew** *v* nguyain
**chick** *n* sisiw
**chicken** *n* manok
**chicken out** *v* umatras
**chicken pox** *n* bulutong
**chide** *v* pagalitan
**chief** *n* pinuno
**chiefly** *adv* pasimuno
**child** *n* bata
**childhood** *n* kabataan
**childish** *adj* ugaling bata
**childless** *adj* walang anak
**children** *n* kabataan
**chill** *n* ginaw
**chill** *v* giniginaw
**chill out** *v* palamigin
**chilly** *adj* malamig
**chimney** *n* tsimeneya
**chimpanzee** *n* inggoy
**chin** *n* baba
**chip** *n* pitsa
**chisel** *n* kikil
**chocolate** *n* tsokolate
**choice** *n* pili
**choir** *n* koro
**choke** *v* sakalin
**cholera** *n* kolera
**cholesterol** *n* kolesterol
**choose** *iv* mamili
**choosy** *adj* mapili
**chop** *v* tadtarin
**chop** *n* tinadtad
**chopper** *n* pagtadtad
**chore** *n* gawain
**christen** *v* binyagan
**christening** *n* binyagan
**christian** *adj* nabinyagan
**Christianity** *n* Kristyanismo

**Christmas** *n* pasko
**chronic** *adj* talamak
**chronology** *n* sunod-sunod
**chubby** *adj* mataba
**chuckle** *v* tumatawa
**chunk** *n* piraso
**church** *n* simbahan
**chute** *n* tubo
**cider** *n* pinaasim; suka
**cigar** *n* tabako
**cigarette** *n* sigarilyo
**cinder** *n* uking
**cinema** *n* sinehan
**cinnamon** *n* kanela
**circle** *n* bilog
**circle** *v* bilugan
**circuit** *n* palibot; paligid
**circular** *adj* paikot; pabilog
**circulate** *v* ipasa
**circulation** *n* pasahan
**circumcise** *v* tuliin
**circumcision** *n* tuli
**circumstance** *n* pangyayari
**circumstancial** *adj* pagkakataon
**circus** *n* sirko
**cistern** *n* tangke ng tubig
**citizen** *n* mamamayan
**city** *n* lungsod
**civic** *adj* panglungsod
**civil** *adj* pambayan
**civilization** *n* sibilisasyon
**civilize** *v* paunlarin
**claim** *v* angkinin
**claim** *n* pag-angkin
**clam** *n* kabibi
**clamor** *v* maghangad
**clamp** *n* pangkapit
**clan** *n* angkan; lahi
**clandestine** *adj* patago
**clap** *v* palakpakan
**clarification** *n* kalinawan
**clarify** *v* liwanagin
**clarinet** *n* klarinet
**clarity** *n* malinaw
**clash** *v* nagbanggaan
**clash** *n* banggaan
**class** *n* kalase
**classic** *adj* tradisyonal
**classify** *v* bigyan-uri
**classmate** *n* kamag-aral
**classroom** *n* silid-aralan
**classy** *adj* mataas na antas
**clause** *n* panag-uri
**claw** *n* matulis na kuko
**claw** *v* kalmutin
**clay** *n* putik
**clean** *adj* malinis
**clean** *v* linisin
**cleaner** *n* panglinis
**cleanliness** *n* kalinisan
**cleanse** *v* nillinis
**cleanser** *n* panglinis
**clear** *adj* maliwanag
**clear** *v* liwanagin

**clearance** *n* pahintulot
**clearly** *adv* malinaw
**clearness** *n* kalinawan
**cleft** *n* hiwa; espasyo
**clemency** *n* kapatawaran
**clench** *v* suntok ; kamao
**clergy** *n* pari; banal
**clergyman** *n* kabanalan
**clerical** *adj* pang-kawani
**clerk** *n* kawani
**clever** *adj* matalino
**click** *v* tunog; kilk
**client** *n* kleyente
**clientele** *n* kleyente
**cliff** *n* bangin
**climate** *n* klima
**climatic** *adj* ayon sa panahon
**climax** *n* kasukdulan
**climb** *v* akyatin
**climbing** *n* paakyat
**clinch** *v* yakapin
**cling** *iv* nakasabit
**clinic** *n* klinika
**clip** *v* gupitin
**clipping** *n* ginupit
**cloak** *n* alampay
**clock** *n* orasan
**clog** *v* bumara
**cloister** *n* monasteryo
**clone** *v* sinipi
**cloning** *n* sipi
**close** *v* pininid
**close** *adj* nakapinid
**close to** *pre* malapit sa
**closed** *adj* nakapinid
**closely** *adv* lapit-lapit
**closet** *n* aparador
**closure** *n* sarado
**clot** *n* bara
**cloth** *n* tela
**clothe** *v* nakadamit
**clothes** *n* damit
**clothing** *n* kadamitan
**cloud** *n* ulap
**cloudless** *adj* walang ulap
**cloudy** *adj* maulap
**clown** *n* payaso
**club** *n* kapisanan; batuta
**club** *v* batutain
**clue** *n* palatandaan
**clumsiness** *n* katangahan
**clumsy** *adj* tanga
**cluster** *n* kumpol; buwig
**cluster** *v* ikumpol
**clutch** *n* pigil; hawak
**coach** *v* sanayin; turuan
**coach** *n* tagasanay; taga turo
**coaching** *n* pagsasanay
**coagulate** *v* mapanis
**coagulation** *n* pagpanis
**coal** *n* uling
**coalition** *n* samahan
**coarse** *adj* magaspang
**coast** *n* aplaya

**coastal** *adj* baybayin
**coat** *n* pangginaw
**coax** *v* suyuin; utuin
**cob** *n* busal
**cobblestone** *n* bato
**cobweb** *n* sapot
**cocaine** *n* bato
**cock** *n* tandang
**cockpit** *n* sabungan
**cockroach** *n* ipis
**cocky** *adj* mayabang
**cocoa** *n* kakaw
**coconut** *n* niyog
**cod** *n* isda
**code** *n* batas
**codify** *v* bigyang sistema
**coerce** *v* pilitin
**coercion** *n* pagpilit
**coexist** *v* kasangga
**coffee** *n* kape
**coffin** *n* kabaong
**cohabit** *v* maki apid
**coherent** *adj* magkadikit
**cohesion** *n* dikit
**coin** *n* barya; sensilyo
**coincide** *v* itaon; isabay
**coincidence** *n* maisabay
**coincidental** *adj* nagkataon
**cold** *adj* malamig
**coldness** *n* lamig
**colic** *n* sakit ng tiyan
**collaborate** *v* makipag alam
**collaboration** *n* pagtutulungan
**collaborator** *n* katulong
**collapse** *v* nagwakas
**collapse** *n* wakas
**collar** *n* kuwelyo
**collarbone** *n* balikat
**collateral** *adj* katabi
**colleague** *n* kasamahan
**collect** *v* likapin
**collection** *n* nakalap
**collector** *n* kolektor
**college** *n* kolehiyo
**collide** *v* banggain
**collision** *n* banggaan
**cologne** *n* pabango
**colon** *n* bituka
**colonel** *n* koronel
**colonial** *adj* makabanyaga
**colonization** *n* pagsakop
**colonize** *v* sinakop
**colony** *n* banyaga
**color** *n* kulay
**color** *v* kulayan
**colorful** *adj* makulay
**colossal** *adj* malawak
**colt** *n* kabayo
**column** *n* hanay; haligi
**coma** *n* kuwit
**comb** *n* suklay
**comb** *v* nagsuklay
**combat** *n* away
**combat** *v* awayin

**combatant** *n* pal; aban
**combination** *n* kombinasyon
**combine** *v* ipagsama
**combustible** *n* maaring sumabog
**combustion** *n* pagsabog
**come** *iv* halika
**come about** *v* lumabas
**come across** *v* nasagupa
**come apart** *v* nahiwa-hiwalay
**come back** *v* bumalik
**come down** *v* bumaba
**come forward** *v* pumarito
**come from** *v* galing sa
**come in** *v* tumuloy
**come out** *v* lumabas
**come over** *v* dumalaw
**come up** *v* dumating
**comeback** *n* balik
**comedian** *n* komikero
**comedy** *n* komedya
**comet** *n* kometa
**comfort** *n* libang; aliw
**comfortable** *adj* maaliw
**comforter** *n* makapal na kumot
**comical** *adj* nakakateawa
**coming** *n* pagdating
**coming** *adj* dadating
**comma** *n* kuwit
**command** *v* utusan
**commander** *n* pangangalaga
**commandment** *n* utos
**commemorate** *v* gunitain
**commence** *v* umpisa
**commend** *v* papuri
**commendation** *n* pagpuri
**comment** *v* purihin
**comment** *n* papuri
**commerce** *n* komersyo
**commercial** *adj* komersyo
**commission** *n* komisyon
**commit** *v* nangako
**commitment** *n* pangako
**committed** *adj* nakapangako
**committee** *n* komite
**common** *adj* pangkaraniwan
**commotion** *n* pagkakagulo
**communication** *n* talsatasan
**communion** *n* komunyon
**communism** *n* komunista
**communist** *adj* komunista
**community** *n* lipunan
**commute** *v* sumakay
**compact** *adj* masikip
**compact** *v* sikipan
**companion** *n* kasama
**companionship** *n* samahan
**company** *n* kumpanya
**comparable** *adj* magkahawig
**comparative** *adj* kahawig
**compare** *v* ipaghawig
**comparison** *n* pagkahawig
**compartment** *n* partisyon
**compass** *n* kompas; aguhon
**compassion** *n* awa

**compassionate** *adj* maawain
**compatibility** *n* magkatapat
**compatible** *adj* bagay
**compatriot** *n* kababayan
**compel** *v* pilitin
**compelling** *adj* napipilitan
**compendium** *n* talata
**compensate** *v* bayaran
**compensation** *n* kabayaran
**competence** *n* karunungan
**competent** *adj* marunong
**competition** *n* paligsahan
**competitor** *n* katunggali
**compile** *v* ipunin
**complain** *v* umangal
**complaint** *n* angal
**complement** *n* suporta
**complete** *adj* sapat
**complete** *v* sapat
**completely** *adv* pagkasapat
**completion** *n* kabuuan
**complex** *adj* masalimuot
**complexion** *n* kutis
**complexity** *n* magusot
**compliance** *n* pagsunod
**compliant** *adj* umayon
**complicate** *v* guluhin
**complication** *n* kaguluhan
**complicity** *n* ksapakat
**compliment** *n* papurihan
**complimentary** *adj* walang bayad
**comply** *v* sumunod
**component** *n* bahagi
**compose** *v* gumawa
**composed** *adj* nagawa
**composer** *n* kompositor
**composition** *n* kompusisyon
**compost** *n* pataba
**composure** *n* katahimikan
**compound** *n* looban; higit sa isa
**compound** *v* ipaloob
**comprehend** *v* unwain
**comprehensive** *adj* pngkalahatan
**compress** *v* pisain
**compression** *n* pinisa
**comprise** *v* kinabibilangan
**compromise** *n* areglo
**compromise** *v* aregluhin
**compulsion** *n* pagkabigla
**compulsive** *adj* biglaan
**compulsory** *adj* obligasyon
**compute** *v* tuusin
**computer** *n* kompyuter
**comrade** *n* kasmahan
**con man** *n* manloloko
**conceal** *v* itago
**concede** *v* sumuko
**conceive** *v* naglilihi
**concentrate** *v* mag-isip
**concentration** *n* pag-iisip
**concentric** *adj* bilugan
**concept** *n* ideya
**conception** *n* napag-isipan
**concern** *v* mag malasakit

C

**concern** *n* malasakit
**concerning** *pre* naayon sa
**concert** *n* konsiyert
**concession** *n* pag bibigay
**conciliate** *v* awatin
**conciliatory** *adj* pang-awat
**concise** *adj* maiksi
**conclude** *v* tapusin
**conclusion** *n* katapusan
**conclusive** *adj* may katapusan
**concoct** *v* maghalo
**concoction** *n* hinalo
**concrete** *n* konkreto
**concrete** *adj* konkreto
**concur** *v* sumang ayon
**concurrent** *adj* pangkasalukuyan
**concussion** *n* maga
**condemn** *v* isumpa
**condemnation** *n* pagsumpa
**condensation** *n* pagkatunaw
**condense** *v* natunaw
**condescend** *v* magpakumbaba
**condiment** *n* pampalasa
**condition** *n* lagay
**conditional** *adj* may pasubali
**conditioner** *n* pampa kondisyon
**condo** *n* tirahan
**condolences** *n* pakiramay
**condone** *v* kunsintihin
**conduct** *n* asal
**conduct** *v* asal
**conductor** *n* konduktor
**cone** *n* hugis tatsulok
**confer** *v* ipagkaloob
**conference** *n* kumperensya
**confess** *v* mangumpisal
**confession** *n* kumpisal
**confessional** *n* pangungumpisal
**confessor** *n* pari
**confidant** *n* kasamahan
**confide** *v* magtiwala
**confidence** *n* kumpiyansa
**confident** *adj* may tiwala
**confidential** *adj* lihim
**confine** *v* ikulong; limitahan
**confinement** *n* kulong
**confirm** *v* kumpilan
**confirmation** *n* kumpil
**confiscate** *v* kumpiskahin
**confiscation** *n* pagkumpiska
**conflict** *n* magkagulo
**conflict** *v* nagkagulo
**conflicting** *adj* nagkakagulo
**conform** *v* sumang-ayon
**conformist** *adj* mapag-sang-ayon
**conformity** *n* pag-sang-ayon
**confound** *v* nalito
**confront** *v* sinita
**confrontation** *n* paghaharap
**confuse** *v* nalilito
**confusing** *adj* nakakalito
**confusion** *n* pagkalito
**congenial** *adj* masaya
**congested** *adj* magulo

**congestion** *n* kaguluhan
**congratulate** *v* binabati
**congratulations** *n* pagbati
**congregate** *v* mag-ipon-ipon
**congregation** *n* kongregasyon
**congress** *n* kongreso
**conjecture** *n* hula
**conjugate** *v* balangkasin
**conjunction** *n* salitang pangkabit
**conjure up** *v* isumpa
**connect** *v* ikabit
**connection** *n* pagkabit
**connive** *v* kasapakat
**connote** *v* ibig - sabihin
**conquer** *v* lupigin
**conqueror** *n* manlulupig
**conquest** *n* paglupig
**conscience** *n* kunsyensya
**conscious** *adj* nakakaalam
**conciousness** *n* kaalaman
**conscript** *n* talaan
**consecrate** *v* gawing banal
**consecration** *n* kabanalan
**consecutive** *adj* magkasunod
**consensus** *n* madla
**consent** *v* payagan
**consent** *n* pagpayag
**consequence** *n* dahilan
**consequent** *adj* kinahinatnan
**conservation** *n* pag sagip
**conservative** *adj* sagipin
**conserve** *v* magtipid
**conserve** *n* pagtitipid
**consider** *v* isa-alang-alang
**considerable** *adj* tamang bilang
**considerate** *adj* mapag-bigay
**consignment** *n* utang
**consist** *v* binubuo
**consistency** *n* langkap
**consistent** *adj* umaayon
**consolation** *n* pakinabang
**console** *v* damayan
**consolidate** *v* pagsamahin
**consonant** *n* katinig
**conspicuous** *adj* hindi halata
**conspiracy** *n* kasapakat
**conspirator** *n* kasapakat
**conspire** *v* kakutsabain
**constancy** *n* katatagan
**constant** *adj* matatag
**consternation** *n* pagkatulala
**constipate** *v* nahirapang dumumi
**constipated** *adj* tibi
**constipation** *n* di makadumi
**constitute** *v* binubuo
**constitution** *n* saligang-batas
**constrain** *v* pigilin
**constraint** *n* pagpigil
**construct** *v* gumawa
**construction** *n* gawain
**consul** *n* konsul
**consulate** *n* konsulado
**consult** *v* magpakonsulta
**consultation** *n* konsulta

**consume** *v* gamitin
**consumer** *n* mamimili
**consumption** *n* nagamit
**contact** *v* makipag-alam
**contact** *n* pakikitungo
**contagious** *adj* nakakahawa
**contain** *v* naglalaman
**container** *n* lalagyan
**contaminate** *v* marumihan
**contamination** *n* pagkarumi
**contemplate** *v* mag-isip
**contempt** *n* paghamak
**contend** *v* di-umano
**contender** *n* kalaban
**content** *adj* nilalaman
**content** *v* magkasya
**contentious** *adj* palasagot
**contents** *n* mga nilalaman
**contest** *n* palaro
**contestant** *n* kasapi
**context** *n* kahulugan
**continent** *n* kontinente
**continental** *adj* kontinental
**contingent** *adj* maaring mangyari
**continuation** *n* pagpapatuloy
**continue** *v* ituloy
**continuity** *n* tuluyan
**continuous** *adj* tuloy-tuloy
**contour** *n* hugis
**contraband** *n* kontrabando
**contract** *v* magkasundo
**contract** *n* kasulatan
**contraction** *n* pina-igsi
**contradict** *v* di sumang-ayon
**contradiction** *n* di pag-sang-ayon
**contrary** *adj* laban sa
**contrast** *v* igahin
**contrast** *n* kaibahan
**contribute** *v* dagdagan
**contribution** *n* dagdag
**contributor** *n* tagapag-gigay
**contrition** *n* pagsisisi
**control** *n* sawata
**control** *v* sawatain
**controversial** *adj* magulo
**controversy** *n* gusot
**convalescent** *adj* pag-galing
**convene** *v* nag-umpisa
**convenience** *n* kaginhawahan
**convenient** *adj* maginhawa
**convent** *n* kumbento
**convention** *n* pagpupulong
**conventional** *adj* ayon sa kaugalian
**converge** *v* magsalubong
**conversation** *n* pag-uusap
**converse** *v* mag-usap
**conversely** *adv* magkasalungat
**conversion** *n* palitan
**convert** *v* nag-palit
**convert** *n* palitan
**convey** *v* sabihin
**convict** *v* sentensyahan
**conviction** *n* sentensya
**convince** *v* kumbinsihin

C

**convincing** *adj* kapani-paniwala
**convoluted** *adj* lukot
**convoy** *n* kasama
**convulse** *v* nanginig
**convulsion** *n* kombulsyon
**cook** *v* magluto
**cook** *n* kusinero
**cookie** *n* kuki
**cooking** *n* pagluluto
**cool** *adj* malamig
**cool** *v* palamigin
**cool down** *v* magpalamig
**cooling** *adj* lumalamig
**coolness** *n* lamig
**cooperate** *v* maki-ayon
**cooperation** *n* kaayunan
**cooperative** *adj* kooperatiba
**coordination** *n* tulong-tulong
**coordinator** *n* namamahala
**cop** *n* pulis
**cope** *v* kayanin
**copier** *n* makinang panipi
**copper** *n* tanso
**copy** *v* sipiin
**copy** *n* sipiin
**copyright** *n* sariling akda
**cord** *n* kawad
**cordial** *adj* magalang
**cordless** *adj* walang kawad
**cordon** *n* kawad
**cordon off** *v* harangan
**core** *n* gitna
**cork** *n* tapon
**corn** *n* mais
**corner** *n* kanto
**cornerstone** *n* palatandaan
**cornet** *n* konela
**corollary** *n* naaayon sa
**coronary** *adj* ukol sa puso
**corporal** *adj* laman
**corporal** *n* kabo
**corporation** *n* korporasyon
**corpse** *n* bangkay
**corpulent** *adj* maskulado
**corpuscle** *n* dugo
**correct** *v* itama
**correct** *adj* tama
**correction** *n* akma
**correlate** *v* pagtugmain
**correspond** *v* tugunin
**correspondent** *n* katalastas
**corresponding** *adj* magkatugma
**corridor** *n* pasilyo; daanan
**corroborate** *v* patunayan
**corrode** *v* kinalawang
**corrupt** *v* suhulan
**corrupt** *adj* kabulukan
**corruption** *n* bulok
**cosmetic** *n* palamuti
**cosmic** *adj* mala kosmos
**cosmonaut** *n* kosmonot
**cost** *iv* halagahan
**cost** *n* halaga
**costly** *adj* mahal

**costume** *n* damit
**cottage** *n* maliit na bahay
**cotton** *n* bulak
**couch** *n* sopa
**cough** *n* ubo
**cough** *v* umubo
**council** *n* konseho
**counsel** *v* payuhan
**counsel** *n* abogado
**counselor** *n* tagapayo
**count** *v* bilangin
**count** *n* bilang
**countdown** *n* pagbilang
**countenance** *n* mukha
**counter** *n* di ayon
**counter** *v* taga bilang
**counteract** *v* igahin
**counterfeit** *v* peke
**counterfeit** *adj* pekein
**counterpart** *n* katulad
**countess** *n* kondesa
**countless** *adj* di mabilang
**country** *n* bansa
**countryman** *n* kababayan
**countryside** *n* bukid
**county** *n* lalawigan
**couple** *n* mag-asawa
**coupon** *n* kupon
**courage** *n* katapangan
**courageous** *adj* matapang
**courier** *n* mensahero
**course** *n* kurso
**court** *n* hukuman; korte
**court** *v* ligawan
**courteous** *adj* magalang
**courtesy** *n* paggalang
**courthouse** *n* bahay hukuman
**courtship** *n* ligawan
**courtyard** *n* palaruan
**cousin** *n* pinsan
**cove** *n* amo
**covenant** *n* kasunsuan
**cover** *n* takip
**cover** *v* takpan
**cover up** *v* pagtakpan
**coverage** *n* nasasakupan
**covert** *adj* lihim
**coverup** *n* patatakip
**covet** *v* agawin
**cow** *n* baka
**coward** *n* duwag
**cowardice** *n* karuwagan
**cowardly** *adv* duwag
**cowboy** *n* bakero
**cozy** *adj* maginhawa
**crab** *n* alimango
**crack** *n* lamat
**crack** *v* lamatan
**cradle** *n* duyan
**craft** *n* kasanayan
**craftsman** *n* espesyalista
**cram** *v* nagmadali
**cramp** *n* paninigas
**cramped** *adj* masikip

**crane** *n* tikling
**crank** *n* loka
**cranky** *adj* masungit
**crap** *n* basura
**crappy** *adj* marumi
**crash** *n* banggaan
**crash** *v* nabangga
**crass** *adj* garapal
**crater** *n* hukay
**crave** *v* nananabik
**craving** *n* pananabik
**crawl** *v* gumapang
**crayon** *n* pangkulay
**craziness** *n* kabaliwan
**crazy** *adj* baliw
**creak** *v* sapa
**creak** *n* langitngit
**cream** *n* krema
**creamy** *adj* makrema
**crease** *n* tupi
**crease** *v* itupi
**create** *v* gumawa
**creation** *n* nilikha
**creative** *adj* masining
**creativity** *n* pagiging malikhain
**creator** *n* Tagapag likha
**creature** *n* nilikha
**credibility** *n* tiwala
**credit** *n* utang
**creditor** *n* nagpapautang
**creed** *n* pananalig
**creek** *n* sapa
**creep** *v* gumapang
**creepy** *adj* nakakakilabot
**cremate** *v* sunugin
**crematorium** *n* krematoryo
**crest** *n* tuktok
**crevice** *n* siwang
**crew** *n* tauhan
**crib** *n* kuna
**cricket** *n* salagubang
**crime** *n* krimen
**criminal** *adj* salarin
**cripple** *adj* pilay
**cripple** *v* pilayin
**crisis** *n* krisis; panganib
**crisp** *adj* malutong
**criss-cross** *v* sala-salabat
**crispy** *adj* malutong
**criterion** *n* pamantayan
**criticism** *n* panunuri
**criticize** *v* suriin
**critique** *n* manunuri
**crockery** *n* paso
**crocodile** *n* buwaya
**crony** *n* alagad
**crook** *n* magnanakaw
**crooked** *adj* tabingi
**crop** *n* pananim
**cross** *n* krus
**cross** *adj* mala krus
**cross** *v* krus
**cross out** *v* guhitan
**crossfire** *n* barilan

C

**crossing** *n* krosing
**crossroads** *n* daan krus
**crosswalk** *n* daanan
**crossword** *n* palaisipan
**crouch** *v* humukot
**crow** *n* uwak
**crowbar** *n* pang hukay
**crowd** *n* matao
**crowd** *v* magpulong
**crowded** *adj* maraming tao
**crown** *n* korona
**crown** *v* koronahan
**crucial** *adj* mahalaga
**crucifix** *n* krus
**crucifixion** *n* pinako sa krus
**crucify** *v* ipako sa krus
**crude** *adj* hindi pino
**cruel** *adj* malupit
**cruelty** *n* kalupitan
**cruise** *v* pasyal
**crumb** *n* mumo; pira-piraso
**crumble** *v* durugin
**crunchy** *adj* malutong
**crusade** *n* krusada
**crush** *v* durugin
**crushing** *adj* nandudurog
**crust** *n* latak
**crutch** *n* malutong na latak
**cry** *n* iyak
**cry** *v* umiyak; tumangis
**cry out** *v* nag-umiyak
**crying** *n* pag-iyak
**crystal** *n* kristal; bubog
**cub** *n* guya
**cube** *n* kubo
**cubic** *adj* kubiko
**cucumber** *n* pipino
**cuddle** *v* yapusin
**cuff** *n* punyas
**cuisine** *n* pagluluto
**culminate** *v* pagtatapos
**culpability** *n* kasalanan
**culprit** *n* may sala
**cult** *n* kulto
**cultivate** *v* magtanim
**cultivation** *n* pananim
**cultural** *adj* kalinangan
**culture** *n* kultura
**cumbersome** *adj* matrabaho
**cunning** *adj* tuso
**cup** *n* tasa
**cupboard** *n* paminggalan
**curable** *adj* malulunasan
**curator** *n* tagapamahala
**curb** *v* ibangketa
**curb** *n* bangketa
**curdle** *v* umasim
**cure** *v* lunasan; gamutin
**cure** *n* gamot
**curfew** *n* takadang oras
**curiosity** *n* pag-uusisa
**curious** *adj* mausisa
**curl** *v* kulutin
**curl** *n* kulot

**curly** *adj* kulot
**currency** *n* pera; salapi
**currently** *adv* sa ngayon
**curse** *v* isumpa
**curtail** *v* pagbawalan
**curtain** *n* kurtina
**curve** *n* kurbada
**curve** *v* iliko
**cushion** *n* alpombra
**cushion** *v* suportahan
**cuss** *v* magmura
**custard** *n* matamis; pamutat
**custȏdian** *n* taga pamahala
**custody** *n* pag-iingat
**custom** *n* nakaugalian
**customary** *adj* ayon sa kaugalian
**customer** *n* mamimili
**custom-made** *adj* pasadya
**customs** *n* adwana
**cut** *n* hiwa
**cut** *iv* putulin
**cut back** *v* bawasan
**cut down** *v* bawasan
**cut off** *v* itigil
**cut out** *v* ginupit
**cute** *adj* maganda
**cutter** *n* maghiwa
**cyanide** *n* lason
**cycle** *n* ikot; bilog
**cyclist** *n* siklista
**cyclone** *n* unos
**cylinder** *n* silindro
**cynic** *adj* nangungutya
**cynicism** *n* di naniniwala
**cypress** *n* halaman
**cyst** *n* bukol
**czar** *n* isang hari

# D

**dad** *n* ama
**dagger** *n* panaksak
**daily** *adv* araw-araw
**dairy farm** *n* bukid
**daisy** *n* bulaklak
**dam** *n* dam
**damage** *n* sira
**damage** *v* nasira
**damaging** *adj* nakakasira
**damn** *v* pasamain
**damnation** *n* kasamaan
**damp** *adj* basa
**dampen** *v* basain
**dance** *n* sayaw
**dance** *v* magsayaw
**dancing** *n* sayawan
**dandruff** *n* balakubak
**danger** *n* delikado
**dangerous** *adj* mapanganib
**dangle** *v* isabit

D

**dare** *v* hamunin
**dare** *n* paghamon
**dark** *adj* madilim
**darken** *v* diliman
**darkness** *n* kadiliman
**darling** *adj* sinta
**darn** *v* sulsihan; tahiin
**dart** *n* palasong maigsi
**dash** *v* tumakbong mabilis
**dashing** *adj* mabilis
**data** *n* datos
**database** *n* basehan ng datos
**date** *n* tagpuan
**date** *v* magtatagpo
**daughter** *n* anak
**daughter-in-law** *n* manugang
**daunt** *v* nahintakutan
**daunting** *adj* kahindik-hindik
**dawn** *n* madaling-araw
**day** *n* araw
**daydream** *v* nananaginip
**daze** *v* hilo
**dazed** *adj* nahilo
**dazzle** *v* silawin
**dazzling** *adj* nakakasilaw
**de luxe** *adj* espsyal
**dead** *adj* patay
**dead end** *n* katapusan
**deaden** *v* patayin
**deadline** *n* takdang araw
**deadlock** *adj* tabla
**deadly** *adj* nakamamatay
**deaf** *adj* bingi
**deafen** *v* nabibingi
**deafening** *adj* nakabibingi
**deafness** *n* pagka bingi
**deal** *iv* makipagkasunduan
**deal** *n* kasunduan
**dealer** *n* mangangalakal
**dealings** *n* pangangalakal
**dean** *n* dekana
**dear** *adj* mahal
**dearly** *adv* mahalin
**death** *n* kamatayan
**death toll** *n* bilang ng namatay
**death trap** *n* patibong
**debase** *v* sirain
**debatable** *adj* mapagtatalunan
**debate** *v* magtalo
**debate** *n* pagtatalo
**debit** *n* tubo
**debrief** *v* igsian
**debris** *n* natira
**debt** *n* utang
**debtor** *n* ang nangungutang
**debunk** *v* sinira
**debut** *n* unang labas
**decade** *n* dekada
**decadence** *n* pagkasira
**decapitate** *v* pugutan
**decay** *v* nabubulok
**decay** *n* bulok
**deceased** *adj* namayapa
**deceit** *n* daya

**deceitful** *adj* madaya
**deceive** *v* dayain
**December** *n* Disyembre
**decency** *n* disente
**decent** *adj* disente
**deception** *n* pandaraya
**deceptive** *adj* madaya
**decide** *v* magpasya
**deciding** *adj* nagpasya
**decimal** *adj* tuldok
**decimate** *v* sugpuin
**decipher** *v* isipin
**decision** *n* pasya
**decisive** *adj* wakas
**deck** *n* kubyerta
**declaration** *n* pagpapahayag
**declare** *v* ipahayag
**decline** *v* tanggihan
**decline** *n* pagtanggi
**decompose** *v* naagnas
**décor** *n* palamuti
**decorate** *v* palamutian
**decorative** *adj* pampalamuti
**decorum** *n* tamang ayos
**decrease** *v* bawasan
**decrease** *n* bawas
**decree** *n* batas; utos
**decree** *v* ipag-utos
**decrepit** *adj* mahina; matanda
**dedicate** *v* ihandog; ialay
**dedication** *n* paghahandog
**deduce** *v* bawasan
**deduct** *v* bawasan
**deductible** *adj* magbababawas
**deduction** *n* bawas
**deed** *n* katibayan; gawain
**deem** *v* ipalagay
**deep** *adj* kalaliman
**deepen** *v* laliman
**deer** *n* usa
**deface** *v* dumihan
**defame** *v* dungisan
**defeat** *v* talunin
**defeat** *n* talo
**defect** *n* takas
**defect** *v* tumakas
**defection** *n* pagtakas
**defective** *adj* may kasiraan
**defend** *v* iapgtanggol
**defendant** *n* manananggol
**defense** *n* laban
**defenseless** *adj* walang laban
**defer** *v* ipag-paliban
**defiance** *n* ipagtanggol
**defiant** *adj* mapagtanggol
**deficiency** *n* kasiraan
**deficient** *adj* kakulangan
**deficit** *n* kulang
**defile** *v* dumihan
**definite** *adj* tiyak
**definition** *n* kahulugan
**definitive** *adj* may kahulugan
**deflate** *v* alisin ang hangin
**deform** *v* pinasama ang ayos

**deformity** *n* kasiraan ng ayos
**defraud** *v* dayain; lokohin
**defray** *v* sagutin
**defrost** *v* tunawin
**deft** *adj* matalas; matalino
**defuse** *v* patayin
**defy** *v* sinuway
**degenerate** *v* lumalala
**degenerate** *adj* malala
**degeneration** *n* paglala
**degradation** *n* malalang kalagayan
**degrade** *v* lumala ang kalagayn
**degree** *n* antas; pinag-aralan
**dehydrate** *v* naubusan ng tubig
**deign** *v* karapat-dapat
**deity** *n* dyosa
**dejected** *adj* pagka bigo
**delay** *v* naantala
**delay** *n* huli
**delegate** *v* i-utos
**delegate** *n* delegado
**delegation** *n* delegasyon
**delete** *v* burahin
**deliberate** *v* pag-usapan
**deliberate** *adj* napa-usapan
**delicacy** *n* kakanin
**delicate** *adj* maselan
**delicious** *adj* masarap
**delight** *n* maaya
**delight** *v* ayahan
**delightful** *adj* malugod
**delinquent** *n* estapadora
**deliver** *v* dalhin
**delivery** *n* paghahatid
**delude** *v* lituhin
**deluge** *n* baha
**delusion** *n* maling paniniwala
**demand** *v* nangangailangan
**demand** *n* panghihingi
**demanding** *adj* mapag hanap
**demean** *v* nagpakumbaba
**demeaning** *adj* bawass pagkatao
**demeanor** *n* magandang ugali
**demented** *adj* makakalimutin
**demise** *n* pagpanaw
**democracy** *n* demokrasya
**democratic** *adj* pantay-pantay
**demolish** *v* gibain
**demolition** *n* pag giba
**demon** *n* demonyo
**demonstrate** *v* ipakita
**demonstrative** *adj* pagpapakita
**demote** *v* ibaba ang ranggo
**den** *n* lungga; kweba
**denial** *n* pagtanggi
**denigrate** *v* siraan
**Denmak** *n* Denmark
**denominator** *n* kabahagdan
**denote** *v* patungkulan
**denounce** *v* isuplong
**dense** *adj* matindi ; makapal
**density** *n* kakapalan
**dent** *v* napingkong
**dent** *n* pingkong

**dental** *adj* dental
**dentist** *n* dentista
**dentures** *n* pustiso
**deny** *v* itanggi
**depart** *v* umalis
**department** *n* departamento
**departure** *n* pag-alis
**depend** *v* umasa; iasa
**dependable** *adj* maasahan
**dependence** *n* nakasalalay
**dependent** *adj* tangkilik
**depict** *v* ilarawan
**deplete** *v* ubusin
**deplorable** *adj* karumal-dumal
**deplore** *v* panghinayangan
**deploy** *v* italaga
**deployment** *n* pag talaga
**deport** *v* palayasin
**deportation** *n* deprtasyon
**depose** *v* patalsikin
**deposit** *n* deposito
**depot** *n* lagakan
**deprave** *adj* malaswa
**depravity** *n* kalaswaan
**depress** *v* nawalan ng sigla
**depressing** *adj* nakakalungkot
**depression** *n* matinding lungkot
**deprive** *v* ipagkait
**deprived** *adj* salat
**deprivation** *n* ipagkait
**depth** *n* lalim
**derail** *v* nadiskarel
**derailment** *n* diskarel
**deranged** *adj* loko-loko
**derelict** *adj* abonado, iniwan
**deride** *v* tuyain
**derivative** *adj* pinagmulan
**derive** *v* galing sa
**derogatory** *adj* pagmumura
**descend** *v* bumaba
**descendant** *n* ninuno
**descent** *n* pagbaba
**describe** *v* ilarawan
**description** *n* paglalarawan
**descriptive** *adj* mapaglarawan
**desecrate** *v* alipustain
**desegregate** *v* paghiwa-hiwalayin
**desert** *n* disyerto
**desert** *v* iwanan
**deserted** *adj* iniwanan
**deserter** *n* tumakas
**deserve** *v* nararapat lamang
**deserving** *adj* karapat-dapat
**design** *n* palamuti
**designate** *v* italaga
**desirable** *adj* kaibig-ibig
**desire** *n* pagnanasa
**desire** *v* pagnasaan
**desist** *v* ayawan
**desk** *n* sulatan
**desolate** *adj* nag-iisa
**desolation** *n* pag-iisa
**despair** *n* kawalang pag-asa
**desperate** *adj* walang pag-asa

D

**despicable** *adj* kalunos-lunos
**despise** *v* hamakin
**despite** *c* bagamat
**despondent** *adj* malungkot
**despot** *n* hari
**despotic** *adj* mala- hari
**dessert** *n* pag-himagas
**destination** *n* patutunguhan
**destiny** *n* tadhana
**destitute** *adj* kahirapan
**destroy** *v* sirain
**destroyer** *n* pangsira
**destruction** *n* pagkasira
**destructive** *adj* mapanira
**detach** *v* tanggalin
**detachable** *adj* natatanggal
**detail** *n* detalye
**detail** *v* idetalye
**detain** *v* ipakulong
**detect** *v* manmanan
**detective** *n* tiktik
**detention** *n* pakakulong
**deter** *v* pigilan
**detergent** *n* panglinis
**deteriorate** *v* nabubulok
**deterioration** *n* pagka bulok
**determine** *v* alamin
**deterrence** *n* sagabal
**detest** *v* kamuhian
**detestable** *adj* kinapopootan
**detonate** *v* pasabugin
**detonation** *n* pagsabog
**detonator** *n* pampasabog
**detour** *n* iwasan, iliko
**detriment** *n* pagkawala
**detrimental** *adj* nakakabawas
**devaluation** *n* pagbaba
**devalue** *v* pawalang-halaga
**devastate** *v* wasakin
**devastating** *adj* sinalanta
**devastation** *n* nasalanta
**develop** *v* pagbutihin
**development** *n* pagpapaganda
**deviation** *n* pag bago
**device** *n* isang makina
**devil** *n* demonyo
**devious** *adj* maligoy
**devise** *v* gumawa
**devoid** *adj* kakulangan
**devote** *v* gamitin ang panahon
**devotion** *n* pagmamahal
**devour** *v* lapain
**devout** *adj* marubdob
**dew** *n* hamog
**diabetes** *n* dyabetes
**diabetic** *adj* may dyabetes
**diabolical** *adj* pahaba
**diagnose** *v* alamin ang kondisyon
**diagonal** *adj* dayagonal
**diagram** *n* plano; balangkas
**dial** *n* dayal
**dial** *v* idayal
**dial tone** *n* tunog
**dialect** *n* wika

**dialogue** *n* dayalogo
**diameter** *n* dayametro
**diamond** *n* dyamante
**diaper** *n* lampin
**diarrhea** *n* pagtatae
**diary** *n* dyari
**dice** *n* days
**dictate** *v* mag-dikta
**dictator** *n* diktador
**dictatorial** *adj* diktadura
**dictatorship** *n* diktador
**dictionary** *n* talasalitaan
**die** *v* patayin
**die out** *v* namatay
**diet** *n* diyeta
**differ** *v* ibahin
**difference** *n* diperensya
**different** *adj* magka-iba
**difficult** *adj* mahirap
**difficulty** *n* kahirapan
**diffuse** *v* ikalat
**dig** *iv* hukayin
**digest** *v* tunawin
**digestion** *n* pagtunaw ng kinain
**digit** *n* bilang
**dignify** *v* bigyan parangal
**dignitary** *n* pinagpipitaganan
**dignity** *n* dignidad
**digress** *v* ibahin
**dike** *n* lawa
**dilapidated** *adj* lumang-luma
**dilemma** *n* pagkakasubo
**diligence** *n* pagsisikap
**diligent** *adj* masikap
**dilute** *v* ihalo
**dim** *adj* madilim
**dim** *v* diliman
**dime** *n* diyes
**dimension** *n* sukat
**diminish** *v* iwala
**dine** *v* kumain
**diner** *n* kainan
**dining room** *n* silid kainan
**dinner** *n* hapunan
**dinosaur** *n* halimaw
**diocese** *n* dayoseso
**diphthong** *n* isang tunog
**diploma** *n* diploma
**diplomacy** *n* diplomasya
**diplomat** *n* diplomatiko
**diplomatic** *adj* madiplomasya
**dire** *adj* terible
**direct** *adj* diretso
**direct** *v* ituro
**direction** *n* direksyon
**director** *n* direktor
**directory** *n* listahan
**dirt** *n* dumi
**dirty** *adj* marumi
**disability** *n* walang kakayanan
**disabled** *adj* baldado
**disadvantage** *n* walang silbi
**disagree** *v* di sumang-ayon
**disagreeable** *adj* di pag-sang-ayon

**disagreement** *n* di pagkakasundo
**disappear** *v* nawala
**disappearance** *n* pagka wala
**disappoint** *v* nabigo
**disappointing** *adj* nakakabigo
**disappointment** *n* pagka bigo
**disapproval** *n* walang pahintulot
**disapprove** *v* hindi pinayagan
**disarm** *v* inalisan ng armas
**disarmament** *n* kulang sa armas
**disaster** *n* salanta
**disastrous** *adj* sumalanta
**disband** *v* mag-hiwalay
**disbelief** *n* di kapani-paniwala
**disburse** *v* maglabas ng pera
**discard** *v* itapon
**discern** *v* isipin
**discharge** *v* palitan; pawalan
**discharge** *n* pagpalit
**disciple** *n* disipolo
**discipline** *n* disiplina
**disclaim** *v* itanggi
**disclose** *v* ilahad
**discomfort** *n* di palagay
**disconnect** *v* ipa-putol
**discontent** *adj* di sang-ayon
**discontinue** *v* itigil
**discord** *n* pagtatalo
**discordant** *adj* di umayon
**discount** *n* diskwento
**discount** *v* bawasan
**discourage** *v* nawalan ng pag-asa
**discourtesy** *n* walang galang
**discover** *v* alamin
**discovery** *n* nalaman
**discredit** *v* siraang puri
**discreet** *adj* ilihim
**discrepancy** *n* kamalian
**discretion** *n* may kapangyarihan
**discriminate** *v* panigan
**discrimination** *n* pagpanig
**discuss** *v* pag-usapan
**discussion** *n* pag-uusap
**disdain** *n* pag-alipusta
**disease** *n* sakit
**disembark** *v* bumaba
**disentangle** *v* inalis ang buhol
**disfigure** *v* sinira; winasak
**disgrace** *n* kahihiyan
**disgrace** *v* nakakahiya
**disgraceful** *adj* walanghiya
**disgruntled** *adj* masama ang loob
**disguise** *v* mag-panggap
**disguise** *n* pag-panggap
**disgust** *n* pagkasuya
**disgusting** *adj* nakakasuya
**dish** *n* pagkain
**dishonest** *adj* mandaraya
**dishonesty** *n* pandaraya
**dishonor** *n* nawalan ng dangal
**dishonorable** *adj* walang dangal
**disinfect** *v* linisin
**disinfectant** *n* panglinis
**disinherit** *v* nawalan ng mana

**disintegrate** *v* pag-hiwa-hiwalayin
**disintegration** *n* paghihiwalay
**disinterested** *adj* walang gana
**disk** *n* lalagyan
**dislike** *v* ayaw
**dislike** *n* pag-ayaw
**dislocate** *v* natanggal sa lugar
**dislodge** *v* naalis
**disloyal** *adj* hindi tapat
**disloyalty** *n* hindi tapat
**dismal** *adj* malungkot
**dismantle** *v* tanggalin
**dismay** *n* bagabag
**dismay** *v* nabagabag
**dismiss** *v* itiwalag; alisin
**dismissal** *n* tiniwalag; inalis
**dismount** *v* bumaba
**disobedience** *n* pag-suway
**disobedient** *adj* masuway
**disobey** *v* suwayin
**disorder** *n* kaguluhan
**disorganized** *adj* magulo
**disoriented** *adj* lito
**disown** *v* iwaksi
**disparity** *n* hindi magkatugma
**dispatch** *v* ipahatid; ipadala
**dispel** *v* ikalat
**dispensation** *n* pagpapatawad
**dispense** *v* ipamahagi
**dispersal** *n* pagpapakalat
**disperse** *v* ikalat
**displace** *v* pinalayas
**display** *n* pagladlad
**display** *v* iladlad
**displease** *v* hindi nagustuhan
**displeasing** *adj* di ka-aya-aya
**displeasure** *n* pagkayamot
**disposable** *adj* pamigay
**disposal** *n* kagustuhan
**dispose** *v* ipamigay
**disprove** *v* di sang-ayunan
**dispute** *n* pagtatalo
**dispute** *v* nagtalo
**disqualify** *v* pinawalang-saysay
**disregard** *v* pinawalang-bisa
**disrespect** *n* paglapastangan
**disrespectful** *adj* walang galang
**disrupt** *v* abalahin
**disruption** *n* pigilan
**dissatisfied** *adj* nabigo
**disseminate** *v* pinamudmod
**dissent** *v* ayaw sumang-ayon
**dissident** *adj* sumalungat
**dissimilar** *adj* magka-iba
**dissipate** *v* isabog
**dissolute** *adj* kakaiba
**dissolution** *n* pagtunaw
**dissolve** *v* tunawin
**dissonant** *adj* salungat
**dissuade** *v* sumalungat
**distance** *n* layo
**distant** *adj* malayo
**distaste** *n* di kanais-nais
**distasteful** *adj* malaswa

D

**distill** *v* salain
**distinct** *adj* kaka-iba
**distinction** *n* parangal
**distinctive** *adj* kakaiba
**distinguish** *v* parangalan
**distort** *v* ibahin
**distortion** *n* pagkakaiba
**distract** *v* lituhin
**distraction** *n* pampalito
**distraught** *adj* nasira ang ulo
**distress** *n* pagkabalisa
**distress** *v* nabalisa
**distressing** *adj* nakakabalisa
**distribute** *v* ipmamahagi
**distribution** *n* pagbahagi
**district** *n* purok
**distrust** *n* walang tiwala
**distrustful** *adj* hinid katiwa-tiwala
**disturb** *v* nag-aalala
**disturbance** *n* kaguluhan
**disturbing** *adj* magulo
**disunity** *n* walang pagkaka-isa
**disuse** *n* tinigi ang paggamit
**ditch** *n* hukay
**dive** *v* sumisid
**diver** *n* maninisid
**diverse** *adj* iba-iba
**diversify** *v* pag-iba-ibahin
**diversion** *n* pag-sanga
**diversity** *n* iba-iba
**divert** *v* iligaw
**divide** *v* hatiin
**dividend** *n* tubo; pakinabang
**divine** *adj* banal
**diving** *n* pagsisid
**divinity** *n* kabanalan
**divisible** *adj* maaring hatiin
**division** *n* paghahati-hati
**divorce** *n* diborsyo
**divorce** *v* maghiwalay
**divorcee** *n* humiwalay
**divulge** *v* isinambulat
**dizziness** *n* pagka hilo
**dizzy** *adj* hilo
**do** *iv* gawin na
**docile** *adj* madaling turuan
**docility** *n* matalas
**dock** *n* daungan
**dock** *v* idaong
**doctor** *n* manggagamot
**doctrine** *n* doktrina
**document** *n* papeles
**documentary** *n* kasulatan
**documentation** *n* papeles
**dodge** *v* ilagan
**dog** *n* aso
**dole out** *v* palimos
**doll** *n* manika
**dollar** *n* dolyar
**dolphin** *n* dolpin
**dome** *n* simboryo
**domestic** *adj* domestiko
**domesticate** *v* paamuhin
**dominate** *v* sakupin

**domination** *n* kapangyarihan
**domineering** *adj* makapangyarihan
**dominion** *n* kaharian
**donate** *v* magbigay
**donation** *n* abuloy
**donkey** *n* buriko
**donor** *n* may bigay
**doom** *n* tadhana
**doomed** *adj* sawi
**door** *n* pinto
**doorbell** *n* timbre
**doorstep** *n* sa may pinto
**doorway** *n* daanan; pasilyo
**dope** *n* sugapa
**dope** *v* apyan
**dormitory** *n* dormitoryo
**dosage** *n* takal ng gamoth
**dossier** *n* papeles
**dot** *n* tuldok
**double** *adj* doble
**double** *v* doble
**double-check** *v* tingnan muli
**double-cross** *v* linlangin
**doubt** *n* walang tiwala
**doubt** *v* alinlangan; duda
**doubtful** *adl* ka-duda-duda
**dough** *n* masa
**dove** *n* kalapati
**down** *adv* baba
**down payment** *n* paunang bayad
**downcast** *adj* pababa
**downfall** *n* pagbagsak
**downhill** *adv* pababa
**downpour** *n* pagbuhos ng ulan
**downsize** *v* bawasan ang sukat
**downstairs** *adv* ibaba
**down-to-earth** *adj* makatotohanan
**downtown** *n* kabayanan; sentro
**downtrodden** *adj* api; aba
**downturn** *n* pag-bagsak
**dowry** *n* dote
**doze** *n* idlip
**doze** *v* napaidlip
**dozen** *n* dosena
**draft** *v* iguhit
**draftsman** *n* delinyante
**drag** *v* hilahin
**dragon** *n* dragon
**drain** *v* salain
**drainage** *n* kanal
**dramatic** *adj* madula
**dramatize** *v* isadula
**drape** *n* kurtina
**drastic** *adj* matindi
**draw** *n* pag-guhit
**draw** *iv* iguhit
**drawback** *n* sagabal
**drawer** *n* hunos
**drawing** *n* guhit; dibuho
**dread** *v* ayawan
**dreaded** *adj* inaayawan
**dreadful** *adj* karumal-dumal
**dream** *iv* nanaginip

D

**dream** *n* pangarap
**dress** *n* damit
**dress** *v* damitan
**dresser** *n* lalagyan ng damit
**dressing** *n* salsa
**dried** *adj* tuyo
**drift** *v* natangay
**drift apart** *v* nagkahiwalay
**drifter** *n* ligaw
**drill** *v* maghukay
**drill** *n* panghukay
**drink** *iv* uminom
**drink** *n* inumin
**drinkable** *adj* maaring inumin
**drinker** *n* manginginom
**drip** *v* tumulo
**drip** *n* tulo
**drive** *n* tsuper
**drive** *iv* mag-maneho
**drive at** *v* tumbukin
**drive away** *v* palayasin
**driver** *n* tsupr
**driveway** *n* daanan
**drizzle** *v* umaambon
**drizzle** *n* ambon
**drop** *n* nahulog
**drop** *v* nahuhulog
**drop in** *v* sumaglit
**drop off** *v* ilagay
**drop out** *v* tumigil
**drought** *n* tag-tuyot
**drown** *v* nalulunod
**drowsy** *adj* lango
**drug** *n* gamot
**drug** *v* gamutin
**drugstore** *n* parmasiya
**drum** *n* tambol
**drunk** *adj* lasing
**drunkenness** *n* kalasingan
**dry** *v* natutuyo
**dry** *adj* natuyo
**dryclean** *v* linisin ng tuyo
**dryer** *n* pampatuyo
**dual** *adj* doble
**dubious** *adj* di tiyak
**duchess** *n* dukesa
**duck** *n* pato
**duck** *v* dumapa
**duct** *n* daluyan
**due** *adj* nakatakda
**duel** *n* duwelo
**dues** *n* bayarin
**duke** *n* duke
**dull** *adj* mapurol; bobo
**duly** *adv* nang nararapat
**dumb** *adj* bingi
**dummy** *n* tanga
**dummy** *adj* modelo; manikin
**dump** *v* itapon
**dump** *n* basura
**dung** *n* dumi ng hayop
**dungeon** *n* bartolina
**dupe** *v* nanloloko
**duplicate** *v* sipiin

**duplication** *n* sipi
**durable** *adj* matibay
**duration** *n* tagal
**during** *pre* sa panahon
**dusk** *n* dapit-hapon
**dust** *n* alikabok
**dusty** *adj* maalikabok
**Dutch** *adj* Olandes
**duty** *n* katungkulan
**dwarf** *n* dwende
**dwell** *iv* tumira; manirahan
**dwelling** *n* bahay
**dwindle** *v* unti-unting maubos
**dye** *v* kulayan
**dye** *n* pangkulay
**dying** *adj* naghihingalo
**dynamic** *adj* masigla
**dynamite** *n* dinamita
**dynasty** *n* dinastiya

**each** *adj* bawat isa
**each other** *adj* isat-isa
**eager** *adj* masigasig
**eagerness** *n* pagkasabik
**eagle** *n* agila
**ear** *n* tainga
**earache** *n* masakit ang tainga
**eardrum** *n* loob ng tainga
**early** *adv* maaga
**earmark** *v* italaga
**earn** *v* kita
**earnestly** *adv* tapat
**earnings** *n* kinita
**earphones** *n* makinang pandinig
**earring** *n* hikaw
**earth** *n* mundo
**earthquake** *n* lindol
**earwax** *n* tutuli
**ease** *v* madaliin
**ease** *n* madali
**easily** *adv* magmadali
**east** *n* silangan
**eastern** *adj* silanganan
**easterner** *n* taga silangan
**eastward** *adv* patungong
**easy** *adj* madali
**eat** *iv* kumain
**eat away** *v* nilamon
**eavesdrop** *v* makinig
**ebb** *v* kati
**eccentric** *adj* makasarili
**echo** *n* alingawngaw
**eclipse** *n* paglalaho
**ecology** *n* ekolohiya
**economical** *adj* matipid
**economize** *v* magtipid
**economy** *n* ekonomiya
**edge** *n* gilid

**edgy** *adj* di mapalagay
**edible** *adj* makakain
**edifice** *n* edipisyo
**edit** *v* baguhin
**edition** *n* binago
**educate** *v* turuan
**eerie** *adj* nakakatakot
**effect** *n* epekto
**effective** *adj* mabisa
**effectiveness** *n* pagkamabisa
**efficiency** *n* kahusayan
**efficient** *adj* mahusay
**effigy** *n* larawan
**effort** *n* pagpupunyagi
**effusive** *adj* garapal
**egg** *n* itlog
**egg white** *n* puti ng itlog
**egoism** *n* pansarili
**egoist** *n* makasarili
**eight** *adj* walo
**eighteen** *adj* labing - walo
**eighth** *adj* pang-walo
**eighty** *adj* walumpu
**either** *adj* kahit alin
**either** *adv* alinman
**eject** *v* tanggihan
**elapse** *v* lumamapas
**elastic** *adj* lastiko
**elated** *adj* nasiyahan
**elbow** *n* siko
**elder** *n* nakatatanda
**elderly** *adj* matanda
**elect** *v* iboto
**election** *n* botohan
**electric** *adj* elektrika
**electrician** *n* elektresista
**electricity** *n* koryente
**electrify** *v* ibitay sa koryente
**electrocute** *v* koryentihin
**electronic** *adj* elektronika
**elegance** *n* elegante
**elegant** *adj* elegante
**element** *n* elemento
**elementary** *adj* elementarya
**elephant** *n* elepante
**elevate** *v* itaas
**elevation** *n* taas
**elevator** *n* makinang pantaas
**eleven** *adj* labing-isa
**eleventh** *adj* pang-labing-isa
**eligible** *adj* nararapat
**eliminate** *v* alisin
**elm** *n* puno
**eloquence** *n* kahusayan
**else** *adv* kung hindi; o kaya
**elsewhere** *adv* kahit saan
**elude** *v* iwasan
**elusive** *adj* mailap
**emaciated** *adj* maputla
**emanate** *v* magmula
**emancipate** *v* palayain
**embalm** *v* embalsamuhin
**embark** *v* sumakay
**embarrass** *v* ipahiya

**embassy** *n* emababahada
**embellish** *v* palamutian
**embers** *n* uling
**embezzle** *v* lustayin
**embitter** *v* galitin
**emblem** *n* sagisag
**embody** *v* kinapapalooban
**emboss** *v* nakakapa
**embrace** *v* yakapin
**embrace** *n* yakap
**embroider** *v* burdahan
**embroidery** *n* burda
**embroil** *v* ihawin
**embryo** *n* sanggol
**emerald** *n* emerald
**emerge** *v* lumabas
**emigrant** *n* dayuhan
**emigrate** *v* mandayuhan
**emission** *n* buga
**emit** *v* bumuga
**emotion** *n* damdamin
**emotional** *adj* maramdamin
**emperor** *n* emperador
**emphasis** *n* pagtuon
**emphasize** *v* ituon
**empire** *n* imperyo
**employ** *v* upahan
**employee** *n* kawani
**employer** *n* amo
**employment** *n* hanap-buhay
**empress** *n* emperatris
**emptiness** *n* emperatris
**empty** *adj* walang laman
**empty** *v* wala
**enable** *v* magbigay-kaya
**enchant** *v* nabighani
**enchanting** *adj* nakbibighani
**encircle** *v* bilugan
**enclave** *n* kabilang bayan
**enclose** *v* palooban
**enclosure** *n* kapalooban
**encompass** *v* napapalooban
**encounter** *v* salubungin
**encounter** *n* salubong
**encourage** *v* palakasin
**encroach** *v* pakialaman
**end** *n* wakas
**end** *v* wakasan
**end up** *v* nag-wakas
**endanger** *v* manganib
**endeavor** *v* magsikap
**endeavor** *n* pagsikapan
**ending** *n* wakasan
**endless** *adj* walang hanggan
**endorse** *v* lagdaan sa likod
**endorsement** *n* nilagdaan
**endure** *v* tiisin
**enemy** *n* kalaban
**energetic** *adj* malakas
**energy** *n* kalakasan
**enforce** *v* ipatupad
**engage** *v* magkasunduan
**engaged** *adj* may kasunduan
**engagement** *n* kasunduan

E

E

**engine** *n* makina
**engineer** *n* inhinyero
**England** *n* Inglatera
**English** *adj* inglis
**engrave** *v* iukit
**engraving** *n* pang-ukit
**engrossed** *adj* abala
**engulf** *v* sakupin
**enhance** *v* pagandahin
**enjoy** *v* sumaya
**enjoyable** *adj* nakakaligaya
**enjoyment** *n* kaligayahan
**enlarge** *v* lumaki
**enlargement** *n* pagka-laki
**enlighten** *v* liwanagin
**enlist** *v* magpatala
**enormous** *adj* malawak
**enough** *adv* sapat
**enrage** *v* magalit
**enrich** *v* magpayaman
**enroll** *v* magpatala
**enrollment** *n* pagpapatala
**ensure** *v* tiyakin
**entail** *v* magkakahalaga
**entangle** *v* buhulin
**enter** *v* pumasok
**enterprise** *n* proyekto
**entertain** *v* libangin
**entertaining** *adj* nakakaaliw
**entertainment** *n* aliw
**enthrall** *v* nabighani
**enthralling** *adj* kabigha-bighani
**enthuse** *v* magpakitang gilas
**enthusiasm** *n* sigasig
**entice** *v* akitin
**enticement** *n* gayuma
**enticing** *adj* kaakit-akit
**entire** *adj* buo
**entirely** *adv* kabuuan
**entrance** *n* pasukan
**entreat** *v* makiusap
**entree** *n* pagpasok
**entrenched** *adj* kublihan
**entrepreneur** *n* mangangalakal
**entrust** *v* ipakatiwala
**entry** *n* pagpasok
**enumerate** *v* isa-isahan
**envelop** *v* paligiran
**envelope** *n* sobre
**envious** *adj* naiinggit
**environment** *n* kapaligiran
**envisage** *v* isaisip
**envoy** *n* sugo
**envy** *n* inggit
**envy** *v* naiinggit
**epidemic** *n* sakit na lumaganap
**epilepsy** *n* epilepsi
**episode** *n* yugto
**epistle** *n* banal na kasulatan
**epitaph** *n* lapida
**epitomize** *v* kasulatan ngpapuri
**epoch** *n* kapanahunan
**equal** *adj* kapantay
**equate** *v* itulad

**equation** *n* pagka-balanse
**equator** *n* ekwador
**equilibrium** *n* pantay
**equip** *v* gamitan
**equipment** *n* gamit
**equivalent** *adj* katumbas
**era** *n* panahon
**eradicate** *v* sawatahin
**erase** *v* burahin
**eraser** *n* pambura
**erect** *v* tumindig
**erect** *adj* nakatindig
**err** *v* nagkamali
**errand** *n* pag-alis
**erroneous** *adj* may mali
**error** *n* mali
**erupt** *v* sumabog
**eruption** *n* pagsabog
**escalate** *v* itaas
**escalator** *n* makingang hagdan
**escapade** *n* kapilyuhan
**escape** *v* tuamakas
**escort** *n* abay
**esophagus** *n* lalamunan
**especially** *adv* lalo na
**espionage** *n* paniniktik
**essay** *n* sanaysay
**essence** *n* ang katotohanan
**essential** *adj* basiko
**establish** *v* itatag; patunayan
**estate** *n* ari-arian
**esteem** *v* pagtatangi
**estimate** *v* tantyahin
**estimation** *n* pagtantya
**estranged** *adj* hiwalay
**estuary** *n* bunganga ng dagat
**eternity** *n* walang hangganan
**ethical** *adj* magandang asal
**ethics** *n* etika
**euphoria** *n* kaluwalhatian
**Europe** *n* Eyuropa
**European** *adj* taga Eyuropa
**evacuate** *v* lumisan
**evade** *v* iwasan
**evaluate** *v* sukatin
**evaporate** *v* naglaho
**evasion** *n* pag-iwas
**evasive** *adj* pala iwas
**eve** *n* gabi
**even** *adj* kahit na
**even if** *c* manapat
**even more** *c* lao pat
**evening** *n* gabi
**event** *n* pangyayari
**ever** *adv* kailan man
**everlasting** *adj* walang hanggan
**every** *adj* bawat
**everybody** *pro* lahat
**everyday** *adj* araw-araw
**everyone** *pro* lahat
**everything** *pro* pangkalahatan
**evict** *v* paalisin
**evidence** *n* katibayan
**evil** *n* demonyo; dyablo

E

**evil** *adj* masama
**evoke** *v* nagpapagunita
**evolution** *n* pag-unlad
**evolve** *v* tumubo
**exact** *adj* tamang-tama
**exaggerate** *v* palakihin
**exalt** *v* purihin
**examination** *n* pagsusulit
**examine** *v* suriin
**example** *n* halimbawa
**exasperate** *v* abalahin
**excavate** *v* hukayin
**exceed** *v* higitan
**exceedingly** *adv* lumampad
**excel** *v* mamayani
**excellence** *n* kagalingan
**excellent** *adj* magaling
**except** *pre* maliban
**exception** *n* maliban sa
**exceptional** *adj* pagkaliban sa
**excerpt** *n* hango
**excess** *n* labis
**excessive** *adj* kalabisan
**exchange** *v* palitan
**excite** *v* panabikin
**excitement** *n* kapanabikan
**exciting** *adj* nananabik
**exclaim** *v* isigaw
**exclude** *v* huwag isali
**excruciating** *adj* napaka sakit
**excuse** *v* idahilan
**excuse** *n* dahilan
**execute** *v* gawin; isagawa
**executive** *n* tagapamahala
**exemplary** *adj* kaibig-ibig
**exempt** *adj* hindi kasali
**exemption** *n* hindi obligado
**exercise** *n* pagsasanay
**exercise** *v* magsanay
**exert** *v* magbigay lakas
**exertion** *n* pagbibigay lakas
**exhaust** *v* gamitin lahat
**exhausting** *adj* nakakapagod
**exhaustion** *n* pagod
**exhibit** *v* pagtatanghal
**exhibition** *n* tanghal
**exhilarating** *adj* nakaka aliw
**exhort** *v* magbabala
**exist** *v* mabuhay
**existence** *n* pagka buhya
**exit** *n* labasan
**exodus** *n* paglabas; pag alis
**exonerate** *v* pawalang sala
**exorbitant** *adj* labsi na halaga
**expand** *v* palakihin
**expansion** *n* paglaki
**expect** *v* umaasa
**expectancy** *n* pag-asa
**expectation** *n* inaasahan
**expediency** *n* pagmamadali
**expedient** *adj* madali
**expedition** *n* paglalakbay
**expel** *v* iluwas; palayasin
**expenditure** *n* gastos

**expense** *n* pagkakagastusan
**expensive** *adj* mahal
**experience** *n* karanasan
**experiment** *n* eksperimento
**expert** *adj* dalubhasa
**expiate** *v* magsisi
**expiation** *n* pagsisisi
**expiration** *n* katapusan
**expire** *v* natapos
**explain** *v* ipaliwanag
**explicit** *adj* maliwanag
**explode** *v* sumabog
**exploit** *v* samantalahin
**exploit** *n* pagsamantala
**explore** *v* tuklasin
**explorer** *n* manunuklas
**explosion** *n* pagsabog
**explosive** *adj* pampasabog
**explotation** *n* pansasamantala
**export** *v* angkat
**expose** *v* ibunyag
**exposed** *adj* pagbunyag
**express** *n* ipaliwanag
**expression** *n* pagpapahayag
**expressly** *adv* pinahayag
**expropriate** *v* magtabi
**expulsion** *n* pagpapatalsik
**exquisite** *adj* ispisyal
**extend** *v* pahahabain; palugitan
**extension** *n* palugit
**extent** *n* laki
**extenuating** *adj* nakakagaan
**exterior** *adj* panlabas na anyo
**exterminate** *v* lipulin
**external** *adj* panlabas
**extinct** *adj* hindi na gumagana
**extinguish** *v* patayin
**extort** *v* kikilan
**extortion** *n* pangingikil
**extra** *adv* labis
**extract** *v* katasin
**extradite** *v* madali
**extradition** *n* pagpapasuko
**extraneous** *adj* galing sa labas
**extravagance** *n* luho
**extravagant** *adj* maluho
**extreme** *adj* sukdulan
**extremist** *adj* kasukdulan
**extremities** *n* mga dulo
**extricate** *v* pakawalan
**extroverted** *adj* pala kaibigan
**exude** *v* umapaw
**exult** *v* sambahin
**eye** *n* mata
**eyebrow** *n* kilay
**eye-catching** *adj* ka-pansin-pansin
**eyeglasses** *n* salamin
**eyelash** *n* pilik-mata
**eyelid** *n* talukap ng mata
**eyesight** *n* paningin
**eyewitness** *n* testigo

F

**fable** *n* pabula
**fabric** *n* tela
**fabricate** *v* gumawa
**fabulous** *adj* di-kapani-paniwala
**face** *n* mukha
**face up to** *v* harapin
**facet** *n* isang gawi
**facilitate** *v* madaliin
**facing** *pre* haharapin
**fact** *n* katotohanan
**factor** *n* sanhi; dahilan
**factory** *n* pabrika
**factual** *adj* makatotohanan
**faculty** *n* guro
**fad** *n* uso
**fade** *v* kumupas
**faded** *adj* kupas
**fail** *v* hindi nagwagi
**failure** *n* talunan
**faint** *v* hinimatay
**faint** *n* himatay
**faint** *adj* mahina
**fair** *n* patas
**fair** *adj* kainaman
**fairness** *n* patas
**fairy** *n* diwata
**faith** *n* sampalataya
**faithful** *adj* tapat; totoo
**fake** *v* dayain
**fake** *adj* huwad
**fall** *n* bagsak
**fall** *iv* bumagsak
**fall back** *v* umatras
**fall behind** *v* nahuli
**fall down** *v* nahulog
**fall through** *v* nawalang saysay
**fallacy** *n* maling akala
**fallout** *n* resulta
**falsehood** *n* kahuwaran
**falsify** *v* gawing huwad
**falter** *v* magkamali
**fame** *n* kabantugan
**familiar** *adj* kilala
**family** *n* pamilya
**famine** *n* tag gutom
**famous** *adj* bantog; kilala
**fan** *n* taga-hanga
**fanatic** *adj* panatiko
**fancy** *adj* guni-guni
**fang** *n* pangil
**fantastic** *adj* di-kapani-paniwala
**fantasy** *n* guni-guni
**far** *adv* malayo
**faraway** *adj* napakalayo
**farce** *n* walang-kabuluhan
**fare** *n* pamasahe
**farewell** *n* paalam
**farm** *n* bukid
**farmer** *n* magbubukid
**farming** *n* pagbubukid
**farmyard** *n* kabukiran

**farther** *adv* sa kalayuan
**fascinate** *v* akitin
**fashion** *n* moda
**fashionable** *adj* sunod sa uso
**fast** *adj* mabilis
**fasten** *v* igapos
**fat** *n* taba
**fat** *adj* mataba
**fatal** *adj* nakamamatay
**fate** *n* kapalaran
**father** *n* ama
**fatherhood** *n* pagiging ama
**father-in-law** *n* amain
**fatherly** *adj* maki ama
**fathom out** *v* arukin
**fatigue** *n* kapaguran
**fatten** *v* patabain
**fatty** *adj* mataba
**faucet** *n* gripo
**fault** *n* kasalanan
**faulty** *adj* pagkukulang
**favor** *n* kagandahang loob
**favorable** *adj* sang-ayon
**favorite** *adj* itinatangi
**fear** *n* takot
**fearful** *adj* nakakatakot
**feasible** *adj* maaring mangyari
**feast** *n* handaan
**feat** *n* dakilang gawa
**feather** *n* balahibo ng ibon
**feature** *n* katangian
**February** *n* Pebrero
**fed up** *adj* sawa na
**federal** *adj* pederal
**fee** *n* kabayaran
**feeble** *adj* mahina
**feed** *iv* pakainin
**feedback** *n* pidbak
**feel** *iv* maramdaman
**feeling** *n* damdamin
**feelings** *n* damdamin
**feet** *n* paa
**feign** *v* magdahilan
**fellow** *n* kasamahan
**fellowship** *n* samahan
**felon** *n* kriminal
**felony** *n* labag sa batas
**female** *n* babae
**feminine** *adj* kababaihan
**fence** *n* bakod
**fencing** *n* bakuran
**fend** *v* iwasan
**fend off** *v* hadlangan
**fender** *n* harang
**ferment** *v* paasimin
**ferment** *n* asim
**ferocious** *cdj* mabangis
**ferocity** *n* kabangisan
**ferry** *n* tawiran
**fertility** *n* maaring magpunla
**fertilize** *v* ipunla
**fervent** *adj* masugid
**fester** *v* nagsugat
**festive** *adj* masaya

F

F

**festivity** *n* kasayahan
**fetid** *adj* masansang
**fetus** *n* bata sa sinapupunan
**feud** *n* matandang alitan
**fever** *n* lagnat
**feverish** *adj* may sinat
**few** *adj* kaunti
**fewer** *adj* mangilan-ngilan
**fiancé** *n* nobya
**fiber** *n* hibla
**fickle** *adj* salawahan
**fiction** *n* likhang -isip
**fiddle** *n* gitara
**fidelity** *n* katapatan
**field** *n* bukid
**fierce** *adj* mabangis
**fiery** *adj* maapoy
**fifteen** *adj* pang-labing-lima
**fifth** *adj* pang-lima
**fifty** *adj* limampu
**fifty-fifty** *adv* limampu't-lima
**fig** *n* igos
**fight** *iv* mag-away
**fight** *n* away
**fighter** *n* palaban
**figure** *n* hugis
**figure out** *v* alamin
**file** *v* ihanay
**fill** *v* punuin
**filling** *n* pampuno
**film** *n* pelikula
**filter** *n* pansala
**filter** *v* salain
**filth** *n* dumi
**filthy** *adj* napakadumi
**fin** *n* palikpik
**final** *adj* kahulihan
**finalize** *v* tapusin
**finance** *v* gugulan
**financial** *adj* pananalapi
**find** *iv* nahanap
**find out** *v* nalaman
**fine** *n* multa
**fine** *v* multahan
**fine** *adv* mapino
**fine** *adj* maganda
**finger** *n* daliri
**fingernail** *n* kuko
**fingerprint** *n* tatak ng daliri
**fingertip** *n* duo ng daliri
**finish** *v* tapusin
**Finland** *n* Pinland
**Finnish** *adj* taga Pinland
**fire** *v* sunugin
**fire** *n* sunog
**firearm** *n* armas
**firecracker** *n* paputok
**firefighter** *n* bumbero
**fireman** *n* bumbero
**fireplace** *n* tsimenea
**fireworks** *n* paputok
**firm** *adj* matatag
**firm** *n* bahay-kalakal
**firmness** *n* katatagan

**first** *adj* una
**fish** *n* isda
**fisherman** *n* mangingisda
**fishy** *adj* malansa
**fist** *n* kamao
**fit** *n* sumpong
**fit** *v* akma
**fitness** *n* pangkalusugan
**fitting** *adj* malandi
**five** *adj* lima
**fix** *v* ayusin
**fjord** *n* baybay; dagat
**flag** *n* bandera
**flagpole** *n* tagdan ng bandera
**flamboyant** *adj* mayabang
**flame** *n* liyab
**flammable** *adj* madaking mag-liyab
**flank** *n* tagiliran
**flare** *n* kislap
**flare-up** *v* kumislap
**flash** *n* bilis; kislap
**flashlight** *n* lampara
**flashy** *adj* makintab
**flat** *n* sapad
**flat** *adj* patag; pantay
**flatten** *v* pantayin
**flattery** *n* pagtuya
**flaunt** *v* magyabang
**flavor** *n* lasa
**flaw** *n* depekto; sira
**flawless** *adj* walang sira
**flea** *n* pulgas
**flee** *iv* tumakas
**fleece** *n* nakawan; lokohan
**fleet** *n* maliksi
**fleeting** *adj* panandalian
**flesh** *n* laman
**flex** *v* itiklop
**flicker** *v* kukutikutitap
**flier** *n* anunsyo
**flight** *n* paglipad
**flimsy** *adj* manipis
**flip** *v* ibiling
**flirt** *v* lumandi
**float** *v* lumutang
**flock** *n* lupon; kawan
**flog** *v* hagupitin
**flood** *v* bumaha
**floodgate** *n* pambara sa baha
**flooding** *n* pagbaha
**floodlight** *n* pantay na ilaw
**floor** *n* sahig
**flop** *n* bigo
**floss** *n* makintab na sinulid
**flour** *n* arina
**flourish** *v* sumagana; dumami
**flow** *v* umagos
**flow** *n* agos
**flower** *n* bulaklak
**flowerpot** *n* paso
**flu** *n* trangkaso
**fluctuate** *v* tumaas o bumaba
**fluently** *adv* mahusay magsalita
**fluid** *n* likido; tubig

F

**flunk** *v* bumagsak sa iksamen
**flush** *v* bugso
**flute** *n* pluta
**flutter** *v* ipagpag
**fly** *iv* lumipad
**fly** *n* lipad
**foam** *n* bula
**focus** *n* nakatuon
**focus on** *v* ituon
**foe** *n* kalaban
**fog** *n* ulap na hamog
**foggy** *adj* maulap
**foil** *v* biguin
**fold** *v* tiklupin; ilupi
**folder** *n* polder
**folks** *n* lipi; lahi
**folksy** *adj* pag-uugali
**follow** *v* sundan
**follower** *n* tagasunod
**folly** *n* kabaliwan
**fond** *adj* mahilig
**fondle** *v* laruin
**fondness** *n* kahiligan
**food** *n* pagkain
**foodstuff** *n* mga kakanin
**fool** *v* ulol; gago
**fool** *adj* ululin
**foolproof** *adj* hinid maloloko
**foot** *n* paa
**football** *n* putbol
**footnote** *n* talababa
**footprint** *n* bakas ng paa
**footstep** *n* yapak
**footwear** *n* sapatos
**for** *pre* para sa
**forbid** *iv* ipinagbawal
**force** *n* lakas
**force** *v* pilitin
**forceful** *adj* malakas
**forcibly** *adv* pinilit
**forecast** *iv* hula
**foreground** *n* sa harapan
**forehead** *n* noo
**foreign** *adj* dayuhan
**foreigner** *n* banyaga
**foreman** *n* kapatas
**foremost** *adj* una sa lahat
**foresee** *iv* nahulaan
**foreshadow** *v* alamin antimano
**forest** *n* gubat
**foretaste** *n* paunang kaalaman
**foretell** *v* hulaan
**forever** *adv* habang panahon
**forewarn** *v* magbabala
**foreword** *n* paunang salita
**forfeit** *v* bawiin
**forge** *v* huwarin
**forgery** *n* huwad
**forget** *v* kalimutan
**forgive** *v* patawarin
**forgiveness** *n* kapatawaran
**fork** *n* tinidor
**form** *n* anyo
**formal** *adj* husto

**formality** *n* katimpian
**formalize** *v* hustuhin
**formally** *adv* naayon
**format** *n* tularan
**formation** *n* pamumuo
**former** *adj* dati; nauna
**formerly** *adv* noong una
**formidable** *adj* kinatatakutan
**formula** *n* pormula
**forsake** *iv* pabayaan
**fort** *n* kuta
**forthcoming** *adj* nalalapit
**forthright** *adj* deretsahan
**fortify** *v* palakasin
**fortitude** *n* katatagan
**fortress** *n* ligtas na lugar
**fortunate** *adj* mapalad
**fortune** *n* kapalaran
**forty** *adj* apanapu
**forward** *adv* pasulong
**fossil** *n* bakas ng nakaraan
**foster** *v* maghasik
**foul** *adj* mabaho
**foundation** *n* pasimula
**founder** *n* nagtatag
**foundry** *n* hurno
**fountain** *n* bukal
**four** *adj* apat
**fourteen** *adj* labing-apat
**fourth** *adj* pang-apat
**fox** *n* lobo
**foxy** *adj* tuso
**fraction** *n* bahagdan
**fracture** *n* bali
**fragile** *adj* maselan
**fragment** *n* bahagi; piraso
**fragrance** *n* bango
**fragrant** *adj* mabango
**frail** *adj* marupok
**frailty** *n* karupukan
**frame** *n* kuwadro
**frame** *v* ikwadro
**framework** *n* balangkas
**France** *n* Pransya
**franchise** *n* prangkisa
**frank** *adj* tapat
**frankly** *adv* tahasan
**frankness** *n* katahasan
**frantic** *adj* kinabahan
**fraternal** *adj* pangkapatid
**fraternity** *n* kapatiran
**fraud** *n* daya; dayaan
**fraudulent** *adj* madaya
**freckle** *n* pekas
**freckled** *adj* mapekas
**free** *v* palayain
**free** *adj* malaya
**freedom** *n* kalayaan
**freeze** *iv* gawing ilado
**freezer** *n* palamigan
**freezing** *adj* nagyeyelo
**freight** *n* kargada
**French** *adj* Pransya
**frenetic** *adj* nahintakutan

**frenzied** *adj* nenerbyos
**frenzy** *n* nerbyos
**frequency** *n* kadalasan
**frequent** *adj* madalas
**frequent** *v* dalasan
**fresh** *adj* sariwa
**freshen** *v* sariwain
**freshness** *n* kasariwaan
**friar** *n* prayle
**friction** *n* nagkiskis
**Friday** *n* Biyernes
**fried** *adj* pinirito
**friend** *n* kaibigan
**friendship** *n* pagkakaibigan
**fries** *n* prito
**frigate** *n* armadong barko
**fright** *n* takot
**frighten** *v* natakot
**frightening** *adj* nakakatakot
**frigid** *adj* napakalamig
**fringe** *n* palamuti; iba
**frog** *n* palaka
**from** *pre* mula sa
**front** *n* harapan
**front** *adj* pangharap
**frontage** *n* hinaharap
**frontier** *n* gilid; harapan
**frost** *n* yelo
**frostbite** *n* pagka ilado
**frostbitten** *adj* ilado
**frosty** *adj* mayelo
**frown** *v* nakasimangot
**frozen** *adj* ilado
**frugal** *adj* matipid
**frugality** *n* katipiran
**fruit** *n* prutas
**fruitful** *adj* nagbunga
**fruity** *adj* mabunga
**frustrate** *v* biguin
**frustration** *n* kabiguan
**fry** *v* iprito
**frying pan** *n* kawali
**fuel** *n* panggatong
**fuel** *v* igatong
**fugitive** *n* pugante
**fulfill** *v* isaganap
**fulfillment** *n* kaganapan
**full** *adj* puno; lipos
**fully** *adv* punong-puno
**fumes** *n* usok
**fumigate** *v* pausukan
**fun** *n* kasayahan
**function** *n* gamit
**fund** *n* pondo
**fund** *v* pondohan
**fundamental** *adj* basehan
**funds** *n* pondo
**funeral** *n* libing
**fungus** *n* pungus
**funny** *adj* nakakatawa
**furious** *adj* nagagalit
**furiously** *adv* galit na galit
**furnace** *n* pugon
**furnish** *v* magkaloob

**furnishings** *n* kasangkapan
**furor** *n* pansamantalang uso
**furrow** *n* daanng araro
**furry** *adj* mabalahibo
**further** *adv* at saka
**furthermore** *adv* ganun pa man
**fury** *n* galit
**fuse** *n* pagdikit
**fusion** *n* pagsasama
**fuss** *n* mainit na usapan
**fussy** *adj* malaking usapan
**futile** *adj* walang saysay
**futility** *n* pagka silbi
**future** *n* kinabukasan
**fuzzy** *adj* malabo

# G

**gadget** *n* gamit
**gag** *n* daldal
**gag** *v* magdaldal
**gage** *v* sukatin
**gain** *v* magtubo
**gain** *n* tubo
**gal** *n* kaibigan
**gale** *n* malakas na hangin
**gall bladder** *n* bato
**gallant** *adj* maginoo
**gallery** *n* mahabang daanan
**gallon** *n* galon
**gallop** *v* lumukso
**gallows** *n* bitayan; bigtihan
**galvanize** *v* koryentehin
**gamble** *v* mag sugal
**game** *n* sugal
**gang** *n* gang
**gangrene** *n* kanggrena
**gangster** *n* sanggano
**gap** *n* siwang
**garage** *n* garahe
**garbage** *n* basura
**garden** *n* hardin
**gardener** *n* hardinero
**gargle** *v* magmumog
**garland** *n* putong ng bulaklak
**garlic** *n* bawang
**garment** *n* damit
**garnish** *v* palamutian
**garnish** *n* palamuti
**garrison** *n* garison
**garrulous** *adj* paligoy-ligoy
**garter** *n* ligas
**gas** *n* gaas
**gash** *n* hiwa; laslas
**gasoline** *n* gasolina
**gasp** *v* humingal
**gastric** *adj* maasim
**gate** *n* tarangkahan
**gather** *v* ipunin
**gathering** *n* salu-salo

G

**gauge** *v* sukatin
**gauze** *n* gasa
**gaze** *v* tumitig
**gear** *n* kambyo
**geese** *n* gansa
**gem** *n* mahalagang bato
**gender** *n* kasarian
**general** *n* heneral
**generalize** *v* lahatin
**generate** *v* tumubo
**generation** *n* saling lahi
**generosity** *n* kabutihang - loob
**genetic** *adj* henetika
**genial** *adj* magiliw
**genius** *n* henyo
**gentle** *adj* mahinahon
**gentleman** *n* ginoo
**gentleness** *n* kahinahunan
**genuflect** *v* lumuhod
**genuine** *adj* tunay
**geography** *n* heograpiya
**geology** *n* Helohiya
**geometry** *n* Heometriya
**germ** *n* mikrobyo
**German** *adj* Aleman
**Germany** *n* Alemanya
**germinate** *v* tumubo
**gestation** *n* pagdadalantao
**gesticulate** *v* magkukumpas
**gesture** *n* kilos
**get** *iv* kunin
**get along** *v* magkasundo
**get away** *v* lumayo
**get back** *v* bumalik
**get by** *v* makatalilis
**get in** *v* pumasok
**get off** *v* bumaba
**get out** *v* umalis
**get over** *v* kalimutan
**get together** *v* mag-umpukan
**get up** *v* tumayo
**geyser** *n* bukal
**ghastly** *adj* maputla
**ghost** *n* multo
**giant** *n* higante
**gift** *n* regalo; handog
**gifted** *adj* matalino; matalas
**gigantic** *adj* napakalaki
**giggle** *v* tawang nakikiliti
**gimmick** *n* gimik
**ginger** *n* luya
**gingerly** *adv* mala-luya
**giraffe** *n* hirapa
**girl** *n* batang babae
**girlfriend** *n* kaibigang babae
**give** *iv* magbigay
**give away** *v* ipamigay
**give back** *v* isauli
**give in** *v* bumigay
**give out** *v* mamigay
**give up** *v* sumuko
**glacier** *n* bundok na yelo
**glad** *adj* natutuwa
**gladiator** *n* taong pinag-aaway

**glamorous** *adj* kahalina-halina
**glance** *v* tumingin sandali
**glance** *n* sulyap
**gland** *n* glandula
**glare** *n* nakasisilaw
**glass** *n* salamin
**glasses** *n* salamin; kristal
**gleam** *n* banaag; sinag
**gleam** *v* suminag
**glide** *v* dumausdos
**glimmer** *n* kutitap
**glimpse** *n* sulayap
**glimpse** *v* sumulyap
**glitter** *v* kumikislap
**globe** *n* globo
**globule** *n* hugis globo
**gloom** *n* lumbay; panglaw
**gloomy** *adj* mapanglaw
**glorify** *v* sambahin
**glorious** *adj* maluwalhati
**glory** *n* kaluwalhatian
**gloss** *n* kintab
**glossary** *n* talasalitaan
**glossy** *adj* makintab
**glove** *n* guwantes
**glow** *v* sinag; baga
**glue** *n* pandikit
**glue** *v* idikit
**glut** *n* paglamon
**glutton** *n* matakaw
**gnaw** *v* kutkutin
**go** *iv* lumakad
**go ahead** *v* ipagpatuloy
**go away** *v* umalis
**go back** *v* bumalik
**go down** *v* bumaba
**go in** *v* pumasok
**go on** *v* mapatuloy
**go out** *v* lumabas
**go over** *v* tingnan muli
**go through** *v* lumampas
**go under** *v* pumailalim
**go up** *v* umakyat
**goad** *v* latiguhin
**goal** *n* hantungan
**goalkeeper** *n* gabay
**goat** *n* kambing
**gobble** *v* lamunin
**God** *n* Panginoon
**goddess** *n* diwata
**godless** *adj* walang Diyos
**goggles** *n* pantakip sa mata
**gold** *n* ginto
**golden** *adj* ginintuan
**good** *adj* mabuti
**good-looking** *adj* magandang tao
**goodness** *n* kagandahan
**goods** *n* kagamitan
**goodwill** *n* kagandahan loob
**goof** *v* magkamali
**goof** *n* pagkakamali
**goose** *n* gansa
**gorge** *n* malaki
**gorgeous** *adj* marikit; marilag

G

**gorilla** *n* gurilya
**gospel** *n* ebanghelyo
**gossip** *v* magtsismis
**gossip** *n* tsismis
**govern** *v* mamahala
**government** *n* pamahalaan
**governor** *n* gobernador
**gown** *n* kauotang promal
**grab** *v* agawin
**grace** *n* grasya
**graceful** *adj* kaaya-aya
**gracious** *adj* mapag-biyaya
**grade** *n* antas
**gradual** *adj* unti-unti
**graduate** *v* nagtapos
**graduation** *n* pagtatapos
**graft** *n* pangunguwarta
**grain** *n* butil
**gram** *n* gramo
**grammar** *n* balarila
**grand** *adj* malaki; dakila
**grandchild** *n* apo
**granddad** *n* lolo
**grandfather** *n* lolo
**grandmother** *n* lola
**grandson** *n* apo
**grandstand** *n* entablado
**granite** *n* granate
**granny** *n* lolo; lola
**grant** *v* ipagkaloob
**grant** *n* kaloob
**grape** *n* ubas
**grapefruit** *n* suha
**grapevine** *n* ubasan
**graphic** *adj* maliwanag
**grasp** *n* paghawak
**grasp** *v* hawakan
**grass** *n* damo
**grassroots** *adj* mga dukha; api
**gratify** *v* pagbigyan
**gratifying** *adj* mapagbigay
**gratitude** *n* pasasalamat
**gratuity** *n* pampalubag-loob
**grave** *adj* malubha
**grave** *n* puntod
**gravel** *n* graba
**gravely** *adv* napakalubha
**gravestone** *n* lapida
**graveyard** *n* libingan; sementeryo
**gravitate** *v* bigatan
**gravity** *n* bigat; kalubhaan
**gravy** *n* kul
**gray** *adj* kulay abo
**grayish** *adj* abuhin
**graze** *n* panginginain
**grease** *v* langisan
**grease** *n* sebo; grasa
**greasy** *adj* masebo
**great** *adj* dakila
**greatness** *n* kadakilaan
**Greece** *n* Greko
**greed** *n* kasuwapangan
**greedy** *adj* suwapang
**Greek** *adj* Griyego

**green** *adj* berde
**green bean** *n* patani
**greenhouse** *n* bahay na berde
**Greenland** *n* Grinlandya
**greet** *v* batiin
**greetings** *n* pagbati
**gregarious** *adj* masaya
**grenade** *n* granada
**grief** *n* dalamhati
**grievance** *n* sumbong
**grieve** *v* magdalamhati
**grill** *v* ihaw
**grill** *n* inihaw
**grim** *adj* mabangis
**grimace** *n* ngiwi
**grime** *n* dumi
**grind** *iv* gilingin
**grip** *v* pisil; hawak
**grip** *n* pag pisil
**gripe** *n* hinanakit
**groan** *v* humalinghing
**groan** *n* halinghing
**groceries** *n* groseri
**groin** *n* singit
**groom** *n* nobyo
**groove** *n* kanal
**gross** *adj* mahalay; kabuan
**grotto** *n* groto
**grouch** *v* magsungit
**grouchy** *adj* masungit
**ground** *n* lapag
**ground floor** *n* unang palapag
**groundless** *adj* walang sahig
**groundwork** *n* haligi ng rpoyekto
**group** *n* pulutong; pangkat
**grow** *iv* lumaki
**grow up** *v* tumubo
**growl** *v* singhal
**grown-up** *n* mga nakatatanda
**growth** *n* paglaki
**grudge** *n* sama ng loob
**grudgingly** *adv* may hinanakit
**gruelling** *adj* nakapapagod
**gruesome** *adj* kalunos-lunos
**grumble** *v* bumubulong
**grumpy** *adj* masungit
**guarantee** *v* siguruhin
**guarantee** *n* sigurado
**guarantor** *n* pyador
**guard** *n* bantayan
**guardian** *n* katiwala
**guerrilla** *n* gerilya
**guess** *v* hulaan
**guess** *n* hula
**guest** *n* panuhin
**guidance** *n* pamatnubay
**guide** *v* patnubayan
**guide** *n* taga patnubay
**guidebook** *n* aklat ng mapa
**guidelines** *n* panuntunan
**guild** *n* kapisanan
**guile** *n* panloloko
**guillotine** *n* gilotina
**guilt** *n* kasalanan

**guilty** *adj* makasalanan
**guise** *n* panggap
**guitar** *n* gitara
**gulf** *n* lambak
**gull** *n* ibong dagat
**gullible** *adj* mapaniwalain
**gulp** *v* lagukin
**gulp** *n* paglagok
**gulp down** *v* lunukin
**gum** *n* gilagid
**gun** *n* baril
**gun down** *v* binaril
**gunfire** *n* pagpapaputok
**gunman** *n* namaril
**gunpowder** *n* pulbura
**gunshot** *n* putok ng baril
**gust** *n* bugso ng hangin
**gusto** *n* ibig
**gut** *n* bituka
**guts** *n* lakas ng loob
**gutter** *n* alulod
**guy** *n* lalaki
**guzzle** *v* tumungga
**gymnasium** *n* dyim
**gynecology** *n* genekolohiya
**gypsy** *n* hilano

**habit** *n* kasanay
**habitable** *adj* maaring tirahan
**habitual** *adj* sanay
**hack** *v* tagain
**haggle** *v* makipagtawaran
**hail** *n* pagka aba
**hail** *v* abahin
**hair** *n* buhok
**hairbrush** *n* panuklay ng buhok
**haircut** *n* mangugupit
**hairdo** *n* ayos ng buhok
**hairdresser** *n* manggugupit
**hairpiece** *n* piluka
**hairy** *adj* mabuhok
**half** *n* kalahati
**half** *adj* kalahati
**hall** *n* bulwagan
**hallucinate** *v* managimit
**hallway** *n* pasilyo
**halt** *v* itigil
**halve** *v* ikalahati
**ham** *n* hamon
**hamburger** *n* hamburger
**hamlet** *n* nayon; baryo
**hammer** *n* martilyo
**hammock** *n* duyan
**hand** *n* kamay
**hand down** *v* ipamana
**hand in** *v* iabot

**hand out** *v* ipamudmod
**hand over** *v* ibigay
**handbag** *n* bag
**handbook** *n* aklat
**handcuff** *v* iposas
**handcuffs** *n* posas
**handful** *n* isang dakot
**handgun** *n* baril
**handicap** *n* may kapansanan
**handkerchief** *n* panyo
**handle** *v* hawakan
**handle** *n* hawakan
**handmade** *adj* yari sa kamay
**handout** *n* babasahin
**handrail** *n* gabay sa hagdan
**handshake** *n* kamayan
**handsome** *adj* guwapo
**handwritting** *n* sulat kamay
**handy** *adj* madaling gamitin
**hang** *iv* isabit
**hang around** *v* umistambay
**hang on** *v* maghintay
**hang up** *v* kakulangan
**hanger** *n* sabitan
**hangup** *n* kakuilangan
**happen** *v* nangyari
**happening** *n* pangyayari
**happiness** *n* kaligayahan
**happy** *adj* masaya
**harass** *v* istorbohin
**harassment** *n* pang-iistorbo
**harbor** *n* pantalan
**hard** *adj* matigas
**harden** *v* patigasin
**hardly** *adv* bahagya
**hardness** *n* katigasan
**hardship** *n* kahirapan
**hardwood** *n* kahoy
**hardy** *adj* malusog
**hare** *n* kuneho
**harm** *v* pinsalain
**harm** *n* kapinsalaan
**harmful** *adj* mapanira
**harmless** *adj* hindi mapanira
**harmonize** *v* pagtugmain
**harmony** *n* pagkakaisa
**harp** *n* gitara ng anghel
**harpoon** *n* paputok
**harrowing** *adj* kinakayod
**harsh** *adj* tampalasan
**harshly** *adv* bastos
**harshness** *n* pambabastos
**harvest** *n* ani
**harvest** *v* umani
**hashish** *n* uri ng damo
**hassle** *v* makipagbunuan
**hassle** *n* bunuan
**haste** *n* pagmamadali
**hasten** *v* bilisan
**hastily** *adv* minadali
**hasty** *adj* mabilis
**hat** *n* sumbrero
**hatchet** *n* palakol
**hate** *v* kamuhian

**hateful** *adj* kamuhi-muhi
**hatred** *n* pagkamuhi
**haughty** *adj* mayabang
**haul** *v* hakutin
**haunt** *v* pagmultuhan
**have** *iv* mayroon
**have to** *v* kailangan
**haven** *n* bahay
**havoc** *n* kaguluhan
**hawk** *n* lawin
**hay** *n* tuyong damo
**hazard** *n* panganib
**hazardous** *adj* mapanganib
**haze** *n* maulap
**hazelnut** *n* uri ng mani
**hazy** *adj* malabo
**he** *pro* siya
**head** *n* pinuno
**head for** *v* patungo
**headache** *n* sakit ng ulo
**heading** *n* pinamumunuan
**head-on** *adv* magkabangga
**headphones** *n* makinang pandinig
**headquarters** *n* punong-tanggapan
**headway** *n* pagsulong
**heal** *v* gamutin
**healer** *n* manggagamot
**health** *n* klalusugan
**healthy** *adj* malusog
**heap** *n* bunton
**heap** *v* itambak
**hear** *iv* narinig
**hearing** *n* pandinig
**hearsay** *n* sabi-sabi
**hearse** *n* karo ng patay
**heart** *n* puso
**heartbeat** *n* pintig ng puso
**heartburn** *n* kabag
**hearten** *v* tapangan
**heartfelt** *adj* taos puso
**hearth** *n* lapag ng apuyan
**heartless** *adj* walang puso
**hearty** *adj* masarap
**heat** *v* initin
**heat** *n* initin
**heater** *n* pang-init
**heathen** *n* pagano
**heating** *n* pag init
**heatwave** *n* sukdulang init
**heaven** *n* kalangitan
**heavenly** *adj* makalangit
**heaviness** *n* kabigatan
**heavy** *adj* mabigat
**heckle** *v* tuyain
**hectic** *adj* abala
**heed** *v* makinig; mag-ingat
**heel** *n* sakong
**height** *n* taas
**heighten** *v* pag alabin
**heinous** *adj* pataasin
**heir** *n* tagapag mana
**heist** *n* pagnanakaw
**helicopter** *n* salipawpaw

**hell** *n* impyerno
**hello** *e* helo
**helm** *n* timon
**helmet** *n* helmet
**help** *v* tulungan
**help** *n* tulong
**helper** *n* katulong
**helpful** *adj* matulungin
**helpless** *adj* mahina
**hem** *n* laylayan ng damit
**hemisphere** *n* kalahati ng mundo
**hen** *n* inahing manok
**hence** *adv* samakatuwid
**henchman** *n* kriminal
**her** *adj* sya
**herald** *v* ibalita
**herald** *n* pamamalita
**herb** *n* halaman
**here** *adv* dito
**hereafter** *adv* sa hinaharap
**hereditary** *adj* namamana
**heretic** *adj* erehe
**heritage** *n* pamanang lahi
**hermetic** *adj* selyado
**hermit** *n* ermitanyo
**hernia** *n* luslos
**hero** *n* bayani
**heroic** *adj* dakila
**heroin** *n* babaeng bayani
**heroism** *n* kabayanihan
**hers** *pro* sa kanya
**herself** *pro* sya
**hesitant** *adj* alumpihit
**hesitate** *v* nagbabago ang isip
**hesitation** *n* pagbabago ng isip
**heyday** *n* rurok ng tagumpay
**hiccup** *n* sinok
**hidden** *adj* nakatago
**hide** *iv* itago
**hideaway** *n* taguan
**hideous** *adj* nakakagulat
**hierarchy** *n* hirarkiya
**high** *adj* mataas
**highly** *adv* kataas-taasan
**Highness** *n* Kamahalan
**highway** *n* lansangang bayan
**hijack** *v* agawin
**hijack** *n* pag-aagaw
**hijacker** *n* magnanakaw
**hike** *v* maglakad
**hike** *n* paglalakad
**hilarious** *adj* nakakatawa
**hill** *n* burol
**hillside** *n* sa gilid ng burol
**hilltop** *n* sa taas ng burol
**hilly** *adj* bulubundukon
**hilt** *n* hawakan ng espada
**hinder** *v* pigilan
**hindrance** *n* sagabal
**hindsight** *n* pangitain
**hinge** *v* lagyan ng bisagra
**hinge** *n* bisagra
**hint** *n* pahiwatig
**hint** *v* ipahiwatig

**hip** *n* balakang
**hire** *v* upahan
**his** *adj* sa kanya
**his** *pro* kanya
**Hispanic** *adj* hispaniko
**hiss** *v* tunog ng ahas
**historian** *n* mananalaysay
**history** *n* Kasaysayan
**hit** *n* pagpapatama
**hit** *iv* tinamaan
**hit back** *v* gumanti
**hitch** *n* pag-angkas
**hitch up** *v* iangkas
**hitchhike** *n* pakikisakay
**hitherto** *adv* hanggang ngayon
**hive** *n* bahay-pukyutan
**hoard** *v* itago
**hoarse** *adj* magasapang
**hoax** *n* pandaraya
**hobby** *n* libangan
**hog** *n* baboy
**hoist** *v* itaas
**hoist** *n* itaas
**hold** *iv* hawakan
**hold back** *v* tigilan
**hold on to** *v* hawakan
**hold out** *v* pigilan
**hold up** *v* agawin
**holdup** *n* pagka antala
**hole** *n* butas
**holiday** *n* pista
**holiness** *n* kabanalan
**Holland** *n* Olanda
**hollow** *adj* mababaw
**holocaust** *n* pagka salanta
**holy** *adj* banal
**homage** *n* bigay pugay
**home** *n* tahanan
**homeland** *n* lupang tinubuan
**homeless** *adj* walang tahanan
**homely** *adj* pangit
**homemade** *adj* gawa sa bahay
**homesick** *adj* sabik sa pag-uwi
**hometown** *n* tubong bayan
**homework** *n* takdang-arakin
**homicide** *n* pagpatay
**homily** *n* ebanghelyo
**honest** *adj* matapat
**honesty** *n* katapatan
**honey** *n* pulot-pukyutan
**honeymoon** *n* pulot-gata
**honk** *v* bumusina
**honor** *n* puri
**hood** *n* talukbong
**hoodlum** *n* masamang tao
**hoof** *n* paa ng hayop
**hook** *n* kawit
**hooligan** *n* magnanakaw
**hop** *v* tumalon
**hope** *n* pag-asa
**hopeful** *adj* umaasa
**hopefully** *adv* sana
**hopeless** *adj* walang pag-asa
**horizon** *n* abot-tanaw

**horizontal** *adj* pahalang
**hormone** *n* hormon
**horn** *n* sungay
**horrendous** *adj* nanagimbal
**horrible** *adj* nakakatakot
**horrify** *v* takutin
**horror** *n* takot
**horse** *n* kabayo
**hose** *n* gomang pandilig
**hospital** *n* pagamutan
**hospitalize** *v* na-ospital
**host** *n* ang may panauhin
**hostage** *n* kulungin
**hostess** *n* babaeng may bisita
**hostile** *adj* kalaban
**hostility** *n* paglaban
**hot** *adj* mainit
**hound** *n* panunurot
**hour** *n* oras
**hourly** *adv* oras-oras
**house** *n* bahay
**household** *n* nauukol sa bahay
**housekeeper** *n* tagalinis ng bahay
**housewife** *n* may bahay
**housework** *n* gawain bahay
**how** *adv* paano
**however** *c* ganunpaman
**howl** *v* tumaghoy
**howl** *n* taghoy
**hub** *n* gitna
**huddle** *v* magkumpulan
**hug** *v* yakapin
**hug** *n* yakap
**huge** *adj* malaki
**hull** *n* hilahin
**hum** *v* humuni
**human** *adj* makatao
**human being** *n* tao
**humankind** *n* sanlibutan
**humble** *adj* mapagpakumbaba
**humbly** *adv* pakumbaba
**humid** *adj* maalinsangan
**humidity** *n* pagka-alinsangan
**humiliate** *v* ipahiya
**humility** *n* pagpapakumbaba
**humor** *n* katatawanan
**humorous** *adj* nakakatawa
**hump** *n* umbok
**hunch** *n* kutob
**hunchback** *n* kuba
**hunched** *adj* nakahukot
**hundred** *adj* isang daan
**hundredth** *adj* pang isang daan
**hunger** *n* gutom
**hungry** *adj* gutom
**hunt** *v* mangaso
**hunter** *n* mangangaso
**hunting** *n* pangangaso
**hurdle** *n* talunan
**hurl** *v* ipukol
**hurricane** *n* bagyo
**hurriedly** *adv* pagmamadali
**hurry** *v* magmadali
**hurry up** *v* bilisan

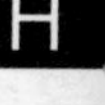

**hurt** *iv* nasaktan
**hurt** *adj* masakit
**hurtful** *adj* nakakasakit
**husband** *n* asawang lalaki
**hush** *n* katahimikan
**hush up** *v* tumahimik
**husky** *adj* matipuno
**hustle** *n* pagpilit
**hut** *n* kubo
**hydrogen** *n* haydrodyen
**hyena** *n* hayena
**hygiene** *n* kalinisan
**hymn** *n* himno
**hyphen** *n* gitling
**hypnosis** *n* hipnosis
**hypnotize** *v* patulugin
**hypocrisy** *n* pagbabalat-kayo
**hypocrite** *adj* mapag-balat-kayo
**hypothesis** *n* palagay
**hysteria** *n* histerya
**hysterical** *adj* histerikal

**I** *pro* ako
**ice** *n* yelo
**ice cream** *n* sorbetes
**ice cube** *n* yelo
**ice skate** *v* sapatos pang yelo
**iceberg** *n* yelo sa dagat
**icebox** *n* lalagyan ng yelo
**ice-cold** *adj* pinalamig
**icon** *n* larawan
**icy** *adj* napaka lamig
**idea** *n* kuro-kuro
**ideal** *adj* uliran; huwaran
**identical** *adj* kapareho
**identify** *v* kilalanin
**identity** *n* pagkakakilanlan
**ideology** *n* ideolohiya
**idiom** *n* idyoma
**idiot** *n* tanga
**idiotic** *adj* pagka tanga
**idle** *adj* walang ginagawa
**idol** *n* idolo
**if** *c* kung
**ignite** *v* sindihan
**ignorance** *n* kamang-mangan
**ignorant** *adj* mangmang
**ignore** *v* huwag pansinin
**ill** *adj* may sakit
**illegal** *adj* labag sa batas
**illegible** *adj* hindi mabasa

**illegitimate** *adj* anak sa labas
**illicit** *adj* labag sa batas
**illiterate** *adj* di nag-aral
**illness** *n* sakit
**illogical** *adj* hinid makatwiran
**illuminate** *v* ilawan
**illusion** *n* maling-akala
**illustrate** *v* biglang halimbawa
**illustration** *n* halimbawa
**image** *n* larawang diwa
**imagination** *n* gunita; guni-guni
**imagine** *v* ipalagay
**imbalance** *n* hindi pantay
**imitate** *v* gayahin
**imitation** *n* pangga-gaya
**immaculate** *adj* dalisay; malinis
**immature** *adj* murang-isipan
**immediately** *adv* karaka-raka
**immense** *adj* walang hanggan
**immerse** *v* ilubog
**immersion** *n* paglubog
**immigrant** *n* dayuhan
**immigrate** *v* dumayo
**immigration** *n* imigrasyon
**imminent** *adj* nalalapit
**immobile** *adj* di gumagalaw
**immoral** *adj* imoral
**immorality** *n* walang moralidad
**immortal** *adj* di namamatay
**immortality** *n* walang kamatayan
**immune** *adj* sanay
**immunity** *n* kasanayan
**immunize** *v* bakunahan
**immutable** *adj* hindi mapapalitan
**impact** *n* matinidng epekto
**impact** *v* banggain
**impair** *v* pahinain
**impartial** *adj* di makatarungan
**impatience** *n* pagka inip
**impatient** *adj* mainipin
**impeccable** *adj* malinis ang budhi
**impediment** *n* balakid; hadlang
**impending** *adj* nagbabanta
**imperfection** *n* kakulangan
**imperial** *adj* mataas na tungkulin
**imperialism** *n* imperyalismo
**impersonal** *adj* walang emosyon
**impertinence** *n* walang kahalagahan
**impertinent** *adj* walang galang
**impetuous** *adj* nauukol sa
**implacable** *adj* di makumbinse
**implant** *v* itanim
**implement** *v* ipatupad
**implicate** *v* isangkot
**implication** *n* pagsangkot
**implicit** *adj* nagpapahiwatig
**implore** *v* hilingin
**imply** *v* bigyan kahulugan
**impolite** *adj* walang galang
**import** *v* angkatin
**importance** *n* kahalagahan
**importation** *n* pagaangkat
**impose** *v* mag atang
**imposing** *adj* igiit

**imposition** *n* pag aatang
**impossible** *adj* di maaari
**impotent** *adj* baog
**impound** *v* ikulong
**impoverished** *adj* mahirap; dukha
**impractical** *adj* hindi praktikal
**imprecise** *adj* hindi eksakto
**impress** *v* magpasikat
**impressive** *adj* kahanga-hanga
**imprison** *v* ikulong
**improbable** *adj* mangyayari
**impromptu** *adv* biglaan
**improper** *adj* di dapat
**improve** *v* baguhin; ayusin
**improvement** *n* pagpapaganda
**impulse** *n* bigla
**impunity** *n* ligtas sa parusa
**impure** *adj* marumi
**in** *pre* sa; sa loob
**in depth** *adv* malalim
**inability** *n* hindi kaya
**inaccessible** *adj* di magamit
**inaccurate** *adj* di tama
**inadequate** *adj* di sapat
**inadmissible** *adj* di karapat-dapat
**inappropriate** *adj* hindi tama
**inasmuch as** *c* dahilan sa
**inaugurate** *v* buksan
**inauguration** *n* pagbubukas
**incalculable** *adj* hindi matantya
**incapable** *adj* hindi kaya
**incarcerate** *v* ikulong
**incense** *n* insenso
**incentive** *n* gantimpala
**inception** *n* sa simula
**incessant** *adj* tuloy-tuloy
**inch** *n* pulagada
**incident** *n* pangyayari
**incidentally** *adv* sa pangyayari
**incision** *n* pagopera
**incite** *v* sulsulan
**incitement** *n* pagsulsol
**inclination** *n* pagka hilig
**incline** *v* ihilig
**include** *v* isama
**inclusive** *adv* kasama ang
**incoherent** *adj* malabo
**income** *n* sahod; kinikita
**incoming** *adj* parating
**incompatible** *adj* di tugma
**incompetent** *adj* di kaya
**incomplete** *adj* kulang
**incontinence** *n* di pagpigil
**inconvenient** *adj* di palagay
**incorporate** *v* isama; isabay
**incorrect** *adj* mali
**incorrigible** *adj* di maitama
**increase** *v* dagdagan
**increase** *n* dagdag
**increasing** *adj* dumadagdag
**increment** *n* tubo
**incriminate** *v* idamay
**incur** *v* nakamit

**incurable** *adj* di na gagaling
**indecency** *n* kalaswaan
**indecisive** *adj* walang desisyon
**indeed** *adv* siya nga
**indefinite** *adj* wlang hanggan
**indemnify** *v* bayaran
**indemnity** *n* kabayaran
**independence** *n* kalayaan
**independent** *adj* nagsarili
**indicate** *v* ipakita; ilagay
**indication** *n* pagpapakita
**indict** *v* akusahan
**indifferent** *adj* kulang sa pansin
**indigent** *adj* mahirap; pobre
**indirect** *adj* di natunawan
**indiscreet** *adj* patago
**indiscretion** *n* lantad
**indisposed** *adj* may sakit
**indisputable** *adj* may bisa
**indivisible** *adj* buo
**indoctrinate** *v* turuan
**indoor** *adv* sa loob
**induce** *v* himukin
**indulge** *v* magpakalabis
**indulgent** *adj* labis-labis
**industrious** *adj* masipag
**industry** *n* industriya
**ineffective** *adj* di mabisa
**inept** *adj* tamad
**inequality** *n* di pantay-pantay
**inevitable** *adj* di maiiwasan
**inexcusable** *adj* walang dahilan
**inexplicable** *adj* mura
**infallible** *adj* di nagkakamali
**infamous** *adj* kilala
**infancy** *n* kabataan
**infant** *n* sanggol
**infantry** *n* sangay ng militar
**infect** *v* hawahan
**infection** *n* nahawa
**infectious** *adj* nakakahawa
**infer** *v* mag husga
**inferior** *adj* mahinang uri
**infertile** *adj* baog
**infested** *adj* sinalanta
**infidelity** *n* pagtataksil
**infiltrate** *v* nasakop
**infiltration** *n* pag sakop
**infinite** *adj* walang katapusan
**infirmary** *n* klinika
**inflammation** *n* pamamaga
**inflate** *v* hanginan
**inflexible** *adj* pagbabang halaga
**inflict** *v* saktan
**influence** *n* impluensa
**influential** *adj* maimluensya
**influenza** *n* trangkaso
**influx** *n* pagdagsa
**inform** *v* ipaalam
**informal** *adj* hindi pormal
**informality** *n* hindi pormal
**informant** *n* taga ulat
**information** *n* balita
**informer** *n* taga balita

**infraction** *n* pag labag
**infrequent** *adj* di madalas
**infuriate** *v* galitin
**infusion** *n* paghahalo
**ingenuity** *n* pagka malikhain
**ingest** *v* lulunin
**ingot** *n* paleta
**ingrained** *adj* nakatanim
**ingredient** *n* sangkap
**inhabit** *v* nakatira
**inhabitable** *adj* di maaring tirahan
**inhabitant** *n* naninieahan
**inhale** *v* langhapin
**inherit** *v* manahin
**inheritance** *n* mana
**inhibit** *v* pigilan
**inhuman** *adj* hindi makatao
**initial** *adj* pauna
**initially** *adv* sa simula
**initials** *n* mga unang titik
**initiate** *v* umpisahan
**initiative** *n* ariling kusa
**inject** *v* mag turok
**injection** *n* pang turok
**injure** *v* sinaktan
**injurious** *adj* nakakaakit
**injustice** *n* pinsala
**ink** *n* tinta
**inkling** *n* may kutob
**inlaid** *adj* nakapaloob
**inland** *adv* sa loob
**inland** *adj* looban
**inmate** *n* preso
**inn** *n* paupahan
**innate** *adj* natural
**inner** *adj* kinapapalooban
**innocent** *adj* walang kamalayan
**innovation** *n* pagbabago
**innuendo** *n* parinig
**innumerable** *adj* napakarami
**input** *n* paglalagay
**inquire** *v* alamin
**inquiry** *n* pag - aalam
**insane** *adj* baliw
**insanity** *n* kabaliwan
**insatiable** *adj* walang kasiyahan
**insect** *n* insekto
**insecurity** *n* walang katiyakan
**insensitive** *adj* walang pakiramdam
**insert** *v* isingit
**insertion** *n* pag singit
**inside** *adj* sa loob
**inside** *pre* looboan
**inside out** *adv* baligtad
**insignificant** *adj* di mahalaga
**insincere** *adj* hindi matapat
**insincerity** *n* walang katapatan
**insinuate** *v* magpahiwatig
**insist** *v* igiit
**insistence** *n* paggigiit
**insolent** *adj* tamad
**insoluble** *adj* di natutunaw
**insomnia** *n* di makatulog
**inspect** *v* rekisahin

**inspection** *n* pag rekisa
**inspector** *n* inspektor
**inspiration** *n* inspirasyon
**instability** *n* magbigay diwa
**install** *v* ikabit
**installation** *n* pagkabit
**installment** *n* hulugan
**instance** *n* isang pangyayari
**instant** *n* daglian
**instantly** *adv* kaagad
**instead** *adv* sa halip
**instigate** *v* umpisahan
**instil** *v* itimo; ilagay sa isip
**instinct** *n* katutubong kilos
**institute** *v* paaralin
**institution** *n* paaralan
**instruct** *v* turuan
**instructor** *n* guro
**insufficient** *adj* di sapat
**insulate** *v* takpan
**insulation** *n* pagtakip
**insult** *v* insiltuhin
**insult** *n* insulto
**insurance** *n* seguro
**insure** *v* ipaseguro
**insurgency** *n* pag-aklas
**insurrection** *n* himagsikan
**intact** *adj* buo
**intake** *n* tinanggap
**integrate** *v* ipagsama
**integration** *n* pagsasama
**intelligent** *adj* matalino
**intend** *v* naisin
**intense** *adj* matindi
**intensify** *v* palakasin
**intensity** *n* lakas
**intensive** *adj* matindi
**intention** *n* hangarin
**intercept** *v* hadlangan
**intercession** *n* namagitan
**interchange** *v* pagpalitin
**interchange** *n* pagpapalitan
**interest** *n* tubo
**interested** *adj* may hilig
**interesting** *adj* mahilig
**interfere** *v* hadlangan
**interference** *n* paghadlang
**interior** *adj* kaloob-looban
**intermediary** *n* tagapamagitan
**intern** *v* nagsasanay
**interpret** *v* pagsasaling wika
**interpretation** *n* pagsasalin
**interpreter** *n* salin-wika
**interrogate** *v* imbestigahan
**interrupt** *v* patigilin; pigilan
**interruption** *n* pag tigil
**intersect** *v* magsalubong
**intertwine** *v* magkabuhol
**interval** *n* pagitan
**intervene** *v* makialam
**intervention** *n* pakikialam
**interview** *n* panayam
**intestine** *n* bituka
**intimacy** *n* magkaniig

**intimate** *adj* kaniig
**intimidate** *v* takutin
**intolerable** *adj* hindi makayanan
**intolerance** *n* hindi makatiis
**intoxicated** *adj* lasing
**intravenous** *adj* pagdaloy sa ugat
**intrepid** *adj* walang takot
**intricate** *adj* masalimuot
**intrigue** *n* intriga
**intriguing** *adj* ma intriga
**intrinsic** *adj* pagka natural
**introduce** *v* ipakilala
**introduction** *n* pakilala
**introvert** *adj* makasarili
**intrude** *v* makialam
**intruder** *n* pakialamero/a
**intrusion** *n* pakikialam
**intuition** *n* pakiramdam
**inundate** *v* kalbuhin
**invade** *v* sugurin
**invader** *n* mananalakay
**invalid** *n* walang halaga
**invalidate** *v* pawalang bisa
**invaluable** *adj* mahalaga
**invasion** *n* sumugod
**invent** *v* imbentuhin
**invention** *n* imbensyon
**inventory** *n* imbentaryo
**invest** *v* mamuhunan
**investigate** *v* mag-imbistiga
**investigation** *n* pag-iimbistiga
**investment** *n* puhunan
**investor** *n* namumuhunan
**invincible** *adj* malakas
**invisible** *adj* di nakikita
**invitation** *n* paanyaya
**invite** *v* anyayahan
**invoice** *n* resibo
**invoke** *v* magdasal ng taimtim
**involve** *v* kasangkot
**involved** *v* nasangkot
**involvement** *n* pagkakasangkot
**inward** *adj* sa dakong loob
**inwards** *adv* paloob
**iodine** *n* yodo
**irate** *adj* nainis
**Ireland** *n* Irlanda
**Irish** *adj* Irlandes
**iron** *n* plantsa
**iron** *v* namalantsa
**irony** *n* kabaligtaran
**irrational** *adj* walang isip
**irrefutable** *adj* di napatunayan
**irregular** *adj* hindi madalas
**irreparable** *adj* di magagawa
**irresistible** *adj* di matanggihan
**irrespective** *adj* di alintana
**irreversible** *adj* di naibabalik
**irrevocable** *adj* di na mababawi
**irrigate** *v* patubigan
**irrigation** *n* patubig
**irritate** *v* inisin
**irritating** *adj* nakakainis
**Islamic** *adj* maka muslim

**island** *n* isla
**isle** *n* isla
**isolate** *v* ihiwalay
**isolation** *n* paghiwalay
**issue** *n* usapin; paksa
**Italian** *adj* Italyano
**Italy** *n* Italya
**itch** *v* kumati
**itchiness** *n* makati
**item** *n* gamit
**itemize** *v* isa-isahin
**itinerary** *n* iteneraryo
**ivory** *n* garik

# J

**jackal** *n* aso
**jacket** *n* dtaket
**jackpot** *n* premyo
**jaguar** *n* hayop sa gubat
**jail** *n* kulungan
**jail** *v* nakakulong
**jailer** *n* preso
**jam** *n* matamis
**janitor** *n* tagalinis
**January** *n* Enero
**Japan** *n* Hapon
**Japanese** *adj* Hapon
**jar** *n* banga
**jasmine** *n* hasmin
**jaw** *n* panga
**jealous** *adj* seloso
**jealousy** *n* selos
**jeans** *n* pantalon
**jeopardize** *v* mamiligro
**jerk** *n* baltak
**jersey** *n* seda
**Jew** *n* hudyo
**jewel** *n* alahas
**jeweler** *n* alahero
**jewelry store** *n* alahasan
**Jewish** *adj* hudyo
**job** *n* trabaho
**jobless** *adj* walang trabaho
**join** *v* sumali
**joint** *n* dugtong
**jointly** *adv* kasugpungan
**joke** *n* biro
**joke** *v* biruin
**jokingly** *adv* nagbiro
**jolly** *adj* masaya
**jolt** *v* yumanig
**jolt** *n* yanig
**journal** *n* sulatin
**journalist** *n* manunulat
**journey** *n* paglalakbay
**jovial** *adj* matuwain
**joy** *n* saya
**joyful** *adj* masayahin
**joyfully** *adv* pagsaya

**jubilant** *adj* nagbunyi
**Judaism** *n* hudyo
**judge** *n* hukom
**judgment** *n* nagpasya
**judicious** *adj* matalino
**jug** *n* pitsel
**juggler** *n* payaso
**juice** *n* inumin
**juicy** *adj* masabaw
**July** *n* Hulyo
**jump** *v* tumalon
**jump** *n* talon
**jumpy** *adj* matalon
**junction** *n* kanto
**June** *n* Hunyo
**jungle** *n* gubat
**junior** *adj* batang anak
**junk** *n* basura
**jury** *n* kagawad
**just** *adj* makatarungan
**justice** *n* hustisya
**justify** *v* patunayan
**justly** *adv* makatarungan
**juvenile** *n* kabataan
**juvenile** *adj* pagkabata

**kangaroo** *n* kanggaro
**karate** *n* karate
**keep** *iv* itago
**keep on** *v* ituloy
**keep up** *v* maki bagay
**keg** *n* barilis
**kennel** *n* bahay ng aso
**kettle** *n* palayok
**key** *n* susi
**key ring** *n* lalagyan ng susi
**keyboard** *n* teklado
**kick** *v* sipain
**kickback** *n* kupit
**kickoff** *n* umpisahan
**kid** *n* bata; biro
**kidnap** *v* agawin
**kidnapper** *n* mang-aagaw
**kidnapping** *n* pag-agaw
**kidney** *n* bato
**kill** *v* patayin
**killer** *n* mamatay-tao
**killing** *n* patayan
**kilogram** *n* kilo
**kilometer** *n* kilometro
**kilowatt** *n* kilowat
**kind** *adj* uri
**kindle** *v* sindihan
**kindly** *adv* kabaitan
**kindness** *n* kabutihan

**king** *n* hari
**kingdom** *n* kaharian
**kinship** *n* kamag-anak
**kiosk** *n* karinderya
**kiss** *v* halikan
**kiss** *n* halik
**kitchen** *n* kusina
**kite** *n* saranggola
**kitten** *n* kuting
**knee** *n* tuhod
**kneecap** *n* tuhod
**kneel** *iv* lumuhod
**knife** *n* kutsilyo
**knight** *n* kabalyero
**knit** *v* maggantsilyo
**knob** *n* agradera
**knock** *n* katok
**knock** *v* kumatok
**knot** *n* buhol
**know** *iv* alamin
**know-how** *n* kaalaman
**knowingly** *adv* sinadya
**knowledge** *n* karunungan

# L

**lab** *n* lab
**label** *n* etiketa
**labor** *n* gawain
**laborer** *n* manggagawa
**lace** *n* laso; panali
**lack** *v* basawan
**lack** *n* kulang
**lad** *n* batang lalaki
**ladder** *n* hagdan; ladera
**laden** *adj* kargado
**lady** *n* binibini
**ladylike** *adj* mahinhin
**lagoon** *n* sapa
**lake** *n* look
**lamb** *n* tupa
**lame** *adj* pilay
**lament** *v* magluksa
**lament** *n* luksa
**lamp** *n* lampara
**lamppost** *n* ilaw sa poste
**lampshade** *n* lampara
**land** *n* lupa
**land** *v* lumapag
**landfill** *n* panambak
**landing** *n* kupain
**landlady** *n* may ari ng bahay
**landlocked** *adj* sarado
**landlord** *n* kasera; may ari
**landscape** *n* tanawin

**lane** *n* daanan
**language** *n* wika
**languish** *v* nagdurusa
**lantern** *n* parol
**lap** *n* kandungan
**lapse** *n* tapos
**lapse** *v* natapos
**larceny** *n* pag-aagaw
**lard** *n* mantika
**large** *adj* malaki
**larynx** *n* lalamunan
**laser** *n* leyser
**lash** *n* hagupit
**lash** *v* hagupitin
**lash out** *v* hinagupit
**last** *v* ihuli
**last** *adj* huli
**last name** *n* apelyido
**last night** *adv* kagabi
**lasting** *adj* pangmatagalan
**lastly** *adv* panghuli
**latch** *n* isabit
**late** *adv* nahuli
**lately** *adv* nakaraan
**later** *adv* mamaya
**later** *adj* huli
**lateral** *adj* gilid
**latest** *adj* pinakahuli
**lather** *n* bula
**latitude** *n* latitud
**latter** *adj* ang nabanggit
**laugh** *v* tumawa
**laugh** *n* tawa
**laughable** *adj* nakakatwa
**laughter** *n* tawa
**launch** *n* simulan
**launch** *v* sinimulan
**laundry** *n* labada
**lavatory** *n* lababo
**lavish** *adj* karangyaan
**lavish** *v* marangya
**law** *n* batas
**lawful** *adj* makatarungan
**lawmaker** *n* mambabatas
**lawn** *n* damuhan
**lawsuit** *n* demanda
**lawyer** *n* abogado
**lax** *adj* pabaya
**laxative** *adj* purga
**lay** *n* ilapag
**lay** *iv* inilapag
**lay off** *v* tanggalin
**layer** *n* suson
**lay-out** *n* salansan
**laziness** *n* katamaran
**lazy** *adj* tamad
**lead** *iv* pasimuno
**lead** *n* pamumuno
**leaded** *adj* pinamunuan
**leader** *n* pinuno
**leadership** *n* pamunuan
**leading** *adj* pinamumunuan
**leaf** *n* dahon
**leaflet** *n* maliit na dahon

L

**league** *n* liga
**leak** *v* tumagas
**leak** *n* tagas
**leakage** *n* pagtagas
**lean** *adj* payat
**lean** *iv* sumandal
**lean back** *v* sumandal
**lean on** *v* umasa
**leaning** *n* sandalan
**leap** *iv* tumalon
**leap** *n* pagtalon
**leap year** *n* lipyir
**learn** *iv* alamin
**learned** *adj* natuto
**learner** *n* mag-aaral
**learning** *n* nag-aaral
**lease** *v* upahan
**lease** *n* upa
**leash** *n* tali
**least** *adj* kaunti
**leather** *n* katad; balat
**leave** *iv* iwan
**leave out** *v* iwanan
**lectern** *n* pulpito
**lecture** *n* pagtuturo
**ledger** *n* listahan
**leech** *n* linta
**leftovers** *n* tira
**leg** *n* binti
**legacy** *n* pamana
**legal** *adj* ayon sa batas
**legalize** *v* iayon sa batas
**legend** *n* alamat
**legible** *adj* nababasa
**legislate** *v* gumawa ng batas
**legislation** *n* paggawa ng batas
**legislature** *n* batasan
**legitimate** *adj* naayon sa batas
**leisure** *n* malayang sandali
**lemon** *n* limon
**lemonade** *n* lemonada
**lend** *iv* hiramin
**length** *n* haba
**lengthen** *v* habaan
**lengthy** *adj* mahaba
**leniency** *n* kaluwagan
**lenient** *adj* maluwag
**lense** *n* lente
**Lent** *n* kwaresma
**lentil** *n* munggo
**leopard** *n* lyopard
**leper** *n* ketongin
**leprosy** *n* ketong
**less** *adj* kaunti
**lessee** *n* nagpapaupa
**lessen** *v* bawasan
**lesser** *adj* kaunti
**lesson** *n* aralin
**lessor** *n* umuupa
**let** *iv* payagan
**let down** *v* binigo
**let go** *v* pakawalan
**let in** *v* papasukin
**let out** *v* palabasin

L

**lethal** *adj* nakamamatay
**letter** *n* sulat
**lettuce** *n* lechugas
**leukemia** *n* sakit sa dugo
**level** *v* ipantay
**level** *n* pantay
**lever** *n* bara
**leverage** *n* lakas
**levy** *v* mangalap
**lewd** *adj* malaswa
**liability** *n* pananagutan
**liable** *adj* mananagot
**liaison** *n* sugo
**liar** *adj* sinungaling
**libel** *n* libelo
**liberate** *v* iligtas
**liberation** *n* pagliligtas
**liberty** *n* kalayaan
**library** *n* aklatan
**lice** *n* kuto
**licence** *n* lisensya
**license** *v* lisensya
**lick** *v* dilaan
**lid** *n* takip
**lie** *iv* magsinungaling
**lie** *v* nagsinungaling
**lie** *n* kasinunalingan
**lieu** *n* sa halip na
**lieutenant** *n* tinyente
**life** *n* buhay
**lifeguard** *n* nanagip buhay
**lifeless** *adj* walang buhay
**lifestyle** *n* pamumuhay
**lifetime** *adj* buong buhay
**lift** *v* angatin
**lift off** *v* iangat
**lift-off** *n* pag-angat
**ligament** *n* litid
**light** *iv* magaan
**light** *adj* maliwanag
**light** *n* ilaw
**lighter** *n* panindi
**lighthouse** *n* parola
**lighting** *n* ilaw
**lightly** *adv* bahagya
**lightning** *n* kidlat
**lightweight** *n* magaan
**likable** *adj* kaibig-ibig
**like** *pre* tulad
**like** *v* itulad
**likelihood** *n* katulad ng
**likely** *adv* malamng
**likeness** *n* kamukha
**likewise** *adv* gayundin
**liking** *n* pagkagusto
**limb** *n* laman
**lime** *n* limon
**limestone** *n* apog
**limit** *n* hangganan
**limit** *v* limitahan
**limitation** *n* limitasyon
**limp** *v* pa-ika-ika
**limp** *n* pilay
**line** *n* linya

**line up** *v* pumila
**linen** *n* tela
**linger** *v* magpa-ulit-ulit
**lingerie** *n* damot panloob
**lingering** *adj* paiko-ikot
**lining** *n* aporo
**link** *v* lumubog
**link** *n* karugtong
**lion** *n* leyon
**lioness** *n* babaeng leyon
**lip** *n* labi
**liqueur** *n* alak
**liquid** *n* likido
**liquidate** *v* tunawin
**liquidation** *n* pag-sasara
**liquor** *n* alak
**list** *v* ilista
**list** *n* lista
**listen** *v* makinig
**listener** *n* tagapakinig
**litany** *n* litanya
**liter** *n* kalat
**literal** *adj* karaniwan
**literature** *n* literatura
**litigate** *v* litisin
**litigation** *n* paglilitis
**litre** *n* litro
**litter** *n* kalat
**little** *adj* maliit
**little bit** *n* kaunti
**little by little** *adv* unti-unti
**liturgy** *n* ebanghelyo
**live** *adj* buhay
**live** *v* nakatira
**live off** *v* mamuhay sa
**live up** *v* pangatawanan
**livelihood** *n* kabuhayan
**lively** *adj* masaya
**liver** *n* atay
**livestock** *n* babuyan
**living room** *n* silid tanggapan
**lizard** *n* butiki
**load** *v* kargahin
**load** *n* kargada
**loaded** *adj* kargado
**loaf** *n* bara ng tinapay
**loan** *v* magpautang
**loan** *n* utang
**loathe** *v* nagalit; nainis
**loathing** *n* pagkagalit
**lobby** *n* bulwagan
**lobby** *v* bulwagan
**lobster** *n* ulang
**local** *adj* pampook
**localize** *v* gawing isang lugar
**locate** *v* hanapin
**located** *adj* nahanap
**location** *n* lugar
**lock** *v* ipinid
**lock** *n* kandado
**lock up** *v* nakakandado
**locker room** *n* sild ng mga aparador
**locksmith** *n* panday-susi
**locust** *n* balang

**lodge** *v* tumitira
**lofty** *adj* matarik
**log** *n* kahoy; sanga
**log** *v* itala
**logic** *n* lohica
**logical** *adj* lohikal
**loin** *n* lomo
**loiter** *v* magpakalat-kalat
**loneliness** *n* kalungkutan
**lonely** *adv* malungkot
**loner** *n* mapag-isa
**lonesome** *adj* malungkot
**long** *adj* mahaba
**long for** *v* nananabik
**longing** *n* pananabik
**longitude** *n* pahaba
**long-standing** *adj* matagal na
**long-term** *adj* pangmatagalan
**look** *n* tingin
**look** *v* tumingin
**look after** *v* alagaan
**look at** *v* tingnan
**look down** *v* abahin
**look for** *v* hanapin
**look forward** *v* umasa
**look into** *v* alamin
**look out** *v* mag-ingat
**look over** *v* tumingin
**look through** *v* tingnan
**looking glass** *n* bolang kristal
**looks** *n* tila
**loom** *n* pagbabadya
**loom** *v* nagbabadya
**loophole** *n* butas; silipan
**loose** *v* luwagan
**loose** *adj* maluwag
**loosen** *v* niluwagan
**loot** *v* magnakaw
**loot** *n* nakaw
**lord** *n* panginoon
**lordship** *n* pag-mamay-ari
**lose** *iv* iwala
**loser** *n* talunan
**loss** *n* kawalan
**lot** *adv* dami
**lotion** *n* losyon
**lots** *adj* marami
**lottery** *n* loterya
**loud** *adj* malakas
**loudly** *adv* kalakasan
**lounge** *n* pahingahan
**louse** *n* kuto
**lousy** *adj* masagwa
**lovable** *adj* kaibig-ibig
**love** *v* mahalin
**love** *n* pag-ibig
**lovely** *adj* maganda
**lover** *n* mangingibig
**loving** *adj* mapagmahal
**low** *adj* mababa
**lower** *adj* mas mababa
**lowkey** *adj* mababang loob
**lowly** *adj* mababng uri
**loyal** *adj* matapat

L

**loyalty** *n* katapatan
**lubricate** *v* langisan
**lubrication** *n* panlangis
**lucid** *adj* maliwanag
**luck** *n* swerte
**lucky** *adj* maswerte
**lucrative** *adj* mapagkakakitaan
**ludicrous** *adj* katawa-tawa
**luggage** *n* maleta
**lukewarm** *adj* maligamgam
**lull** *n* ipaghele
**lumber** *n* tabla
**luminous** *adj* makintab
**lump** *n* bukol
**lump sum** *n* buo
**lump together** *v* kumpol
**lunacy** *n* kabaliwan
**lunatic** *adj* baliw
**lunch** *n* pananghalian
**lung** *n* baga
**lure** *v* akitin
**lurid** *adj* namumula
**lurk** *v* napipinto
**lush** *adj* sariwang gulay
**lust** *v* lumibog
**lust** *n* kamunduhan
**lustful** *adj* malibog
**luxurious** *adj* maluho
**luxury** *n* luho
**lynch** *v* ibitay; patayin
**lynx** *n* hayop na tila pusa
**lyrics** *n* liriko

**machine** *n* makina
**machine gun** *n* baril
**mad** *adj* galit
**madam** *n* ginang
**madden** *v* nabaliw
**madly** *adv* nagpakabaliw
**madman** *n* taong baliw
**madness** *n* kabaliwan
**magazine** *n* babasahin
**magic** *n* salamangka
**magical** *adj* kaakit-akit
**magician** *n* salamangkero
**magistrate** *n* hukom
**magnet** *n* batu-balani
**magnetic** *adj* may balani
**magnetism** *n* pagka balani
**magnificent** *adj* dakila
**magnify** *v* palakihin
**magnitude** *n* kalawakan
**mahagony** *n* mahogani
**maid** *n* katulong
**maiden** *n* tagalinis
**mail** *v* sulatan
**mail** *n* sulat
**mailbox** *n* buson
**mailman** *n* kartero
**maim** *v* napilay
**main** *adj* panguna
**mainland** *n* gitnang bayan

**mainly** *adv* higit sa kahat
**maintain** *v* panatilihin
**maintenance** *n* pagpapanatili
**majestic** *adj* marangal
**majesty** *n* kamahal-mahalan
**major** *n* kumandante
**major** *adj* higit
**majority** *n* karamihan
**make** *n* gawa
**make** *iv* gawin
**make up** *v* bumawi
**make up for** *v* bawiin sa
**maker** *n* tagag-likha
**makeup** *n* pampaganda
**malaria** *n* malarya
**male** *n* lalaki
**malevolent** *adj* naghihiganti
**malfunction** *v* di gumagana
**malfunction** *n* hinid paggana
**malice** *n* malisya
**malign** *v* manirang puri
**malignancy** *n* nakamamatay
**malignant** *adj* nakamamatay
**mall** *n* pamilihan
**malnutrition** *n* malnutrisyon
**malpractice** *v* gawing mali
**mammal** *n* hayop na may suso
**mammoth** *n* malaking elepante
**man** *n* tao
**manage** *v* mangasiwa
**management** *n* pangasiwaan
**manager** *n* tagapangasiwa
**mandate** *n* utos
**mandatory** *adj* sapilitan
**maneuver** *n* maneobra
**manger** *n* sabsaban
**mangle** *v* putulin
**manhandle** *v* manakit
**manhunt** *n* paghahanap
**maniac** *adj* manyak
**manifest** *v* nahlata
**manipulate** *v* pangasiwaan
**mankind** *n* sankatauhan
**manliness** *n* pagkalalaki
**manly** *adj* maginoo
**manner** *n* paraan
**mannerism** *n* pag-uugali
**manners** *n* asal
**manpower** *n* trabahador
**mansion** *n* palasyo
**manslaughter** *n* pagpatay
**manual** *n* pangkamay
**manual** *adj* kinamay
**manufacture** *v* gumawa
**manure** *n* pataba; abono
**manuscript** *n* kopya; papel
**many** *adj* marami
**map** *n* mapa
**marble** *n* marmol
**march** *v* magmartsa
**march** *n* Marso
**March** *n* marso
**mare** *n* babaeng kabayo
**margin** *n* gilid

**marginal** *adj* sapat lamang
**marinate** *v* ibabad
**marine** *adj* pandagat
**mark** *n* tandaan
**mark** *v* tandaan
**mark down** *v* ibaba
**marker** *n* palatandaan
**market** *n* palengke
**marksman** *n* taga tatak
**marmalade** *n* marmalada
**marriage** *n* kasalan
**married** *adj* kasal
**marrow** *n* utak
**marry** *v* pakasalan
**Mars** *n* Marso
**marshal** *n* opisyal sa hukbo
**martyr** *n* martir
**martyrdom** *n* kabayanihan
**marvel** *n* kababakaghan
**marvelous** *adj* kahanga-hanga
**masculine** *adj* maskulado
**mash** *v* lamasin
**mask** *n* maskara
**masochism** *n* pananakit sa sarili
**mason** *n* mason
**masquerade** *v* parada
**mass** *n* misa
**massacre** *n* pagpatay ng marami
**massage** *n* masahe
**massage** *v* minasahe
**masseur** *n* lalaking masahista
**masseuse** *n* babaeng masahista
**massive** *adj* malawak
**mast** *n* haligi
**master** *n* panginoon; amo
**master** *v* isaulo
**mastermind** *n* utak; pinuno
**mastermind** *v* namuno
**mastery** *n* kaalaman
**mat** *n* banig
**match** *n* magkatapat
**match** *v* pinagtapat
**material** *n* materyal
**materialism** *n* materyalismo
**maternal** *adj* tungkol sa ina
**maternity** *n* pagdadalantao
**math** *n* matematika
**matriculate** *v* magpatala
**matrimony** *n* kasalan
**matter** *n* bagay
**mattress** *n* kutson
**mature** *adj* nasa hustong isip
**maturity** *n* may isip
**maul** *v* bugbugin
**maxim** *n* kasabihan
**maximum** *adj* pinaka marami
**May** *n* Mayo
**may** *iv* mayroon
**may-be** *adv* marahil
**mayhem** *n* pagsasakit sa sarili
**mayor** *n* alkalde
**maze** *n* nakalilito
**meadow** *n* damuhan
**meager** *adj* kakaunti

**meal** *n* pagkain
**mean** *iv* hangarin
**mean** *adj* malupit
**meaning** *n* kahulugan
**meaningful** *adj* mahalaga
**meaningless** *adj* wealang halaga
**meanness** *n* kalupitan
**means** *n* kakayahn
**meantime** *adv* samantala
**meanwhile** *adv* habang
**measles** *n* tigdas
**measure** *v* sukatin
**measurement** *n* panukat
**meat** *n* karne
**mechanic** *n* mekaniko
**mechanism** *n* mekanismo
**mechanize** *v* gawin sa makina
**medal** *n* medalya
**medallion** *n* malaking medalya
**meddle** *v* makialam
**mediate** *v* awatin
**mediator** *n* pag-aawat
**medication** *n* gamot
**medicinal** *adj* mabisang gamot
**medicine** *n* medisina
**medieval** *adj* makaluma
**mediocre** *adj* pangkaraniwang tao
**meditate** *v* magnilay-nilay
**meditation** *n* pagninilay-nilay
**medium** *adj* kainaman
**meek** *adj* maamo
**meekness** *n* kababaang-loob

**meet** *iv* salubungin
**meeting** *n* pagpupulong
**melancholy** *n* kalungkutan
**mellow** *adj* malambot; hinog
**mellow** *v* pahinugin
**melodic** *adj* may himig
**melody** *n* himig
**melon** *n* cantaloupe
**melt** *v* natunaw
**member** *n* kasapi
**membership** *n* pagsapi
**membrane** *n* lamad
**memento** *n* ala-ala
**memoirs** *n* talaarawan
**memorable** *adj* mahalaga
**memorize** *v* kabisahin
**memory** *n* gunita
**men** *n* mga lalaki
**menace** *n* panganib
**mend** *v* tagpian
**meningitis** *n* minighitis
**mental** *adj* mental
**mentality** *n* kaisipan
**mentally** *adv* nasa isip
**mention** *v* banggitin
**mention** *n* pagbanggit
**menu** *n* menu
**merchandise** *n* kalakal
**merchant** *n* mangangalakal
**merciful** *adj* mapagpatawad
**merciless** *adj* walang awa
**mercury** *n* asoge

**mercy** *n* awa
**merely** *adv* lamang
**merge** *v* idugtong
**merger** *n* pang-dugtong
**merit** *n* halaga
**merit** *v* pahalagahan
**mermaid** *n* sirena
**merry** *adj* maligaya
**mesh** *n* sinulid
**mesmerize** *v* naakit
**mess** *n* kalat
**mess around** *v* magkalat
**mess up** *v* nagkamali
**message** *n* mensahe
**messenger** *n* mensahero
**Messiah** *n* tagapag-ligtas
**messy** *adj* madumi
**metal** *n* metal
**metallic** *adj* mala-lata
**metaphor** *n* paghahambing
**meteor** *n* maliit na bituin
**meter** *n* metro
**method** *n* paraan
**methodical** *adj* maparaan
**meticulous** *adj* maselan
**metric** *adj* metro
**metropolis** *n* karatig
**Mexican** *adj* meksikano
**mice** *n* daga
**microbe** *n* mikrobyo
**microphone** *n* mikropono
**microscope** *n* mikrospkopyo
**midair** *n* sa gitna
**midday** *n* gitnang araw
**middle** *n* gitna
**middleman** *n* ahente
**midget** *n* unano
**midnight** *n* hatinggabi
**midsummer** *n* tag-araw
**midwife** *n* komadrona
**mighty** *adj* malakas
**migrant** *n* dayuhan
**migrate** *v* dumayo
**mild** *adj* mahinay
**mildew** *n* hamog
**mile** *n* milya
**mileage** *n* milyahe
**milestone** *n* kaganapan
**militant** *adj* militante
**milk** *n* gatas
**milky** *adj* tila gatas
**mill** *n* gilingan
**millennium** *n* libong taon
**milligram** *n* sanlibong gramo
**millimeter** *n* sanlibong metro
**million** *n* milyon
**millionaire** *n* milyonaryo
**mime** *v* maym
**mince** *v* tadtarin
**mincemeat** *n* giniling
**mind** *v* isipin
**mind** *n* isip
**mindful** *adj* pansinin
**mindless** *adj* walang isip

**mine** *n* akin; mina
**mine** *v* angkinin
**mine** *pro* akin; mina
**minefield** *n* minahan
**miner** *n* minero
**mineral** *n* mineral
**mingle** *v* maki-halubilo
**miniature** *n* malilit
**minimize** *v* sagarin
**minimum** *n* pinaka kaunti
**miniskirt** *n* maiksiing palda
**minister** *n* ministro
**minister** *v* ministro
**ministry** *n* ministeryo
**minor** *adj* menor de edad
**minus** *adj* bawas
**minute** *n* minuto
**miracle** *n* milagro
**miraculous** *adj* milagroso
**mirage** *n* pangitain
**mirror** *n* salamin
**misbehave** *v* walang asal
**miscalculate** *v* magkamali
**miscarriage** *n* nakunan
**miscarry** *v* di madala
**mischief** *n* kapilyuhan
**mischievous** *adj* pilyo
**misconduct** *n* maling ugali
**misconstrue** *v* nagkamali
**misdemeanor** *n* pagkakamali
**miser** *n* suwapang
**miserable** *adj* kalunos-lunos
**misery** *n* kahirapan
**misfit** *adj* hindi bagay
**misfortune** *n* kamalasan
**misgiving** *n* hindi mapatawad
**misguided** *adj* naligaw ng landas
**misinterpret** *v* maling akala
**misjudge** *v* hatulan ng mali
**mislead** *v* nalito
**misleading** *adj* nakakalito
**misplace** *v* nawala
**misprint** *n* maling paglimbag
**miss** *v* nananabik
**miss** *n* binibini
**missile** *n* misel
**missing** *adj* nawawala
**mission** *n* misyon
**missionary** *n* misyonaryo
**mist** *n* muog
**mistake** *iv* namali
**mistake** *n* nagkamali
**mistaken** *adj* mali
**mister** *n* ginoo
**mistreat** *v* pagmalupitan
**mistreatment** *n* kalupitan
**mistress** *n* kabit
**mistrust** *n* walang tiwala
**misty** *adj* maulap
**misuse** *n* maling paggamit
**mitigate** *v* ibsan
**mix** *v* haluin
**mixed-up** *adj* naihalo
**mixer** *n* pang-halo

**mixture** *n* halo
**mix-up** *n* pag-halo-halo
**moan** *v* umungol
**moan** *n* ungol
**mob** *n* matao
**mobile** *adj* magalaw
**mobilize** *v* galawin
**mobster** *n* mga taong nagagalit
**mock** *v* tuyain
**mockery** *n* panunuya
**mode** *n* paraan
**model** *n* modelo
**moderate** *adj* katamtaman
**moderation** *n* pagka katamtaman
**modern** *adj* moderno
**modernize** *v* gawing moderno
**modest** *adj* mahihin
**modesty** *n* kahinhinan
**modify** *v* binago
**module** *n* modyul
**moisten** *v* basain
**moisture** *n* hamog
**molar** *n* bagang
**mold** *v* inamag
**mold** *n* amag
**moldy** *adj* maamag
**mole** *n* nunal
**molecule** *n* maliit na bahagi
**molest** *v* molstyahin
**mom** *n* inay
**moment** *n* sandali
**momentarily** *adv* pansamantala
**momentous** *adj* napaka halaga
**monarch** *n* hari
**monarchy** *n* kaharian
**monastery** *n* monasteryo
**monastic** *adj* pagka banal
**Monday** *n* Lunes
**money** *n* pera; salapi
**money order** *n* pagpapadala
**monitor** *v* bantayan
**monk** *n* pari
**monkey** *n* unggoy
**monopolize** *v* solohin
**monopoly** *n* monopolyo
**monotonous** *adj* na-inip
**monotony** *n* pagka - inip
**monster** *n* halimaw
**monstrous** *adj* mala halimaw
**month** *n* buwan
**monthly** *adv* buwanan
**monument** *n* monumento
**monumental** *adj* napaka laki
**mood** *n* gana
**moody** *adj* may sumpong
**moon** *n* buwan
**moor** *v* dumaong
**mop** *v* panlinis
**moral** *adj* mabuti; mabait
**moral** *n* kaugaliang wagas
**morality** *n* moralidad
**more** *adj* higt sa
**moreover** *adv* ganundin
**morning** *n* umaga

**moron** *adj* tanga
**morphine** *n* morpina
**morsel** *n* kapiraso; kaunti
**mortal** *adj* mortal
**mortality** *n* may hangganan
**mortar** *n* lusong; almires
**mortgage** *n* utang
**mortification** *n* pagtitika
**mortify** *v* gawin ang pinagtika
**mortuary** *n* morge
**mosaic** *n* desenyo
**mosque** *n* simbahan ng muslim
**mosquito** *n* lamok
**moss** *n* lumot
**most** *adj* karamihan
**mostly** *adv* karamihan
**motel** *n* motel
**moth** *n* paru-paro
**mother** *n* ina; nanay
**motherhood** *n* pagiging ina
**mother-in-law** *n* byenan
**motion** *n* paggalaw
**motionless** *adj* di gumagalaw
**motivate** *v* pagganyakin
**motive** *n* motibo
**motor** *n* motor
**motorcycle** *n* motorsiklo
**motto** *n* kasabihan
**mouldy** *adj* maamag
**mount** *n* pagtayo
**mount** *v* itayo
**mountain** *n* bundok
**mountainous** *adj* bulubundukin
**mourn** *v* magluksa
**mourning** *n* pagluluksa
**mouse** *n* daga
**mouth** *n* bibig
**move** *n* galaw
**move** *v* galawin
**move back** *v* umatras
**move forward** *v* umabante
**move out** *v* umalis
**move up** *v* tumaas
**movement** *n* galaw
**movie** *n* pelikula
**mow** *v* araruhin
**much** *adv* marami
**mucus** *n* sipon
**mud** *n* putik
**muddle** *n* pagkalito
**muddy** *adj* maputik
**muffle** *v* balutin
**muffler** *n* tambutso
**mug** *n* tasa
**mug** *v* itasa
**mugging** *n* bugbugan
**mule** *n* mula
**multiple** *adj* karamihan
**multiplication** *n* pagpaparami
**multiply** *v* doblehin
**multitude** *n* karamihan
**mumble** *v* bumulong
**mumps** *n* beke
**munch** *v* nguyain

**munitions** *n* armas
**murder** *n* pagpatay
**murderer** *n* mamamatay tao
**murky** *adj* napaka lungkot
**murmur** *v* bumubulong
**murmur** *n* bulong
**muscle** *n* kalamnan
**museum** *n* museyo
**mushroom** *n* kabute
**music** *n* musika
**musician** *n* musikero
**Muslim** *adj* muslim
**must** *iv* dapat
**mustache** *n* bigote
**mustard** *n* mustasa
**mutate** *v* manganak
**mute** *adj* pipi
**mutilate** *v* putol-putulin
**mutiny** *n* gulo
**mutually** *adv* isa't- isa
**muzzle** *v* ngusuin
**muzzle** *n* busal
**my** *adj* akin
**myself** *pro* sarili
**mysterious** *adj* misteryoso
**mystery** *n* misteryo
**mystic** *adj* nakapagtataka
**mystify** *v* pagtakahan
**myth** *n* alamat

# N

**nag** *v* bwisitin; yamutin
**nagging** *adj* nakakabwisit
**nail** *n* pako
**naive** *adj* mahiyain
**naked** *adj* hubad
**name** *n* pangalan
**namely** *adv* mga sumusunod:
**nanny** *n* yaya
**nap** *n* idlip
**napkin** *n* pamunas na papel
**narcotic** *n* narkotiko
**narrate** *v* magkuwento
**narrow** *adj* makitid
**narrowly** *adv* pagkakitid
**nasty** *adj* masagwa
**nation** *n* bansa
**national** *adj* pambansa
**nationality** *n* lahi
**native** *adj* tubo
**natural** *adj* natural
**nature** *n* kalikasan
**naughty** *adj* pilyo
**nausea** *n* duwal
**navel** *n* pusod
**navigate** *v* layagin
**navigation** *n* paglalayag
**navy** *n* sundalong pandagat
**navy blue** *adj* asul
**near** *pre* malapit

**nearby** *adj* malapit
**nearly** *adv* halos
**neat** *adj* malinis
**neatly** *adv* may kaayusan
**necessary** *adj* kailangan
**necessitate** *v* kinailangan
**necessity** *n* kailangan
**neck** *n* leeg
**necklace** *n* kwintas
**necktie** *n* kurbata
**need** *v* kinailangan
**need** *n* kailangan
**needle** *n* karayom
**needless** *adj* mga karayom
**needy** *adj* nangangailangan
**negative** *adj* negatibo
**neglect** *v* pabayaan
**neglect** *n* kapabayaan
**negligence** *n* pagpapabaya
**negligent** *adj* pabaya
**negotiate** *v* makipag-alam
**negotiation** *n* pakkipag-alaman
**neighbor** *n* kapit-bahay
**neighborhood** *n* kabahayan
**neither** *adj* alinma'y hindi
**neither** *adv* hindi
**nephew** *n* pamangkin
**nerve** *n* litid; lakas - loob
**nervous** *adj* nerbyos
**nest** *n* pugad
**net** *n* lambat; tubo
**Netherlands** *n* Nederland
**network** *n* pagkaka-kabit-kabit
**neurotic** *adj* nerbyosos
**neutral** *adj* patas
**neutralize** *v* gawing walang bisa
**never** *adv* hinid kailanman
**nevertheless** *adv* bagaman
**new** *adj* bago
**newborn** *n* bagng panganak
**newcomer** *n* bagong salta
**newly** *adv* bago
**newlywed** *adj* bagong kasal
**news** *n* balita
**newscast** *n* balita
**newsletter** *n* maliit na babasahin
**newspaper** *n* dyaryo
**newsstand** *n* tindahan ng dyaryo
**next** *adj* kasunod
**next door** *adj* sa kabila
**nibble** *v* tamilmil
**nice** *adj* mabuti
**nicely** *adv* kalugod-lugod
**nickel** *n* singko
**nickname** *n* palayaw
**nicotine** *n* nikotina
**niece** *n* pamangkin
**night** *n* gabi
**nightfall** *n* takip silim
**nightgown** *n* pantulog
**nightingale** *n* ibon
**nightmare** *n* bangungot
**nine** *adj* siyam
**nineteen** *adj* labingsiyam

**ninety** *adj* siyamnapu
**ninth** *adj* pang-siyam
**nip** *n* naputol
**nip** *v* putulin
**nipple** *n* utong
**nitpicking** *adj* nanghihinguto
**nitrogen** *n* nitroheno
**nobility** *n* kagitingan
**noble** *adj* magiting
**nobleman** *n* maharlika
**nobody** *pro* wala ninuman
**nocturnal** *adj* panggabi
**nod** *v* tumango
**noise** *n* ingay
**noisily** *adv* nag-iingay
**noisy** *adj* maingay
**nominate** *v* maghirang
**none** *pre* wala
**nonetheless** *c* ganunpaman
**nonsense** *n* walang kahulugan
**nonsmoker** *n* di nagsisgarilyo
**nonstop** *adv* walang humpay
**noon** *n* tanghali
**noose** *n* lubid
**no one** *pro* wala
**nor** *c* ni hindi
**norm** *n* kalakaran
**normal** *adj* normal
**normalize** *v* gawing normal
**normally** *adv* pangkaraniwan
**north** *n* hilaga
**northeast** *n* hilagangsilangan
**northern** *adj* nasa hilaga
**northerner** *adj* taga hilaga
**Norway** *n* Norwey
**Norwegian** *adj* taga Norwey
**nose** *n* ilong
**nosedive** *v* magpatihulog
**nostril** *n* butas ng ilong
**nosy** *adj* tsismosa
**not** *adv* hinid
**notable** *adj* kilala
**notably** *adv* pagkakakilala
**notary** *n* notaryo
**notation** *n* paliwanag
**note** *v* nota
**notebook** *n* kwaderno
**noteworthy** *adj* kansin-pansin
**nothing** *n* wala
**notice** *v* napansin
**notice** *n* babala
**noticeable** *adj* kapansin-pansin
**notification** *n* babala
**notify** *v* pinaalam
**notion** *n* akala
**noun** *n* pangngalan
**nourish** *v* pakainin
**novel** *n* nobela
**novelist** *n* nobelista
**novelty** *n* bago
**November** *n* Nobyembre
**novice** *n* bagito
**now** *adv* ngayong
**nowhere** *adv* kahit saan

**noxious** *adj* masama
**nozzle** *n* nguso
**nuance** *n* kulay
**nuclear** *adj* nukleyar
**nude** *adj* hubad
**nudism** *n* paghuhubad
**nudist** *n* pala hubad
**nudity** *n* hubad
**nuisance** *n* taong nakakainis
**nullify** *v* pawalang bisa
**numb** *adj* manhid
**number** *n* bilang
**numbness** *n* manhid
**numerous** *adj* marami
**nun** *n* madre
**nurse** *n* narses
**nurse** *v* mag alaga
**nursery** *n* bahay halaman
**nurture** *v* alagaan
**nut** *n* mani
**nutrition** *n* pagkain
**nutritious** *adj* masustansya
**nut-shell** *n* balat ng mani
**nutty** *adj* maraming mani

**oak** *n* kahoy
**oar** *n* sagwan
**oath** *n* sumpa
**oatmeal** *n* pagkaing butil
**obedience** *n* sundin
**obedient** *adj* masuburin
**obese** *adj* mataba
**obey** *v* sundin
**object** *n* bagay
**objection** *n* di pag sang ayon
**objective** *n* layunin
**obligate** *v* piliting magpagawa
**obligation** *n* katungkulan
**obligatory** *adj* sa pilitan
**oblige** *v* pinilit
**obliged** *adj* sapilitan
**oblique** *adj* nakapahalang
**obliterate** *v* pag pawi
**oblivion** *n* paghihiwalay
**oblivious** *adj* halata
**oblong** *adj* bilohaba
**obnoxious** *adj* masama
**obscene** *adj* mahalay
**obscenity** *n* kahalayn
**obscure** *adj* malabo
**obscurity** *n* kalabuan
**observation** *n* pagpansin
**observatory** *n* obserbatoryo
**observe** *v* pagmasdan

**obsess** *v* naisin ng matindi
**obsession** *n* matinidng pananais
**obsolete** *adj* kalumaan
**obstacle** *n* balakid
**obstinacy** *n* katigasan ng ulo
**obstinate** *adj* matigas ang ulo
**obstruct** *v* barahan
**obstruction** *n* bara
**obtain** *v* makuha
**obvious** *adj* halata
**obviously** *adv* pagkahalata
**occasion** *n* okasyon
**occasionally** *adv* paminsan-minsan
**occult** *adj* mahiwaga
**occupant** *n* may tao
**occupation** *n* trabaho
**occupy** *v* saklawin; tirahan
**occur** *v* maganap
**ocean** *n* malawak na dagat
**October** *n* Oktubre
**octopus** *n* pugita
**ocurrence** *n* pangyayari
**odd** *adj* kakaiba
**oddity** *n* pagkakaiba
**odds** *n* kakaibahan
**odious** *adj* kamuhi-muhi
**odor** *n* amoy
**of** *pre* ng
**off** *adv* patay
**offensive** *adj* nakainis
**offer** *v* ialay
**offer** *n* alay
**offering** *n* pag-aalay
**office** *n* opisina
**officer** *n* opisyal
**official** *adj* opisyal
**officiate** *v* pangasiwaan
**offset** *v* bayaran
**offspring** *n* anak
**off-the-record** *adj* hindi naka tala
**often** *adv* madalas
**oil** *n* langis
**ointment** *n* pamahid
**okay** *adv* ayos
**old** *adj* matanda
**old age** *n* katandaan
**old-fashioned** *adj* makaluma
**olive** *n* oliba
**olympics** *n* olimpyada
**omelette** *n* torta
**ominous** *adj* maliwanag
**omission** *n* pagkakalaktaw
**omit** *v* laktawan
**on** *pre* nasa
**once** *adv* minsan
**once** *c* isang beses
**one** *adj* isa
**oneself** *pre* mag-isa
**ongoing** *adj* sa kasalukuyan
**onion** *n* sibuyas
**onlooker** *n* manonod
**only** *adv* lamang
**onset** *n* sa umpisa
**onslaught** *n* paglusob

**onwards** *adv* pasulong
**opaque** *adj* makapal
**open** *v* buksan
**open** *adj* bukas
**open up** *v* magbukas
**opening** *n* pagbukas
**open-minded** *adj* malawak ang isip
**openness** *n* bukas na kaisipan
**opera** *n* opera
**operate** *v* tistisin; magpalakad
**operation** *n* patitistis
**opinion** *n* palagay
**opium** *n* opyo
**opponent** *n* katunggali
**opportune** *adj* napapanahon
**opportunity** *n* pagkakataon
**oppose** *v* salungatin
**opposite** *adj* kasalungat
**opposite** *adv* pagkasalungat
**opposite** *n* kabaligtaran
**opposition** *n* kalaban
**oppress** *v* apihin
**oppression** *n* pang-aapi
**opt for** *v* pinili
**optical** *adj* tungkol sa mata
**optician** *n* optiko
**optimism** *n* mapagkatiwala
**optimistic** *adj* may tiwala
**option** *n* pagpipilian
**optional** *adj* di sapilitan
**opulence** *n* karangyaan
**or** *c* o



**oracle** *n* hula
**orally** *adv* bigkasin
**orange** *n* kular dalandan
**orangutan** *n* unggoy
**orbit** *n* pag-inog
**orchard** *n* taniman
**orchestra** *n* orkestra
**ordain** *v* italaga
**ordeal** *n* pagpapahirap
**order** *n* utos
**ordinarily** *adv* karaniwan
**ordinary** *adj* pangkaraniwan
**ordination** *n* pagtatalaga
**ore** *n* uling
**organ** *n* kasangkapan
**organism** *n* organismo
**organist** *n* organista
**organization** *n* samahan
**organize** *v* magtayo
**orient** *n* Silangan
**oriental** *adj* silanganan
**orientation** *n* kaalaman
**oriented** *adj* may alam
**origin** *n* pinagmulan
**original** *adj* orihinal
**originally** *adv* kalikasan
**originate** *v* pinagmulan
**ornament** *n* palamuti
**ornamental** *adj* pampalamuti
**orphan** *n* ulila
**orphanage** *n* bahay ampunan
**ostentatious** *adj* mapag balatkayo

**ostrich** *n* malaking ibon
**other** *adj* iba
**otherwise** *adv* kung hindi
**otter** *n* oter
**ought to** *iv* dapat
**ounce** *n* onsa
**our** *adj* natin
**ours** *pro* atin
**ourselves** *pro* tayo
**oust** *v* paalisin
**out** *adv* labas
**outbreak** *n* paglaganap
**outburst** *n* bulaslas
**outcast** *adj* palaboy
**outcome** *n* kinahinatnan
**outdated** *adj* luma
**outdo** *v* talunin
**outdoor** *adv* panlabas
**outdoors** *adv* sa labas
**outer** *adj* sa paligid
**outfit** *n* kasuotan
**outgoing** *adj* papalabas
**outgrow** *v* kakalakihan
**outing** *n* iskursyon
**outlaw** *v* magnakaw
**outlast** *v* tumagal
**outlet** *n* lagusan
**outline** *n* balangkas
**outline** *v* ibalangkas
**outlook** *n* tanawin
**outmoded** *adj* naluma
**outnumber** *v* mas marami
**outpatient** *n* uwiang pasyente
**outperform** *v* matalo
**outpouring** *n* pagdagsa
**output** *n* resulta ng ginawa
**outrage** *n* pagka galit
**outrageous** *adj* nagalit
**outright** *adj* sa pangkalahatan
**outrun** *v* naunahan
**outset** *n* umpisa
**outside** *adv* sa labas
**outsider** *n* taga labas
**outskirts** *n* karatig
**outspoken** *adj* palasalita
**outstanding** *adj* bukod tangi
**outstretched** *adj* kalabisan na
**outward** *adj* palabas
**outweigh** *v* lumabis
**oval** *adj* bilo haba
**oven** *n* pugon
**over** *pre* labis
**overall** *adv* pangkalahatan
**overbearing** *adj* dominante
**overcast** *adj* maulap
**overcharge** *v* singilin ng labis
**overcoat** *n* kapote; balabal
**overcome** *v* daigin; supilin
**overcrowded** *adj* maraming tao
**overdo** *v* gawing kalabisan
**overdone** *adj* ginawang labis
**overdue** *adj* atrasado; huli
**overflow** *v* umagos
**overhaul** *v* baguhin; linisin

**overlap** *v* takpan ang bahagi
**overlook** *v* hindi nakita
**overnight** *adv* magdamag
**overpower** *v* nagapi
**overrule** *v* natalo sa desisyon
**overrun** *v* sinugod
**overseas** *adv* ibang bansa
**oversee** *v* pangasiwaan
**overshadow** *v* nasapawan
**oversight** *n* pagkakamali
**overstate** *v* labis na pagsasalita
**overstep** *v* sapawan ang iba
**overtake** *v* unahan
**overthrow** *v* patalsikin
**overthrow** *n* pagpapatalsik
**overtime** *adv* lampas sa oras
**overturn** *v* tumiwarik
**overview** *n* balangkas
**overweight** *adj* sobrang bigat
**owe** *v* umutang
**owing to** *adv* dahilan sa
**owl** *n* kuwago
**own** *v* nag-may-ari
**own** *adj* may-ari
**owner** *n* may-ari
**ownership** *n* pag-aari
**ox** *n* kinapong baka
**oxygen** *n* oksidyen
**oyster** *n* talaba

**pace** *v* ihakbang
**pace** *n* hakbang
**pacify** *v* patahimikin
**pack** *v* balutin
**package** *n* binalot na padala
**pact** *n* kasunduan
**pad** *v* isapin
**padding** *n* pampakapal
**paddle** *v* isagwan
**padlock** *n* kandado
**pagan** *adj* pagano
**page** *n* pahina
**pail** *n* timba
**pain** *n* sakit
**painful** *adj* masakit
**painless** *adj* di masakit
**paint** *v* pintahan
**paint** *n* pintura
**paintbrush** *n* brocha
**painter** *n* pintor
**painting** *n* sining ng pagpinta
**pair** *n* pares
**pajamas** *n* damit pantulog
**pal** *n* kaibigan
**palace** *n* palasyo
**palate** *n* ngala-ngala
**pale** *adj* maputla
**paleness** *n* kaputlaan
**palm** *n* palad

**palpable** *adj* nakakapa
**paltry** *adj* walang kabuluhan
**pamper** *v* bigyan ng labis
**pamphlet** *n* polyito
**pan** *n* kawali
**pancreas** *n* lapay
**pander** *v* ibugaw
**pang** *n* sakit
**panic** *n* gulo; pagkagulat
**panorama** *n* tanawin
**panther** *n* puma; kugar
**pantry** *n* paminggalan
**pants** *n* pantalon
**pantyhose** *n* medyas
**papacy** *n* kabanalan; Papa
**paper** *n* papel
**paperclip** *n* pang-ipit ng papel
**paperwork** *n* mga panulat
**parable** *n* pabula
**parachute** *n* parakayda
**parade** *n* parada
**paradise** *n* kaluwalhatian
**paradox** *n* kabalituanan
**paragraph** *n* talata
**parakeet** *n* ibon
**parallel** *n* pagkahalintulad
**paralysis** *n* pagkapararalitiko
**paralyze** *v* nabalda
**parameters** *n* sukatan
**paramount** *adj* pinakamahalaga
**paranoid** *adj* loko-loko
**paratrooper** *n* sundalo
**parcel** *n* bahagi
**parcel post** *n* koreo
**parch** *v* patuyuin
**pardon** *v* patawarin
**pardon** *n* patawad
**parenthesis** *n* panaklong
**parents** *n* magulang
**parish** *n* paroko
**parity** *n* pagkakatulad
**park** *v* igarahe
**park** *n* parke
**parking** *n* hintuan
**parliament** *n* batasan
**parochial** *adj* parokya
**parrot** *n* loro
**parsley** *n* kinchay
**parsnip** *n* singkamas
**part** *v* bahaginan
**part** *n* bahagi
**partial** *adj* bahagi
**partially** *adv* kabahaginan
**participate** *v* sumali
**participation** *n* pagsali
**participle** *n* pandiwari
**particle** *n* katiting
**particular** *adj* bukod; tangi
**particularly** *adv* lalong-lalo na
**parting** *n* paghihiwalay
**partisan** *n* kapanalig
**partition** *n* paghahati-hati
**partly** *adv* sa isang banda
**partner** *n* kasama

**partnership** *n* pagkakasosyo
**partridge** *n* ibon
**party** *n* salu-salo
**pass** *n* daanan
**pass** *v* umaan
**pass around** *v* ipasa
**pass out** *v* hinimatay
**passage** *n* daan
**passenger** *n* pasahero
**passer-by** *n* dumadaan
**passion** *n* masidhing damdamin
**passionate** *adj* mapusok
**passport** *n* pasaporte
**password** *n* hudyat
**past** *adj* nakalipas
**paste** *v* idikit
**paste** *n* pandikit
**pasteurize** *v* gawing panis
**pastime** *n* aliwan
**pastor** *n* pastor
**pastoral** *adj* mabukirin
**pastry** *n* matamis
**pasture** *n* pastulan
**pat** *n* tapik
**patch** *v* tagpi
**patch** *n* tagpian
**patent** *n* pag-aari ng ideya
**patent** *adj* iptala ang pag-aari
**paternity** *n* panig ng ama
**path** *n* daan
**pathetic** *adj* nakakaawa
**patience** *n* pasensya
**patient** *adj* matiyaga
**patio** *n* pahingahan
**patriarch** *n* patriyarka
**patrimony** *n* lupang minana
**patriot** *n* bayani
**patriotic** *adj* makabayan
**patrol** *n* patrolya
**patron** *n* taga kalinga
**patronage** *n* pagtangkilik
**patronize** *v* tangkilikin
**pattern** *n* dibuho
**pavement** *n* bangketa
**pavilion** *n* gusali
**paw** *n* paa ng hayop
**pawn** *v* isangla
**pawnbroker** *n* sanglaan
**pay** *n* bayad
**pay** *iv* bayaran
**pay back** *v* pag bayaran
**pay off** *v* bayaran
**payable** *adj* babayaran
**paycheck** *n* tseke
**payee** *n* binayaran
**payment** *n* kabayaran
**payroll** *n* listahan ng sweldo
**payslip** *n* sipi ng ginana
**pea** *n* gisantes; patani
**peace** *n* kapayapaan
**peaceful** *adj* mapayapa
**peach** *n* milokoton
**peacock** *n* tandang
**peak** *n* rurok

**peanut** *n* mani
**pear** *n* peras
**pearl** *n* perlas
**peasant** *n* dukha
**pebble** *n* bato
**peck** *v* tukain
**peck** *n* tuka
**peculiar** *adj* kakaiba
**pedagogy** *n* pagtuturo
**pedal** *n* pedal
**pedantic** *adj* malalim
**pedestrian** *n* taong naglalakad
**peel** *v* balatan
**peel** *n* balat
**peep** *v* silipin
**peer** *n* kaibigan
**pelican** *n* ibon
**pellet** *n* patuka
**pen** *n* pluma
**penalize** *v* parusahan
**penalty** *n* parusa
**penance** *n* parusa
**pencil** *n* lapis
**pendant** *n* palawit
**pending** *adj* nakabinbin
**pendulum** *n* pendyulum
**penetrate** *v* pasukin
**penguin** *n* penggwin
**penicillin** *n* pinisilin
**peninsula** *n* peninsula
**penitent** *n* pagsisisi
**penniless** *adj* walang pera
**penny** *n* sentimo
**pension** *n* pensyon
**pentagon** *n* pintagono
**pent-up** *adj* naipong emosyon
**people** *n* madla
**pepper** *n* sili
**per** *pre* bawat
**perceive** *v* nalaman
**percent** *adv* porsyento
**percentage** *n* bahagdan
**perception** *n* pag-iisip
**perennial** *adj* palagian
**perfect** *adj* perpekto
**perfection** *n* pagkaperpekto
**perforate** *v* butasin
**perforation** *n* may butas
**perform** *v* magsagawa
**performance** *n* pagkakagawa
**perfume** *n* pabango
**perhaps** *adv* marahil
**peril** *n* pangamba
**perilous** *adj* mapanganib
**perimeter** *n* buong paligid
**period** *n* tuldok
**perish** *v* nabulok
**perishable** *adj* nabubulok
**perjury** *n* kasinungalinan
**permanent** *adj* pangmatagalan
**permeate** *v* itagos
**permission** *n* pahintulot
**permit** *v* pahintulutan
**pernicious** *adj* delikado

**perpetrate** *v* gawin
**persecute** *v* bitayin
**persevere** *v* magsikap
**persist** *v* ipagpatuloy
**persistence** *n* pagpilit
**persistent** *adj* mapilit
**person** *n* tao
**personal** *adj* sarili
**personality** *n* pagkatao
**personify** *v* isatao
**personnel** *n* tauhan
**perspective** *n* ideya
**perspiration** *n* pawis
**perspire** *v* namamawis
**persuade** *v* kumbinsihin
**persuasion** *n* pagkumbinsi
**persuasive** *adj* makumbinsi
**pertain** *v* nauukol sa
**pertinent** *adj* may kinalaman
**perturb** *v* guluhin
**perverse** *adj* kakaiba sa normal
**pervert** *v* gumawa ng di dapat
**pervert** *adj* di normal
**pessimism** *n* pagiging negatibo
**pest** *n* peste
**pester** *v* pestehin
**pesticide** *n* lason
**pet** *n* alaga
**petal** *n* talulot
**petite** *adj* maliit; pandak
**petition** *n* kahilingan
**petrified** *adj* pinatigas
**petroleum** *n* petrolyo
**petty** *adj* walang halaga
**pew** *n* luhuran
**phantom** *n* multo
**pharmacist** *n* parmasyotika
**pharmacy** *n* botika; parmasya
**phase** *n* army
**pheasant** *n* dukha
**philosopher** *n* pilosopo
**philosophy** *n* pilospiya
**phobia** *n* matinding takot
**phone** *n* telepono
**phone** *v* tawagan
**phoney** *adj* huwad
**phosphorus** *n* posporo
**photo** *n* larawan
**photocopy** *n* kopya; sipi
**photograph** *v* potograpiya
**photographer** *n* letratista
**photography** *n* mga larawan
**phrase** *n* parirala
**physically** *adv* pangangatawan
**physician** *n* manggagamot
**pianist** *n* pyanista
**piano** *n* pyano
**pick** *v* piliin
**pick up** *v* pulutin
**pickpocket** *n* mandurukot
**pickup** *n* pulutin
**picture** *n* larawan
**picture** *v* ipalagay
**picturesque** *adj* malarawan

P

**pie** *n* empanada
**piece** *n* piraso
**piecemeal** *adv* unit-unti
**pier** *n* pantalan
**pierce** *v* tusukin
**piercing** *n* tumatagos
**piety** *n* kabanalan
**pig** *n* baboy
**pigeon** *n* kalapati
**piggy bank** *n* alkansya
**pile** *v* isalansan
**pile** *n* salansan
**pile up** *v* tumambak
**pilfer** *v* burikiin
**pilgrim** *n* peregrino
**pilgrimage** *n* paglalakbay
**pill** *n* pildora
**pillage** *v* sirain; nakawan
**pillar** *n* haligi
**pillow** *n* unan
**pillowcase** *n* punda
**pilot** *n* piloto
**pimple** *n* tagihawat
**pin** *n* aspili
**pincers** *n* sipit; tyani
**pinch** *v* kurutin
**pinch** *n* kurot
**pine** *n* bunga ng pino
**pineapple** *n* pinya
**pink** *adj* rosas
**pinpoint** *v* ituro
**pint** *n* pinto
**pioneer** *n* pangunahin
**pious** *adj* madasalin
**pipe** *n* pipa
**pipeline** *n* tubo
**piracy** *n* pamimirata
**pirate** *n* pirata
**pistol** *n* pistola
**pit** *n* butas
**pitch-black** *adj* maitim
**pitfall** *n* patibong
**pitiful** *adj* naka-awa
**pity** *n* awa
**placard** *n* paskel; kartelon
**placate** *v* kalmahin
**place** *n* lunan
**placid** *adj* tahimik
**plague** *n* peste
**plain** *n* kalinawan
**plain** *adj* malinaw
**plainly** *adv* pagkalinaw
**plan** *v* magbalak
**plan** *n* balak
**plane** *n* eroplano
**planet** *n* palneta
**plant** *v* itanim
**plant** *n* tanim
**plaster** *n* pagtapal
**plaster** *v* tapalan
**plastic** *n* plastik
**plate** *n* plato
**plateau** *n* patag na lupa
**platform** *n* entablado

**platinum** *n* tingga
**platoon** *n* pulutong
**plausible** *adj* maaasahan
**play** *v* maglaro
**play** *n* laro
**player** *n* manlalaro
**playful** *adj* pala-laro
**playground** *n* palaruan
**plea** *n* tawad
**plead** *v* makiusap
**pleasant** *adj* kaaya-aya
**please** *v* pakibagayan
**pleasing** *adj* kaaya-aya
**pleasure** *n* aliw
**pleat** *n* tupi
**pleated** *adj* naka tupi
**pledge** *v* sumumpa
**pledge** *n* sumpa
**plentiful** *adj* marami
**plenty** *n* dami
**pliable** *adj* malambot
**pliers** *n* plays
**plot** *v* magbalak
**plot** *n* balangaka
**plow** *v* araruhin
**ploy** *n* taktika
**pluck** *v* pitasin
**plug** *v* isaksak
**plug** *n* pangsaksak
**plum** *n* sinigwelas
**plumber** *n* tubero
**plumbing** *n* koneksyon ng tubo
**plummet** *v* tantyahin
**plump** *adj* mataba
**plunder** *v* nagnakaw
**plunge** *v* ilubog
**plunge** *n* pag lubog
**plural** *n* marami
**plus** *adv* at saka
**plush** *adj* mayaman
**plutonium** *n* plutonyum
**pneumonia** *n* pulmonya
**pocket** *n* bulsa
**poem** *n* tula
**poet** *n* manunula
**poetry** *n* tula
**poignant** *adj* matindi
**point** *n* dulo
**point** *v* ituro
**pointed** *adj* matulis
**pointless** *adj* walang saysay
**poise** *n* tatag; katatagan
**poison** *v* nilason
**poison** *n* lason
**poisoning** *n* nilalason
**poisonous** *adj* nakalalason
**Poland** *n* Poland
**polar** *adj* magkaiba
**pole** *n* haligi; dulo ng mundo
**police** *n* pulis
**policeman** *n* alagad ng batas
**policy** *n* patakaran
**Polish** *adj* taga Poland
**polish** *n* kintab

**polish** *v* pakintabin
**polite** *adj* magalang
**politeness** *n* paggalang
**politician** *n* pulitiko
**politics** *n* pulitika
**poll** *n* paghalal
**pollen** *n* pukyutan
**pollute** *v* dumihan
**pollution** *n* pagdudumi
**polygamist** *adj* maraming asawa
**pomegranate** *n* granada
**pomposity** *n* marangya
**pond** *n* palaisdaan
**ponder** *v* mag-isip
**pontiff** *n* papa; obispo
**pool** *n* grupo ng tao
**pool** *v* mag grupo
**poor** *n* dukha
**poorly** *adv* masamang pakita
**popcorn** *n* papkorn
**Pope** *n* santo papa
**poppy** *n* halamang opyo
**popular** *adj* kilala
**popularize** *v* gawing kilala
**population** *n* mamamayan
**porcelain** *n* porselana
**porch** *n* beranda
**porcupine** *n* matinik na hayop
**pore** *n* maliliit na butas
**pork** *n* baboy
**porous** *adj* butas-butas
**port** *n* daungan
**portable** *adj* mabibitbit
**portent** *n* babala
**porter** *n* kargador
**portion** *n* bahagi; kaputol
**portrait** *n* larawan
**portray** *v* isalarawan
**Portugal** *n* portugal
**Portuguese** *adj* Portuges
**pose** *v* tumayo ng maganda
**pose** *n* tindig
**posh** *adj* mamahalin
**position** *n* katungkulan
**positive** *adj* tiyak
**possess** *v* ariin
**possession** *n* pag-aari
**possibility** *n* ikaspangyayari
**possible** *adj* maaring mangyari
**post** *n* poste
**post office** *n* bahay postal
**postage** *n* selyo
**postcard** *n* poskard
**poster** *n* malaking larawan
**posterity** *n* kamag-anakan
**postman** *n* kartero
**postmark** *n* tatak ng postal
**postpone** *v* ipagpaliban
**postponement** *n* pagpapaliban
**pot** *n* palayok
**potato** *n* patatas
**potent** *adj* mabisa
**potential** *adj* natatagong lakas
**pothole** *n* butas

**poultry** *n* manukan
**pound** *v* pukpukin
**pound** *n* libra
**pour** *v* ibuhos
**poverty** *n* kahirapan
**powder** *n* pulbo
**power** *n* lakas
**powerful** *adj* malakas
**powerless** *adj* walang lakas
**practical** *adj* praktikal
**practice** *n* magsanay
**practise** *v* sanayin
**practising** *adj* nagsasanay
**pragmatist** *adj* praktikal
**prairie** *n* damuhan
**praise** *v* purihin
**praise** *n* papuri
**prank** *n* kalokohan
**prawn** *n* sugpo
**pray** *v* magdasal
**prayer** *n* dasal; panalangin
**preach** *v* mangaral
**preacher** *n* tagapangaral
**preaching** *n* nangangaral
**preamble** *n* paunang salita
**precarious** *adj* walang katiyakan
**precaution** *n* pag-iingat
**precede** *v* sinundan
**precedent** *n* pagkasunod
**preceding** *adj* sinusundan
**precept** *n* utos
**precious** *adj* mahalaga

**precipice** *n* bangin
**precipitate** *v* nag tubig
**precise** *adj* wasto; tama
**precision** *n* pagka wasto
**precocious** *adj* maingat
**precursor** *n* pinagpalitan
**predecessor** *n* sinundan
**predicament** *n* kapalaran
**predict** *v* hulaan
**prediction** *n* hula
**predilection** *n* hula
**predisposed** *adj* nahihilig sa
**predominate** *v* nag domina
**preempt** *v* tirahan
**prefabricate** *v* biling yari
**preface** *n* paunang salita
**prefer** *v* piliin; gustuhin
**preference** *n* kagustuhan
**prefix** *n* unlapi
**pregnancy** *n* magdalantao
**pregnant** *adj* buntis
**prehistoric** *adj* kasaysayan
**preliminary** *adj* una; simula
**prelude** *n* paunang kaganapan
**premature** *adj* di pa dapat
**premeditate** *v* unang plano
**premier** *adj* pangunahin
**premise** *n* paniniwala
**premises** *n* kapaligiran
**premonition** *n* kutob; kaba
**preoccupy** *v* mag-abala
**preparation** *n* paghahanda

**prepare** *v* maghanda
**preposition** *n* pang-ukol
**prerequisite** *n* lagay
**prerogative** *n* pribilehyo
**prescribe** *v* ireseta
**prescription** *n* reseta
**presence** *n* pagharap
**present** *adj* sa kasalukuyan
**present** *v* sa ngayon
**presentation** *n* pag-aalay
**preserve** *v* pangalagaan
**preside** *v* pamunuan
**presidency** *n* panguluhan
**president** *n* pangulo
**press** *n* mamamamahayag
**press** *v* ihayag
**pressing** *adj* mabigat
**pressure** *v* ipabigat
**pressure** *n* bigat
**prestige** *n* reputasyon
**presume** *v* akalain
**presumption** *n* sapantaha; akala
**presuppose** *v* mag-akala
**presupposition** *n* pag aakala
**pretend** *v* magkunwari
**pretense** *n* pagkukunwari
**pretension** *n* kunwari
**pretty** *adj* maganda
**prevail** *v* umiral
**prevalent** *adj* nananaig
**prevent** *v* sugpuin
**prevention** *n* pagsugpo
**preventive** *adj* umiwas
**previous** *adj* nakaraan
**previously** *adv* nauna
**prey** *n* biktima
**price** *n* halaga
**pricey** *adj* mahal
**prick** *v* tusukin
**pride** *n* hiya
**priest** *n* pari
**priesthood** *n* pagpapari
**primacy** *n* pangunahin
**primarily** *adv* una sa lahat
**prime** *adj* pangunahin
**primitive** *adj* sina una
**prince** *n* prinsipe
**princess** *n* prinsesa
**principal** *adj* pinaka puno
**principle** *n* alituntunin
**print** *v* iguhit
**print** *n* imprenta
**printing** *n* paglilimbag
**prior** *adj* nauna
**priority** *n* kahalagahan
**prism** *n* prismo
**prison** *n* kulungan
**prisoner** *n* preso
**privacy** *n* pribado
**private** *adj* pribado
**privilege** *n* pribilehyo
**prize** *n* premyo
**probable** *adj* maaring mangyari
**probe** *v* magimbestiga

P

**probing** *n* pagiimbestiga
**problem** *n* suliranin
**problematic** *adj* problemado
**procedure** *n* paraan
**proceed** *v* magpatuloy
**proceeds** *n* mga kinita
**process** *v* gawain
**process** *n* palakad; paraan
**procession** *n* prusisyon
**proclaim** *v* ipahayag
**proclamation** *n* pagpapahayag
**procrastinate** *v* ipagpaliban
**procreate** *v* manganak
**procure** *v* kumuha
**prod** *v* pilitin
**prodigious** *adj* kagiliw-giliw
**prodigy** *n* henyo
**produce** *v* gumawa
**produce** *n* paggawa
**product** *n* ani
**production** *n* paggawa
**productive** *adj* malikhain
**profane** *adj* walang galang
**profess** *v* magkunwari
**profession** *n* propesyon
**professional** *adj* propesyonal
**professor** *n* propesor
**proficiency** *n* pagiging bihasa
**proficient** *adj* bihasa
**profile** *n* hugis
**profit** *v* tumubo
**profit** *n* tubo
**profitable** *adj* may kita
**profound** *adj* kalaliman
**program** *n* programa
**programmer** *n* programer
**progress** *v* sumulong
**progress** *n* pagsulong
**progressive** *adj* maunlad
**prohibit** *v* ipagbawal
**prohibition** *n* pagbabawal
**project** *v* iwasto
**project** *n* proyekto
**projectile** *n* bala
**prologue** *n* paunang salita
**prolong** *v* pahabain
**promenade** *n* parada
**prominent** *adj* kilala
**promiscuous** *adj* malandi
**promise** *n* pangako
**promote** *v* iangat
**promotion** *n* pag-angat
**prompt** *adj* nasa oras
**prone** *adj* pagkahilig
**pronoun** *n* panghalip
**pronounce** *v* bigkasin
**proof** *n* ebidensya
**propagate** *v* magparami
**propel** *v* paikutin
**propensity** *n* pagkahilig
**proper** *adj* tama
**properly** *adv* karapat-dapat
**property** *n* pag-aari
**prophecy** *n* hula

**prophet** *n* manghuhula
**proportion** *n* sukat
**proposal** *n* mungkahi
**propose** *v* magmungkahi
**proposition** *n* panukala
**prose** *n* tuluyan
**prosecute** *v* usigin
**prosecutor** *n* piskal; taga-usig
**prospect** *n* pag-asa
**prosper** *v* umunlad
**prosperity** *n* pagunlad
**prosperous** *adj* maunlad
**prostate** *n* prosteyt
**prostrate** *v* dumapa
**protect** *v* ikubli; kalingain
**protection** *n* kalinga
**protein** *n* prutina
**protest** *v* maghimagsik
**protest** *n* paghihimagsik
**prototype** *n* modelo
**protract** *v* pahabain ang oras
**protracted** *adj* mahabang oras
**protrude** *v* lumuwa
**proud** *adj* mayabang
**proudly** *adv* pagyabang
**prove** *v* patunayan
**proven** *adj* napatunayan
**proverb** *n* kasabihan
**provide** *v* magalay
**providence** *n* Diyos; Bathala
**providing that** *c* sa isang kondisyon
**province** *n* probinsya
**provision** *n* may nakaabang
**provisional** *adj* pansamantal
**provocation** *n* pagpukaw
**provoke** *v* pukawin; galitin
**prow** *n* harapan ng barko
**prowl** *v* maghanap
**prowler** *n* pulbos
**proximity** *n* kalapitan
**proxy** *n* kahalili; kinatawan
**prudence** *n* kahinahunan
**prudent** *adj* mahinahon
**prune** *v* putulin ang sanga
**prune** *n* pinatuyong sinigwelas
**prurient** *adj* malibog
**pseudonym** *n* alyas
**psychiatry** *n* sikayatri
**psychic** *adj* manghuhula
**psychology** *n* sikolohiya
**psychopath** *n* sira ang ulo
**puberty** *n* pagbibinata
**public** *adj* madla
**publication** *n* paglalahatla
**publicity** *n* lathala
**publicly** *adv* hayagan; lantaran
**publish** *v* ilathala;ilimbag
**publisher** *n* naglilimbag
**pudding** *n* matamis na tinapay
**puerile** *adj* isip bata
**puff** *n* pag ihip
**puffy** *adj* hinihingal
**pull** *v* hilahin

P

**pull ahead** *v* umabante
**pull down** *v* ibaba
**pull out** *v* hugutin
**pulp** *n* ubod; laman
**pulpit** *n* pulpito
**pulsate** *v* tumibok
**pulse** *n* pagtibok
**pulverize** *v* pulbusin
**pump** *v* bombahin
**pump** *n* bomba
**pumpkin** *n* kalabasa
**punch** *v* suntukin
**punch** *n* suntok
**punctual** *adj* nasa oras
**puncture** *n* butasin
**punish** *v* parusahan
**punishable** *adj* may parusa
**punishment** *n* parusa
**pupil** *n* mag-aaral
**puppet** *n* tau-tauhan
**puppy** *n* tuta
**purchase** *v* bumili
**purchase** *n* bilihin
**pure** *adj* dalisay
**puree** *n* dinurog na prutas
**purgatory** *n* purgatoryo
**purge** *n* paglinis
**purge** *v* linisin
**purification** *n* paglilinis ng budhi
**purify** *v* linisin ang budhi
**purity** *n* kalinisan
**purple** *adj* lila;kulay ube
**purpose** *n* hangad;balak
**purposely** *adv* binalak; hinangad
**purse** *n* bag
**pursue** *v* habulin; sundan
**pursuit** *n* pagtugis
**pus** *n* nana
**push** *v* itulak
**pushy** *adj* pala utos
**put** *iv* ilagay
**put aside** *v* itabi
**put away** *v* itago
**put off** *v* itigil
**put out** *v* patayin
**put up** *v* magtiis
**put up with** *v* tiisin
**putrid** *adj* naagnas
**puzzle** *n* palaisipan
**puzzling** *adj* nakakalito
**pyramid** *n* piramida
**python** *n* ahas

**quagmire** *n* pagkalito
**quail** *n* pugo
**quake** *v* lindol
**quality** *n* kalidad
**qualm** *n* ligalig; balisa

**quandary** *n* pagaalinlangan
**quantity** *n* dami
**quarrel** *v* mag-away
**quarrel** *n* away
**quarrelsome** *adj* pala-away
**quarry** *n* hukayan ng bato
**quarterly** *adj* tuwing ika-apat
**quarters** *n* tuluyan
**quash** *v* durugin
**queen** *n* reyna
**queer** *adj* kakatwa
**quell** *v* pigilin
**quench** *v* sugpuin; patdin
**quest** *n* paghahanap
**question** *v* tanungin
**question** *n* tanong
**questionable** *adj* kaduda-duda
**queue** *n* pila
**quick** *adj* mabilis
**quicken** *v* bilisan
**quickly** *adv* bilisan
**quicksand** *n* kamunoy
**quiet** *adj* tahimik
**quietness** *n* katahimikan
**quit** *iv* umayaw
**quite** *adv* bahagya
**quiver** *v* manginig
**quiz** *v* maigsing pagsusulit
**quotation** *n* sinipi
**quote** *v* sabihin
**quotient** *n* sagot sa paghahati

**rabbi** *n* pari
**rabbit** *n* kuneho
**rabies** *n* rabis
**race** *v* karera
**race** *n* lahi
**racist** *adj* rasista
**racket** *n* raketa
**racketeering** *n* panlilinlang
**radar** *n* radar
**radiation** *n* radyesyon
**radical** *adj* makabago
**radio** *n* radyo
**radish** *n* rabanos
**radius** *n* radyos
**raffle** *n* ripa
**raft** *n* balsa
**rag** *n* basahan
**rage** *n* galit
**ragged** *adj* marumi
**raid** *n* paglusob
**raid** *v* lusubin
**raider** *n* manlulusob
**rail** *n* riles
**railroad** *n* riles ng tren
**rain** *n* ulan
**rain** *v* umulan
**rainbow** *n* bahag-hari
**raincoat** *n* kapote
**rainfall** *n* pag-ulan

**rainy** *adj* maulan
**raise** *n* taas
**raise** *v* itaas
**raisin** *n* pasas
**rake** *n* kalaykay
**rally** *n* pagtitipon-tipon
**ram** *n* lalaking tupa
**ram** *v* nabangga
**ramification** *n* kalalabasan
**ramp** *n* rmapa
**rampage** *v* mag wala
**rampant** *adj* laganap
**ramson** *n* bawang
**ranch** *n* rantso
**rancor** *n* galit
**range** *n* kalan; hanay
**rank** *n* ranggo
**rank** *v* ihanay
**ransack** *v* hinalughog
**rape** *v* nilaspatangan
**rape** *n* pag lapastangan
**rapid** *adj* mabilis
**rapist** *n* manggagahasa
**rapport** *n* pakikisama
**rare** *adj* bihira
**rarely** *adv* madalang
**rascal** *n* pagka tampalasan
**rash** *v* magmadali
**rash** *n* pantal-pantal
**raspberry** *n* aratiles
**rat** *n* daga
**rate** *n* marka
**rather** *adv* higit pa; lalo
**ratification** *n* pagpapatibay
**ratify** *v* pagtibayin
**ratio** *n* proporsyon
**ration** *v* rasyonan
**ration** *n* rasyon
**rational** *adj* may isip
**rationalize** *v* magdahilan
**rattle** *v* kalampagin
**ravage** *v* wasakin
**ravage** *n* pagkakawasak
**rave** *v* magalit ng husto
**raven** *n* itim na ibon
**ravine** *n* bangin
**raw** *adj* hilaw
**ray** *n* sinag; silahis
**raze** *v* wasakin
**razor** *n* pang ahit
**reach** *v* abutin
**reach** *n* abot
**react** *v* gumanti
**reaction** *n* pagganti
**read** *iv* basahin
**reader** *n* babasahin
**readiness** *n* handa
**reading** *n* pagbasa
**ready** *adj* nakahanda
**real** *adj* tunay
**realism** *n* pagkatotoo
**reality** *n* katotohanan
**realize** *v* akalain
**really** *adv* totoo

**realm** *n* kaharian
**realty** *n* ari-arian
**reap** *v* umani
**reappear** *v* lumabas ulit
**rear** *v* tumalikod
**rear** *n* likod
**rear** *adj* talikod
**reason** *v* idahilan
**reason** *n* dahilan
**reasonable** *adj* tama lamang
**reasoning** *n* kapasyahan
**reassure** *v* sinigurado
**rebate** *n* diskwento
**rebel** *v* nagrebelde
**rebel** *n* rebelde
**rebellion** *n* pag-aklas
**rebound** *v* tumalbog
**rebuff** *v* sinopla
**rebuff** *n* pagsusuplada
**rebuild** *v* gawin muli
**rebuke** *v* libakin
**rebuke** *n* libak
**rebut** *v* sagutin
**recall** *v* tawagin ulit
**recant** *v* baguhin
**recap** *v* tapalan
**recapture** *v* dakpin muli
**recede** *v* bumaba
**receipt** *n* resibo
**receive** *v* tanggapin
**recent** *adj* kamakailan
**reception** *n* tanggapan
**receptive** *adj* bukas ang isip
**recess** *n* pahinga
**recital** *n* pagsasalaysay
**recite** *v* magsalaysay
**reckless** *adj* walang ingat
**reckon** *v* kilanin
**reckon on** *v* isipin
**reclaim** *v* ayusin; tubusin
**recline** *v* isandal
**recluse** *n* ermitanyo
**recognition** *n* pagkilala
**recognize** *v* kilalanin
**recollect** *v* gunitain
**recollection** *n* pag gunita
**recommend** *v* itagubilin
**recompense** *v* bayaran
**recompense** *n* pagbabayad
**reconcile** *v* magkasundo
**reconstruct** *v* gawin muli
**record** *v* isulat
**record** *n* kasulatan
**recorder** *n* makinang pantala
**recording** *n* pagtatala
**recount** *n* bilangin muli
**recoup** *v* ipunin
**recourse** *v* hiningan ng tulong
**recourse** *n* paghingi ng tulong
**recover** *v* gumagaling
**recovery** *n* paggaling
**recreate** *v* gawin muli
**recreation** *n* aliwan
**recruit** *v* magpatala

**recruit** *n* pagpapatala
**recruitment** *n* talaan
**rectangle** *n* pagkaparihaba
**rectangular** *adj* parihaba
**rectify** *v* ayusin
**rector** *n* tagapagsalita
**rectum** *n* kuyukot
**recuperate** *v* gumagaling
**recur** *v* umulit
**recurrence** *n* ulit
**recycle** *v* gamitin ulit
**red** *adj* pula
**red tape** *n* red teyp
**redden** *v* pumula
**redeem** *v* bawiin; tubusin
**redemption** *n* pagbawi
**red-hot** *adj* maanghang
**redo** *v* gawin muli
**redouble** *v* gawin ulit
**redress** *v* aregluhin
**reduce** *v* bawasan
**redundant** *adj* pauli-ulit
**reed** *n* tambo
**reef** *n* bato sa dagat
**reel** *n* ikiran
**reelect** *v* muling ihalal
**reentry** *n* muling pagpasok
**refer to** *v* patungkol sa
**referee** *n* tagapamagitan
**reference** *n* sanggunian
**referendum** *n* pag halal
**refill** *v* punuing muli
**refinance** *v* pautangin muli
**refine** *v* gawin pino
**refinery** *n* bahay pantining
**reflect** *v* naaninag
**reflection** *n* aninag
**reflexive** *adj* tumalbog
**reform** *v* baguhin
**reform** *n* pagbabago
**refrain** *v* iwasan
**refresh** *v* magpaginhawa
**refreshing** *adj* nagpapaginhawa
**refreshment** *n* pamatid-uhaw
**refrigerate** *v* palamigin
**refuel** *v* maglagay ng gas
**refuge** *n* kanlungan
**refugee** *n* nagkubli
**refund** *v* bayaran
**refund** *n* pagbabayad
**refurbish** *v* kumpunihin
**refusal** *n* tanggi
**refuse** *v* tinaggihan
**refuse** *n* basurahan
**refute** *v* pawalang saysay
**regain** *v* bawiin
**regal** *adj* makahari
**regard** *v* masid; tingin
**regarding** *pre* ukol sa
**regardless** *adv* sa kabila ng
**regards** *n* pag-aalala
**regime** *n* pamamahala
**regiment** *n* dalawang batalyon
**region** *n* rehyon

**regional** *adj* pampook
**register** *v* magpatala
**registration** *n* talaan
**regret** *v* nagsisisi
**regret** *n* pagsisisi
**regrettable** *adj* nakakapagsisi
**regularity** *n* kadalasan
**regularly** *adv* palagi
**regulate** *v* pangasiwaan
**regulation** *n* palakad
**rehearsal** *n* pagsasanay
**rehearse** *v* magsanay
**reign** *v* maghari
**reign** *n* paghahari
**reimburse** *v* bayaran
**reimbursement** *n* pagbabayad
**rein** *v* rendahan
**rein** *n* renda
**reindeer** *n* usa
**reinforce** *v* palakasin
**reinforcements** *n* pampalakas
**reiterate** *v* ulitin
**reject** *v* tanggihan
**rejection** *n* ayawan
**rejoice** *v* magbunyi
**rejoin** *v* magdugtong
**rejuvenate** *v* magpabata
**relapse** *n* naulit
**related** *adj* may kaugnayan
**relationship** *n* may kaugnayan
**relative** *adj* kamag-anak
**relative** *n* kamag-anak
**relax** *v* magpahinga
**relaxation** *n* pahinga
**relaxing** *adj* nakakapahinga
**relay** *v* ipaabot
**release** *v* pawalan
**relegate** *v* iatas
**relent** *v* umayon
**relentless** *adj* walang tigil
**relevant** *adj* may kinalaman
**reliable** *adj* maaasahan
**reliance** *n* pagtitiwala
**relief** *n* lumang bagay
**relieve** *v* ibsan
**religion** *n* relihiyon
**religious** *adj* banal
**relinquish** *v* ipamana
**relish** *v* palamutian
**relive** *v* buhayin
**relocate** *v* lumipat
**relocation** *n* lipat
**reluctant** *adj* alumpihit
**reluctantly** *adv* mag-alinlangan
**rely on** *v* umasa sa
**remain** *v* iniwan
**remainder** *n* naiwan
**remaining** *adj* iiwanan
**remains** *n* iwan
**remake** *v* gawin muli
**remark** *v* punahin
**remark** *n* puna
**remarkable** *adj* kapuri-puri
**remarry** *v* mag-asawa muli

**remedy** *v* gamutin
**remedy** *n* gamot
**remember** *v* alalahanin
**remembrance** *n* ala-ala
**remind** *v* paalalahanan
**reminder** *n* paalala
**remission** *n* nawala
**remit** *v* magpadala
**remittance** *n* padala
**remnant** *n* tira
**remodel** *v* gawin muli
**remorse** *n* sisi
**remorseful** *adj* nagsisisi
**remote** *adj* malayo
**removal** *n* pag-alis
**remove** *v* alisin
**remunerate** *v* bayaran
**renew** *v* gawin muli
**renewal** *n* pagbabago
**renounce** *v* tanggihan
**renovate** *v* ayusin
**renovation** *n* pag-ayos
**renowned** *adj* kilala
**rent** *v* upahan
**rent** *n* upa
**reorganize** *v* ayusin
**repair** *v* ayusin
**reparation** *n* bayad pinsala
**repatriate** *v* pabalikin
**repay** *v* bayaran
**repayment** *n* kabayaran
**repeal** *v* ipawalag-bisa
**repeat** *v* ulitin
**repel** *v* hinadlangan
**repent** *v* magsisi
**repentance** *n* pagsisisi
**repetition** *n* pauli-ulit
**replace** *v* palitan
**replacement** *n* kapalit
**replay** *n* ulitin
**replenish** *v* palitan
**replete** *adj* punung-puno
**replica** *n* katulad
**replicate** *v* gayahin
**reply** *v* sagutin
**reply** *n* sagot
**report** *v* nag-uulat
**report** *n* ulat
**reportedly** *adv* inulat
**reporter** *n* tagapa-ulat
**repose** *v* pagtahimik
**repose** *n* matahimik
**represent** *v* kumatawan
**repress** *v* pigilin
**repression** *n* pagpigil
**reprieve** *n* ipagpaliban
**reprint** *v* limbagin muli
**reprisal** *n* higanti
**reproach** *v* sisihin
**reproach** *n* paninisi
**reproduce** *v* magparami
**reproduction** *n* pagpaparami
**reptile** *n* reptila
**republic** *n* republika

R

**repudiate** *v* itakwil
**repugnant** *adj* di sang-ayon
**repulse** *v* di sumang ayon
**repulse** *n* pagkasuklam
**repulsive** *adj* kauklam-suklam
**reputation** *n* puri
**reputedly** *adv* pagkakakilala
**request** *v* humiling
**request** *n* hiling
**require** *v* kailanganin
**requirement** *n* kailangan
**rescue** *v* sagipin
**rescue** *n* sagip
**research** *v* nagsaliksik
**research** *n* saliksik
**resemblance** *n* katulad
**resemble** *v* tularan
**resent** *v* ayawan
**resentment** *n* ayaw
**reservation** *n* paglalaan
**reserve** *v* ilaan
**reservoir** *n* imbakan ng tubis
**reside** *v* tumira
**residence** *n* nakatira
**residue** *n* latak
**resign** *v* nagbitiw
**resignation** *n* pagbibitiw
**resilient** *adj* matatag
**resist** *v* labanan
**resistance** *n* paglaban
**resolute** *adj* nakahanda
**resolution** *n* pasya
**resolve** *v* gawan ng aksyon
**resort** *v* magpasya
**resounding** *adj* dumadagundong
**respect** *v* igalang
**respect** *n* pag-galang
**respectful** *adj* magalang
**respective** *adj* kagalang-galang
**respiration** *n* paghinga
**respite** *n* pagpahinga
**respond** *v* sagutin
**response** *n* sagot
**responsibility** *n* pananagutan
**responsible** *adj* maaasahan
**responsive** *adj* laging handa
**rest** *v* magpahinga
**rest** *n* pahinga
**rest room** *n* palikuran
**restaurant** *n* restorante
**restful** *adj* maginhawa
**restless** *adj* di mapalagay
**restore** *v* panumbalikin
**restrain** *v* pigilin
**restraint** *n* pagpipigil
**restrict** *v* pagbawalan
**result** *n* resulta
**resume** *v* ipagpatuloy
**resumption** *n* pagpapatuloy
**resurface** *v* lumabas muli
**resuscitate** *v* bigyang buhay
**retain** *v* panatilihin
**retaliate** *v* gumanti
**retaliation** *n* ganti

**retarded** *adj* hinid normal
**retention** *n* pagpapanatili
**retire** *v* retiro
**retirement** *n* retirido
**retract** *v* bawiin
**retreat** *v* binawi
**retreat** *n* bawi
**retrieval** *n* muling pagkuha
**retrieve** *v* kunin muli
**return** *v* ibalik
**return** *n* pagbalik
**reunion** *n* pagkikita-kita
**reveal** *v* ibunyag
**revealing** *adj* matapat
**revel** *v* nagsaya
**revelation** *n* paghahayag
**revenge** *v* gumanti
**revenge** *n* ganti
**revenue** *n* kinita
**reverence** *n* pag-galang
**reversal** *n* kabaligtaran
**reverse** *n* baligtad
**reversible** *adj* baliktarin
**revert** *v* ibalik
**review** *v* muling pag-aralan
**review** *n* balik-aral
**revise** *v* baguhin
**revision** *n* pagbabago
**revive** *v* buhayin muli
**revoke** *v* bawiin
**revolt** *v* mag-alsa
**revolt** *n* pag-alsa
**revolting** *adj* naghimagsik
**revolve** *v* paikutin
**revolver** *n* pistola
**revue** *n* palabas
**revulsion** *n* biglang pagkagalit
**reward** *v* bigyang pabuya
**reward** *n* pabuya
**rewarding** *adj* kapaki-pakinabang
**rheumatism** *n* rayuma
**rhinoceros** *n* hayop
**rhyme** *n* ritmo
**rhythm** *n* ritmo
**rib** *n* buto
**ribbon** *n* laso
**rice** *n* bigas
**rich** *adj* mayaman
**rid of** *iv* iwasan
**riddle** *n* bugtong
**ride** *iv* sumakay
**ridge** *n* gilid
**ridicule** *v* pagtawanan
**ridicule** *n* katatawanan
**ridiculous** *adj* nakakatawa
**rifle** *n* sandata
**rift** *n* alitan
**right** *adv* kanan
**right** *adj* tama; kanan
**right** *n* karapatan
**rigid** *adj* masusi
**rigor** *n* pagka strikto
**rim** *n* gilid
**ring** *iv* paligiran

R

**ring** *n* singsing
**ringleader** *n* puno ng
**rinse** *v* banlawan
**riot** *v* nagkagulo
**riot** *n* gulo
**rip** *v* punitin
**rip apart** *v* pirasuhin
**rip off** *v* singilin ng sobra
**ripe** *adj* hinog
**ripen** *v* nahinog
**ripple** *n* maliit na alon
**rise** *iv* tumaas
**risk** *v* isubo sa panganib
**risk** *n* panganib
**risky** *adj* mapanganib
**rite** *n* seremonya
**rival** *n* karibal
**rivalry** *n* paglalabanan
**river** *n* ilog
**rivet** *v* ikabit
**riveting** *adj* pangkabit
**road** *n* lansangan; daan
**roam** *v* maglayas
**roar** *v* umungol
**roar** *n* pag sigaw
**roast** *v* ihawin
**roast** *n* inihaw
**rob** *v* magnakaw
**robber** *n* magnanakaw
**robbery** *n* nakawan
**robe** *n* bata
**robust** *adj* matipuno
**rock** *n* bato
**rocket** *n* raket
**rocky** *adj* mabato
**rod** *n* patpat
**rodent** *n* daga
**roll** *v* gumulong
**romance** *n* pag-ibig
**roof** *n* bubong
**room** *n* silid
**roomy** *adj* maalwan
**rooster** *n* tandang
**root** *n* ugat
**rope** *n* lubid
**rosary** *n* rosaryo
**rose** *n* bulaklak
**rosy** *adj* mamula
**rot** *v* nabulok
**rot** *n* bulok
**rotate** *v* paikutin
**rotation** *n* pag-ikot
**rotten** *adj* kabulkan
**rough** *adj* magasapang
**round** *adj* bilog
**roundup** *n* lipulin
**rouse** *v* gisingin
**rousing** *adj* gumigising
**route** *n* daan; ruta
**routine** *n* mga kostumbre
**row** *v* mag-away
**row** *n* hanay
**rowdy** *adj* garapal
**royalty** *n* kataas-taasan

**rub** *v* ikiskis
**rubber** *n* goma
**rubbish** *n* basura
**rubble** *n* pira-pirasong bato
**ruby** *n* pulang bato
**rudder** *n* kambyo
**rude** *adj* bastos
**rudeness** *n* kagaspangan
**rug** *n* tapete
**ruin** *v* sinira
**ruin** *n* nasira
**rule** *v* ipasya
**rule** *n* patakaran
**ruler** *n* panukat
**rum** *n* alak
**rumble** *v* idagundong
**rumble** *n* pagdagundong
**rumor** *n* balita
**run** *iv* tumakbo
**run away** *v* lumayas
**run into** *v* nasalubong
**run out** *v* naubusan
**run over** *v* sagasaan
**run up** *v* akyatin
**runner** *n* utusan
**runway** *n* naglayas
**rupture** *n* putok
**rupture** *v* pumutok
**rural** *adj* ukol sa bukid
**ruse** *n* patibong
**rush** *v* bilisan
**Russia** *n* Ruso
**Russian** *adj* taga Rusya
**rust** *v* kalawangin
**rust** *n* kalawang
**rustic** *adj* pambukid
**rusty** *adj* kalawangin
**ruthless** *adj* malupit
**rye** *n* arina

# S

**sabotage** *v* isabotahe
**sabotage** *n* sabotahe
**sack** *v* isako
**sack** *n* sako
**sacrament** *n* sakramento
**sacred** *adj* banal
**sacrifice** *n* magtiis
**sad** *adj* malungkot
**sadden** *v* nalungkot
**saddle** *n* siya ng kabayo
**sadist** *n* malungkutin
**sadness** *n* kalungkutan
**safe** *adj* ligtas
**safeguard** *n* pangalagaan
**safety** *n* kaligtasan
**sail** *v* maglayag
**sail** *n* paglalayag
**sailboat** *n* bangka

**sailor** *n* marinero
**saint** *n* santo
**salad** *n* salad
**salary** *n* sweldo; gana
**sale** *n* benta
**sale slip** *n* resibo
**saliva** *n* dura
**salmon** *n* salmon
**saloon** *n* salon
**salt** *n* asin
**salty** *adj* maalat
**salvage** *v* sagipin
**salvation** *n* pagliligtas
**same** *adj* pareho
**sample** *n* halimbawa
**sanctify** *v* gawing banal
**sanction** *v* saklawan
**sanction** *n* saklaw
**sanctity** *n* kabanalan
**sanctuary** *n* silungan
**sand** *n* buhangin
**sandal** *n* sandalyas
**sandpaper** *n* papel de liha
**sane** *adj* kaisipan
**sanity** *n* pag-iisip
**sap** *n* katas
**sap** *v* kinatas
**sapphire** *n* batong asul
**sarcasm** *n* panunuya
**sarcastic** *adj* mapanuya
**sardine** *n* sardinas
**satanic** *adj* satananiko
**satellite** *n* buwan
**satire** *n* dulang satiriko
**satisfaction** *n* kaiyahan
**satisfactory** *adj* kasiya-siya
**satisfy** *v* masiyahan
**saturate** *v* ihalo; ibabad
**Saturday** *n* Sabado
**sauce** *n* salsa
**saucepan** *n* sarten
**saucer** *n* platito
**sausage** *n* soriso
**savage** *adj* di sibilisado
**savagery** *n* hampas-lupa
**save** *v* magtipid
**savings** *n* ipon
**savior** *n* manunubos
**savor** *v* lasahan
**saw** *iv* lagariin
**saw** *n* lagare
**say** *iv* sabihin
**saying** *n* kasabihan
**scald** *v* banlian
**scale** *v* timbangin
**scale** *n* timbangan
**scalp** *n* anit
**scam** *n* panloloko
**scan** *v* hanapin
**scandal** *n* iskandalo
**scandalize** *v* iskandaluhin
**scapegoat** *n* dahilan
**scar** *n* peklat
**scarce** *adj* bihira

**scarcely** *adv* kawalan
**scarcity** *n* mangilan-ngilan
**scare** *v* natakot
**scare** *n* takot
**scare away** *v* natakot
**scarf** *n* alampay
**scary** *adj* nakakatakot
**scatter** *v* ikalat
**scenario** *n* mga pangyayari
**scene** *n* eksena
**scenery** *n* tanawin
**scenic** *adj* malarawan
**scent** *n* halimuyak
**schedule** *v* takdaan
**schedule** *n* talatakdaan
**scheme** *n* pagpapanukala
**scholarship** *n* karunungan
**school** *n* paaralan
**science** *n* syensa
**scientific** *adj* maka-agham
**scissors** *n* gunting
**scoff** *v* kutyain
**scold** *v* pinagalitan
**scolding** *n* pagpagalit
**scooter** *n* motorsiklo
**scope** *n* lawak
**scorch** *v* initin
**score** *n* bilang
**score** *v* bilangin
**scorn** *v* hamakin
**scornful** *n* paghamak
**scorpion** *n* alupihan
**scour** *v* kuskusin
**scourge** *n* pag bugbog
**scout** *n* taga tuklas
**scramble** *v* batihin
**scrap** *n* kapiraso; tira
**scrap** *v* tirahan
**scrape** *v* kayurin
**scratch** *v* kamutin
**scratch** *n* gasgas
**scream** *v* sigaw
**scream** *n* sumigaw
**screech** *v* tumili
**screen** *n* pangsala; tabing
**screen** *v* salain; tabingan
**screw** *v* turnilyuhin
**screw** *n* turnilyo
**screwdriver** *n* pang-ikot ng turnilyo
**scribble** *v* magsulat
**script** *n* skirp; manuskrito
**scroll** *n* rolyo ng kasulatan
**scrub** *v* kuskusin
**scruples** *n* sukat ng bigat
**scrupulous** *adj* maingat
**scrutiny** *n* pagsusuri
**scuffle** *n* pagbubuno
**sculptor** *n* eskultor
**sculpture** *n* eskultura
**sea** *n* dagat
**seafood** *n* pagkaing dagat
**seagull** *n* ibong dagat
**seal** *v* tatak
**seal** *n* tatakan

**seal off** *v* bakuran
**seam** *n* laylayan ng damit
**seamless** *adj* walang laylayan
**seamstress** *n* mananahi
**search** *v* hagilapin
**search** *n* hagilap
**seashore** *n* aplaya
**seasick** *adj* nalulula sa barko
**seaside** *adj* tabing dagat
**season** *n* panahon
**seasonal** *adj* pan-panahon
**seasoning** *n* pampalasa
**seat** *n* upuan
**seated** *adj* nakaupo
**secede** *v* tumiwalag
**secluded** *adj* nakahiwalay
**seclusion** *n* paghiwalay
**second** *n* pangalawa
**secondary** *adj* sekundarya
**secrecy** *n* paglilihim
**secret** *n* lihim
**secretary** *n* sekretarya
**secretly** *adv* palihim
**sect** *n* sekto
**section** *n* bahagi
**sector** *n* bahagi
**secure** *v* kumuha
**secure** *adj* matatag
**security** *n* seguridad
**sedate** *v* patulugin
**sedation** *n* pampatulog
**seduce** *v* akitin
**seduction** *n* akit
**see** *iv* nakita
**seed** *n* punla
**seedless** *adj* walang punla
**seedy** *adj* mabuto
**seek** *iv* hanapin
**seem** *v* tila
**see-through** *adj* aninag
**segment** *n* isang bahagi
**segregate** *v* ihiwalay
**segregation** *n* paghihiwalay
**seize** *v* ikulong
**seizure** *n* pagkulong
**seldom** *adv* bihira
**select** *v* piliin
**selection** *n* pagpili
**self-concious** *adj* maisip sa sarili
**self-esteem** *n* hiya
**self-evident** *adj* halata
**selfish** *adj* madamot
**selfishness** *n* karamutan
**self-respect** *n* sariling paggalang
**sell** *iv* itinda
**seller** *n* tindera
**sellout** *n* nabili lahat
**semblance** *n* katulad
**semester** *n* semestre
**seminary** *n* seminaryo
**senate** *n* senado
**senator** *n* senador
**send** *iv* ipadala
**sender** *n* nagpadala

**senile** *adj* matanda na
**senior** *adj* nakatatanda
**seniority** *n* matagal na
**sensation** *n* pakiramdam
**sense** *v* damahin
**sense** *n* pandama
**senseless** *adj* walanga kabuluhan
**sensible** *adj* may kabuluhan
**sensitive** *adj* sensitibo
**sensual** *adj* senswal
**sentence** *v* mangusap
**sentence** *n* pangungusap
**sentiment** *n* sentimyento
**sentimental** *adj* sentimental
**sentry** *n* bantay; gwardya
**separate** *v* ihiwalay
**separate** *adj* hiwalay
**separation** *n* paghihiwalay
**September** *n* Setyembre
**sequel** *n* kabanata
**serenade** *n* harana
**serene** *adj* matahimik
**serenity** *n* pagka mahinahon
**sergeant** *n* sarhento
**series** *n* serye
**serious** *adj* malubha
**seriousness** *n* kalubhaan
**sermon** *n* sermon
**serpent** *n* ahas
**serum** *n* sirum
**servant** *n* naninilbihan
**serve** *v* magsilbi
**service** *n* silbi
**service** *v* serbisyo
**session** *n* pulong
**set** *n* ayos
**set** *iv* iayos
**set about** *v* ayusin
**set off** *v* umpisahan
**set out** *v* humayo
**set up** *v* itatag
**setback** *n* kakukalangan
**setting** *n* tagpuan
**settle** *v* lutasin; manirahan
**settle down** *v* lumagay sa tahimik
**settle for** *v* magkasya sa
**settlement** *n* tirahan; pagtutubos
**settler** *n* naninirahan
**setup** *n* ayusin
**seven** *adj* pito
**seventeen** *adj* labing-pito
**seventh** *adj* pang-pito
**seventy** *adj* pitumpo
**sever** *v* humiwalay
**several** *adj* mangilan-ngilan
**severe** *adj* malala
**severity** *n* pagka lala
**sew** *v* magtahi
**sewage** *n* lagusan ng dumi
**sewer** *n* imburnal
**sewing** *n* pananahi
**sex** *n* pagtatalik
**sexuality** *n* pagkalalaki
**shabby** *adj* gusgusin

**shack** *n* dampa
**shackle** *n* posas
**shade** *n* lilim
**shadow** *n* anino
**shady** *adj* malabo
**shake** *iv* kalugin
**shaken** *adj* nakalog
**shaky** *adj* makalog
**shallow** *adj* mababaw
**sham** *n* pagkukunwari
**shambles** *n* bahay matadero
**shame** *v* mahiya
**shame** *n* hiya
**shameful** *adj* nahihiya
**shameless** *adj* walang hiya
**shape** *v* ihugis
**shape** *n* hugis
**share** *v* ibahagi
**share** *n* bahagi
**shareholder** *n* kabahagi
**shark** *n* pating
**sharp** *adj* matalas
**sharpen** *v* talasan
**sharpener** *n* panghasa
**shatter** *v* durugin; basagin
**shattering** *adj* nadudurog
**shave** *v* mag ahit
**she** *pro* sya
**shear** *iv* gupitin
**shed** *iv* maglagas
**sheep** *n* tupa
**sheets** *n* kumot; piraso
**shelf** *n* istante
**shell** *n* kabibi
**shellfish** *n* talaba
**shelter** *v* sumilong
**shelter** *n* silungan
**shelves** *n* istante
**shepherd** *n* taga pastol
**sherry** *n* alak
**shield** *v* tabingan
**shield** *n* tabing
**shift** *n* pagpalit
**shift** *v* palitan
**shine** *iv* pakintabin
**shiny** *adj* makintab
**ship** *n* barko
**shipment** *n* kargamento
**shipwreck** *n* lumubog na barko
**shipyard** *n* pantalan
**shirk** *v* umilag
**shirt** *n* kamisadentro
**shiver** *v* nanginig
**shiver** *n* panginginig
**shock** *v* nagulat; nabigla
**shock** *n* pagkagulat
**shocking** *adj* nagulat; nabigla
**shoddy** *adj* huwad
**shoe** *n* sapatos
**shoelace** *n* sintas
**shoepolish** *n* biton
**shoestore** *n* tindahan ng sapatos
**shoot** *iv* barilin
**shoot down** *v* mamaril

**shop** *v* mamili
**shop** *n* bilihan
**shoplifting** *n* mandurukot
**shopping** *n* pamimili
**shore** *n* aplaya
**short** *adj* maiksi
**shortage** *n* kakulangan
**shortcoming** *n* pagkukulang
**shortcut** *n* maigsing daan
**shorten** *v* liitan
**shorthand** *n* takigrapiya
**shortlived** *adj* maigsing buhay
**shortly** *adv* sumandali
**shorts** *n* maikling pantalon
**shot** *n* binaril
**shotgun** *n* baril
**shoulder** *n* balikat
**shout** *v* sigawan
**shout** *n* sigaw
**shouting** *n* sigawan
**shove** *v* palahin
**shove** *n* pagpalis
**shovel** *n* pala
**show** *iv* ipakita
**show off** *v* magyabang
**show up** *v* duamating
**showdown** *n* pakikipagtuos
**shower** *n* dutsa
**shrapnel** *n* laman ng bomba
**shred** *v* pira-pirasuhin
**shred** *n* pagpipira-piraso
**shrewd** *adj* tuso
**shriek** *v* sumigaw; tumili
**shriek** *n* pagsigaw; pag tili
**shrimp** *n* hipon
**shrine** *n* banal na lugar
**shrink** *iv* umurong
**shrouded** *adj* binalot; tinakpan
**shrub** *n* halaman
**shrug** *v* kibit balikat
**shudder** *n* pagka takot
**shudder** *v* natakot; nanginig
**shuffle** *v* balasahin
**shun** *v* umilag
**shut** *iv* isara
**shut off** *v* sinara
**shut up** *v* tumigil
**shuttle** *v* saksakyan
**shy** *adj* mahiyain
**shyness** *n* hiya
**sick** *adj* masakit
**sicken** *v* magkasakit
**sickening** *adj* nakaririmarim
**sickle** *n* kalawit
**sickness** *n* sakit
**side** *n* gilid
**sidewalk** *n* bangketa
**sideways** *adv* patagilid
**siege** *n* huli
**siege** *v* hinuli
**sift** *v* salain
**sigh** *n* daing
**sigh** *v* dumaing
**sight** *n* paningin

**sign** *v* lagdaan
**sign** *n* lagda; pirma
**signal** *n* pahiwatig
**signature** *n* pirma
**significance** *n* kahalagahan
**significant** *adj* mahalaga
**signify** *v* bigyang halaga
**silence** *n* katahimikan
**silence** *v* tumahimik
**silent** *adj* matahimik
**silhouette** *n* anino
**silk** *n* seda
**silly** *adj* ulol
**silver** *n* pilak
**silverplated** *adj* nabalot ng pilak
**similar** *adj* katulad
**similarity** *n* magkatulad
**simmer** *v* kumulo
**simple** *adj* simple
**simplicity** *n* kapayakan
**simplify** *v* gawing payak
**simply** *adv* kapayakan
**simulate** *v* mag kunwari
**simultaneous** *adj* sabay
**sin** *v* magkasala
**sin** *n* kasalanan
**since** *c* simula ng
**since** *pre* sapagkat
**since then** *adv* simula noon
**sincere** *adj* matapat
**sincerity** *n* taimtim
**sinful** *adj* makasalanan
**sing** *iv* umawit
**singer** *n* mang-aawit
**single** *n* dalaga/binata
**single** *adj* nag-iisa
**singlehanded** *adj* isang kamay
**singleminded** *adj* isang kaisipan
**singular** *adj* isa
**sink** *iv* ilubog
**sink in** *v* lumubog
**sinner** *n* makasalanan
**sip** *v* higupin
**sip** *n* higop
**sir** *n* ginoo
**siren** *n* sirena
**sirloin** *n* laman
**sissy** *adj* duwag
**sister** *n* kapatid
**sister-in-law** *n* hipag
**sit** *iv* umupo
**site** *n* pagtatayuan
**sitting** *n* umuupo
**situated** *adj* kalagayan
**situation** *n* kalagayan
**six** *adj* anim
**sixteen** *adj* labing-anim
**sixth** *adj* pang anim
**sixty** *adj* animnapu
**sizable** *adj* kainaman
**size** *n* sukat
**size up** *v* sukatin
**skate** *v* magpadausdos
**skeleton** *n* kalansay

**skeptic** *adj* alinlangan
**sketch** *v* iguhit
**sketch** *n* dibuho
**sketchy** *adj* magulo
**skill** *n* kaalaman
**skillful** *adj* bihasa
**skim** *v* sagipin
**skin** *v* balatan
**skin** *n* balat
**skinny** *adj* payat
**skip** *v* lagpasan
**skip** *n* lagpasan
**skirmish** *n* pag sagupa
**skirt** *n* palda
**skull** *n* bungo
**sky** *n* langit
**slab** *n* batong makapal
**slack** *adj* pantalon
**slacken** *v* magpatalo
**slacks** *n* pantalon
**slam** *v* malakas na tunog
**slander** *n* paninirang puri
**slanted** *adj* lihis

**slap** *n* sampal
**slap** *v* sampalin
**slash** *n* laslas
**slash** *v* laslasin
**slate** *n* munting pisara
**slaughter** *v* patayin
**slaughter** *n* pagpatay
**slave** *n* alipin
**slavery** *n* pang-aalipin
**slay** *iv* patayin; pumatay
**sleazy** *adj* manipis na tela
**sleep** *iv* matulog
**sleep** *n* tulog
**sleeve** *n* manggas
**sleeveless** *adj* walang manggas
**slender** *adj* balingkinitan
**slice** *v* hiwain
**slice** *n* hiwa
**slide** *iv* ipadulas
**slightly** *adv* bahagya
**slim** *adj* payat
**slip** *v* nadulas
**slip** *n* dulas
**slipper** *n* tsinelas
**slippery** *adj* madulas
**slit** *iv* hiwain
**slob** *n* salaula
**slogan** *n* salawikain
**slope** *n* libis; gulod
**sloppy** *adj* marumi
**slot** *n* bakas; puwang
**slow** *adj* mabagal
**slow down** *v* bagalan
**slow motion** *n* pagkabagal
**slowly** *adv* bagalan
**sluggish** *adj* tamad; antukin
**slump** *v* bumagsak
**slump** *n* pagbagsak
**slur** *v* umuutal
**sly** *adj* matalino
**smack** *n* pagpalo

**smack** *v* pinalo
**small** *adj* maliit
**small print** *n* maliliit na titik
**smallpox** *n* bulutong
**smart** *adj* matalino
**smash** *v* basagin
**smear** *n* pagmantsa
**smear** *v* mantsahan
**smell** *iv* amuyin
**smelly** *adj* mabaho
**smile** *v* ngumiti
**smile** *n* ngiti
**smith** *n* panday
**smoke** *v* umusok
**smoked** *adj* pausukan
**smoker** *n* pagsisigarilyo
**smoking gun** *n* pambaril
**smooth** *v* pakinisin
**smooth** *adj* makinis
**smoothly** *adv* pakinisin
**smoothness** *n* kinis
**smother** *v* sakalin
**smuggler** *n* kontrabandista
**snail** *n* suso
**snake** *n* ahas
**snapshot** *n* kuha ng larawan
**snare** *v* siluin
**snare** *n* bitag; silo
**snatch** *v* agawin
**sneak** *v* silipin; bilisan
**sneeze** *v* bumahin
**sneeze** *n* bahin
**sniff** *v* singhutin
**sniper** *n* asintado
**snitch** *v* nakawin
**snooze** *v* idlip
**snore** *v* humilik
**snore** *n* hilik
**snow** *v* nyebe
**snow** *n* nyebe
**snowfall** *n* pagpatak ng nyebe
**snowflake** *n* nyebe
**snub** *v* magsuplada
**snub** *n* suplada
**soak** *v* ibabad
**soak in** *v* ibabad
**soak up** *v* magsanay
**soar** *v* sumahimpapawid
**sob** *v* humagulgol
**sob** *n* hagulgol
**sober** *adj* hindi lasing
**so-called** *adj* kilala sa
**sociable** *adj* pala kaibigan
**socialism** *n* sosyalismo
**socialize** *v* makipag-kaibigan
**society** *n* lipunan
**sock** *n* medyas
**sod** *n* damuhan
**soda** *n* inumin
**sofa** *n* sopa
**soft** *adj* malambot
**soften** *v* palambutin
**softly** *adv* kalambutan
**softness** *n* pagka malambot

**soggy** *adj* malabsa
**soil** *v* basain
**soil** *n* lupa
**soiled** *adj* mamasa-masa
**solace** *n* ligaya
**solar** *adj* maaraw
**solder** *v* sulda
**soldier** *n* sundalo
**sold-out** *adj* nabili lahat
**sole** *n* mag-isa
**sole** *adj* nag-isa
**solely** *adv* isa lamang
**solemn** *adj* matahimik
**solicit** *v* manghingi
**solid** *adj* buo
**solidarity** *n* pagkakaisa
**solitary** *adj* nag-iisa
**solitude** *n* pag-iisa
**soluble** *adj* matutunaw
**solution** *n* solusyon
**solve** *v* lunasan
**solvent** *adj* pampatunaw
**somber** *adj* kulimlim
**some** *adj* alinman
**somebody** *pro* isang tao
**someday** *adv* balang-araw
**somehow** *adv* kahit papano
**someone** *pro* isang tao
**something** *pro* isang bagay
**sometimes** *adv* kung minsan
**someway** *adv* isang paraan
**somewhat** *adv* tila
**son** *n* anak na lalaki
**song** *n* awit
**son-in-law** *n* manugang
**soon** *adv* kaagad
**soothe** *v* ibsan
**sorcerer** *n* mangkukulam
**sorcery** *n* kulam
**sore** *n* maga
**sore** *adj* namamaga
**sorrow** *n* lungkot
**sorrowful** *adj* kalungkutan
**sorry** *adj* malungkot
**sort** *n* piliin
**sort out** *v* piliin
**soul** *n* kaluluwa
**sound** *n* tumog
**sound** *v* tumunog
**sound out** *v* isgaw; sabihin
**soup** *n* sabaw
**sour** *adj* maasim
**source** *n* pinanggalingan
**south** *n* timog
**southbound** *adv* patungong timog
**southeast** *n* timog - silangan
**southern** *adj* patungong timog
**southerner** *n* tiga timog
**southwest** *n* timog-
**souvenir** *n* ala-ala
**soviet** *adj* sobyet
**sow** *iv* magtanim
**spa** *n* spa
**space** *n* kalawakan; pagitan

S

**spacious** *adj* malawak
**spade** *n* pala
**Spain** *n* Espanya
**span** *v* lawakan
**span** *n* lawak
**Spaniard** *n* espanyol
**Spanish** *adj* espanyol
**spank** *v* paluin
**spanking** *n* palo
**spare** *v* ibigay
**spare** *adj* reserba
**sparingly** *adv* tipirin
**spark** *n* panindi
**spark off** *v* sindihan
**spark plug** *n* spark plag
**sparkle** *v* pakintabin
**sparrow** *n* ibon
**sparse** *adj* nakakalat
**spasm** *n* pulikat
**speak** *iv* magsalita
**speaker** *n* tapag-salita
**spear** *n* sibat
**spearhead** *v* simulan
**special** *adj* natatangi
**specialize** *v* magpaka dalubhasa
**specialty** *n* espesyalidad
**species** *n* uri
**specific** *adj* bukod tangi
**specimen** *n* uri ng materyal
**speck** *n* gabutil
**spectacle** *n* kakaibang palabas
**spectator** *n* manonood
**speculate** *v* akalain
**speculation** *n* hinuha
**speech** *n* talumpati
**speechless** *adj* walang masabi
**speed** *iv* bilisan
**speed** *n* bilis
**speedily** *adv* nagmamadali
**speedy** *adj* mabilis
**spell** *iv* baybayin
**spell** *n* pagbaybay; engkanto
**spelling** *n* pagbabaybay
**spend** *iv* gumastos
**spending** *n* paggastos
**sperm** *n* semilya
**sphere** *n* mundo; globo
**spice** *n* silis
**spicy** *adj* maanghang
**spider** *n* gagamba
**spiderweb** *n* sapot ng gagamba
**spill** *iv* natapon
**spill** *n* kalat
**spin** *iv* ikutin
**spine** *n* gulugod
**spineless** *adj* walang gulugod
**spinster** *n* matandang dalaga
**spirit** *n* kaluluwa
**spiritual** *adj* madasalin
**spit** *iv* lumura
**spite** *n* sama ng loob
**spiteful** *adj* masama ang loob
**splash** *v* basyahan ng tubig
**splendid** *adj* kaaya-aya

**splendor** *n* kairlagan
**splint** *n* sapin sa napilayan
**splinter** *n* paghihiwalay
**splinter** *v* humiwalay
**split** *n* paghihiwalay
**split** *iv* paghiwalayin
**split up** *v* naghiwalay
**spoil** *v* sirain
**spoils** *n* pagkasira
**sponge** *n* espongha
**sponsor** *n* ang may panukala
**spontaneity** *n* pagka natural
**spontaneous** *adj* natural
**spooky** *adj* multo
**spool** *n* sinulid
**spoon** *n* kutsara
**spoonful** *n* isang kutsara
**sporadic** *adj* pabugsu-bugso
**sport** *n* laro
**sportman** *n* manlalaro
**sporty** *adj* atleta
**spot** *v* mantsahan
**spot** *n* batik; mantsa
**spotless** *adj* malinis
**spouse** *n* asawa
**sprain** *v* pilay
**sprawl** *v* humilata
**spray** *v* diligin
**spread** *iv* ikalat; isabog
**spring** *iv* luksuhin
**spring** *n* bukal
**springboard** *n* tablang talunan
**sprinkle** *v* diligin
**sprout** *v* umusbong
**spruce up** *v* gawan
**spur** *v* itali
**spur** *n* panali
**spy** *v* nagespiya
**spy** *n* espiya
**squalid** *adj* nanggigitata
**squander** *v* gastosin
**square** *adj* kwadrado
**square** *n* kuwadrado
**squash** *v* pisain; durugin
**squeak** *v* lumalangitngit
**squeaky** *adj* malangitngit
**squeamish** *adj* makaluma
**squeeze** *v* pigain
**squeeze in** *v* sumingit
**squeeze up** *v* pigain
**squid** *n* pusit
**stab** *v* saksakin
**stab** *n* saksak
**stability** *n* katatagan
**stable** *adj* matatag
**stable** *n* kawadra
**stack** *v* sinalansan
**stack** *n* salansan
**staff** *n* tungkod; baston
**stage** *n* entablado
**stage** *v* itanghal
**stagger** *v* saksakin
**staggering** *adj* nangangapa
**stagnant** *adj* nakatigil

**stagnate** *v* tumigil
**stagnation** *n* pagtigil
**stain** *v* mantsahan
**stain** *n* mantsa
**stair** *n* hagdan
**staircase** *n* hagdanan
**stairs** *n* hagdanan
**stake** *n* nakataya
**stake** *v* itinaya
**stale** *adj* ilado
**stalemate** *n* naipit
**stalk** *v* sinundan
**stalk** *n* sundan
**stall** *n* pasilyo
**stall** *v* patayung-tayungin
**stammer** *v* ma utal
**stamp** *v* tatakan
**stamp** *n* tatak; selyo
**stamp out** *v* tatakan
**stampede** *n* takbuhan
**stand** *iv* tumayo
**stand** *n* tayo
**stand for** *v* ipaglaban
**stand out** *v* pumaibabaw
**stand up** *v* tumayo
**standard** *n* pamantayan
**standardize** *v* gawing huwaran
**standing** *n* pagtayo; pagtindig
**standpoint** *n* sariling pananaw
**standstill** *adj* nakatigil
**stapler** *n* pang ipit
**star** *n* bituin
**starch** *n* gawgaw
**starchy** *adj* malagkit
**stare** *v* tumitig
**stark** *adj* madilim
**start** *v* sinimulan
**start** *n* simulan
**startle** *v* nilito
**startled** *adj* nalito
**starvation** *n* gutom
**starve** *v* nagutom
**state** *n* kalagayan
**state** *v* sabihin
**statement** *n* sanaysay
**station** *n* istasyon
**stationary** *adj* di gumagalaw
**stationery** *n* papel
**statistics** *n* bilang
**statue** *n* estatwa
**status** *n* kalagayan
**statute** *n* batas
**staunch** *adj* masugid
**stay** *v* tumigil
**stay** *n* pagtigil
**steady** *adj* matatag
**steak** *n* uri ng pagluluto
**steal** *iv* nakawin
**steam** *n* singaw
**steel** *n* bakal
**steep** *adj* matarik
**stem** *n* sanga
**stem** *v* magsanga
**stench** *n* masangsang

S

**step** *n* hakbang
**step down** *v* bumaba
**step out** *v* lumabas
**step up** *v* umakyat
**stepbrother** *n* kinakapatid
**step-by-step** *adv* isa-isa
**stepdaughter** *n* anak na babae
**stepfather** *n* amain
**stepladder** *n* pang akyat
**stepmother** *n* madrasta
**stepson** *n* anak na lalaki
**sterile** *adj* baog; malinis
**sterilize** *v* linisin; pakuluan
**stern** *n* pagka mahigpit
**stern** *adj* mahigpit; matindi
**sternly** *adv* strikto
**stew** *n* nilaga
**stewardess** *n* serbidora
**stick** *n* magdikit
**stick** *iv* idikit
**stick around** *v* maghintay
**stick out** *v* nakikita
**stick to** *v* maging tapat
**sticker** *n* pandikit na papel
**sticky** *adj* malagkit
**stiff** *adj* matigas
**stiffen** *v* tigasan
**stiffness** *n* matigas
**stifle** *v* napilay
**stifling** *adj* nakapipilay
**still** *adj* tahimik
**still** *adv* matahimik
**stimulant** *n* pampagana
**stimulate** *v* paganahin
**stimulus** *n* pampagana
**sting** *iv* kagatin; sundutin
**sting** *n* pag kagat
**stinging** *adj* nakaka tusok
**stingy** *adj* kuripot
**stink** *iv* mabaho
**stink** *n* pagkabaho
**stinking** *adj* bunmabaho
**stipulate** *v* isaad
**stir** *v* haluin
**stir up** *v* pukawin
**stitch** *v* magsulsi
**stitch** *n* pagsulsi
**stock** *v* isalansan; iayos
**stock** *n* produkto; paninda
**stocking** *n* medyas
**stockpile** *n* reserbang produkto
**stockroom** *n* bodega
**stoic** *adj* walang pakiramdam
**stomach** *n* tiyan
**stone** *n* bato
**stone** *v* binato
**stool** *n* upuan
**stop** *v* tumigil
**stop** *n* tigil
**stop by** *v* tinigil
**stop over** *v* hintayan
**storage** *n* taguan
**store** *v* tinago
**store** *n* tindahan

**storm** *n* bagyo
**stormy** *adj* mabagyo
**story** *n* kuwento
**stove** *n* pugon
**straight** *adj* tuwid
**straighten out** *v* ayusin
**strain** *v* salain; bistayin;
**strain** *n* pagsala; pag bistay
**strained** *adj* may sala
**strainer** *n* salaan
**strait** *n* kipot; kanal
**stranded** *adj* naantala
**strange** *adj* kakaiba
**stranger** *n* banyaga
**strangle** *v* sakalin
**strap** *n* pantali
**strategy** *n* pamamaraan
**straw** *n* pansipsip
**strawberry** *n* prutas na mapula
**stray** *adj* naligaw
**stray** *v* iligaw
**stream** *n* sapa
**street** *n* kalye
**streetlight** *n* ilaw sa kalye
**strength** *n* lakas
**strengthen** *v* laksan
**strenuous** *adj* nakakapagod
**stress** *n* bigyang halaga
**stressful** *adj* mahalaga
**stretch** *n* hila; banat
**stretch** *v* hilahin; banatin
**strict** *adj* strikto
**strife** *n* alitan
**strike** *n* welga
**strike** *iv* humampas; paluin
**strike back** *v* lumaban
**strike out** *v* pinalabas sa laro
**strike up** *v* umawit
**striking** *adj* kakaiba
**string** *n* pisi; tali
**stringent** *adj* malala; matindi
**strip** *n* pira-piraso
**strip** *v* pag piraprasuhin
**stripe** *n* guhit
**striped** *adj* guhitan
**strive** *iv* magsumikap
**stroke** *n* paghaplos
**stroll** *v* ipasyal
**strong** *adj* malakas
**structure** *n* balangkas
**struggle** *v* makibaka
**struggle** *n* pakikibaka
**stub** *n* upos; natira
**stubborn** *adj* matigas ang ulo
**student** *n* mag-aaral
**study** *v* mag-aral
**stuff** *n* bagay-bagay
**stuff** *v* barado
**stuffing** *n* palaman
**stuffy** *adj* barado
**stumble** *v* natalisod
**stun** *v* nabigla
**stunning** *adj* nakakabigla
**stupid** *adj* tanga

**stupidity** *n* katangahan
**sturdy** *adj* matibay
**stutter** *v* nautal
**style** *n* stilo
**subdue** *v* pigilan
**subdued** *adj* napigilan
**subject** *v* dominahin
**subject** *n* paksa; asignatura
**sublime** *adj* nakahihigit
**submerge** *v* ilubog
**submissive** *adj* masunurin
**submit** *v* sumailalim
**subscribe** *v* kumuha
**subscription** *n* pagkuha
**subsidiary** *adj* karagdagan
**subsidize** *v* bigyan ng tulong
**subsidy** *n* tulong
**subsist** *v* mabuhay
**substance** *n* kayamanan
**substandard** *adj* mababang antas
**substantial** *adj* malaman
**substitute** *v* palitan
**substitute** *n* kapalit
**subtle** *adj* banayad
**subtract** *v* bawasan
**subtraction** *n* pagbabawas
**suburb** *n* karatig
**subway** *n* daan sa ilalim
**succeed** *v* nagwagi
**success** *n* pagwawagi
**successful** *adj* nagwagi
**successor** *n* sinundan
**succulent** *adj* makatas
**succumb** *v* sumuko, natalo
**such** *adj* ganyan; gayon
**suck** *v* sipsipin
**sucker** *n* manghuhuthot
**sudden** *adj* bigla
**suddenly** *adv* nabigla
**sue** *v* maghabla
**suffer** *v* magdusa
**suffer from** *v* nagdurusa
**suffering** *n* pagdurusa
**sufficient** *adj* sapat
**suffocate** *v* masakal
**sugar** *n* asukal
**suggest** *v* imungkahi
**suggestion** *n* mungkahi
**suicide** *n* pagpapakamatay
**suit** *n* terno
**suitable** *adj* karapat-dapat
**suitcase** *n* maleta
**sullen** *adj* malalim
**sulphur** *n* asupre
**sum** *n* kabuuan; suma
**sum up** *v* isuma
**summarize** *v* ibigay ang buod
**summary** *n* buod
**summer** *n* tag-araw
**summit** *n* tuktok
**summon** *v* tawagin
**sumptuous** *adj* masarap
**sun** *n* araw
**sunblock** *n* taakpan sa araw

**sunburn** *n* nasunog sa araw
**Sunday** *n* Linggo
**sundown** *n* paglubog ng araw
**sunken** *adj* lubog
**sunny** *adj* maaraw
**sunrise** *n* bukang liway-way
**sunset** *n* bikang liwayway
**superb** *adj* napakaganda
**superfluous** *adj* labis sa kailangan
**superior** *adj* napaka-galing
**superiority** *n* kataas-taasan
**supermarket** *n* pamilihan
**supersede** *v* sinundan
**superstition** *n* pamahiin
**supervise** *v* pangasiwaan
**supervision** *n* pamamahala
**supper** *n* hapunan
**supple** *adj* malambot
**supplier** *n* taga tustos
**supplies** *n* mga kailangan
**supply** *v* bigyan ng kailangan
**support** *v* alalay
**supporter** *n* taga alalay
**suppose** *v* akala
**supposing** *c* nag-aakala
**supposition** *n* mga akala
**suppress** *v* pigilin
**supremacy** *n* pamamayani
**supreme** *adj* kataas-taasan
**surcharge** *n* dagdag na bayarin
**sure** *adj* tiyak; sigurado
**surely** *adv* siyang tunay
**surface** *n* labas
**surge** *n* pagtaas
**surgeon** *n* siruhano
**surname** *n* apelyido
**surpass** *v* lampasan
**surplus** *n* sobra
**surprise** *v* nagulat
**surprise** *n* gulat
**surrender** *v* sumuko
**surrender** *n* suko
**surround** *v* paligiran
**surroundings** *n* paligid
**surveillance** *n* pagmamatyag
**survey** *n* magmasid
**survival** *n* pagka ligtas
**survive** *v* mailigtas
**survivor** *n* nakaligtas
**susceptible** *adj* madaling mahawa
**suspect** *v* paghinalaan
**suspend** *v* ibitin; suspindihin
**suspenders** *n* tirante
**suspense** *n* kapanabikan
**suspension** *n* pagbibitin
**suspicion** *n* hinala
**suspicious** *adj* mapaghinala
**sustain** *v* panatilihin
**sustenance** *n* pagpapanatili
**swallow** *v* lulunin
**swamp** *n* sapa
**swamped** *adj* napaliligiran
**swan** *n* gansa
**swap** *v* magpalit

S

**swap** *n* palit
**swarm** *n* pulutong ng bubuyog
**sway** *v* umuga
**swear** *iv* mangako
**sweat** *n* pawis
**sweat** *v* pina wisan
**sweater** *n* pangginaw
**Sweden** *n* Sweden
**Sweedish** *adj* taga Seweden
**sweep** *iv* magwalis
**sweet** *adj* matamis
**sweeten** *v* imatamis
**sweetheart** *n* giliw
**sweetness** *n* katamisan
**sweets** *n* matamis
**swell** *iv* namaga
**swelling** *n* maga
**swift** *adj* mabilis
**swim** *iv* lumangoy
**swimmer** *n* manlalangoy
**swimming** *n* paglangoy
**swindle** *v* lokohin
**swindle** *n* nagantso
**swindler** *n* manggagantso
**swing** *iv* iduyan
**swing** *n* duyan
**Swiss** *adj* Swiso
**switch** *v* isaksak
**switch** *n* saksakan
**switch off** *v* patayin
**switch on** *v* buksan
**Switzerland** *n* Switserland
**swivel** *v* paikutin
**swollen** *adj* maga
**sword** *n* espada
**swordfish** *n* isdang espada
**syllable** *n* kataga
**symbol** *n* simbolo
**symbolic** *adj* mahalaga
**sympathize** *v* makiramay
**sympathy** *n* pakikiramay
**symptom** *n* palatandaan
**synagogue** *n* simbahan
**synchronize** *v* isabay
**synonym** *n* kasintulad
**synthesis** *n* pagsasama sama
**syphilis** *n* sipilis
**syringe** *n* hiringgilya
**syrup** *n* pulot; arnibal
**system** *n* sistema
**systematic** *adj* mapamaraan

# T

**table** *n* mesa
**tablecloth** *n* mantel
**tablespoon** *n* kutsara
**tablet** *n* tableta
**tack** *n* pako
**tackle** *v* kayanin

**tact** *n* pag galang
**tactful** *adj* magalang
**tactical** *adj* mapamaraan
**tactics** *n* paraan
**tag** *n* tanda; pananda
**tail** *n* buntot
**tail** *v* bumuntot
**tailor** *n* sastre
**tainted** *adj* mantsahan
**take** *iv* kunin
**take apart** *v* paghiwa-hiwalayin
**take away** *v* alisin
**take back** *v* isauli
**take in** *v* ipasok
**take off** *v* alisin
**take out** *v* iuwi
**take over** *v* palitan
**tale** *n* kathang salaysay
**talent** *n* talino; karunungan
**talk** *v* magsalita
**talkative** *adj* madaldal
**tall** *adj* matangkad
**tame** *v* paamuhin
**tangent** *n* pagkakadikit
**tangerine** *n* dalanghita
**tangible** *adj* kita
**tangle** *n* buhol
**tank** *n* tangke
**tanned** *adj* kinulayan
**tantamount to** *adj* katulad ng
**tantrum** *n* sumpong
**tap** *n* kalabit; tapik
**tap into** *v* katukin
**tape** *n* sintas, medida
**tape recorder** *n* teyp rekorder
**tar** *n* alkitran
**tarantula** *n* gagamba
**tardy** *adv* huli
**target** *n* pag asinta
**tarnish** *v* papusyawin
**tart** *n* kaasiman
**tartar** *n* tartar
**task** *n* atas
**taste** *v* lasahan
**taste** *n* lasahan
**tasteful** *adj* malasa
**tasteless** *adj* walang lasa
**tasty** *adj* malinamnam
**tavern** *n* bahay tuluyan
**tax** *n* buwis
**tea** *n* tsaa
**teach** *iv* ituro
**teacher** *n* guro
**team** *n* grupo
**teapot** *n* kapitera
**tear** *iv* punitin
**tear** *n* punitin
**tearful** *adj* luhaan
**tease** *v* biruin
**teaspoon** *n* kutsarita
**technical** *adj* teknikal
**technicality** *n* kasilimuutan
**technician** *n* tekniko
**technique** *n* pamamaraan

T

**technology** *n* teknolohiya
**tedious** *adj* nakakainip
**tedium** *n* kapaguran
**teenager** *n* pagdadalaga
**teeth** *n* ngipin
**telegram** *n* telegrama
**telephone** *n* telepono
**telescope** *n* teleskopyo
**televise** *v* isa telebisyon
**television** *n* telebisyon
**tell** *iv* sabihin
**teller** *n* kawani sa bangko
**telling** *adj* sinasabi
**temper** *n* init ng ulo
**temperature** *n* temeperatura
**tempest** *n* sigwa
**temple** *n* simbahan
**temporary** *adj* di pangmatagalan
**tempt** *v* akitin; tuksuhin
**temptation** *n* pang-aakit
**tempting** *adj* nakakaakit
**ten** *adj* sampu
**tenacity** *n* pagka matatag
**tenant** *n* nangungupahan
**tendency** *n* hilig
**tender** *adj* malambot
**tenderness** *n* kalambutan
**tennis** *n* tenis
**tenor** *n* himig
**tense** *adj* malubha
**tension** *n* pagka bahala
**tent** *n* tolda
**tentacle** *n* galamay
**tentative** *adj* pansamantala
**tenth** *adj* pang sampu
**tenuous** *adj* balingkinitan
**tepid** *adj* maligamgam
**term** *n* takdang panahon
**terminate** *v* wakasan
**terminology** *n* terminolohiya
**termite** *n* anay
**terms** *n* kasunduan
**terrestrial** *adj* taga lupa
**terrible** *adj* terible
**terrific** *adj* matindi
**terrify** *v* takutin
**terrifying** *adj* nakakatakot
**territory** *n* teritoryo
**terror** *n* malaking takot
**terrorism** *n* pananakot
**terrorist** *n* nananakot
**terrorize** *v* takutin
**terse** *adj* galit
**test** *v* subukin
**test** *n* pagsusulit
**testament** *n* testamento
**testify** *v* sumaksi
**testimony** *n* saksi
**text** *n* nilalaman
**textbook** *n* aklat
**texture** *n* hipo; lagay
**thank** *v* magpasalamat
**thankful** *adj* pasalamat
**thanks** *n* salamat

**that** *adj* iyon
**thaw** *v* tunawin
**thaw** *n* tunawin
**theater** *n* teatro
**theft** *n* pagnanakaw
**theme** *n* tema
**themselves** *pro* sila
**then** *adv* pagkatapos
**theory** *n* palagay; teorya
**therapy** *n* gamot
**there** *adv* doon
**therefore** *adv* samakatuwid
**thermometer** *n* termometro
**these** *adj* ang mga ito
**thesis** *n* tisis
**they** *pro* sila
**thick** *adj* makapal
**thicken** *v* kapalan
**thickness** *n* makapal
**thief** *n* magnanakaw
**thigh** *n* hita
**thin** *adj* payat; manipis
**thing** *n* gamit
**think** *iv* isipin
**thinly** *adv* kanipisan
**third** *adj* pangatlo
**thirst** *v* inuhaw
**thirsty** *adj* uhaw
**thirteen** *adj* labing tatlo
**thirty** *adj* tatlumpo
**this** *adj* ito
**thorn** *n* tinik
**thorny** *adj* matinik
**thorough** *adj* masusi
**those** *adj* yaon
**though** *c* kahit na
**thought** *n* isip
**thoughtful** *adj* maalalahanin
**thousand** *adj* libo
**thread** *v* pagkabit-kabitin
**thread** *n* sinulid
**threat** *n* banta
**threaten** *v* nagbanta
**three** *adj* tatlo
**thresh** *v* himayin
**threshold** *n* bungad
**thrifty** *adj* matipid
**thrill** *v* kiligin
**thrill** *n* kaagtingan
**thrive** *v* lumaki
**throat** *n* lalamunan
**throb** *n* tibok
**throb** *v* tumitibok
**thrombosis** *n* bara sa ugat
**throne** *n* trono
**throng** *n* bunton ng tao
**through** *pre* sa pamamagitan
**throw** *iv* tapunan
**throw away** *v* itapon
**throw up** *v* sumuka
**thug** *n* kriminal
**thumb** *n* hinlalaki
**thumbtack** *n* panusok
**thunder** *n* kulog

**thunderbolt** *n* kidlat
**thunderstorm** *n* bagyo
**Thursday** *n* Huwebes
**thus** *adv* samakatwid
**thwart** *v* biguin
**thyroid** *n* tayroyd
**tickle** *v* kilitiin
**tickle** *n* kilitiin
**ticklish** *adj* nakakakiliti
**tidal wave** *n* tsunami
**tide** *n* kati
**tidy** *adj* malinis
**tie** *v* itali
**tie** *n* tali
**tiger** *n* tigre
**tight** *adj* masikip
**tighten** *v* sikipan
**tile** *n* baldosa
**till** *pre* hanggang sa
**till** *v* maghukay
**tilt** *v* ibaling
**timber** *n* kahoy
**time** *n* oras
**time** *v* orasan
**timeless** *adj* walang oras
**timely** *adj* nasa oras
**times** *n* panahon
**timetable** *n* ulat ng oras
**timid** *adj* mahiyain
**timidity** *n* pagka mahiyain
**tin** *n* lata
**tiny** *adj* maliit
**tip** *n* dulo
**tiptoe** *n* tingkayad
**tired** *adj* pagod
**tiredness** *n* kapaguran
**tireless** *adj* walang pagod
**tiresome** *adj* nakakapagod
**tissue** *n* papel
**title** *n* pangalan
**to** *pre* sa
**toad** *n* palaka
**toast** *v* tinusta
**toast** *n* taostado
**toaster** *n* tostrador
**tobacco** *n* tabako
**today** *adv* ngayon
**toddler** *n* bata
**toe** *n* daliri sa paa
**toenail** *n* kuko sa paa
**together** *adv* magkasama
**toil** *v* gawain
**toilet** *n* kasilyas
**token** *n* ala-ala
**tolerable** *adj* matitiis
**tolerance** *n* patitiis
**tolerate** *v* pahintulutan
**toll** *n* bayad
**toll** *v* bayarin
**tomato** *n* kamatis
**tomb** *n* nitso
**tombstone** *n* lapida
**tomorrow** *adv* bukas
**ton** *n* tonelada

T

**tone** *n* tono
**tongs** *n* pang-ipit
**tongue** *n* dila
**tonic** *n* tonika
**tonight** *adv* mamayang gabi
**tonsil** *n* tonsil
**too** *adv* din
**tool** *n* gamit
**tooth** *n* ngipin
**toothache** *n* masakit ang ngipin
**toothpick** *n* palito
**top** *n* ibabaw
**topic** *n* buod
**topple** *v* lupigin
**torch** *n* sulo
**torment** *v* magdusa
**torment** *n* pagdurusa
**torrid** *adj* matindi
**torso** *n* katawan
**tortoise** *n* pagong
**torture** *v* parusahan
**torture** *n* pagparusa
**toss** *v* magpukol
**total** *adj* kabuuan
**totality** *n* kabuuan
**touch** *n* pag hipo
**touch** *v* hipuin
**touch on** *v* banggitin
**touch up** *v* pagandahin
**touching** *adj* hinihipo
**tough** *adj* matatag
**toughen** *v* patatagin
**tour** *n* paglalakbay
**tourism** *n* turismo
**tourist** *n* turista
**tournament** *n* torneyo
**tow** *v* hilahin
**tow truck** *n* trak na panghila
**towards** *pre* tungo sa
**towel** *n* tuwalya
**tower** *n* tore
**towering** *adj* nangingibabaw
**town** *n* bayan
**toxic** *adj* nakakalason
**toxin** *n* lason
**toy** *n* laruan
**trace** *v* tandaan
**track** *n* riles
**track** *v* sundan
**tractor** *n* trak
**trade** *n* pangangalakal
**trade** *v* mangalakal
**trader** *n* mangangalakal
**tradition** *n* kaugalian
**traffic** *n* trapiko
**traffic** *v* trapiko
**tragedy** *n* trahedya
**tragic** *adj* malungkot
**trail** *v* landas
**trail** *n* taluntunin
**trailer** *n* pang hakot
**train** *n* tren
**train** *v* sanayin
**trainee** *n* nagsasanay

**trainer** *n* taga sanay
**training** *n* pagsasanay
**trait** *n* ugali
**traitor** *n* traydor
**trajectory** *n* daan ng raket
**tram** *n* maliit na saksakyan
**trample** *v* tapakan
**trance** *n* sinapian ng espiritu
**tranquility** *n* katahimijan
**transaction** *n* kasunduan
**transcend** *v* higitan
**transcribe** *v* isulat
**transfer** *v* lumipat
**transfer** *n* paglipat
**transform** *v* palitan
**transformation** *n* pagpapalit
**transfusion** *n* pagsasalin
**transient** *adj* pansamantala
**transit** *n* sasakyan
**transition** *n* pagbabago
**translate** *v* isalin
**translator** *n* mananalin
**transmit** *v* ipasa
**transparent** *adj* kita
**transplant** *v* itanim muli
**transport** *v* isakay
**trap** *n* patibong
**trash** *n* basura
**trash can** *n* basurahan
**traumatize** *v* parusahan
**travel** *v* maglakbay
**traveler** *n* manlalakbay
**tray** *n* bandehado
**treacherous** *adj* mandaraya
**treachery** *n* pandaraya
**tread** *iv* yapakan
**treason** *n* daya
**treasure** *n* kayamanan
**treasurer** *n* ingat - yaman
**treat** *v* gamutin
**treat** *n* paggamot
**treatment** *n* panggagamot
**treaty** *n* unawaan
**tree** *n* puno
**tremble** *v* nanginig
**tremor** *n* panginginig
**trend** *n* uso
**trendy** *adj* sunod sa uso
**trial** *n* paglilitis
**triangle** *n* tatsulok
**tribe** *n* tribo
**tribulation** *n* pagsubok
**tribunal** *n* hukuman
**tribute** *n* papuri; parangal
**trick** *v* paglalangan
**trick** *n* pandaraya
**trickle** *v* patak-patak
**tricky** *adj* mandaraya
**trigger** *v* umpisahan
**trigger** *n* gatilyo
**trim** *v* putulan
**trimester** *n* tatlong bahagi
**trimmings** *n* palamuti
**trip** *n* paglalakbay

**trip** *v* maglakbay
**triple** *adj* tatluhan
**triumph** *n* tagumpay
**triumphant** *adj* nagwag
**trivial** *adj* hindi mahalaga
**trolley** *n* pang hatak
**troop** *n* tropa
**trophy** *n* tropeyo
**tropic** *n* tropiko
**tropical** *adj* nasa tropiko
**trouble** *n* panggulo
**trouble** *v* manggulo
**troublesome** *adj* pala away
**trousers** *n* pantalon
**trout** *n* isda
**truce** *n* tigil putukan
**truck** *n* trak
**trumped-up** *adj* manggagantso
**trumpet** *n* trompeta
**trunk** *n* puno
**trust** *v* magtiwala
**trust** *n* tiwala
**truth** *n* katotohanan
**truthful** *adj* makatotohanan
**try** *v* subukan
**tub** *n* batya
**tuberculosis** *n* tb; sakit sa baga
**Tuesday** *n* Martes
**tulip** *n* bulaklak
**tumble** *v* mabuwal
**tummy** *n* tyan
**tumor** *n* tumor
**tumult** *n* pagkakagulo
**tumultuous** *adj* magulo
**tuna** *n* tuna
**tune** *n* tono
**tune** *v* itono
**tune up** *v* tyun ap; iayos
**tunic** *n* kasuotan
**tunnel** *n* lagusan
**turbulence** *n* sama ng panahon
**Turk** *adj* turko
**Turkey** *n* Turkya
**turmoil** *n* madulo
**turn** *n* pag-ikot
**turn** *v* ikotin
**turn back** *v* lumingon
**turn down** *v* tanggihan
**turn in** *v* ibigay
**turn off** *v* patayin
**turn on** *v* buksan
**turn out** *v* sawatahin
**turn over** *v* baligtarin
**turn up** *v* dumating
**turret** *n* tore
**turtle** *n* pagong
**tweezers** *n* tyani
**twelfth** *adj* pang labing dalawa
**twelve** *adj* labing dalawa
**twentieth** *adj* pangdalawampu
**twenty** *adj* dalawampu
**twice** *adv* dalawang beses
**twilight** *n* takip silim
**twin** *n* kambal

**twinkle** *v* kumisla-kislap
**twist** *v* pilipitin
**twist** *n* pag pilipit
**twisted** *adj* pinilipit
**twister** *n* pampilipit
**two** *adj* dalawa
**tycoon** *n* mayaman
**type** *n* anyo; uri; klae
**type** *v* makinilyahin
**typical** *adj* nahahalintulad
**tyranny** *n* kalupitan; paniniil
**tyrant** *n* manlulupig

# U

**ugliness** *n* kapangitan
**ugly** *adj* pangit
**ulcer** *n* ulser; sugat
**ultimate** *adj* wakas
**ultimatum** *n* huling babala
**ultrasound** *n* rayos ng tunog
**umbrella** *n* payong
**umpire** *n* taga hatol ng laro
**unable** *adj* hindi kaya
**unanimity** *n* pagkaka-isa
**unarmed** *adj* walang sandata
**unavoidable** *adj* di maiiwasan
**unaware** *adj* di alam
**unbearable** *adj* di matitiis
**unbeatable** *adj* di matalo
**unbiased** *adj* makatarungan
**unbroken** *adj* di masira
**unbutton** *v* hindi naka butones
**uncertain** *adj* di tiyak
**uncle** *n* tiyo
**uncomfortable** *adj* di mapalagay
**uncommon** *adj* di pangkaraniwan
**unconscious** *adj* walang malay
**uncover** *v* alsin ang takip
**undeniable** *adj* tunay na tunay
**under** *pre* ilalim
**undercover** *adj* tiktik
**underdog** *n* api
**undergo** *v* sumailalim
**underground** *adj* sa ilalim
**underlie** *v* ipinailalim
**underline** *v* salungguhitan
**underlying** *adj* nakapilalim
**underneath** *pre* sa ilalim
**underpass** *n* daan sa ilalim
**understand** *v* unawain
**understanding** *n* maunawain
**undertake** *v* gawin
**underwear** *n* damit na panloob
**underwrite** *v* i-seguro
**undeserved** *adj* di karapat dapat
**undesirable** *adj* di kanais-nais
**undo** *v* kalasin
**undoubtedly** *adv* tiyak na tiyak
**undress** *v* maghubad

**undue** *adj* hinid dapat
**unearth** *v* nahukay
**uneasiness** *n* di palagay
**uneasy** *adj* balisa
**unemployed** *adj* walang trabaho
**unemployment** *n* walang trabaho
**unending** *adj* walang katapusan
**unequal** *adj* di pantay
**uneven** *adj* hindi pantay
**uneventful** *adj* hindi mahalaga
**unexpected** *adj* di inaasahan
**unfailing** *adj* maasahan
**unfair** *adj* di makatarungan
**unfairly** *adv* patas
**unfairness** *n* hindi patas
**unfaithful** *adj* taksil
**unfamiliar** *adj* di kilala
**unfasten** *v* kalagin
**unfavorable** *adj* di kanais-nais
**unfit** *adj* hindi nababagay
**unfold** *v* ibulgar
**unforeseen** *adj* di inaasahan
**unforgettable** *adj* di malilimutan
**unhappiness** *n* kalungkutan
**unhappy** *adj* di masaya
**unharmed** *adj* di nasaktan
**unhealthy** *adj* masakitin
**unheard-of** *adj* hindi totoo
**unhurt** *adj* di nasaktan
**unification** *n* pakikipag-isa
**uniform** *n* pare-pareho
**unify** *v* pagkaisahin
**unilateral** *adj* isang bahagi
**union** *n* unyon
**unique** *adj* kaisa-isa
**unit** *n* bahagi
**unite** *v* magkasundo
**unity** *n* pagkakaisa
**universe** *n* sansinukob
**university** *n* dalubhasaan
**unjustified** *adj* di makatarungan
**unknown** *adj* di kilala
**unlawful** *adj* labag sa batas
**unleaded** *adj* walang metal
**unleash** *v* pakawalan
**unless** *c* bagamat
**unlike** *adj* di katulad
**unlikely** *adj* di mangyayari
**unlimited** *adj* walang hangganan
**unload** *v* ibaba; ilabas
**unlock** *v* buksan
**unlucky** *adj* malas
**unmarried** *adj* di kasal
**unmask** *v* ilantad
**unnecessary** *adj* di kailangan
**unnoticed** *adj* di napansin
**unoccupied** *adj* di abala
**unofficially** *adv* hindi opisyal
**unpack** *v* alisan ng laman
**unpleasant** *adj* di kaaya-aya
**unplug** *v* tanggalin
**unpopular** *adj* di kilala
**unpredictable** *adj* di mahulaan
**unprofitable** *adj* di tumutubo

**unravel** *v* isiwalat
**unreal** *adj* hindi tunay
**unrealistic** *adj* di makatotohanan
**unreasonable** *adj* di makatarungan
**unrelated** *adj* walang kinalaman
**unreliable** *adj* di maasahan
**unrest** *n* kaguluhan
**unsafe** *adj* delikado
**unselfish** *adj* mapagbigay
**unstable** *adj* walang tibay
**unsteady** *adj* hindi matatag
**unsuitable** *adj* hindi dapat
**unthinkable** *adj* di maisip
**untie** *v* kalagin
**until** *pre* hanggang sa
**untimely** *adj* wala sa panahon
**untouchable** *adj* hindi mahipo
**untrue** *adj* di totoo
**unusual** *adj* di pangkaraniwan
**unveil** *v* alisan ng belo
**unwillingly** *adv* di payag
**unwind** *v* magpahinga
**unwise** *adj* di matalino
**unwrap** *v* tanggalin ang balot
**upbringing** *n* pagpapalaki
**upcoming** *adj* napipinto
**update** *v* mag ulat
**upgrade** *v* iangat
**upheaval** *n* pag-aklas
**uphill** *adv* pataas
**uphold** *v* panindigan
**upkeep** *n* pag-aalaga
**upon** *pre* sa ibabaw ng
**upper** *adj* pang itaas
**upright** *adj* tuwid
**uprising** *n* pag-aaklas
**uproar** *n* pagkakagulo
**uproot** *v* bunutin
**upset** *v* nagalit
**upside-down** *adv* nakabaligtad
**uptight** *adj* pigil na pigil
**up-to-date** *adj* nasa panahon
**upturn** *n* pagpalit
**upwards** *adv* pataas
**urban** *adj* taga syudad
**urge** *n* simbuyo
**urge** *v* himukin
**urgency** *n* pag apura
**urgent** *adj* madalian
**urinate** *v* umihi
**urine** *n* ihi
**us** *pro* tayo
**usage** *n* pag-gamit
**use** *v* gamitin
**use** *n* pag gamit
**used to** *adj* sanay
**useful** *adj* may gamit
**usefulness** *n* pag gamit
**useless** *adj* walang silbi
**user** *n* gumagamit
**usher** *n* tagahatid
**usual** *adj* karaniwan
**usurp** *v* kamkamin
**utensil** *n* kagamitan

**utilize** *v* gamitin
**utmost** *adj* pinala marami
**utter** *v* magsalita

**vacancy** *n* bakante
**vacant** *adj* nakalaan
**vacate** *v* umalis
**vacation** *n* bakasyon
**vaccinate** *v* bakunahan
**vaccine** *n* bakuna
**vacillate** *v* magsalawahan
**vagrant** *n* bagansya
**vague** *adj* malabo
**vain** *adj* banidosa
**vainly** *adv* pagka banidosa
**valiant** *adj* matapang
**valid** *adj* nararapat
**validate** *v* pagindapatin
**validity** *n* ligal
**valley** *n* lambak
**valuable** *adj* mahalaga
**value** *n* halaga
**valve** *n* balbula
**vampire** *n* bampira
**van** *n* ban
**vanguard** *n* pambato
**vanish** *v* nawala
**vanity** *n* banidad
**vanquish** *v* talunin
**vaporize** *v* tunawin
**variable** *adj* paiba-iba
**varied** *adj* iba-iba
**variety** *n* pagkakaiba-iba
**various** *adj* sari-sari
**varnish** *v* barnisan
**varnish** *n* barnisado
**vary** *v* magbago
**vase** *n* plorera
**vast** *adj* malawak
**veal** *n* karneng malambot
**veer** *v* lumiko
**vegetable** *v* gulayin
**vegetarian** *n* mahilig sa gulay
**vegetation** *n* gulayan
**vehicle** *n* sasakyan
**veil** *n* belo
**vein** *n* ugat
**velocity** *n* bilis
**velvet** *n* pelus; tersyo pelo
**venerate** *v* samabahin
**vengeance** *n* pagganti
**venison** *n* karne ng usa
**venom** *n* kamandag
**vent** *n* butas
**ventilation** *n* lagusan ng hangin
**venture** *v* makipag-sapalaran
**verb** *n* pandiwa
**verbally** *adv* sa salita

**verbatim** *adv* bawat salita
**verdict** *n* hatol; pasya
**verge** *n* bingit
**verification** *n* pagpapatunay
**verify** *v* patunayan
**verse** *n* tula; taludtod
**versed** *adj* matulain
**version** *n* salin
**versus** *pre* laban sa
**vertebra** *n* buto sa likod
**very** *adv* napaka
**vessel** *n* sasakyan
**vest** *n* tsaleko
**vestige** *n* bakas
**veteran** *n* beterano
**veto** *v* pawalang halaga
**viaduct** *n* tulay
**vibrant** *adj* puno ng buhay
**vibrate** *v* manginig
**vibration** *n* panginginig
**vice** *n* bisyo
**vicinity** *n* paligid
**vicious** *adj* mabisyo
**victim** *n* biktima
**victimize** *v* biktimahin
**victor** *n* pagwagi
**victorious** *adj* nagwagi
**victory** *n* wagi
**view** *n* sa paningin
**view** *v* tingnan
**viewpoint** *n* palagay
**vigil** *n* lamay
**village** *n* nayon
**villager** *n* taga nayon
**villain** *n* kontra-bida
**vindicate** *v* ipag-higante
**vindictive** *adj* benggadora
**vinegar** *n* suka
**vineyard** *n* taniman ng ubas
**violate** *v* labagin
**violence** *n* dahas
**violent** *adj* marahas
**violet** *n* byoleta; lila
**violin** *n* biyolin
**violinist** *n* byolinista
**viper** *n* ahas
**virgin** *n* birhen
**virile** *adj* tunay na lalaki
**virility** *n* pagkalalaki
**virtue** *n* kanutihan
**virtually** *adv* sa kabuuan
**virtuous** *adj* malinis; banal
**virulent** *adj* nakalalason
**virus** *n* mikrobyo
**visibility** *n* tanaw
**visible** *adj* nakikita
**vision** *n* pangitain
**visit** *n* pagdalaw
**visit** *v* dalawin
**visitor** *n* panauhin
**visual** *adj* nakikita
**visualize** *v* pansinin
**vital** *adj* mahalaga
**vitality** *n* lakas

**vitamin** *n* bitamina
**vivacious** *adj* masigla
**vivid** *adj* matingkad
**vocabulary** *n* talasalitaan
**vocation** *n* hilig; tungkulin
**vogue** *n* uso; moda
**voice** *n* tinig; boses
**void** *adj* walang-laman
**volatile** *adj* salawahan
**volcano** *n* bulkan
**volleyball** *n* balibol
**voltage** *n* boltahe
**volume** *n* lakas ng tunog
**volunteer** *n* kusang-loob
**vomit** *v* nagsuka
**vomit** *n* suka
**vote** *v* bumoto
**vote** *n* boto
**voting** *n* bumuboto
**vouch for** *v* patunayan
**voucher** *n* resibo
**vow** *v* sumumpa
**vowel** *n* patinig
**voyage** *n* ngalakbay
**voyager** *n* manlalakbay
**vulgar** *adj* bulgar
**vulgarity** *n* kalaswaan
**vulnerable** *adj* mahina
**vulture** *n* malaking ibon

**wafer** *n* apa
**wag** *v* ipaspas
**wage** *n* sweldo
**wagon** *n* bagol
**wail** *v* manangis
**wail** *n* pag tangis
**waist** *n* baywang
**wait** *v* maghintay
**waiter** *n* serbedor
**waiting** *n* paghihintay
**waitress** *n* serbedora
**waive** *v* magpaubaya
**wake up** *iv* gumising
**walk** *v* lumakad
**walk** *n* lakad
**walkout** *n* welga
**wall** *n* dingding
**wallet** *n* pitaka
**walnut** *n* uri ng mani
**walrus** *n* walrus
**waltz** *n* balse
**wander** *v* magpagala-gala
**wanderer** *n* gala
**wane** *v* nawawala
**want** *v* ibig
**war** *n* digmaan; gera
**ward** *n* alaga
**wardrobe** *n* aparador ng damit
**warehouse** *n* bodega; kamalig

**warfare** *n* magkaaway
**warm** *adj* mainit
**warm up** *v* painitin
**warmth** *n* init
**warn** *v* bigyang babala
**warning** *n* babala
**warp** *v* nabingkong
**warped** *adj* bingkong
**warrant** *v* tiyakin
**warrant** *n* patotoo
**warranty** *n* patunay
**warrior** *n* mandirigma
**warship** *n* barkong pandigma
**wart** *n* kulugo
**wary** *adj* maingat
**wash** *v* labahan
**washable** *adj* maaring labahan
**wasp** *n* putakti
**waste** *v* ibasura
**waste** *n* basura
**waste basket** *n* basurahan
**wasteful** *adj* bulagsak
**watch** *n* relo; orasan
**watch** *v* bantayan, tingnan
**watch out** *v* mag-ingat
**watchful** *adj* maingat
**watchmaker** *n* relohero
**water** *n* tubig

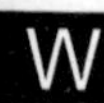

**water** *v* diligan
**water down** *v* pinahina
**waterfall** *n* taktak
**waterheater** *n* pang-init ng tubig
**watermelon** *n* pakwan
**watershed** *n* lagusan ng tubig
**watertight** *adj* di matatalo
**watery** *adj* matubig
**watt** *n* wat
**wave** *n* alon
**waver** *v* magduda
**wavy** *adj* maalon
**wax** *n* pagkit; waks
**way** *n* paraan
**way in** *n* papasok
**way out** *n* palabas
**we** *pro* kami
**weak** *adj* mahina
**weaken** *v* nanghina
**weakness** *n* kahinaan
**wealth** *n* kayamanan
**wealthy** *adj* mayaman
**weapon** *n* sandata
**wear** *n* suot
**wear** *iv* isuot
**wear out** *v* nasira sa kalumaan
**weary** *adj* pagod
**weather** *n* panahon
**weave** *iv* ihabi
**web** *n* bahay ng gagamba
**web site** *n* websayt
**wed** *iv* ikasal
**wedding** *n* kasalan
**wedge** *n* kalang
**Wednesday** *n* Miyerkoles
**weed** *n* damo

**weed** *v* damuhan
**week** *n* linggo
**weekday** *adj* araw
**weekly** *adv* lingguhan
**weep** *iv* umiyak
**weigh** *v* timbangin
**weight** *n* bigat
**weird** *adj* di pangkaraniwan
**welcome** *v* salubungin
**welcome** *n* pagsalubong
**weld** *v* suldahin
**welder** *n* tagapag-sulda
**welfare** *n* kalagayan
**well** *n* mabuti
**well-known** *adj* kilala
**well-to-do** *adj* mayaman
**west** *n* kanluran
**westbound** *adv* patungong kanluran
**western** *adj* pang kanluran
**westerner** *adj* taga kanluran
**wet** *adj* basa
**whale** *n* balyena
**wharf** *n* pantalan, daungan
**what** *adj* ano
**whatever** *adj* kahit ano
**wheat** *n* arina
**wheel** *n* gulong
**wheelbarrow** *n* pang hakot
**wheelchair** *n* silyang di gulong
**wheeze** *v* paghingang may huni
**when** *adv* kailan
**whenever** *adv* kahit kailan
**where** *adv* saan
**whereabouts** *n* kinalaman
**whereas** *c* subalit
**whereupon** *c* gayunpaman
**wherever** *c* saan man
**whether** *c* kahit na ano
**which** *adj* alin
**while** *c* habang
**whim** *n* kapritso
**whine** *v* umangal
**whip** *v* hagupitin
**whip** *n* hagupit
**whirl** *v* paikutin
**whirlpool** *n* paliguan
**whiskers** *n* sungot
**whisper** *v* bumulong
**whisper** *n* bulong
**whistle** *v* sumipol
**whistle** *n* sipol
**white** *adj* puti
**whiten** *v* paputiin
**whittle** *v* putulin
**who** *pro* sino
**whoever** *pro* kahit sino
**whole** *adj* buo
**wholehearted** *adj* buong - puso
**wholesale** *adj* pakyawan
**wholesome** *adj* kaaya-aya
**whom** *pro* kung sinu-sino
**why** *adv* bakit
**wicked** *adj* makasalanan
**wide** *adj* malapad

**widely** *adv* kalaparan
**widen** *v* laparan
**widespread** *adj* laganap
**widow** *n* balong babae; byuda
**widower** *n* balong lalake; byudo
**width** *n* lapad
**wield** *v* iumang ang sandata
**wife** *n* asawang babae
**wig** *n* piluka
**wiggle** *v* wisikin
**wild** *adj* mabangis
**wild boar** *n* baboy ramo
**wilderness** *n* gubat; sukal
**wildlife** *n* hayop sa gubat
**will** *n* loobin; kalooban
**willfully** *adv* kusang binigay
**willing** *adj* pumapayag
**willingly** *adv* kusang-loob
**willingness** *n* pagpayag
**willow** *n* puno
**wimp** *adj* mahina; lampa
**win** *iv* nanalo
**win back** *v* pabalikin
**wind** *n* hangin
**wind** *iv* humangin
**wind up** *v* tapusin
**winding** *adj* pag-ikot
**window** *n* bintana
**windpipe** *n* lalamunan
**windy** *adj* mahangin
**wine** *n* alak
**winery** *n* pagawaan ng alak
**wing** *n* pakpak
**wink** *n* kindat
**wink** *v* kumindat
**winner** *n* panalo
**winter** *n* taglamig
**wipe** *v* punasan
**wipe out** *v* nasalanta
**wire** *n* alambre
**wireless** *adj* walang alambre
**wisdom** *n* karunungan
**wise** *adj* matalino
**wish** *v* humiling
**wish** *n* kahilingan
**wit** *n* talino
**witch** *n* bruha
**witchcraft** *n* kulam
**with** *pre* kasama
**withdraw** *v* bawiin
**withdrawal** *n* pag bawi
**withdrawn** *adj* binawi
**wither** *v* nalanta
**withhold** *iv* ibinbin
**within** *pre* nakapaloob
**without** *pre* nakapalabas
**withstand** *v* tiisin
**witness** *n* testigo
**witty** *adj* matalino
**wives** *n* mga maybahay
**wizard** *n* mahikero
**wobble** *v* umuuga
**woes** *n* hinaing
**wolf** *n* lobo

**woman** *n* babae
**womb** *n* sinapupunan
**women** *n* kababaihan
**wonder** *v* nagtaka
**wonder** *n* nakapagtataka
**wonderful** *adj* kagila-gilalas
**wood** *n* kahoy
**wooden** *adj* yari sa kahoy
**wool** *n* lana
**woolen** *adj* mala lana
**word** *n* salita
**wording** *n* salita
**work** *n* trabaho
**work** *v* magtrabaho
**work out** *v* bigyang lunas
**workable** *adj* maaring gawin
**worker** *n* trabahador
**workshop** *n* pagawaan
**world** *n* mundo
**worldly** *adj* makamundo
**worldwide** *adj* sa buong mundo
**worm** *n* uod
**worn-out** *adj* sira
**worrisome** *adj* nakakapag-alala
**worry** *v* mag-alala
**worry** *n* pag-alala
**worse** *adj* malala
**worsen** *v* lumala
**worship** *n* samba
**worst** *adj* malala
**worth** *n* halaga
**worthless** *adj* walang halaga
**worthwhile** *adj* mahalaga
**worthy** *adj* karapat-dapat
**would-be** *adj* nagpapanggap
**wound** *n* sugat
**wound** *v* nasugat
**woven** *adj* hinabi
**wrap** *v* balutin
**wrap up** *v* tapusin
**wrapping** *n* pagbalot
**wrath** *n* poot
**wreath** *n* korona ng bulaklak
**wreck** *v* wasakin
**wreckage** *n* nawasak
**wrestle** *v* bunuin
**wrestler** *n* mabubuno
**wrestling** *n* pagbubuno
**wretched** *adj* hamal.
**wring** *iv* pigain
**wrinkle** *v* kumulubot
**wrinkle** *n* kulubot
**wrist** *n* puno ng kamay
**write** *iv* magsulat
**write down** *v* isulat
**writer** *n* manunulat
**writhe** *v* namimilipit
**writing** *n* sulatin
**written** *adj* nakasulat
**wrong** *adj* mali

**X-mas** *n* pasko
**X-ray** *n* rayo-ekis

**yacht** *n* yate
**yam** *n* kamote
**yard** *n* yarda
**yarn** *n* sinulid
**yawn** *n* hikab
**yawn** *v* naghikab
**year** *n* taon
**yearly** *adv* taun-taon
**yearn** *v* nananabik
**yeast** *n* amag
**yell** *v* sumigaw
**yellow** *adj* dilaw
**yes** *adv* oo
**yesterday** *adv* kahapon
**yet** *c* pa
**yield** *v* umilag
**yield** *n* pag-ilag
**yoke** *n* singkaw
**yolk** *n* yema
**you** *pro* ikaw
**young** *adj* bata
**youngster** *n* kabataan
**your** *adj* iyo
**yours** *pro* sa iyo
**yourself** *pro* ikaw
**youth** *n* kabataan
**youthful** *adj* bata

**zeal** *n* sigla
**zealous** *adj* masigasig
**zero** *n* sero
**zest** *n* lakas
**zinc** *n* yero
**zip code** *n* kodigo postal
**zipper** *n* siper
**zone** *n* sona
**zoology** *n* soolohiya

# Tagalog-English

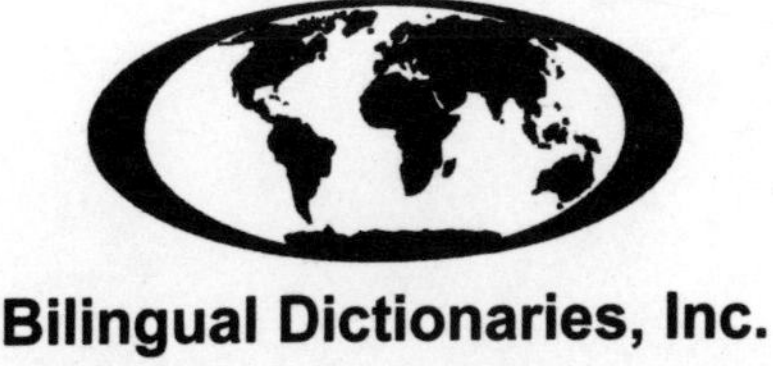

Bilingual Dictionaries, Inc.

## Abbreviations

**a -** article - pantukoy
**adj -** adjective - pang-uri
**adv -** adverb - pang- abay
**c -** conjunction - pang-ugnay
**e -** exclamation
**n -** noun - pangngalan
**pre -** preposition - pang-ukol
**pro -** pronoun - panghalip
**v -** verb - pandiwa

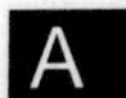

**abahin** *v* hail
**abala** *adv* busily
**abala** *adj* busy, hectic
**abalahin** *v* bother
**abay** *n* best man
**abo** *n* ash
**abogado** *n* attorney
**abonado** *adj* derelict
**abono** *n* manure
**abot** *n* reach
**abot-tanaw** *n* horizon
**abraso** *v* arm
**Abril** *n* April
**abuhin** *adj* grayish
**abuloy** *n* alms
**abutin** *v* reach
**adres** *n* address
**adwana** *n* customs
**agawin** *v* abduct, kidnap
**agila** *n* eagle
**agos** *n* flow
**Agosto** *n* August
**agradera** *n* knob
**ahas** *n* serpent, snake
**ahedres** *n* chess
**ahensya** *n* agency
**ahente** *n* agent
**akademya** *n* academy
**akala** *n* presumption
**akalain** *v* presume
**akin** *adj* my, mine
**akit** *n* charm
**akitin** *v* attract, entice
**aklat** *n* book
**aklat ng mapa** *n* guidebook
**aklatan** *n* library
**akma** *n* correction
**akma** *v* fit
**ako** *pro* I
**akordyon** *n* accordion
**aksento** *n* accent
**aksidente** *n* accident
**aksyon** *n* action
**akusahan** *v* indict
**akusasyon** *n* accusation
**akustika** *adj* acoustic
**akwaryum** *n* aquarium
**akyatin** *v* climb, run up
**ala-ala** *n* remembrance
**alaga** *n* pet
**alagaan** *v* care, look after
**alagad** *n* apostle
**alagad ng batas** *n* policeman
**alahas** *n* jewel
**alahasan** *n* jewelry store
**alahero** *n* jeweler
**alak** *n* booze, liquor
**alalahanin** *v* remember
**alalay** *v* support
**alamat** *n* legend, myth
**alambre** *n* wire

**alamin** *v* discover, learn
**alamin antimano** *v* foreshadow
**alampay** *n* cloak, scarf
**alarma** *n* alarm
**alas** *n* ace
**alay** *n* offer
**Aleman** *adj* German
**Alemanya** *n* Germany
**alerhiya** *adj* allergic
**alerhiya** *n* allergy
**alikabok** *n* dust
**alimango** *n* crab
**alin** *adj* which
**alingawngaw** *n* echo
**alinlangan** *adj* skeptic
**alinlangan** *v* doubt
**alinman** *pro* anything
**alinman** *adv* either
**alinman** *adj* some
**alinma'y hindi** *adj* neither
**alipin** *n* slave
**alipusta** *n* blasphemy
**alipustahin** *v* blaspheme
**alipustain** *v* desecrate
**alisan ng belo** *v* unveil
**alisan ng laman** *v* unpack
**alisin** *v* eliminate
**alisin ang hangin** *v* deflate
**alitan** *n* rift, strife
**alituntunin** *n* principle
**aliw** *n* entertainment
**aliwan** *n* amusement
**aliwin** *v* amuse
**alkalde** *n* mayor
**alkansya** *n* piggy bank
**alkitran** *n* tar
**almanak** *n* almanac
**almirante** *n* admiral
**almon** *n* almond
**almusal** *n* breakfast
**alon** *n* wave
**aloy** *n* alloy
**alpabeto** *n* alphabet
**alpombra** *n* cushion
**alsin ang takip** *v* uncover
**altar** *n* altar
**alulod** *n* gutter
**aluminyo** *n* aluminum
**alumpihit** *adj* hesitant
**alupihan** *n* scorpion
**alyas** *n* pseudonym
**ama** *n* dad
**amag** *n* yeast
**amain** *n* father-in-law
**ambisyoso** *adj* ambitious
**ambon** *n* drizzle
**ambulansya** *n* ambulance
**amerikano** *adj* American
**amo** *n* boss
**amonya** *n* ammonia
**amoy** *n* odor
**ampon** *n* adoption
**amuyin** *v* smell
**anak** *n* daughter

**anak na lalaki** *n* son
**anak sa labas** *adj* illegitimate
**analohiya** *n* analogy
**anarkista** *n* anarchist
**anarkiya** *n* anarchy
**anatomya** *n* anatomy
**anay** *n* termite
**anemya** *n* anemia
**anestisya** *n* anesthesia
**ang** *a* a, an
**ang katotohanan** *n* essence
**ang may panauhin** *n* host
**ang may panukala** *n* sponsor
**ang mga ito** *adj* these
**ang nabanggit** *adj* latter
**ang nabanggit** *n* debtor
**angal** *n* complaint
**angatin** *v* lift
**anggulo** *n* angle
**anghel** *n* angel
**angkan** *n* clan
**angkat** *v* export
**angkatin** *v* import
**angkinin** *v* claim
**angliko** *adj* Anglican
**ani** *n* harvest
**anibersaryo** *n* anniversary
**anim** *adj* six
**animnapu** *adj* sixty
**aninag** *n* reflection
**anino** *n* shadow
**anit** *n* scalp
**ano** *adj* what
**antas** *n* category
**antena** *n* antenna
**antimano** *adv* beforehand
**anunsyo** *n* flier
**anyayahan** *v* invite
**anyo** *n* form, type
**apa** *n* wafer
**apanapu** *adj* forty
**aparador** *n* closet
**apat** *adj* four
**apdo** *n* bile, bladder
**apelyido** *n* last name
**apendiks** *n* appendix
**apendisitis** *n* appendicitis
**api** *adj* downtrodden
**apihin** *v* oppress
**apila** *n* appeal
**aplaya** *n* coast
**aplikante** *n* applicant
**apo** *n* grandchild
**apog** *n* limestone
**aporo** *n* lining
**aprikot** *n* apricot
**aprtamento** *n* apartment
**apyan** *v* dope
**Arabo** *adj* Arabic
**aralin** *n* lesson
**aranya** *n* chandelier
**araruhin** *v* mow, plow
**aratiles** *n* raspberry
**araw** *n* sun, day

**araw-araw** *adv* daily
**areglo** *n* compromise
**aregluhin** *v* compromise
**arestuhin** *v* inhibit
**ari-arian** *n* estate
**ariin** *v* possess
**ariling kusa** *n* initiative
**arina** *n* flour, wheat
**aristokrasya** *n* aristocracy
**aristokrata** *n* aristocrat
**arkeyolohiya** *n* archaeology
**arkitekto** *n* architect
**arkitektura** *n* architecture
**arko** *n* arc, ark
**arkong biyolin** *n* bow
**armado** *adj* armed
**armadong barko** *n* frigate
**armas** *n* firearm
**army** *n* phase
**arsenik** *n* arsenic
**arsobispo** *n* archbishop
**artikulo** *n* article
**artista** *n* artist
**artistang babae** *n* actress
**artistang lalaki** *n* actor
**artritis** *n* arthritis
**arukin** *v* fathom out
**asal** *n* conduct, manners
**asal** *v* conduct
**asal barbaro** *n* barbarism
**asawa** *n* spouse
**asawang babae** *n* wife
**asawang lalaki** *n* husband
**asignatura** *n* subject
**asilo** *n* asylum
**asim** *n* acid, ferment
**asin** *n* salt
**asintado** *n* sniper
**aso** *n* dog, jackal
**asoge** *n* mercury
**aspalto** *n* asphalt
**asparagus** *n* asparagus
**aspeto** *n* aspect
**aspili** *n* pin
**aspirin** *n* aspirin
**asterisko** *n* asterisk
**astrolohiya** *n* astrology
**astronomiya** *n* astronomy
**astronot** *n* astronaut
**asukal** *n* sugar
**asul** *adj* blue
**asupre** *n* sulphur
**at** *c* and
**at saka** *adv* further, plus
**atake sa puso** *n* cardiac arrest
**atas** *n* task
**ataul** *n* casket
**atay** *n* liver
**atin** *pro* ours
**atleta** *adj* sporty
**atrasado** *adj* overdue
**awa** *n* compassion
**awatin** *v* conciliate
**away** *n* brawl

**away ng kalabaw** *n* bull fight
**awayin** *v* antagonize
**awir** *n* chant, song
**awto** *n* auto
**awtomatik** *adj* automatic
**awtoridad** *n* authority
**ay** *v* be
**ayahan** *v* delight
**ayaw** *v* dislike
**ayawan** *v* desist
**ayin sa bibliya** *adj* biblical
**ayon sa** *adv* according to
**ayon sa batas** *adj* legal
**ayon sa panahon** *adj* climatic
**ayos** *adv* set
**ayos ng buhok** *n* hairdo
**ayusin** *v* arrange, fix

# B

**baba** *n* chin
**baba** *adv* down
**babae** *n* female, woman
**babaeng bayani** *n* heroin
**babaeng kabayo** *n* mare
**babaeng leyon** *n* lioness
**babala** *n* notice, sign
**babasagin** *adj* breakable
**babasahin** *n* magazine
**babayaran** *adj* payable
**babolgam** *n* bubble gum
**baboy** *n* hog, pig
**baboy ramo** *n* boar
**babuyan** *n* livestock
**bag** *n* bag, purse
**bagabag** *n* dismay
**bagahe** *n* baggage
**bagalan** *v* slow down
**bagalan** *adv* slowly
**bagaman** *adv* nevertheless
**bagamat** *c* despite, unless
**bagang** *n* molar
**bagansya** *n* vagrant
**bagay** *adj* compatible
**bagay** *n* matter, object
**bagay-bagay** *n* stuff
**baget** *n* baguette
**bagito** *n* novice
**bagng panganak** *n* newborn
**bago** *pre* before
**bago** *adj* new
**bago** *n* novelty
**bagol** *n* wagon
**bagong kasal** *adj* newlywed
**bagong salta** *n* newcomer
**bagsak** *n* fall
**baguhan** *n* apprentice
**baguhin** *v* amend, edit, improve, revise
**bagyo** *n* hurricane

**baha** *n* deluge
**bahagdan** *n* fraction
**bahag-hari** *n* rainbow
**bahagi** *n* fragment, share
**bahaginan** *v* part
**bahagya** *adv* hardly, quite
**bahay** *n* dwelling, house
**bahay ampunan** *n* orphanage
**bahay halaman** *n* nursery
**bahay hukuman** *n* courthouse
**bahay matadero** *n* shambles
**bahay na berde** *n* greenhouse
**bahay ng aso** *n* kennel
**bahay ng gagamba** *n* web
**bahay pantining** *n* refinery
**bahay postal** *n* post office
**bahay sa bukid** *n* chalet
**bahay tanghalan** *n* auditorium
**bahay tuluyan** *n* tavern
**bahay-bata** *n* ovary
**bahay-kalakal** *n* firm
**bahay-pukyutan** *n* beehive
**bahin** *n* sneeze
**bahiran** *v* blemish
**baka** *n* cattle, cow
**bakal** *n* steel
**bakante** *n* vacancy
**bakas** *n* vestige
**bakas ng paa** *n* footprint
**bakasyon** *n* vacation
**bakero** *n* cowboy
**bakit** *adv* why
**bako-bako** *adj* bumpy
**bakod** *n* fence
**bakuna** *n* vaccine
**bakunahan** *v* immunize
**bakuran** *n* seal off
**bala** *n* bullet
**balahibo ng ibon** *n* feather
**balak** *n* plan
**balakang** *n* hip
**balakid** *n* obstacle
**balakin** *v* aim
**balakubak** *n* dandruff
**balang** *n* locust
**balangaka** *n* plot
**balang-araw** *adv* someday
**balangkas** *n* framework
**balangkasin** *v* conjugate
**balarila** *n* grammar
**balasahin** *v* shuffle
**balat** *n* skin, peel
**balat ng mani** *n* nut-shell
**balatan** *v* peel, skin
**balat-kayo** *n* camouflage
**balbas** *n* beard
**balbula** *n* valve
**baldado** *adj* disabled
**baldosa** *n* tile
**bali** *n* fracture
**balibol** *n* volleyball
**baligtad** *adv* inside out
**baligtad** *n* reverse
**baligtarin** *v* turn over

**balik** *n* comeback
**balik-aral** *n* review
**balikat** *n* shoulder
**balikatin** *v* bear
**baliktarin** *adj* reversible
**balingkinitan** *adj* slender
**balisa** *adj* anxious, uneasy
**balita** *n* advertising
**baliw** *adj* crazy, insane
**balkonahe** *n* balcony
**balong babae** *n* widow
**balota** *n* ballot
**balsa** *n* barge, raft
**balse** *n* waltz
**baltak** *n* jerk
**balutin** *v* pack, wrap
**balyena** *n* whale
**bam** *n* balm
**bampira** *n* vampire
**ban** *n* van
**banaag** *n* gleam
**banal** *adj* ascetic, sacred
**banal na lugar** *n* shrine
**banatin** *v* stretch
**banayad** *adj* subtle
**banda** *n* band
**bandehado** *n* tray
**bandera** *n* banner, flag
**bandido** *n* bandit
**bang** *v* bang
**banga** *n* jar
**banggaan** *n* clash, collision
**banggitin** *v* mention
**bangin** *n* chasm, cliff
**bangka** *n* canoe, sailboat
**bangkarote** *n* bankruptcy
**bangkay** *n* carcass, corpse
**bangketa** *n* pavement
**bangko** *n* bank, bench
**bangungot** *n* nightmare
**banidad** *n* vanity
**banidosa** *adj* vain
**banig** *n* mat
**banlawan** *v* rinse
**banlian** *v* scald
**bansa** *n* country, nation
**bantaan** *v* bulldoze
**bantayan** *n* guard
**bantayan** *v* monitor, watch
**bantog** *adj* famous
**banyaga** *n* foreigner
**baog** *adj* impotent, infertile
**baon** *v* carry on
**bar** *n* bar
**bara** *n* blockage
**bara ng tinapay** *n* loaf
**bara sa ugat** *n* thrombosis
**barado** *v* stuff
**barado** *adj* stuffy
**baraha** *n* card
**barahan** *v* obstruct
**barangay** *n* borough
**baratilyo** *n* bargain
**z** *v* bargain

**barbaro** *n* barbarian, barber
**barbikyu** *n* barbecue
**baril** *n* gun
**barilan** *n* crossfire
**barilin** *v* shoot
**barilis** *n* barrel, keg
**barko** *n* boat
**barkong pandigma** *n* warship
**barnisado** *n* varnish
**barnisan** *v* varnish
**bartolina** *n* dungeon
**barya** *n* coin
**basa** *adj* damp, wet
**basagin** *v* smash
**basahan** *n* rag
**basahin** *v* read
**basain** *v* dampen, moisten
**basawan** *v* lack
**basehan** *n* basis
**basehan** *adj* fundamental
**basehan ng datos** *n* database
**basiko** *adj* basic, essential
**basiko** *n* basics
**basket** *n* basket
**basketbol** *n* basketball
**bastarda** *n* bastard
**bastos** *adv* harshly
**bastos** *adj* rude
**bastusin** *v* affront
**basura** *n* crap, garbage
**basurahan** *n* bin, trash can
**basyahan ng tubig** *v* splash
**bat** *n* bat
**bata** *n* child, robe
**bata** *adj* young, youthful
**bata de banyo** *n* bathrobe
**batalyon** *n* battalion
**batang anak** *adj* junior
**batang babae** *n* girl
**batang lalaki** *n* boy, lad
**batas** *n* statute, law
**batasan** *n* legislature
**baterya** *n* battery
**Bathala** *n* providence
**batihin** *v* scramble
**batiin** *n* greet
**batik** *n* spot
**bato** *n* stone, rock
**bato sa dagat** *n* reef
**baton** *n* baton
**batong asul** *n* sapphire
**batong makapal** *n* slab
**batu-balani** *n* magnet
**batutain** *v* club
**batya** *n* tub
**bawal** *n* ban
**bawang** *n* garlic
**bawas** *n* decrease
**bawas** *adj* minus
**bawasan** *v* decrease, discount
**bawass pagkatao** *adj* demeaning
**bawat** *adj* every
**bawat** *pre* per
**bawat isa** *adv* apiece

**bawat isa** *adj* each
**bawat salita** *adv* verbatim
**bawi** *n* retreat
**bawiin** *v* forfeit, redeem
**bawiin sa** *v* make up for
**bayad** *n* charge, pay
**bayad pinsala** *n* reparation
**bayan** *n* town
**bayani** *n* hero, patriot
**bayaran** *v* compensate, refund, repay
**bayarin** *n* dues, toll
**bayas** *n* bias
**bayaw** *n* brother-in-law
**baybay** *adv* ashore, fjord
**baybayin** *adj* coastal
**baybayin** *v* spell
**baylinggwal** *adj* bilingual
**bayolente** *adj* bloodthirsty
**bayoneta** *n* bayonet
**baywang** *n* waist
**beke** *n* mumps
**bekon** *n* bacon
**Belgium** *n* Belgium
**belo** *n* veil
**benda** *n* bandage
**bendahan** *v* bandage
**bendisyon** *n* blessing
**bendisyunan** *v* benefit
**benggadora** *adj* vindictive
**benta** *n* sale
**beranda** *n* porch
**berde** *adj* green
**berey** *n* beret
**beterano** *n* veteran
**beysbol** *n* baseball
**bibig** *n* mouth
**bibliya** *n* bible
**bigamya** *n* bigamy
**bigas** *n* rice
**bigat** *n* gravity, pressure
**bigatan** *v* gravitate
**bigay pugay** *n* homage
**bighani** *n* allure
**bigkasin** *adv* orally
**bigkasin** *v* pronounce
**bigkisin** *v* bind
**bigla** *n* impulse
**biglaan** *adj* compulsive
**bigo** *n* flop
**bigote** *n* mustache
**biguin** *v* foil, frustrate
**bigyan buhay** *n* animation
**bigyan kahulugan** *v* imply
**bigyan ng labis** *v* pamper
**bigyan ng tulong** *v* subsidize
**bigyan pabuya** *v* award
**bigyan parangal** *v* dignify
**bigyang babala** *v* warn
**bigyang buhay** *v* resuscitate
**bigyang halaga** *v* signify
**bigyang halaga** *n* stress
**bigyang lunas** *v* work out
**bigyang pabuya** *v* reward

**bigyang sistema** *v* codify
**bigyan-uri** *v* classify
**bihag** *n* capture
**bihagin** *v* capture
**bihasa** *adj* proficient
**bihira** *adj* rare, scarce
**bihira** *adv* seldom
**bikang liwayway** *n* sunset
**biktima** *n* casualty, victim
**biktimahin** *v* victimize
**bilang** *n* number, count
**bilanggo** *n* captive
**bilangin** *v* count, score
**bilangin muli** *n* recount
**bilihan** *n* shop
**bilihin** *v* purchase
**biling yari** *v* prefabricate
**bilis** *n* velocity
**bilisan** *v* hasten, rush
**bilo haba** *adj* oval
**bilog** *n* circle
**bilog** *adj* round
**bilohaba** *adj* oblong
**bilugan** *v* circle
**bilugan** *adj* concentric
**bilyar** *n* billiards
**bilyon** *n* billion
**binabati** *v* congratulate
**binago** *n* edition
**binago** *v* modify
**binalot** *adj* shrouded
**binalot na padala** *n* package
**binaril** *v* gun down
**binaril** *n* shot
**binata** *n* bachelor
**binato** *v* stone
**binawasan** *adj* attenuating
**binawi** *v* retreat
**binawi** *adj* withdrawn
**binayaran** *n* payee
**bingi** *adj* deaf, dumb
**bingid** *n* brink
**bingit** *n* verge
**bingkong** *adj* warped
**binibini** *n* lady, miss
**binigo** *v* let down
**bintana** *n* window
**bintang** *n* allegation
**binti** *n* leg
**binubuo** *v* consist
**binyag** *n* baptism
**binyagan** *v* baptize
**birhen** *n* virgin
**biro** *n* joke
**biruin** *v* joke, tease
**bisagra** *n* hinge
**bisikleta** *n* bicycle
**bisiro** *n* calf
**biskwit** *n* biscuit
**bisyo** *n* vice
**bitag** *n* snare
**bitamina** *n* vitamin
**bitayan** *n* gallows
**bitayin** *v* persecute

**biton** *n* shoepolish
**bituin** *n* star
**bituka** *n* intestine, gut
**Biyernes** *n* Friday
**biyolin** *n* violin
**biyolohiya** *n* biology
**blangko** *adj* blank
**bloke** *n* block
**blusa** *n* blouse
**bodega** *n* stockroom
**boksing** *n* boxing
**boksingero** *n* boxer
**bola** *n* ball
**bolang kristal** *n* looking glass
**boltahe** *n* voltage
**bomba** *n* bomb, pump
**bombahan** *n* bombing
**bombahin** *v* bomb, pump
**bonus** *n* bonus
**bota** *n* boot
**botanya** *n* botany
**bote** *n* bottle
**boto** *n* vote
**botohan** *n* election
**botones** *n* button
**boykot** *v* boycott
**bra** *n* bra
**braso** *n* arm
**brigada** *n* brigade
**Britanya** *n* Britain
**brocha** *n* paintbrush
**brongkitis** *n* bronchitis
**bruha** *n* witch
**brusko** *adj* brusque
**brutal** *adj* brutal
**bubong** *n* roof
**bubuyog** *n* bee
**buga** *n* emission
**bugbugan** *n* mugging
**bugbugin** *v* batter, maul
**bugso** *v* flush
**bugso ng hangin** *n* gust
**bugtong** *n* riddle
**buhangin** *n* sand
**buhay** *n* life
**buhay** *adj* live
**buhayin** *v* animate
**buhayin muli** *v* revive
**buhok** *n* hair
**buhol** *n* knot
**buhulin** *v* entangle
**bukal** *n* fountain, spring
**bukang liway-way** *n* sunrise
**bukas** *adj* open
**bukas ang isip** *adj* receptive
**bukas na kaisipan** *n* openness
**bukid** *n* barn, farm
**bukod** *adv* aside
**bukod** *pre* besides
**bukod tangi** *adv* specific
**bukol** *n* cyst, lump
**bukong-bukong** *n* ankle
**buksan** *v* inaugurate
**bula** *n* lather, foam

**bulag** *n* blindness
**bulagan** *adv* blindly
**bulagin** *v* blind
**bulagin** *adj* blind
**bulagsak** *adj* wasteful
**bulak** *n* cotton
**bulaklak** *v* blossom
**bulaslas** *n* outburst
**bulgar** *adj* vulgar
**bulkan** *n* volcano
**bulok** *n* corruption, rot
**bulong** *n* murmur, whisper
**bulsa** *n* pocket
**bulubundukin** *adj* mountainous
**bulubundukon** *adj* hilly
**bulutong** *n* chicken pox
**bulwagan** *n* ballroom, hall
**bumaba** *adv* descend, go down
**bumagsak** *v* fall, slump
**bumaha** *v* flood
**bumahin** *v* sneeze
**bumalik** *v* go back
**bumara** *v* clog
**bumawi** *v* make up
**bumbero** *n* fireman
**bumbilya** *n* bulb
**bumigay** *v* give in
**bumili** *v* buy, purchase
**bumoto** *v* vote
**bumuboto** *n* voting
**bumubulong** *v* grumble
**bumuga** *v* emit
**bumulong** *v* mumble
**bumuntot** *v* tail
**bumusina** *v* honk
**bundok** *n* mountain
**bundok na yelo** *n* glacier
**bunga** *n* acorn
**bunga ng pino** *n* pine
**bungad** *n* threshold
**bungang butil** *n* cereal
**bungkos** *n* batch, bundle
**bungo** *n* skull
**bunmabaho** *adj* stinking
**buntis** *adj* pregnant
**bunton** *n* heap
**bunton ng tao** *n* throng
**buntot** *n* tail
**bunuan** *n* hassle
**bunuin** *v* wrestle
**bunutin** *v* uproot
**buo** *adj* entire
**buod** *n* summary
**buong - puso** *adj* wholehearted
**buong buhay** *adj* lifetime
**buong paligid** *n* perimeter
**burahin** *v* abolish, delete
**burda** *n* embroidery
**burdahan** *v* embroider
**burikiin** *v* pilfer
**buriko** *n* donkey
**burol** *n* hill
**bus** *n* bus
**busal** *n* muzzle

**buson** *n* mailbox
**butas** *n* cavity, hole; loophole
**butas ng botones** *n* buttonhole
**butas ng ilong** *n* nostril
**butas-butas** *adj* porous
**butasin** *v* perforate
**butiki** *n* lizard
**butil** *n* grain
**buto** *n* bone, rib
**buto sa likod** *n* vertebra
**buwan** *n* month, moon
**buwanan** *adv* monthly
**buwaya** *n* alligator
**buwis** *n* tax
**bwisitin** *v* nag
**byenan** *n* mother-in-law
**byoleta** *n* violet
**byolinista** *n* violinist
**byudo** *n* widower

# C

**cantaloupe** *n* melon
**Carolina** *n* carol

**daan** *n* path, passage
**daan** *n* access, route
**daan krus** *n* crossroads
**daan ng raket** *n* trajectory
**daan sa ilalim** *n* subway
**daanan** *n* crosswalk, lane
**daang taon** *n* century
**daanng araro** *n* furrow
**dadating** *adj* coming
**daga** *n* mice, rodent
**dagat** *n* bay
**dagdag** *n* contribution, increase
**dagdag na bayarin** *n* surcharge
**dagdag tulong** *adj* auxiliary
**dagdagan** *v* contribute
**daglian** *n* instant
**dahas** *n* violence
**dahil sa** *pre* because of
**dahilan** *n* cause, reason
**dahilan sa** *c* inasmuch as
**dahon** *n* leaf
**daigin** *v* overcome
**daigin** *n* sigh
**dakila** *adj* great, heroic
**dakilang gawa** *n* feat
**dakpin muli** *v* recapture
**dalaga/binata** *n* single
**dalahin** *v* bring
**dalamhati** *n* grief

**dalampasigan** *n* beach
**dalanghita** *n* tangerine
**dalasan** *v* frequent
**dalawa** *adj* two
**dalawampu** *adj* twenty
**dalawang beses** *adv* twice
**dalawang bundok** *n* canyon
**dalawin** *v* call on, visit
**daldal** *n* gag
**dalhin** *v* deliver
**daliri** *n* finger
**daliri sa paa** *n* toe
**dalisay** *adj* pure
**dalubhasa** *adj* expert, genius
**dalubhasaan** *n* university
**daluyan** *n* duct
**daluyan ng tubig** *n* aqueduct
**dam** *n* dam
**damahin** *v* sense
**damayan** *v* console
**damdamin** *n* emotion, feeling
**dami** *n* bulk, quantity
**dami** *adv* lot
**damit** *n* garment
**damit ng pari** *n* cassock
**damit pantulog** *n* pajamas
**damitan** *v* dress
**damo** *n* grass, weed
**damot panloob** *n* lingerie
**dampa** *n* shack
**damuhan** *n* lawn, meadow
**dapat** *v* must, ought to
**dapit-hapon** *n* dusk
**dasal** *n* prayer
**dati** *adv* already
**dati** *adj* former
**datos** *n* data
**daungan** *n* dock, port
**daya** *n* betrayal, deceit
**dayagonal** *adj* diagonal
**dayain** *v* cheat, deceive
**dayal** *n* dial
**dayalogo** *n* dialogue
**dayametro** *n* diameter
**dayoseso** *n* diocese
**days** *n* dice
**dayuhan** *n* alien
**de- lata** *adj* canned
**dekada** *n* decade
**dekana** *n* dean
**delegado** *n* delegate
**delegasyon** *n* delegation
**delikado** *n* danger
**delikado** *adj* unsafe
**delinyante** *n* draftsman
**demanda** *n* lawsuit
**demokrasya** *n* democracy
**demonyo** *n* demon, devil
**Denmark** *n* Denmak
**dental** *adj* dental
**dentista** *n* dentist
**departamento** *n* department
**depekto** *n* flaw
**deposito** *n* deposit

**deprtasyon** *n* deportation
**deretsahan** *adj* forthright
**desenyo** *n* mosaic
**detalye** *n* detail
**di abala** *adj* unoccupied
**di alam** *adj* unaware
**di alintana** *adj* irrespective
**di ayon** *pre* against
**di ayon** *n* counter
**di dapat** *adj* improper
**di gumagalaw** *adj* immobile
**di gumagana** *v* malfunction
**di inaasahan** *adj* unexpected
**di kaaya-aya** *adj* unpleasant
**di ka-aya-aya** *adj* displeasing
**di kailangan** *adj* unnecessary
**di kanais-nais** *n* distaste, disbelief
**di kanais-nais** *adj* undesirable
**di karapat dapat** *adj* undeserved
**di kasal** *adj* unmarried
**di katulad** *adj* unlike
**di kaya** *adj* incompetent
**di kilala** *n* anonymity
**di kilala** *adj* anonymous
**di kinakalawang** *adj* rust-proof
**di maaari** *adj* impossible
**di maasahan** *adj* unreliable
**di mabilang** *adj* countless
**di mabisa** *adj* ineffective
**di madala** *v* miscarry
**di madalas** *adj* infrequent
**di magagawa** *adj* irreparable
**di magamit** *adj* inaccessible
**di mahalaga** *adj* insignificant
**di mahulaan** *adj* unpredictable
**di maiiwasan** *adj* inevitable
**di maisip** *adj* unthinkable
**di maitama** *adj* incorrigible
**di makadumi** *n* constipation
**di makatarungan** *adj* impartial
**di makatulog** *n* insomnia
**di makumbinse** *adj* implacable
**di malilimutan** *adj* unforgettable
**di maliwanag** *adj* incoherent
**di mangyayari** *adj* unlikely
**di mapalagay** *adj* restless
**di masakit** *adj* painless
**di masaya** *adj* unhappy
**di masira** *adj* unbroken
**di matalino** *adj* unwise
**di matalo** *adj* unbeatable
**di matanggihan** *adj* irresistible
**di matatalo** *adj* invincible
**di matitiis** *adj* unbearable
**di na gagaling** *adj* incurable
**di na mababawi** *adj* irrevocable
**di nag-aral** *adj* illiterate
**di nagkakamali** *adj* infallible
**di nagkaunawaan** *v* misunderstand
**di nagsisgarilyo** *n* nonsmoker
**di naibabalik** *adj* irreversible
**di nakikita** *adj* invisible
**di namamatay** *adj* immortal

D

**di naniniwala** *n* cynicism
**di napansin** *adj* unnoticed
**di napatunayan** *adj* irrefutable
**di nasaktan** *adj* unharmed
**di natunawan** *adj* indirect
**di natutunaw** *adj* insoluble
**di normal** *adj* pervert
**di pa dapat** *adj* premature
**di pag sang ayon** *n* objection
**di pagkakasundo** *n* disagreement
**di pagpigil** *n* incontinence
**di pag-sang-ayon** *n* bigotry
**di pag-sang-ayon** *adj* disagreeable
**di palagay** *n* discomfort
**di pangkaraniwan** *adj* bizarre
**di pangmatagalan** *adj* temporary
**di pantay** *adj* unequal
**di pantay-pantay** *n* inequality
**di payag** *adv* unwillingly
**di sang-ayon** *adj* discontent
**di sang-ayunan** *v* disprove
**di sapat** *adj* inadequate
**di sapilitan** *adj* optional
**di sibilisado** *adj* savage
**di sumang ayon** *v* disagree
**di tama** *adj* inaccurate
**di tiyak** *adj* ambivalent
**di totoo** *adj* artificial
**di tugma** *adj* incompatible
**di tumutubo** *adj* unprofitable
**di umano** *adv* allegedly
**di umayon** *adj* discordant
**dibdib** *n* bosom, breast
**diborsyo** *n* divorce
**dibuho** *n* pattern, sketch
**dighay** *n* belch, burp
**digmaan** *n* war
**dignidad** *n* dignity
**dikit** *n* cohesion
**diktador** *n* dictator
**diktadura** *adj* dictatorial
**dila** *n* tongue
**dilaan** *v* lick
**dilaw** *adj* yellow
**diligan** *v* water
**diligin** *v* sprinkle, spray
**diliman** *v* darken, dim
**dilis** *n* anchovy
**din** *adv* also, too
**dinadaanan** *adj* accessible
**dinamita** *n* dynamite
**dinastiya** *n* dynasty
**dingding** *n* wall
**dinurog na prutas** *n* puree
**diperensya** *n* difference
**diploma** *n* diploma
**diplomasya** *n* diplomacy
**diplomatiko** *n* diplomat
**direksyon** *n* direction
**direktor** *n* director
**diretso** *adj* direct
**disente** *adj* decency
**di-sinasadya** *adj* accidental
**disiplina** *n* discipline

**disipolo** *n* disciple
**diskarel** *n* derailment
**diskwento** *n* discount
**Disyembre** *n* December
**disyerto** *n* desert
**dito** *adv* here
**di-umano** *v* contend
**diwata** *n* fairy, goddess
**diyes** *n* dime
**diyeta** *n* diet
**doble** *adj* double, dual
**doblehin** *v* multiply
**doktrina** *n* doctrine
**dolpin** *n* dolphin
**dolyar** *n* dollar
**domestiko** *adj* domestic
**dominahin** *v* subject
**dominante** *adj* overbearing
**doon** *adv* there
**dormitoryo** *n* dormitory
**dosena** *n* dozen
**dote** *n* dowry
**dragon** *n* dragon
**dtaket** *n* jacket
**duamating** *v* show up
**dugo** *n* blood
**dugtong** *n* joint
**duguan** *n* bleeding
**duguan** *adj* bloody
**duhat** *n* blackberry
**duke** *n* duke
**dukesa** *n* duchess
**dukha** *n* peasant, poor
**dulang satiriko** *n* satire
**dulas** *n* slip
**dulo** *n* apex, tip
**dulo ng mundo** *n* pole
**dumadaan** *n* passer-by
**dumadagdag** *adj* increasing
**dumaing** *v* sigh
**dumalaw** *v* come over
**dumalo** *v* attend
**dumaong** *v* moor
**dumapa** *v* duck, prostrate
**dumating** *v* arrive, turn up
**dumausdos** *v* glide
**dumayo** *v* immigrate
**dumi** *n* dirt, filth
**dumi ng hayop** *n* dung
**dumighay** *v* belch, burp
**dumihan** *v* deface, defile
**dumugo** *v* bleed
**dungisan** *v* defame
**duo ng daliri** *n* fingertip
**dura** *n* saliva
**durugin** *v* crumble, crush
**dutsa** *n* shower
**duwag** *n* coward
**duwag** *adv* cowardly
**duwal** *n* nausea
**duwelo** *n* duel
**duyan** *n* cradle, swing
**dwende** *n* dwarf
**dyabetes** *n* diabetes

D E

**dyamante** *n* diamond
**dyari** *n* diary
**dyaryo** *n* newspaper
**dyim** *n* gymnasium
**dyosa** *n* deity

**ebanghelyo** *n* gospel
**ebidensya** *n* proof
**edipisyo** *n* edifice
**ekolohiya** *n* ecology
**ekonomiya** *n* economy
**eksamen** *n* check up
**eksena** *n* scene
**eksperimento** *n* experiment
**ekwador** *n* equator
**elegante** *n* elegance
**elegante** *adj* elegant
**elektresista** *n* electrician
**elektrika** *adj* electric
**elektronika** *adj* electronic
**elementarya** *adj* elementary
**elemento** *n* element
**elepante** *n* elephant
**emabahada** *n* embassy
**embahador** *n* ambassador
**embalsamuhin** *v* embalm
**emerald** *n* emerald
**empanada** *n* pie
**emperador** *n* emperor
**emperatris** *n* empress
**Enero** *n* January
**engkanto** *n* spell
**entablado** *n* grandstand
**epekto** *n* effect
**epilepsi** *n* epilepsy
**epron** *n* apron
**erehe** *adj* heretic
**ermitanyo** *n* hermit
**eroplano** *n* plane
**eskultor** *n* sculptor
**eskultura** *n* sculpture
**espada** *n* sword
**Espanya** *n* Spain
**espanyol** *n* Spaniard
**espanyol** *adj* Spanish
**espesyalidad** *n* specialty
**espesyalista** *n* craftsman
**espitritu** *n* spirit
**espiya** *n* spy
**espongha** *n* sponge
**espsyal** *adj* de luxe
**estapadora** *n* delinquent
**estatwa** *n* statue
**estima** *adj* approximate
**estima** *n* calculation
**estimahin** *v* calculate
**etika** *n* ethics
**etiketa** *n* label

**eyker** *n* acre
**Eyuropa** *n* Europe

# G

**gaas** *n* gas
**gabay** *n* goalkeeper
**gabay sa hagdan** *n* handrail
**gabi** *n* evening, night
**gabutil** *n* speck
**gagamba** *n* spider
**gahaman** *adj* avaricious
**gala** *n* wanderer
**galamay** *n* tentacle
**galaw** *n* move, movement
**galawin** *v* mobilize, move
**galing sa** *v* come from
**galing sa labas** *adj* extraneous
**galit** *n* anger, rage
**galit** *adj* angry, mad
**galit na galit** *adv* furiously
**galitin** *v* embitter
**galon** *n* gallon
**gamit** *n* equipment
**gamit pangkama** *n* bedding
**gamitan** *v* equip
**gamitin** *v* use, utilize
**gamitin lahat** *v* exhaust
**gamitin ulit** *v* recycle
**gamot** *n* cure, remedy
**gampanan** *v* assume
**gamutin** *v* heal, treat
**gana** *n* appetite
**ganap** *n* accuracy
**ganda** *n* beauty
**gang** *n* gang
**gansa** *n* geese, goose
**ganti** *n* retaliation
**gantihan** *v* recompense
**gantimpala** *n* incentive
**ganun pa man** *adv* furthermore
**ganundin** *adv* moreover
**ganunpaman** *c* however
**ganyan** *adj* such
**garahe** *n* garage
**garapal** *adj* rowdy
**garik** *n* ivory
**garison** *n* garrison
**gasa** *n* gauze
**gasgas** *n* scratch
**gasolina** *n* gasoline
**gastos** *n* expenditure
**gastosin** *v* squander
**gatas** *n* milk
**gatilyo** *n* trigger
**gawa** *n* make
**gawa sa bahay** *adj* homemade
**gawain** *n* affair, deed
**gawain** *v* toil
**gawain bahay** *n* housework

E G

G

**gawan** *v* spruce up
**gawan ng aksyon** *v* resolve
**gawgaw** *n* starch
**gawin** *v* achieve, make, execute
**gawin muli** *v* remodel
**gawin na** *v* do, rebuild
**gawin pino** *v* refine
**gawin sa makina** *v* mechanize
**gawin ulit** *v* redouble
**gawing banal** *v* sanctify
**gawing huwad** *v* falsify
**gawing huwaran** *v* standardize
**gawing ilado** *v* freeze
**gawing kalabisan** *v* overdo
**gawing kilala** *v* popularize
**gawing mali** *v* malpractice
**gawing moderno** *v* modernize
**gawing normal** *v* normalize
**gawing panis** *v* pasteurize
**gawing payak** *v* simplify
**gawint banal** *v* canonize
**gayahin** *v* replicate
**gayuma** *n* enticement
**gayundin** *adv* likewise
**gayunpaman** *c* whereupon
**genekolohiya** *n* gynecology
**gera** *n* battle
**gerahin** *v* battle
**gerilya** *n* guerrilla
**gibain** *v* demolish
**gilagid** *n* gum
**gilid** *n* border, edge
**gilingan** *n* mill
**gilingin** *v* grind
**giliw** *n* sweetheart
**gilotina** *n* guillotine
**gimbalin** *v* astound
**gimik** *n* gimmick
**ginang** *n* madam
**ginaw** *n* chill
**ginawa** *v* accomplish
**ginawang labis** *adj* overdone
**giniginaw** *v* chill
**giniling** *n* mincemeat
**ginintuan** *adj* golden
**ginising** *v* awake
**ginoo** *n* gentleman, sir
**ginto** *n* gold
**ginupit** *n* clipping, cut out
**gisantes** *n* pea
**gising** *adj* awake
**gisingin** *v* await, rouse
**gitara** *n* guitar
**gitara ng anghel** *n* harp
**gitling** *n* hyphen
**gitna** *n* axis, center
**gitnang araw** *n* midday
**gitnang bayan** *n* mainland
**glandula** *n* gland
**globo** *n* globe, sphere
**gobernador** *n* governor
**goma** *n* rubber
**gomang pandilig** *n* hose
**gora** *n* cap

**graba** *n* gravel
**gramo** *n* gram
**granada** *n* grenade
**granate** *n* granite
**grasa** *n* grease
**grasya** *n* grace
**Greko** *n* Greece
**Grinlandya** *n* Greenland
**gripo** *n* faucet
**Griyego** *adj* Greek
**groseri** *n* groceries
**groto** *n* grotto
**grupo** *n* team
**grupo ng tao** *n* pool
**gubat** *n* forest, jungle
**gugulan** *v* finance
**guhit** *n* drawing
**guhitan** *v* cross out
**guhitan** *adj* striped
**gulang** *n* age
**gulat** *n* surprise
**gulatin** *v* astonish
**gulay** *n* artichoke, beet
**gulayan** *n* vegetation
**gulayin** *v* vegetable
**gulo** *n* mutiny, riot
**gulong** *n* wheel
**gulugod** *n* spine
**guluhin** *v* complicate
**gumagaling** *v* recover
**gumagamit** *n* user
**gumanap** *v* act
**gumanti** *v* avenge, hit back
**gumapang** *v* crawl, creep
**gumastos** *v* spend
**gumawa** *v* compose, create
**gumawa ng batas** *v* legislate
**gumigising** *adj* rousing
**gumising** *v* wake up
**gumulong** *v* roll
**guni-guni** *adj* fancy
**guni-guni** *n* fantasy
**gunita** *n* memory
**gunitain** *v* recollect
**gunting** *n* scissors
**gupitin** *v* clip, shear
**gurilya** *n* gorilla
**guro** *n* teacher
**gusali** *n* building
**gusgusin** *adj* shabby
**gusot** *n* controversy
**gutom** *n* hunger
**gutom** *adj* hungry
**guwantes** *n* glove
**guwapo** *adj* handsome
**guya** *n* cub
**gwardya** *n* sentry

H

**haba** *n* length
**habaan** *v* lengthen
**habang** *adv* meanwhile
**habang** *c* while
**habang panahon** *adv* forever
**habol** *n* chase
**habulin** *v* pursue
**hadlangan** *v* block
**hagdan** *n* stair
**hagdanan** *n* stairs
**hagilap** *n* search
**hagilapin** *v* search
**hagulgol** *n* sob
**hagupit** *n* lash, whip
**hagupitin** *v* flog, lash
**hahabol** *v* catch up
**haharapin** *pre* facing
**hakbang** *n* pace, step
**hakutin** *v* haul
**halaga** *n* amount, cost
**halagahan** *v* cost
**halaman** *n* shrub
**halamanan** *n* bush
**halamang opyo** *n* poppy
**halata** *adj* obvious
**haligi** *n* foundation
**halik** *n* kiss
**halika** *v* come
**halikan** *v* kiss
**halimaw** *n* dinosaur
**halimbawa** *n* example
**halimuyak** *n* scent
**halina** *v* charm
**halinghing** *n* groan
**halo** *n* blend, mixture
**halos** *adv* almost, nearly
**haluan** *v* adulterate
**haluin** *v* mix, stir
**hamak** *v* base
**hamak** *adj* wretched
**hamakin** *v* despise
**hamburger** *n* hamburger
**hamog** *n* dew, moisture
**hamon** *n* ham
**hampas-lupa** *n* savagery
**hamunin** *v* challenge
**hanap-buhay** *n* employment
**hanapin** *v* browse, seek
**hanay** *n* column
**handa** *n* readiness
**handaan** *n* feast
**hangad** *n* purpose
**hangarin** *n* intention
**hangarin** *v* mean
**hanggahan** *n* base
**hangganan** *n* boundary
**hanggang sa** *pre* till
**hangin** *n* air
**hanginan** *v* air
**hango** *n* excerpt
**hantungan** *n* goal

**hapag** *n* banquet
**haplusin** *v* caress
**hapon** *n* Japan
**hapon** *adj* Japanese
**hapunan** *n* dinner
**harana** *n* serenade
**harang** *n* barrier
**harangan** *pre* barring
**harangan** *v* cordon off
**harapan** *n* bumper, front
**harapan ng barko** *n* prow
**harapin** *v* face up to
**hardin** *n* garden
**hardinero** *n* gardener
**hari** *n* king
**hasmin** *n* jasmine
**hatiin** *v* divide
**hatinggabi** *n* midnight
**hatol** *n* verdict
**hatulan ng mali** *v* misjudge
**hawahan** *v* infect
**hawak** *v* grip, grasp
**hawakan** *v* handle
**hawla** *n* cage
**hayagan** *adv* publicly
**haydrodyen** *n* hydrogen
**hayena** *n* hyena
**hayop** *n* animal
**hayop sa gubat** *n* wildlife
**helmet** *n* helmet
**helo** *e* hello
**Helohiya** *n* geology
**heneral** *n* general
**henetika** *adj* genetic
**henyo** *n* genius
**heograpiya** *n* geography
**Heometriya** *n* geometry
**hibla** *n* fiber
**higad** *n* caterpillar
**higante** *n* giant
**higanti** *n* reprisal
**higit** *adj* better, major
**higit pa** *adv* rather
**higit sa isa** *n* compound
**higit sa kahat** *adv* mainly
**higitan** *v* exceed
**higop** *n* sip
**higt sa** *adj* more
**higupin** *v* sip
**hika** *n* asthma
**hikab** *n* yawn
**hikain** *adj* asthmatic
**hikaw** *n* earring
**hila** *n* stretch
**hilaga** *n* north
**hilahin** *v* drag, pull
**hilano** *n* gypsy
**hilaw** *adj* raw
**hilig** *n* tendency
**hilik** *n* snore
**hiling** *n* request
**hilingin** *v* implore
**hilo** *v* daze
**hilo** *adj* dizzy

H

**himagsikan** *n* insurrection
**himasin** *v* caress
**himatay** *n* faint
**himayin** *v* thresh
**himig** *n* melody
**himno** *n* hymn
**himukin** *v* induce, urge

**hinabi** *adj* woven
**hinadlangan** *v* repel
**hinagupit** *v* lash out
**hinaharap** *n* frontage
**hinaing** *n* woes
**hinala** *n* suspicion
**hinalo** *n* concoction
**hinalughog** *v* ransack
**hinanakit** *n* gripe
**hinangad** *adv* purposely
**hinarangan** *v* blockade
**hindi** *adv* neither
**hindi bagay** *adj* misfit
**hindi dapat** *adj* unsuitable
**hindi eksakto** *adj* imprecise
**hindi halata** *adj* conspicuous
**hindi kasali** *adj* exempt
**hindi kaya** *n* inability
**hindi kaya** *adj* incapable
**hindi lasing** *adj* sober
**hindi mabasa** *adj* illegible
**hindi madalas** *adj* irregular
**hindi madalas** *n* disparity
**hindi mahalaga** *adj* trivial
**hindi mahipo** *adj* untouchable
**hindi makatao** *adj* inhuman
**hindi makatiis** *n* intolerance
**hindi makayanan** *adj* intolerable
**hindi mapanira** *adj* harmless
**hindi mapapalitan** *adj* immutable
**hindi mapatawad** *n* misgiving
**hindi matantya** *adj* incalculable
**hindi matapat** *adj* insincere
**hindi matatag** *adj* unsteady
**hindi nababagay** *adj* unfit
**hindi nagustuhan** *v* displease
**hindi nagwagi** *v* fail
**hindi naka tala** *adj* off-the-record
**hindi nakita** *v* overlook
**hindi naniniwala** *n* atheist
**hindi normal** *adj* abnormal
**hindi obligado** *n* exemption
**hindi opisyal** *adv* unofficially
**hindi pantay** *n* imbalance
**hindi patas** *n* unfairness
**hindi pinayagan** *v* disapprove
**hindi pino** *adj* crude
**hindi pormal** *adj* informal
**hindi pormal** *n* informality
**hindi praktikal** *adj* impractical
**hindi sang-ayon** *adj* bigot
**hindi tama** *adj* inappropriate
**hindi tapat** *adj* disloyal
**hindi tapat** *n* disloyalty
**hindi totoo** *adj* unheard-of
**hindi tunay** *adj* unreal
**hinging** *n* buzz

**hinid** *adv* not
**hinid dapat** *adj* undue
**hinid kailanman** *adv* never
**hinid kailanman** *adj* distrustful
**hinid makatwiran** *adj* illogical
**hinid maloloko** *adj* foolproof
**hinid normal** *adj* retarded
**hinid paggana** *n* malfunction
**hinihingal** *adj* puffy
**hinihipo** *adj* touching
**hinimatay** *v* faint
**hininga** *n* breath
**hiniram** *v* borrow
**hinlalaki** *n* thumb
**hinog** *adj* ripe
**hintayan** *v* stop over
**hintuan** *n* parking
**hinuha** *n* speculation
**hinuli** *v* catch, siege
**hipag** *n* sister-in-law
**hipan** *v* blow
**hipnosis** *n* hypnosis
**hipo** *n* texture
**hipon** *n* shrimp
**hipuin** *v* touch
**hiramin** *v* lend, appoint
**hirapa** *n* giraffe
**hirarkiya** *n* hierarchy
**hiringgilya** *n* syringe
**hispaniko** *adj* Hispanic
**histerikal** *adj* hysterical
**histerya** *n* hysteria
**hita** *n* thigh
**hiwa** *n* cut, slice
**hiwain** *v* slice, slit
**hiwalay** *adj* estranged
**hiya** *n* blush, shyness
**hormon** *n* hormone
**hubad** *adj* bare, naked
**hudyat** *n* password
**hudyo** *n* Jew, Jewish
**hugis** *n* contour
**hugis globo** *n* globule
**hugis tatsulok** *n* cone
**hugutin** *v* pull out
**hugutin** *n* crater, ditch
**hukayan ng bato** *n* quarry
**hukayin** *v* dig
**hukbo** *n* judge
**hukuman** *n* court, tribunal
**hula** *v* forecast, guess
**hulaan** *n* anticipation
**hulaan** *v* guess, predict, anticipate
**huli** *n* delay
**huli** *adj* last
**hulihin** *v* apprehend
**huling babala** *n* ultimatum
**hulugan** *n* installment
**Hulyo** *n* July
**humagulgol** *v* sob
**humahabol** *adj* catching
**humalinghing** *v* groan
**humampas** *v* strike

**humandusay** *v* sprawl
**humanga** *v* admire
**humangin** *v* wind
**humayo** *v* set out
**humilata** *v* sprawl
**humilik** *v* snore
**humiling** *v* request, wish
**huminga** *v* breathe
**humingal** *v* gasp
**humiwalay** *n* sever
**humiwalay** *v* splinter
**humukot** *v* crouch
**humuni** *v* hum
**hunos** *n* drawer
**Hunyo** *n* June
**huramentado** *adv* berserk
**hurno** *v* bake
**hustisya** *n* justice
**husto** *adj* formal
**hustuhin** *v* formalize
**hutukin** *v* bend down
**huwad** *adj* fake, phoney
**huwad** *n* forgery
**huwag isali** *v* exclude
**huwag pansinin** *v* ignore
**huwarin** *v* forge
**Huwebes** *n* Thursday

**iabot** *v* hand in
**ialay** *v* dedicate
**iangat** *v* promote, upgrade
**iangkas** *v* hitch up
**iapgtanggol** *v* defend
**iatas** *v* relegate
**iatras** *adv* backwards
**iayon sa batas** *v* legalize
**iayos** *v* adjust, set
**iba** *adj* other
**iba** *n* aversion
**ibaba** *n* bottom
**ibaba** *v* bring down
**ibaba** *adv* downstairs
**ibaba** *v* unload
**ibaba ang ranggo** *v* demote
**ibabad** *v* marinate, soak
**ibabaw** *n* top
**ibahagi** *v* share
**ibahin** *v* distort, differ
**iba-iba** *adj* diverse
**iba-iba** *n* diversity
**ibalangkas** *v* outline
**ibalik** *v* bring back
**ibaling** *v* tilt
**ibalita** *v* herald
**ibang bansa** *adv* overseas
**ibangketa** *v* curb
**ibasura** *v* waste

**ibig** *n* gusto
**ibig** *v* want
**ibig - sabihin** *v* connote
**ibigay** *v* hand over
**ibigay ang buod** *v* summarize
**ibilad** *v* bask
**ibiling** *v* flip
**ibinbin** *v* withhold
**ibitay** *v* lynch
**ibitay sa koryente** *v* electrify
**ibitin** *v* suspend
**ibon** *n* bird, sparrow
**ibong dagat** *n* gull
**ibote** *v* bottle
**iboto** *v* elect
**ibsan** *v* alleviate
**ibugaw** *v* pander
**ibuhos** *v* pour
**ibulgar** *v* unfold
**i-bungkos** *v* bundle
**ibunyag** *v* expose
**idagundong** *v* rumble
**idahilan** *v* excuse
**idamay** *v* incriminate
**idaong** *v* dock
**idayal** *v* dial
**i-de lata** *v* can
**ideolohiya** *n* ideology
**idetalye** *v* detail
**ideya** *n* concept
**idikit** *v* adhere
**idlip** *n* doze
**idolo** *n* idol
**idugtong** *v* merge
**iduyan** *v* swing
**idyoma** *n* idiom
**igahin** *v* contrast
**igalang** *v* respect
**igapos** *v* bind
**igarahe** *v* park
**igatong** *v* fuel
**igiit** *adj* imposing
**i-gitna** *v* center
**igos** *n* fig
**igsian** *v* debrief
**iguhit** *v* draft
**ihabi** *v* weave
**ihagis** *v* cast
**ihakbang** *v* pace
**ihalo** *v* blend
**ihanay** *v* file
**ihandog** *v* dedicate
**ihaw** *v* grill
**ihawin** *v* broil
**ihayag** *v* press
**ihi** *n* urine
**ihilig** *v* incline
**ihip** *n* blow
**ihiwalay** *v* isolate
**ihugis** *v* cast
**ihuli** *v* last
**iiwanan** *adj* remaining
**ikabit** *v* attach, connect
**ikadena** *v* chain

**ikalahati** *v* halve
**ikalat** *v* disperse, scatter, spread
**ikandado** *v* bolt
**ikariton** *v* cart
**ikasal** *v* wed
**ikaspangyayari** *n* possibility
**ikaw** *pro* you, yourself
**ikiran** *n* reel
**ikiskis** *v* rub
**iklian** *adv* briefly
**ikot** *n* cycle
**ikotin** *v* turn
**ikula** *v* bleach
**ikulong** *v* imprison, confine
**ikumpol** *v* cluster
**ikutin** *v* spin
**ikwadro** *v* frame
**ilaan** *v* reserve
**iladlad** *v* display
**ilado** *adj* frozen, stale
**ilagan** *v* dodge
**ilagay** *v* indicate, put
**ilagay sa isip** *v* instil
**ilahad** *v* disclose
**ilalim** *pre* under, below
**ilantad** *v* unmask
**ilapag** *n* lay
**ilarawan** *v* describe
**ilaw** *n* beam, light
**ilaw sa kalye** *n* streetlight
**ilaw sa poste** *n* lamppost
**ilawan** *v* illuminate
**ilibing** *v* bury
**iligaw** *v* stray, divert
**iligtas** *v* liberate
**ilihim** *adj* discreet
**iliko** *v* curve
**ilimbag** *v* publish
**ilista** *v* list
**ilog** *n* river
**ilong** *n* nose
**ilubog** *v* sink, plunge, submerge
**ilupi** *v* fold
**iluwas** *v* expel
**imatamis** *v* sweeten
**imbakan ng tubis** *n* reservoir
**imbensyon** *n* invention
**imbentaryo** *n* inventory
**imbentuhin** *v* invent
**imbestigahan** *v* interrogate
**imbi** *v* base
**imburnal** *n* sewer
**imigrasyon** *n* immigration
**imoral** *adj* immoral
**imperyalismo** *n* imperialism
**impluensa** *n* influence
**imprenta** *n* print
**impyerno** *n* hell
**imungkahi** *v* suggest
**ina** *n* mother
**inaalam** *adv* abreast
**inaasahan** *n* expectation
**inaayawan** *adj* dreaded
**inahing manok** *n* hen

**inakusahan** *v* accuse
**inalis ang buhol** *v* disentangle
**inalisan ng armas** *v* disarm
**inamag** *v* mold
**inawat** *v* arbitrate
**inay** *n* mom
**industriya** *n* industry
**ingat - yaman** *n* treasurer
**ingatan** *v* care
**ingay** *n* noise
**inggit** *n* envy
**inggoy** *n* chimpanzee
**Inglatera** *n* England
**inglis** *adj* English
**inhinyero** *n* engineer
**iniba** *v* avert
**inihaw** *n* grill, roast
**iniksian** *v* brief
**inilapag** *v* lay
**inisin** *v* annoy, irritate
**init** *n* warmth
**init ng ulo** *n* temper
**initin** *v* heat, scorch
**initin** *n* heat
**iniwan** *v* remain
**iniwanan** *adj* deserted
**insekto** *n* bug, insect
**insenso** *n* incense
**insiltuhin** *v* insult
**inspektor** *n* inspector
**inspirasyon** *n* inspiration
**insulto** *n* insult
**intriga** *n* intrigue
**inuhaw** *v* thirst
**inukit** *v* carve
**inulat** *adv* reportedly
**inumin** *n* drink, juice
**ipaabot** *v* relay
**ipaalam** *v* inform
**ipabigat** *v* pressure
**ipadala** *v* dispatch, send
**ipadulas** *v* slide
**ipagawa** *v* assign
**ipagbawal** *v* ban, prohibit
**ipagdiwang** *v* celebrate
**ipaghawig** *v* compare
**ipaghele** *n* lull
**ipag-higante** *v* vindicate
**ipagitna** *v* centralize
**ipagkait** *v* deprive
**ipagkait** *n* deprivation
**ipagkaloob** *v* bestow, grant
**ipagkanulo** *v* betray
**ipaglaban** *v* stand for
**ipagpag** *v* flutter
**ipagpaliban** *v* postpone
**ipagpaliban** *n* reprieve
**ipag-paliban** *v* defer
**ipagpatuloy** *v* persist, resume
**ipagsama** *v* assimilate
**ipagtanggol** *n* defiance
**ipag-utos** *v* decree
**ipahatid** *v* dispatch
**ipahayag** *v* declare

I

**ipahiwatig** *v* hint
**ipahiya** *v* embarrass
**ipakatiwala** *v* entrust
**ipakilala** *v* introduce
**ipakita** *v* demonstrate
**ipako sa krus** *v* crucify
**ipakulong** *v* detain
**ipalagay** *v* imagine, picture
**ipalit** *n* change
**ipaliwanag** *v* explain
**ipaloob** *v* compound
**ipamahagi** *v* dispense
**ipamalita** *v* advertise
**ipamana** *v* bequeath
**ipamigay** *v* dispose
**ipamudmod** *v* hand out
**ipanganak** *v* be born
**ipanganak** *n* birth
**ipantay** *v* balance, level
**ipa-putol** *v* disconnect
**ipasa** *v* transmit
**ipaseguro** *v* insure
**ipasok** *v* take in
**ipaspas** *v* wag
**ipasya** *v* rule
**ipasyal** *v* stroll
**ipatupad** *v* enforce, implement
**ipawalag-bisa** *v* repeal
**ipawalang-bisa** *v* annul
**ipinagbawal** *v* forbid
**ipinailalim** *v* underlie
**ipinid** *v* lock
**ipis** *n* cockroach
**ipmamahagi** *v* distribute
**ipon** *n* savings
**iposas** *v* handcuff
**i-preno** *v* brake
**iprito** *v* fry
**ipukol** *v* hurl
**ipunin** *v* compile, gather
**ipunla** *v* fertilize
**ireseta** *v* prescribe
**Irlanda** *n* Ireland
**Irlandes** *adj* Irish
**isa** *adj* one, singular
**isa lamang** *adv* solely
**isa telebisyon** *v* televise
**isaad** *v* stipulate
**isa-alang-alang** *v* consider
**isabay** *v* synchronize
**isabit** *v* dangle, hang
**isabit** *n* latch
**isabog** *v* dissipate
**isabotahe** *v* sabotage
**isadula** *v* dramatize
**isaganap** *v* fulfill
**isagwan** *v* paddle
**isa-isa** *adv* step-by-step
**isa-isahan** *v* enumerate
**isa-isahin** *v* itemize
**isa-isan tabi** *v* brush aside
**isaisip** *v* envisage
**isakay** *v* transport
**isako** *v* sack

**isaksak** *v* plug, switch
**isalansan** *v* amass, stock
**isalarawan** *v* portray
**isalin** *v* translate
**isama** *v* include, affix
**isandal** *v* recline
**isang bagay** *pro* something
**isang bahagi** *n* segment
**isang beses** *c* once
**isang daan** *adj* hundred
**isang dakot** *n* handful
**isang gawi** *n* facet
**isang hari** *n* czar
**isang kaisipan** *adj* singleminded
**isang kamay** *adj* singlehanded
**isang kutsara** *n* spoonful
**isang lalaki** *n* buck
**isang makina** *n* device
**isang pangyayari** *n* instance
**isang paraan** *adv* someway
**isang tao** *pro* somebody
**isang tunog** *n* diphthong
**isangkot** *v* implicate
**isangla** *v* pawn
**isapin** *v* pad
**isara** *v* shut
**isa't- isa** *adv* mutually
**isatao** *v* personify
**isat-isa** *adj* each other
**isatitik** *v* abbreviate
**isauli** *v* take back
**isaulo** *v* master
**isda** *n* cod, fish, trout
**isdang espada** *n* swordfish
**i-seguro** *v* underwrite
**isgaw** *v* sound out
**isigaw** *v* exclaim
**isinambulat** *v* divulge
**isingit** *v* insert
**isip** *n* thought, mind
**isip bata** *adj* puerile
**isipin** *v* decipher, discern
**isiwalat** *v* unravel
**iskandalo** *n* scandal
**iskandaluhin** *v* scandalize
**iskinita** *n* alley
**iskursyon** *n* outing
**isla** *n* island
**ispisyal** *adj* exquisite
**istambay** *n* bystander
**istante** *n* shelf, shelves
**istasyon** *n* station
**istorbohin** *v* harass
**isuko** *v* abdicate
**isulat** *v* record, transcribe
**isuma** *v* sum up
**isumpa** *v* condemn, curse
**isunod** *v* back up
**isuot** *v* wear
**isuplong** *v* denounce
**itaas** *v* hoist, raise
**itaas ang antas** *v* boost
**itabi** *v* put aside
**itago** *v* conceal, hide

**itagos** *v* permeate
**itagubilin** *v* recommend
**itakda** *v* assign
**itakwil** *v* repudiate
**italaga** *v* designate, ordain
**italastas** *v* announce
**itali** *v* buckle up, tie
**italikod** *v* back
**Italya** *n* Italy
**Italyano** *adj* Italian
**itama** *v* correct
**itambak** *v* heap, pile
**itanggi** *v* deny, disclaim
**itanghal** *v* stage
**itanim** *v* implant, plant
**itanim muli** *v* transplant
**itaon** *v* coincide
**itapat** *v* align
**itapon** *v* discard, dump
**itasa** *v* mug
**itatag** *v* establish
**itayo** *v* mount
**iteneraryo** *n* itinerary
**itigil** *v* cease, halt
**itiklop** *v* flex
**itim na ibon** *n* raven
**itimo** *v* instil
**itinatangi** *adj* favorite
**itinaya** *v* stake
**itinda** *v* sell
**itinigil** *v* adjourn
**itiwalag** *v* dismiss
**itlog** *n* egg
**ito** *adj* this
**itono** *v* tune
**itsura** *n* appearance
**itulad** *v* equate, like
**itulak** *v* push
**ituloy** *v* continue
**ituon** *v* focus on
**itupi** *v* crease
**ituro** *v* direct, teach
**iukit** *v* engrave
**iuna** *v* advance
**i-utos** *v* delegate
**iuwi** *v* carry out
**iwaksi** *v* disown
**iwala** *v* diminish, lose
**iwan** *v* leave
**iwan** *n* remains
**iwanan** *v* abandon, elude
**iwasto** *v* project
**iyak** *n* cry
**iyo** *adj* your
**iyon** *adj* that

# K

**kaagad** *adv* abruptly
**kaagtingan** *n* thrill
**kaakit-akit** *adj* magical
**ka-akit-akit** *adj* attractive
**kaalaman** *n* mastery, skill
**kaasiman** *n* acidity
**kaaya-aya** *adj* graceful
**kaayunan** *n* cooperation
**kababaang-loob** *n* meekness
**kababaihan** *adj* feminine
**kababakaghan** *n* marvel
**kababayan** *n* countryman
**kabag** *n* heartburn
**kabahagdan** *n* denominator
**kabahagi** *n* shareholder
**kabahaginan** *adv* partially
**kabahayan** *n* neighborhood
**kabaitan** *adv* kindly
**kabaligtaran** *n* opposite
**kabaliktaran** *adj* averse
**kabalituanan** *n* paradox
**kabaliwan** *n* craziness, folly
**kabalyero** *n* knight
**kabanalan** *n* sanctity, piety
**kabanata** *n* sequel
**kabangisan** *n* ferocity
**kabantugan** *n* fame
**kabaong** *n* casket, coffin
**kabataan** *n* childhood, youth
**kabayanan** *n* downtown
**kabayanihan** *n* heroism
**kabayaran** *n* fee, payment
**kabayo** *n* colt, horse
**kabibi** *n* clam, shell
**kabigatan** *n* heaviness
**kabigha-bighani** *adj* alluring
**kabiguan** *n* frustration
**kabilang bayan** *n* enclave
**kabinete** *n* cabinet
**kabisahin** *v* memorize
**kabit** *n* mistress
**kable** *n* cable
**kabo** *n* corporal
**kabuan** *adj* gross
**kabuhayan** *n* business
**kabukiran** *adj* agricultural
**kabulkan** *adj* rotten
**kabulukan** *adj* corrupt
**kabute** *n* mushroom
**kabutihan** *n* kindness
**kabutihang - loob** *n* generosity
**kabuuan** *adj* absolute, total
**kadakilaan** *n* greatness
**kadalasan** *n* frequency
**kadamitan** *n* clothing
**kadena** *n* chain
**kadiliman** *n* darkness
**ka-duda-duda** *adl* doubtful
**kagabi** *adv* last night
**kagahaman** *n* avarice
**kagalingan** *n* excellence

**kagamitan** *n* belongings
**kaganapan** *n* fulfillment
**kagandahan** *n* goodness
**kagaspangan** *n* rudeness
**kagatin** *n* bit, bite, sting
**kagawad** *n* jury
**kagila-gilalas** *adj* wonderful
**kagiliw-giliw** *adj* prodigious
**kagimba-gimbal** *adj* astounding
**kaginhawahan** *n* convenience
**kagitingan** *n* nobility
**kagulat-gulat** *n* amazement
**kaguluhan** *n* chaos, havoc
**kagustuhan** *n* preference
**kaha** *n* case
**kahalagahan** *n* priority
**kahalayn** *n* obscenity
**kahalili** *n* proxy
**kahanga-hanga** *adj* marvelous
**kahapon** *adv* yesterday
**kaharian** *n* kingdom
**kahawig** *adj* comparative
**kahera** *n* cashier
**kahihiyan** *n* disgrace
**kahiligan** *n* fondness
**kahilingan** *n* petition, wish
**kahinaan** *n* weakness
**kahinahunan** *n* prudence
**kahindik-hindik** *adj* daunting
**kahinhinan** *n* modesty
**kahirapan** *adj* destitute
**kahirapan** *n* hardship
**kahit alin** *adj* either
**kahit ano** *adj* whatever
**kahit kailan** *adv* whenever
**kahit na** *adj* even
**kahit na** *c* though
**kahit na ano** *c* whether
**kahit papano** *pro* anyhow
**kahit saan** *adv* elsewhere
**kahit sino** *pro* anybody
**kahon** *n* box
**kahoy** *n* wood, timber
**kahulihan** *adj* final
**kahulugan** *n* definition
**kahusayan** *n* eloquence
**kahuwaran** *n* falsehood
**kaibahan** *n* contrast
**kaibigan** *n* friend, pal
**kaibigang babae** *n* girlfriend
**kaibiganin** *v* befriend
**kaibig-ibig** *adj* amiable
**kailaliman** *pre* below
**kailan** *adv* when
**kailan man** *adv* ever
**kailangan** *v* have to
**kailangan** *n* necessity, need
**kailanganin** *v* require
**kainaman** *adj* fair, sizable
**kainan** *n* diner
**kairlagan** *n* splendor
**kaisa-isa** *adj* unique
**kaisipan** *n* mentality
**kaitaasan** *n* altitude

**kaitiman** *n* blackness
**kaiyahan** *n* satisfaction
**kakaiba** *adj* authentic; odd, strange, striking
**kaka-iba** *adj* distinct
**kakaibahan** *n* odds
**kakalakihan** *v* outgrow
**kakampi** *n* ally
**kakanin** *n* delicacy
**kakapalan** *n* density
**kakatwa** *adj* queer
**kakaunti** *adj* meager
**kakaw** *n* cocoa
**kakayahn** *n* means
**kakayanan** *n* ability
**kakayanan** *adj* affordable
**kakilala** *n* acquaintance
**kakuilangan** *n* hangup
**kakukalangan** *n* setback
**kakulangan** *adj* deficient
**kakulangan** *v* hang up
**kakutsabain** *v* conspire
**kalaban** *n* adversary
**kalaban** *adj* hostile
**kalabasa** *n* pumpkin
**kalabaw** *n* buffalo
**kalabisan** *adj* excessive
**kalabisan na** *adj* outstretched
**kalabit** *n* tap
**kalabuan** *adj* bleak
**kalagayan** *n* situation, status
**kalagin** *v* unfasten
**kalagitnaan** *adj* central
**kalahati** *n* half
**kalakal** *n* merchandise
**kalakaran** *n* norm
**kalakasan** *n* energy
**kalalabasan** *n* ramification
**kalaliman** *adj* profound, deep
**kalamanan** *n* carnage
**kalambutan** *n* tenderness
**kalamidad** *n* calamity
**kalamnan** *n* muscle
**kalampagin** *v* rattle
**kalan** *n* range
**kalang** *n* wedge
**kalangitan** *n* heaven
**kalansay** *n* skeleton
**kalaparan** *adv* widely
**kalapati** *n* dove, pigeon
**kalapitan** *n* proximity
**kalase** *n* class
**kalasin** *v* undo
**kalasingan** *n* drunkenness
**kalaswaan** *n* depravity
**kalat** *n* mess, spill
**kalawakan** *n* magnitude
**kalawang** *n* rust
**kalawangin** *adj* rusty
**kalawit** *n* sickle
**kalayaan** *n* freedom
**kalaykay** *n* rake
**kalbo** *adj* bald
**kalbuhin** *v* inundate

K

**kaldero** *n* boiler
**kalendaryo** *n* calendar
**kalibre** *n* caliber
**kalidad** *n* quality
**kaligayahan** *n* happiness
**kaligtasan** *n* safety
**kalikasan** *n* nature
**kalimutan** *v* forget
**kalinangan** *adj* cultural
**kalinawan** *n* clarification
**kalinga** *n* protection
**kalingain** *v* protect
**kalinisan** *n* cleanliness
**kalis** *n* chalice
**kalmahin** *v* placate
**kalmutin** *v* claw
**kalokohan** *n* prank
**kaloob** *n* grant
**kaloob-looban** *adj* interior
**kaloriya** *n* calorie
**kalubhaan** *n* gravity
**kalugin** *v* shake
**kalugod-lugod** *adv* nicely
**kaluluwa** *n* soul
**kalumaam** *n* antiquity
**kalumaan** *adj* obsolete
**kalungkutan** *n* loneliness
**kalungkutan** *adj* sorrowful
**kalunos-lunos** *adj* miserable
**kalupitan** *n* atrocity
**kaluwagan** *n* leniency
**kaluwalhatian** *n* glory
**kalye** *n* avenue, stree
**kalyo** *adj* callous
**kama** *n* bed
**kamag-anak** *n* relative
**kamag-aral** *n* classmate
**Kamahalan** *n* Highness
**kamahal-mahalan** *n* majesty
**kamakailan** *adj* recent
**kamalasan** *n* adversity
**kamalian** *n* discrepancy
**kamandag** *n* venom
**kamang-mangan** *n* ignorance
**kamao** *n* fist
**kamatayan** *n* death
**kamatis** *n* tomato
**kamay** *n* hand
**kamayan** *n* handshake
**kambal** *n* twin
**kambing** *n* goat
**kambyo** *n* rudder, gear
**kamelyo** *n* camel
**kamera** *n* camera
**kami** *pro* we
**kamisadentro** *n* shirt
**kamkamin** *v* usurp
**kamote** *n* yam
**kampana** *n* bell
**kampanya** *n* campaign
**kampeon** *n* champ
**kampihan** *v* ally
**kampo** *n* camp
**kamuhian** *v* detest, hate

**kamuhi-muhi** *adj* hateful
**kamukha** *n* likeness
**kamunoy** *n* quicksand
**kamutin** *v* scratch
**kanal** *n* canal, groove
**kanan** *adv* right
**kanaryo** *n* canary
**kandado** *n* bolt, lock
**kandidato** *n* candidate
**kandila** *n* candle
**kandungan** *n* lap
**kanela** *n* cinnamon
**kanggaro** *n* kangaroo
**kanggrena** *n* gangrene
**kanibal** *n* cannibal
**kaniig** *adj* intimate
**kanipisan** *adv* thinly
**kanlungan** *n* refuge
**kanluran** *n* west
**kanselahin** *v* cancel
**kanser** *n* cancer
**kansin-pansin** *adj* noteworthy
**kantina** *n* canteen
**kanto** *n* corner
**kanutihan** *n* virtue
**kanya** *pro* his
**kanyon** *n* cannon
**kapabayaan** *n* neglect
**kapaguran** *n* fatigue
**kapaitan** *n* bitterness
**kapal** *n* bulk
**kapalan** *v* thicken
**kapalaran** *n* fate, fortune
**kapaligiran** *n* atmosphere
**kapalit** *adj* alternate
**kapalit** *n* alternative
**kapalooban** *n* enclosure
**kapanabikan** *n* suspense
**kapanahunan** *n* epoch
**kapanalig** *n* partisan
**kapanganakan** *n* birthday
**kapangitan** *n* ugliness
**kapangyarihan** *n* domination
**kapani-paniwala** *adj* believable
**kapantay** *adj* equal
**kapareho** *adj* identical
**kapasyahan** *n* reasoning
**kapatas** *n* foreman
**kapatawaran** *n* forgiveness
**kapatid** *n* sister
**kapatid na lalaki** *n* brother
**kapatiran** *n* brotherhood
**kapayakan** *n* simplicity
**kapayakan** *adv* simply
**kapayapaan** *n* peace
**kape** *n* coffee
**kapeyn** *n* caffeine
**kapihan** *n* cafeteria
**kapilya** *n* chapel
**kapilyuhan** *n* escapade
**kapinsalaan** *n* harm
**kapiraso** *n* morsel
**kapisanan** *n* guild, club
**kapitalismo** *n* capitalism

**kapitan** *n* captain
**kapit-bahay** *n* neighbor
**kapitera** *n* teapot
**kapote** *n* overcoat
**kapritso** *n* whim
**kapsula** *n* capsule
**kapulungan** *n* chamber
**kapural** *n* agitator
**kapurihan** *n* bestiality
**kapuri-puri** *adj* remarkable
**kapurulan** *n* bluntness
**kaputlaan** *n* paleness
**karagdagan** *adj* additional
**karaka-raka** *adv* immediately
**karamihan** *n* majority
**karamutan** *n* selfishness
**karangyaan** *n* opulence
**karaniwan** *adj* literal, usual
**karapat-dapat** *v* deign
**karapat-dapat** *adj* deserving
**karat** *n* carat
**karate** *n* karate
**karatig** *n* suburb
**karayom** *n* needle
**karburador** *n* carburetor
**kardiyolohiya** *n* cardiology
**karera** *n* career, race
**kargada** *n* freight, load
**kargado** *adj* loaded
**kargador** *n* porter
**kargahin** *v* carry, load
**kargamento** *n* cargo

**karibal** *n* rival
**karinderya** *n* kiosk
**karisma** *n* charisma
**kariton** *n* cart
**karne** *n* meat
**karne ng usa** *n* venison
**karneng baka** *n* beef
**karneysyon** *n* carnation
**karo ng patay** *n* hearse
**karot** *n* carrot
**kartelon** *n* placard
**kartero** *n* mailman
**karton** *n* cardboard
**kartrids** *n* cartridge
**karugtong** *n* annex, link
**karumal-dumal** *adj* dreadful
**karunungan** *n* knowledge
**karupukan** *n* frailty
**karuwagan** *n* cowardice
**kasabihan** *n* maxim, saying
**kasaganaan** *n* amenities
**kasal** *adj* married
**kasalan** *n* marriage
**kasalanan** *n* fault, guilt
**kasalungat** *adj* opposite
**kasama** *n* partner
**kasama** *pre* with
**kasama ang** *adv* inclusive
**kasamaan** *n* damnation
**kasamahan** *n* colleague
**kasanay** *n* habit
**kasanayan** *n* immunity

**kasangga** *v* coexist
**kasangkapan** *n* organ
**kasangkot** *v* involve
**kasapakat** *n* conspiracy
**kasapi** *n* contestant
**kasarapan** *n* ecstasy
**kasarian** *n* gender
**kasariwaan** *n* freshness
**kasayahan** *n* festivity
**kasaysayan** *n* history
**kasaysayan** *adj* prehistoric
**kaseguruhan** *adj* collateral
**kasera** *n* landlord
**kaserola** *n* casserole
**kasilimuutan** *n* technicality
**kasilyas** *n* toilet
**kasino** *n* casino
**kasintahan** *n* boyfriend
**kasintulad** *n* synonym
**kasinunalingan** *n* lie
**kasiraan** *n* deficiency
**kasiya-siya** *adj* satisfactory
**kasmahan** *n* comrade
**kastanyas** *n* chestnut
**kastilyo** *n* castle
**kasugpungan** *adv* jointly
**kasukdulan** *n* climax
**kasulatan** *n* chart, record
**kasunduan** *n* agreement
**kasunod** *adj* adjoining, next
**kasunsuan** *n* covenant
**kasuotan** *n* outfit, tunic
**kasuwapangan** *n* greed
**kataas-taasan** *n* chancellor, superiority
**kataas-taasan** *adv* highly
**katab** *adj* collateral
**katabi** *adj* adjacent
**katabi** *pre* along, beside
**katad** *n* leather
**kataga** *n* syllable
**katahasan** *n* frankness
**katahimijan** *n* tranquility
**katahimikan** *n* calm, silence
**katalastas** *n* correspondent
**katalogo** *n* catalog
**katamaran** *n* laziness
**katamtaman** *n* average
**katandaan** *n* old age
**katangahan** *n* stupidity
**katangian** *v* attribute
**katapangan** *n* boldness
**katapat** *pre* across
**katapatan** *n* allegiance
**katapusan** *n* conclusion
**katarata** *n* cataract
**katas** *n* sap
**katasin** *v* extract
**katatagan** *n* fortitude
**katatawanan** *n* ridicule
**katauhan** *n* being
**katawan** *n* body, torso
**katawa-tawa** *adj* ludicrous
**katedral** *n* cathedral

**katekismo** *n* catechism
**kathang salaysay** *n* tale
**kati** *v* ebb, tide
**katigasan** *n* hardness
**katigasan ng ulo** *n* obstinacy
**katimpian** *n* formality
**katinig** *n* consonant
**katipiran** *n* frugality
**katiting** *n* particle
**katiwala** *n* guardian
**katiyakan** *n* assurance
**katok** *n* knock
**katoliko** *adj* catholic
**Katolisismo** *n* Catholicism
**katotohanan** *n* fact, truth
**katukin** *v* tap into
**katulad** *n* replica
**katulad** *adj* similar, alike
**katulad ng** *n* likelihood
**katulad ng** *adj* tantamount to
**katulong** *n* aide, helper
**katumbas** *adj* equivalent
**katunayan** *adj* affirmative
**katunggali** *n* competitor
**katungkulan** *n* duty
**katutubong kilos** *n* instinct
**kaugalian** *n* tradition
**kauklam-suklam** *adj* repulsive
**kaunti** *adj* least, less, few
**kaunti** *n* morsel
**kauotang promal** *n* gown
**kauri** *n* caste
**kawad** *n* cord, cordon
**kawadra** *n* stable
**kawalan** *n* loss
**kawalang pag-asa** *n* despair
**kawali** *n* frying pan
**kawani** *n* employee
**kawani sa bangko** *n* teller
**kawanihan** *n* bureau
**kawayan** *n* bamboo
**kawit** *n* hook
**kaya** *v* afford
**kaya** *adj* capable
**kayamanan** *n* wealth
**kayanin** *v* cope, tackle
**kayurin** *v* scrape
**kemikal** *adj* chemical
**kemistri** *n* chemistry
**kendi** *n* candy
**keso** *n* cheese
**ketong** *n* leprosy
**ketongin** *n* leper
**keyk** *n* cake
**kibit balikat** *v* shrug
**kidlat** *n* lightning
**kikil** *n* chisel
**kikilan** *v* extort
**kilala** *n* celebrity
**kilala** *adj* prominent
**kilala** *v* acclaim
**kilala sa** *adj* so-called
**kilalanin** *v* acquaint
**kilanin** *v* reckon

**kilay** *n* eyebrow
**kiligin** *v* thrill
**kilikili** *n* armpit
**kilitiin** *v* tickle
**kilitiin** *n* tickle
**kilo** *n* kilogram
**kilometro** *n* kilometer
**kilos** *n* gesture
**kilowat** *n* kilowatt
**kimiko** *n* chemist
**kinabahan** *adj* frantic
**kinabibilangan** *v* comprise
**kinabukasan** *n* future
**kinagat** *v* bite
**kinahinatnan** *adj* consequent
**kinahinatnan** *n* outcome
**kinailangan** *v* need
**kinakapatid** *n* stepbrother
**kinakayod** *adj* harrowing
**kinalaman** *n* whereabouts
**kinalawang** *v* corrode
**kinamay** *adj* manual
**kinapapalooban** *v* embody
**kinapapalooban** *adj* inner
**kinapong baka** *n* ox
**kinapopootan** *adj* detestable
**kinatas** *v* sap
**kinatatakutan** *adj* formidable
**kinchay** *n* parsley
**kindat** *v* blink, wink
**kinikita** *n* income
**kinis** *n* smoothness
**kinita** *n* earnings
**kintab** *n* gloss, polish
**kintsay** *n* celery
**kinulayan** *adj* tanned
**kipot** *n* strait
**kisame** *n* ceiling
**kislap** *n* flare
**kita** *adj* tangible
**kita** *v* earn
**klalusugan** *n* health
**klarinet** *n* clarinet
**kleyente** *n* client
**klima** *n* climate
**klinika** *n* clinic
**kodigo postal** *n* zip code
**kolehiyo** *n* college
**kolektor** *n* collector
**kolera** *n* cholera
**kolesterol** *n* cholesterol
**komadrona** *n* midwife
**kombinasyon** *n* combination
**kombulsyon** *n* convulsion
**komedya** *n* comedy
**komersyo** *n* commerce
**kometa** *n* comet
**komikero** *n* comedian
**komisyon** *n* commission
**komite** *n* committee
**kompas** *n* compass
**kompositor** *n* composer
**kompusisyon** *n* composition
**kompyuter** *n* computer

**komunista** *n* communism
**komunista** *adj* communist
**komunyon** *n* communion
**kondesa** *n* countess
**konduktor** *n* conductor
**konela** *n* cornet
**kongregasyon** *n* congregation
**kongreso** *n* congress
**konkreto** *adj* concrete
**konseho** *n* council
**konsiyert** *n* concert
**konsul** *n* consul
**konsulado** *n* consulate
**konsulta** *n* consultation
**kontinental** *adj* continental
**kontinente** *n* continent
**kontra** *n* antipathy
**kontrabandista** *n* smuggler
**kontrabando** *n* contraband
**kontra-bida** *n* villain
**kooperatiba** *adj* cooperative
**kopya** *n* photocopy
**koreo** *n* parcel post
**koro** *n* choir
**korona** *n* crown, wreath
**koronahan** *v* crown
**koronel** *n* colonel
**korporasyon** *n* corporation
**korte** *n* court
**koryente** *n* electricity
**koryentehin** *v* galvanize
**koryentihin** *v* electrocute
**kosmonot** *n* cosmonaut
**kotongan** *v* blackmail
**kotse** *n* car
**krema** *n* cream
**krematoryo** *n* crematorium
**krimen** *n* crime
**kriminal** *n* felon
**krisis** *n* crisis
**kristal** *n* crystal
**Kristyanismo** *n* Christianity
**krosing** *n* crossing
**krus** *n* cross, crucifix
**krus** *v* cross
**krusada** *n* crusade
**ksapakat** *n* complicity
**kuba** *n* hunchback
**kubiko** *adj* cubic
**kubkubin** *v* besiege
**kublihan** *adj* entrenched
**kubo** *n* cube, hut
**kubyerta** *n* deck
**kudlit** *n* apostrophe
**kuha ng larawan** *n* snapshot
**kuki** *n* cookie
**kuko** *n* fingernail
**kuko sa paa** *n* toenail
**kukutikutitap** *v* flicker
**kul** *n* gravy
**kula** *n* bleach
**kulam** *n* sorcery
**kulang** *n* deficit
**kulang** *adj* incomplete, lack

**kulang sa armas** *n* disarmament
**kulang sa dugo** *adj* anemic
**kulang sa pansin** *adj* indifferent
**kular dalandan** *n* orange
**kulay** *n* color
**kulay abo** *adj* gray
**kulay kape** *adj* brown
**kulayan** *v* color, dye
**kulimlim** *adj* somber
**kulog** *n* thunder
**kulong** *n* confinement
**kulot** *n* curl
**kulot** *adj* curly
**kulto** *n* cult
**kultura** *n* culture
**kulubot** *n* wrinkle
**kulugo** *n* wart
**kulungan** *n* jail, prison
**kulungin** *v* besiege
**kulungin** *n* hostage
**kulutin** *v* curl
**kumain** *v* dine, eat
**kumandante** *n* major
**kumapit** *v* brace for
**kumatawan** *v* represent
**kumati** *v* itch
**kumatok** *v* knock
**kumbento** *n* convent
**kumbinsihin** *v* persuade
**kumikislap** *v* glitter
**kumindat** *v* wink
**kumisla-kislap** *v* twinkle
**kumislap** *v* flare-up
**kumot** *n* blanket, sheets
**kumpanya** *n* company
**kumperensya** *n* conference
**kumpil** *n* confirmation
**kumpilan** *v* confirm
**kumpisal** *n* confession
**kumpiskahin** *v* confiscate
**kumpiyansa** *n* confidence
**kumpol** *v* lump together
**kumpol** *n* cluster
**kumpunihin** *v* refurbish
**kumuha** *v* secure, procure
**kumulo** *v* boil, simmer
**kumulubot** *v* wrinkle
**kumupas** *v* fade
**kuna** *n* crib
**kuneho** *n* hare
**kung** *c* if
**kung hindi** *adv* otherwise
**kung minsan** *adv* sometimes
**kung sinu-sino** *pro* whom
**kunin** *v* get, take
**kunin muli** *v* retrieve
**kunsintihin** *v* condone
**kunsyensya** *n* conscience
**kunwari** *n* pretension
**kupain** *n* landing
**kupas** *adj* faded
**kupit** *n* kickback
**kupon** *n* coupon
**kura paroko** *n* abbot

**kurbada** *n* curve
**kurbata** *n* necktie
**kuripot** *adj* stingy
**kuro-kuro** *n* idea
**kurot** *n* pinch
**kurso** *n* course
**kurtina** *n* curtain, drape
**kurutin** *v* pinch
**kusang binigay** *adv* willfully
**kusang-loob** *n* volunteer
**kusang-loob** *adv* willingly
**kusina** *n* kitchen
**kusinero** *n* cook
**kuskusin** *v* scour, scrub
**kuta** *n* fort
**kuting** *n* kitten
**kutis** *n* complexion
**kutitap** *n* glimmer
**kutkutin** *v* gnaw
**kuto** *n* lice, louse
**kutob** *n* hunch
**kutsara** *n* spoon
**kutsarita** *n* teaspoon
**kutsilyo** *n* knife
**kutson** *n* mattress
**kutyain** *v* scoff
**kuwadrado** *n* square
**kuwadro** *n* frame
**kuwago** *n* owl
**kuwarta** *n* cash
**kuwelyo** *n* collar
**kuwento** *n* story
**kuwit** *n* coma, comma
**kuyukot** *n* rectum
**kwaderno** *n* notebook
**kwadrado** *adj* square
**kwaresma** *n* Lent
**kweba** *n* cave
**kwenta** *n* bill
**kwintas** *n* necklace

# L

**lab** *n* lab
**lababo** *n* lavatory
**labada** *n* laundry
**labag sa batas** *n* felony
**labag sa batas** *adj* unlawful
**labagin** *v* violate
**labahan** *v* wash
**laban** *n* defense
**laban sa** *adj* contrary
**labanan** *v* resist
**labas** *adv* out
**labasan** *n* exit
**labi** *n* lip
**labing - walo** *adj* eighteen
**labing dalawa** *adj* twelve
**labing tatlo** *adj* thirteen
**labing-anim** *adj* sixteen

**labing-apat** *adj* fourteen
**labing-isa** *adj* eleven
**labing-pito** *adj* seventeen
**labingsiyam** *adj* nineteen
**labis** *n* excess
**labis** *adv* extra
**labis** *pre* over
**labis-labis** *adj* indulgent
**labsi na halaga** *adj* exorbitant
**ladera** *n* ladder
**ladrilyador** *n* bricklayer
**ladrilyo** *n* brick
**lagakan** *n* depot
**laganap** *adj* rampant
**lagare** *n* saw
**lagariin** *v* saw
**lagay** *n* condition
**lagda** *n* sign
**lagdaan** *v* sign
**lagdaan sa likod** *v* endorse
**laging handa** *adj* responsive
**lagnat** *n* fever
**lagpasan** *v* skip
**lagpasan** *n* skip
**lagukin** *v* gulp
**lagusan** *n* tunnel
**lagusan ng dumi** *n* sewage
**lagusan ng tubig** *n* watershed
**lagyan ng bisagra** *v* hinge
**lahat** *adj* all
**lahat** *pro* everybody
**lahatin** *v* generalize
**lahat-lahat** *adj* altogether
**lahi** *n* breed, race
**lakad** *n* walk
**lakas** *n* power, strength
**lakas ng loob** *n* audacity
**lakas ng tunog** *n* volume
**laki** *n* bulk, extent
**laksan** *v* strengthen
**laktawan** *v* omit
**lalagyan** *n* container
**lalagyan ng abo** *n* ashtray
**lalagyan ng aklat** *n* bookcase
**lalagyan ng damit** *n* dresser
**lalagyan ng yelo** *n* icebox
**lalaki** *n* guy, male
**lalaking baka** *n* bull
**lalaking tupa** *n* ram
**lalamunan** *n* larynx, throat
**lalawigan** *n* county
**lalim** *n* depth
**laliman** *v* deepen
**lalo na** *adv* especially
**lalong-lalo na** *adv* particularly
**lamad** *n* membrane
**laman** *adj* corporal
**laman** *n* flesh, limb
**laman ng bomba** *n* shrapnel
**lamang** *adv* merely, only
**lamasin** *v* mash
**lamat** *n* crack
**lamatan** *v* crack
**lamay** *n* vigil

L

**lambak** *n* gulf, valley
**lamig** *n* coolness
**lamok** *n* mosquito
**lampara** *n* lamp
**lampas** *n* bypass
**lampas sa oras** *adv* overtime
**lampasan** *v* bypass
**lampin** *n* diaper
**lamunin** *v* gobble
**lana** *v* budge
**lana** *n* wool
**landas** *v* trail
**langgam** *n* ant
**langhapin** *v* inhale
**langis** *n* oil
**langisan** *v* grease
**langit** *n* sky
**langitngit** *n* creak
**langkap** *n* consistency
**lango** *adj* drowsy
**lansangan** *n* boulevard
**lansangang bayan** *n* highway
**lantad** *adv* barely
**lantad** *adj* indiscretion
**lao pat** *c* even more
**lapad** *n* width
**lapag** *n* ground
**lapag ng apuyan** *n* hearth
**lapain** *v* devour
**laparan** *v* widen
**lapastangan** *n* abuse
**lapay** *n* pancreas
**lapida** *n* gravestone
**lapis** *n* pencil
**lapitan** *v* approach
**lapit-lapit** *adv* closely
**larawan** *n* effigy, picture
**larawang diwa** *n* image
**larga bista** *n* binoculars
**laro** *n* play, sport
**laruan** *n* toy
**laruin** *v* fondle
**lasa** *n* flavor
**lasahan** *v* savor, taste
**lasing** *adj* drunk
**laslas** *n* slash
**laslasin** *v* slash
**laso** *n* ribbon, lace
**lason** *n* poison, toxin
**lastiko** *adj* elastic
**lasunin ang isip** *v* brainwash
**lata** *n* can, tin
**latak** *n* crust, residue
**lathala** *n* publicity
**latiguhin** *v* goad
**latitud** *n* latitude
**lawa** *n* dike
**lawak** *n* scope, span
**lawakan** *v* span
**lawin** *n* hawk
**layagin** *v* navigate
**layo** *n* distance
**layunin** *n* objective
**lechugas** *n* lettuce

**leeg** *n* neck
**lemonada** *n* lemonade
**lente** *n* lense
**letratista** *n* photographer
**leyon** *n* lion
**leyser** *n* laser
**libak** *n* rebuke
**libakin** *v* rebuke
**libang** *n* comfort
**libangan** *n* hobby
**libangin** *v* entertain
**libelo** *n* libel
**libing** *n* funeral
**libingan** *n* cemetery
**libis** *n* slope
**libo** *adj* thousand
**libog** *n* lust
**libong taon** *n* millennium
**libra** *n* pound
**libreta** *n* checkbook
**liga** *n* league
**ligal** *n* validity
**ligalig** *n* qualm
**ligas** *n* garter
**ligaw** *n* drifter
**ligawan** *v* court
**ligawan** *n* courtship
**ligaya** *n* solace
**ligtas** *adj* safe
**ligtas na lugar** *n* fortress
**ligtas sa parusa** *n* impunity
**lihim** *adj* confidential
**lihis** *adj* slanted
**liitan** *v* shorten
**likapin** *v* collect
**likhang -isip** *n* fiction
**likido** *n* fluid, liquid
**likod** *n* back, rear
**lila** *adj* purple
**lilim** *n* shade
**lima** *adj* five
**limampu** *adj* fifty
**limampu't-lima** *adv* fifty-fifty
**limbagin muli** *v* reprint
**limitahan** *v* confine, limit
**limitasyon** *n* limitation
**limon** *n* lemon, lime
**lindol** *n* earthquake
**Linggo** *n* Sunday, week
**lingguhan** *adv* weekly
**linisin** *v* disinfect, clean
**linisin ang budhi** *v* purify
**linisin ng tuyo** *v* dryclean
**linlangin** *v* double-cross
**linta** *n* leech
**linya** *n* line
**lipad** *n* fly
**lipat** *n* relocation
**lipi** *n* folks
**lipulin** *v* exterminate
**lipunan** *n* society
**lipyir** *n* leap year
**liriko** *n* lyrics
**lisensya** *n* licence

L

**lisensya** *v* license
**lista** *n* list
**listahan** *n* directory
**listo** *adj* alert
**litanya** *n* litany
**literatura** *n* literature
**litid** *n* ligament
**litisin** *v* litigate
**lito** *adj* disoriented
**litro** *n* litre
**lituhin** *v* delude, distract
**liwanagin** *v* clarify, clear
**liyab** *n* flame
**lobo** *n* fox, wolf
**lohica** *n* logic
**lohikal** *adj* logical
**loka** *n* crank
**lokohin** *v* swindle
**loko-loko** *adj* deranged
**lola** *n* grandmother
**lolo** *n* grandfather
**lomo** *n* loin
**lona** *n* awning, canvas
**lonahan** *v* canvas
**loob ng tainga** *n* eardrum
**looban** *n* compound
**looban** *adj* inland
**loobin** *n* will
**looboan** *pre* inside
**look** *n* lake
**loro** *n* parrot
**syon** *n* lotion
**loterya** *n* lottery
**lubid** *n* noose, rope
**lubog** *adj* sunken
**lugar** *n* location
**luhaan** *adj* tearful
**luho** *n* luxury
**luhuran** *n* pew
**lukot** *adj* convoluted
**luksa** *n* lament
**luksuhin** *v* spring
**lulunin** *v* ingest, swallow
**luma** *adj* ancient, outdated
**lumaban** *v* strike back
**lumabas** *v* emerge
**lumabas muli** *v* resurface
**lumabas ulit** *v* reappear
**lumabis** *v* outweigh
**lumabo** *v* blur, settle down
**lumakad** *v* go, walk
**lumaki** *v* enlarge, grow
**lumala** *v* worsen
**lumalala** *v* degenerate
**lumalamig** *adj* cooling
**lumalangitngit** *v* squeak
**lumamapas** *v* elapse
**lumampad** *adv* exceedingly
**lumampas** *v* go through
**lumandi** *v* flirt
**lumang bagay** *n* relief
**lumang-luma** *adj* dilapidated
**lumangoy** *v* swim
**lumapag** *v* land

**lumayag** *v* embark
**lumayo** *v* get away
**lumbay** *n* gloom
**lumibog** *v* lust
**lumiko** *v* veer
**lumingon** *v* turn back
**lumipad** *v* fly
**lumipat** *v* transfer
**lumisan** *v* evacuate
**lumot** *n* moss
**lumubog** *v* link, sink in
**lumuhod** *v* genuflect
**lumukso** *v* gallop
**lumura** *v* spit
**lumutang** *adv* afloat
**lumutang** *v* float
**lumuwa** *v* protrude
**lunan** *n* area, place
**lunasan** *v* cure, solve
**Lunes** *n* Monday
**lungga** *n* den
**lungkot** *n* sorrow
**lungsod** *n* city
**lunukin** *v* gulp down
**lupa** *n* land, soil
**lupang minana** *n* patrimony
**lupang tinubuan** *n* homeland
**lupigin** *v* conquer
**lupon** *n* flock
**luslos** *n* hernia
**lusong** *n* mortar
**lustayin** *v* embezzle
**lusubin** *v* raid
**lutasin** *v* settle
**luwagan** *v* loose
**luya** *n* ginger
**lyopard** *n* leopard

**ma intriga** *adj* intriguing
**ma utal** *v* stammer
**maaari** *v* can
**maaaring gamitin** *adj* applicable
**maaasahan** *adj* plausible
**maaayos** *adj* adjustable
**maaga** *adv* early
**maalaga** *adj* caring
**maalalahanin** *adj* thoughtful
**maalat** *adj* salty
**maalikabok** *adj* dusty
**maalinsangan** *adj* humid
**maaliw** *adj* comfortable
**maalon** *adj* wavy
**maalwan** *adj* roomy
**maamag** *adj* moldy
**maamo** *adj* meek
**maanghang** *adj* spicy
**maapoy** *adj* fiery
**maaraw** *adj* solar, sunny

**maaring gawin** *adj* workable
**maaring hatiin** *adj* divisible
**maaring inumin** *adj* drinkable
**maaring labahan** *adj* washable
**maaring magpunla** *n* fertility
**maaring mangyari** *adj* feasible
**maaring tirahan** *adj* habitable
**maasahan** *adj* unfailing
**maasim** *adj* gastric
**maawain** *adj* compassionate
**maaya** *n* delight
**mababa** *adj* low
**mababang antas** *adj* substandard
**mababang loob** *adj* lowkey
**mababaw** *adj* hollow, shallow
**mababng uri** *adj* lowly
**mabagal** *adj* slow
**mabagyo** *adj* stormy
**mabahala** *v* concern
**mabaho** *adj* foul, smelly
**mabalahibo** *adj* furry
**mabangis** *adj* ferocious
**mabango** *adj* fragrant
**mabato** *adj* rocky
**mabibitbit** *adj* portable
**mabigat** *adj* heavy
**mabilis** *adj* brisk, fast
**mabini** *adj* gentle
**mabisa** *adj* effective
**mabisang gamot** *adj* medicinal
**mabisyo** *adj* vicious
**mabubuno** *n* wrestler
**mabuhay** *v* exist
**mabuhok** *adj* hairy
**mabukirin** *adj* pastoral
**mabunga** *adj* fruity
**mabuti** *adj* good, moral
**mabuti** *n* well
**mabuto** *adj* seedy
**mabuwal** *v* tumble
**madalang** *adv* rarely
**madalas** *adj* frequent
**madaldal** *adj* talkative
**madali** *adj* easy
**madali** *v* extradite, ease
**madalian** *adj* urgent
**madaliin** *v* facilitate
**madaling gamitin** *adj* handy
**madaling lapitan** *adj* approachable
**madaling mahawa** *adj* susceptible
**madaling turuan** *adj* docile
**madaling-araw** *n* dawn
**madamot** *adj* selfish
**madasalin** *adj* pious
**madaya** *adj* deceitful
**madikit** *adj* adhesive
**madilim** *adj* dark, dim
**madiplomasya** *adj* diplomatic
**madla** *n* people
**madla** *adj* public
**madrasta** *n* stepmother
**madre** *n* nun
**madula** *adj* dramatic
**madulas** *adj* slippery

**madulo** *n* turmoil
**madumi** *adj* messy
**mag ahit** *v* shave
**mag alaga** *v* nurse
**mag atang** *v* impose
**mag grupo** *v* pool
**mag husga** *v* infer
**mag kunwari** *v* simulate
**mag sugal** *v* gamble
**mag turok** *v* inject
**mag ulat** *v* update
**mag wala** *v* rampage
**maga** *n* swelling, sore
**maga** *adj* swollen
**magaan** *v* light
**mag-aaral** *n* student, pupil
**mag-abala** *v* preoccupy
**mag-alaga** *v* breed
**mag-alala** *v* worry
**magalang** *adj* cordial, polite
**magalaw** *adj* active, mobile
**magalay** *v* provide
**magaling** *adj* excellent
**mag-alinlangan** *adv* reluctantly
**magalit** *v* enrage
**magalit ng husto** *v* rave
**mag-alsa** *v* revolt
**mag-ampon** *v* adopt
**maganap** *v* occur
**maganda** *adj* beautiful, cute
**magandang asal** *adj* ethical
**magandang tao** *adj* good-looking
**magandang ugali** *n* demeanor
**mag-apila** *v* advocate
**mag-aral** *v* study
**magasapang** *adj* hoarse, rough
**mag-asawa** *n* couple
**mag-asawa muli** *v* remarry
**magaspang** *adj* coarse
**mag-away** *v* quarrel, fight
**magbabala** *v* exhort
**magbabawas** *adj* deductible
**magbago** *v* vary
**magbalak** *v* plan, plot
**magbigay** *v* donate, give
**magbigay diwa** *n* inspire
**magbigay lakas** *v* exert
**magbigay-kaya** *v* enable
**magbubukid** *n* farmer
**magbukas** *v* open up
**magbunyi** *v* rejoice
**mag-bus** *v* bus
**magdahilan** *v* cause, feign
**magdalamhati** *v* grieve
**magdalantao** *n* pregnancy
**magdaldal** *v* chat
**magdamag** *adv* overnight
**magdasal** *v* pray
**magdaya** *v* cheat
**magdikit** *n* stick
**mag-dikta** *v* dictate
**magduda** *v* waver
**magdugtong** *v* rejoin
**magdusa** *v* suffer, torment

**maggagawa** *n* builder
**maggantsilyo** *v* knit
**maghabla** *v* sue
**maghalo** *v* concoct
**maghanap** *v* prowl
**maghanda** *v* prepare
**maghangad** *v* clamor
**maghari** *v* reign
**maghasik** *v* foster
**maghilamos** *v* brush up
**maghimagsik** *v* protest
**maghintay** *v* stick around, wait
**maghirang** *v* nominate
**maghiwa** *n* cutter
**maghiwalay** *v* divorce
**mag-hiwalay** *v* disband
**maghubad** *v* undress
**maghukay** *v* drill, till
**magiliw** *adj* charismatic
**magimbestiga** *v* probe
**mag-imbistiga** *v* investigate
**maging** *v* become
**maging tapat** *v* stick to
**mag-ingat** *v* beware
**maginhawa** *adj* convenient
**maginoo** *adj* gallant, manly
**mag-ipon-ipon** *v* congregate
**mag-isa** *pre* oneself
**mag-isip** *v* contemplate
**magiting** *adj* noble
**magkaaway** *n* warfare
**magkabangga** *adv* head-on
**magkabuhol** *v* intertwine
**magkadikit** *adj* coherent
**magkagulo** *n* conflict
**magkahawig** *adj* comparable
**magkahiwalay** *adv* apart
**magkaiba** *adj* polar
**magka-iba** *adj* different
**magkakahalaga** *v* entail
**magkalat** *v* mess around
**magkaloob** *v* furnish
**magkamali** *v* falter
**magkamit** *v* acquire
**magkaniig** *n* intimacy
**magkasakit** *v* sicken
**magkasala** *v* sin
**magkasalungat** *adv* conversely
**magkasama** *adv* together
**magkasira** *v* break up
**magkasundo** *v* reconcile
**magkasunduan** *v* engage
**magkasunod** *adj* consecutive
**magkasya** *v* content
**magkasya sa** *v* settle for
**magkatapat** *n* compatibility
**magkatugma** *adj* corresponding
**magkatulad** *n* similarity
**magkukumpas** *v* gesticulate
**magkumpulan** *v* huddle
**magkunwari** *v* pretend
**magkuwento** *v* narrate
**maglabas ng pera** *v* disburse
**maglagas** *v* shed

**maglagay ng gas** *v* refuel
**maglakad** *v* hike
**maglakbay** *v* travel
**maglaro** *v* play
**maglayag** *v* sail
**magluksa** *v* lament, mourn
**magluto** *v* cook
**magmadali** *v* hurry, rash
**mag-maneho** *v* drive
**magmartsa** *v* march
**magmasid** *n* survey
**magmula** *v* emanate
**magmumog** *v* gargle
**magmungkahi** *v* propose
**magmura** *v* cuss
**magnakaw** *v* loot, rob
**magnanakaw** *n* burglar, thief
**magnilay-nilay** *v* meditate
**magpabata** *v* rejuvenate
**magpadala** *v* remit
**magpadausdos** *v* skate
**magpagala-gala** *v* wander
**magpaginhawa** *v* refresh
**magpahinga** *v* relax, rest
**magpahiwatig** *v* insinuate
**magpakain** *v* blow out
**magpakalabis** *v* indulge
**magpakalat-kalat** *v* loiter
**magpakonsulta** *v* consult
**magpakumbaba** *v* condescend
**magpalakad** *v* operate
**magpalakas** *v* beef up
**magpalamig** *v* cool down
**magpalit** *v* swap
**mag-panggap** *v* disguise
**magparami** *v* propagate
**magpasalamat** *v* thank
**magpasikat** *v* impress
**magpasya** *v* decide
**magpatala** *v* enlist, enroll
**magpatalo** *v* slacken
**magpatihulog** *v* nosedive
**magpatotoo** *v* assert
**magpatuloy** *v* proceed
**magpatunay** *v* certify
**magpaubaya** *v* waive
**magpa-ulit-ulit** *v* linger
**magpaumanhin** *v* apologize
**magpautang** *v* loan
**magpayaman** *v* enrich
**magpugay** *v* bow
**magpukol** *v* toss
**magpulong** *v* crowd
**magsagawa** *v* perform
**magsalawahan** *v* vacillate
**magsalaysay** *v* recite
**magsalita** *v* speak, talk
**magsalubong** *v* converge
**magsanay** *v* exercise
**mag-sanga** *v* branch out
**magsayaw** *v* dance
**magsikap** *v* apply
**magsilbi** *v* serve
**magsinungaling** *v* lie

**magsisi** *v* repent
**magsulat** *v* write
**magsulsi** *v* stitch
**magsumikap** *v* strive
**magsungit** *v* grouch
**magsuplada** *v* snub
**magtabi** *v* expropriate
**magtagumpay** *v* attest
**magtahi** *v* sew
**magtalo** *v* debate
**magtanim** *v* cultivate
**magtatagpo** *v* date
**magtayo** *v* organize
**magtiis** *n* sacrifice
**magtipid** *v* economize, save
**magtiwala** *v* trust
**magtrabaho** *v* work
**magtsismis** *v* gossip
**magtubo** *v* gain
**magulang** *n* parents
**magulo** *adj* chaotic
**mag-umpukan** *v* gather
**mag-usap** *v* converse
**magusot** *n* complexity
**magwalis** *v* sweep
**magyabang** *v* brag, show off
**mahaba** *adj* lengthy
**mahabang daanan** *n* gallery
**mahabang oras** *adj* protracted
**mahal** *adj* costly, dear
**mahalaga** *adj* vital, crucial
**mahalagang bato** *n* gem
**mahalay** *adj* gross
**mahalin** *adv* dearly
**mahalin** *v* love
**mahalina** *adj* charming
**mahangin** *adj* windy
**maharlika** *n* nobleman
**mahigpit** *adj* stern
**mahihin** *adj* modest
**mahikero** *n* wizard
**mahilig** *adj* fond
**mahilig sa gulay** *n* vegetarian
**mahilig sa laro** *adj* athletic
**mahina** *adj* feeble, weak
**mahinahon** *adj* gentle
**mahinang uri** *adj* inferior
**mahinay** *adj* mild
**mahinhin** *adj* ladylike
**mahirap** *adj* indigent
**mahirap gawin** *adj* arduous
**mahiwaga** *adj* occult
**mahiya** *v* shame
**mahiyain** *adj* bashful, shy
**mahogani** *n* mahagony
**mahusay** *adj* efficient
**maigsing buhay** *adj* shortlived
**maigsing daan** *n* shortcut
**maiiwasan** *adj* avoidable
**maikling pantalon** *n* shorts
**maikling salita** *n* briefs
**maiksi** *adj* brief, short
**maiksiing palda** *n* miniskirt
**mailap** *adj* aloof, elusive

**mailigtas** *v* survive
**maimluensya** *adj* influential
**maingat** *adj* careful, cautious
**maingay** *adj* noisy
**mainipin** *adj* impatient
**mainit** *adj* hot, warm
**mainit na usapan** *n* fuss
**maipapayo** *adj* advisable
**mais** *n* corn
**maisabay** *n* coincidence
**maisip sa sarili** *adj* self-concious
**maitim** *adj* black
**maka muslim** *adj* Islamic
**maka-agham** *adj* scientific
**makabago** *adj* radical
**makabanyaga** *adj* colonial
**makabayan** *adj* patriotic
**makahari** *adj* regal
**makahayop** *adj* bestial
**makakain** *adj* edible
**makakalimutin** *adj* demented
**makakamit** *adj* attainable
**makalangit** *adj* heavenly
**makalog** *adj* shaky
**makaluma** *adj* medieval
**makamundo** *adj* worldly
**makapal** *adj* dense, thick
**makasalanan** *adj* sinful
**makasalanan** *n* sinner
**makasarili** *adj* eccentric
**makatalilis** *v* get by
**makatao** *adj* human
**makatarungan** *adj* just, lawful
**makatas** *adj* succulent
**makati** *n* itchiness
**makatotohanan** *adj* truthful
**maki ama** *adj* fatherly
**maki apid** *v* cohabit
**maki bagay** *v* keep up
**makialam** *v* intervene
**maki-ayon** *v* cooperate
**makibaka** *v* struggle
**maki-halubilo** *v* mingle
**makina** *n* machine
**makinang** *adj* brilliant
**makinang panipi** *n* copier
**makinang pantaas** *n* elevator
**makinang pantala** *n* recorder
**makinig** *v* eavesdrop
**makinilyahin** *v* type
**makinis** *adj* smooth
**makintab** *adj* glossy
**makipag alam** *v* collaborate
**makipag-alam** *v* contact, negotiate
**makipagbunuan** *v* hassle
**makipag-kaibigan** *v* socialize
**makipagtawaran** *v* haggle
**makiramay** *v* sympathize
**makitid** *adj* narrow
**makiusap** *v* plead
**makompromiso** *adj* binding
**makrema** *adj* creamy
**makuha** *v* obtain

**makulay** *adj* colorful
**makumbinsi** *adj* persuasive
**mala anghel** *adj* angelic
**mala halimaw** *adj* monstrous
**mala- hari** *adj* despotic
**mala kosmos** *adj* cosmic
**mala krus** *adj* cross
**mala lana** *adj* woolen
**malabo** *adj* vague, fuzzy
**malabsa** *adj* soggy
**malagkit** *adj* sticky
**malakas** *adj* forceful
**malakas na putok** *n* boom
**malakas na tunog** *v* slam

**malaki** *adj* big, huge
**malaking ibon** *n* vulture
**malaking kuweba** *n* cavern
**malaking larawan** *n* poster
**malaking takot** *n* terror
**malaking usapan** *adj* fussy
**malala** *n* aggravation
**malala** *adj* severe, worse
**malalaking titik** *n* capital letter
**mala-lata** *adj* metallic
**malalim** *adv* in depth
**malalim** *adj* pedantic
**mala-luya** *adv* gingerly
**malaman** *adj* substantial
**malambot** *adj* soft, supple
**malamig** *adj* cold, chilly
**malamng** *adv* likely
**malandi** *adj* fitting
**malangitngit** *adj* squeaky
**malansa** *adj* fishy
**malapad** *adj* wide
**malapit** *pre* near
**malapit** *adj* nearby
**malapit sa** *pre* close to
**malarawan** *adj* scenic
**malarya** *n* malaria
**malas** *adj* unlucky
**malasa** *adj* tasteful
**malasakit** *n* concern
**malaswa** *adj* distasteful
**mala-uling** *adj* charbroil
**malawak** *adj* enormous
**malawak na dagat** *n* ocean
**malaya** *adj* free
**malayang sandali** *n* leisure
**malayo** *adv* away, distant
**maleta** *n* luggage
**mali** *n* error
**mali** *adj* mistaken
**maliban** *adj* absent
**maliban** *pre* except
**maliban sa** *n* exception
**malibog** *adj* lustful
**maligamgam** *adj* tepid
**maligaya** *adj* merry
**maligo** *v* bathe
**maligoy** *adj* devious
**maliit** *adj* small, tiny, petite
**maliit na aklat** *n* booklet
**maliit na alon** *n* ripple

**maliit na bahagi** *n* molecule
**maliit na bahay** *n* cottage
**maliit na bituin** *n* meteor
**maliit na dahon** *n* leaflet
**maliit na planeta** *n* asteroid
**maliit na silid** *n* attic
**malikhain** *adj* productive
**malik-mata** *n* apparition
**maliksi** *adj* agile
**maliksi** *n* fleet
**maliliit na butas** *n* pore
**maliliit na titik** *n* small print
**malilit** *n* miniature
**malinamnam** *adj* tasty
**malinaw** *n* clarity
**malinaw** *adv* clearly
**malinaw** *adj* plain
**malinaw na kopya** *n* fine print
**maling akala** *n* fallacy
**maling akala** *v* misinterpret
**maling paggamit** *n* misuse
**maling ugali** *n* misconduct
**maling-akala** *n* illusion
**malinis** *adj* clean, neat
**malisya** *n* malice
**maliwanag** *adj* bright, clear
**malnutrisyon** *n* malnutrition
**malubha** *adj* grave, serious
**malugod** *adj* delightful
**maluho** *adj* luxurious
**malulunasan** *adj* curable
**malungkot** *adj* sad, sorry
**malungkutin** *n* sadist
**malupit** *adj* brute, cruel
**malusog** *adj* healthy
**malutong** *adj* crispy, crunchy
**malutong na latak** *adj* crusty
**maluwag** *adj* lenient
**maluwalhati** *adj* glorious
**mamahala** *v* govern
**mamahalin** *adj* posh
**mamalimos** *v* beg
**mamamahayag** *n* press
**mamamatay-tao** *n* assassin
**mamamayan** *n* citizen
**mamaril** *v* shoot down
**mamasa-masa** *adj* soiled
**mamatay-tao** *n* killer
**mamaya** *adv* later
**mamayang gabi** *adv* tonight
**mamayani** *v* excel
**mambabatas** *n* lawmaker
**mamigay** *v* give out
**mamili** *v* shop, choose
**mamiligro** *v* jeopardize
**mamimili** *n* consumer
**mamuhay sa** *v* live off
**mamuhunan** *v* invest
**mamula** *adj* rosy
**mamuno** *v* boss around
**mana** *n* inheritance
**managimit** *v* hallucinate
**manahin** *v* inherit
**manakit** *v* manhandle

**mananagot** *adj* liable
**mananahi** *n* seamstress
**mananalakay** *n* invader
**mananalastas** *n* broadcaster
**mananalaysay** *n* historian
**mananalin** *n* translator
**manananggol** *n* defendant
**manangis** *v* wail
**manapat** *c* even if
**mandaraya** *adj* dishonest
**mandayuhan** *v* emigrate
**mandirigma** *n* warrior
**mandurukot** *n* pickpocket
**maneobra** *n* maneuver
**mang-aagaw** *n* kidnapper
**mang-aawit** *n* singer
**mangako** *v* swear
**mangalakal** *v* trade
**mangalap** *v* levy
**mangampanya** *v* campaign
**manganak** *v* mutate
**mangangalakal** *n* dealer
**mangangaso** *n* hunter
**manganib** *v* endanger
**mangaral** *v* preach
**mangarap** *v* aspire
**mangasiwa** *v* manage
**mangaso** *v* hunt
**manggagahasa** *n* rapist
**manggagamot** *n* doctor
**manggagantso** *n* swindler
**manggagawa** *n* laborer
**manggas** *n* sleeve
**manggugupit** *n* hairdresser
**manggulo** *v* trouble
**mangha** *n* awe
**manghingi** *v* solicit
**manghuhula** *n* prophet
**manghuhuthot** *n* sucker
**mangilan-ngilan** *adj* fewer
**mangiling** *v* abstain
**mangingibig** *n* lover
**manginginom** *n* drinker
**mangingisda** *n* fisherman
**manginig** *v* quiver
**mangkok** *n* bowl
**mangkukulam** *n* sorcerer
**mangmang** *adj* ignorant
**mangugupit** *n* haircut
**mangumpisal** *v* confess
**mangusap** *v* sentence
**mangyayari** *adj* improbable
**manhid** *n* numbness
**mani** *n* nut, peanut
**manika** *n* doll
**manikin** *adj* dummy
**maninisid** *n* diver
**manipis** *adj* flimsy, thin
**manipis na tela** *adj* sleazy
**manirahan** *v* settle
**manirang puri** *v* malign
**maniwala** *v* believe
**manlalakbay** *n* traveler
**manlalangoy** *n* swimmer

**manlalaro** *n* athlete
**manloloko** *n* con man
**manlulupig** *n* tyrant
**manlulusob** *n* raider
**manmanan** *v* detect
**manok** *n* chicken
**manonod** *n* onlooker
**manonood** *n* audience
**mansanas** *n* apple
**mantekilya** *n* butter
**mantel** *n* tablecloth
**mantika** *n* lard
**mantsa** *n* blot, stain
**mantsahan** *v* smear
**mantsahan** *adj* tainted
**manugang** *n* son-in-law
**manukan** *n* poultry
**manunubos** *n* savior
**manunugod** *n* attacker
**manunuklas** *n* explorer
**manunula** *n* poet
**manunulat** *n* writer
**manununog** *n* arsonist
**manunuri** *n* critique
**manyak** *adj* maniac
**mapa** *n* map
**mapag balatkayo** *adj* ostentatious
**mapag hanap** *adj* demanding
**mapag-ayon** *adj* adaptable
**mapag-balat-kayo** *adj* hypocrite
**mapagbigay** *n* bounty
**mapagbigay** *adj* charitable
**mapag-bigay** *adj* considerate
**mapag-biyaya** *adj* gracious
**mapaghinala** *adj* suspicious
**mapag-isa** *n* loner
**mapagkatiwala** *n* optimism
**mapaglarawan** *adj* descriptive
**mapagmahal** *adj* loving
**mapagpatawad** *adj* merciful
**mapag-sang-ayon** *adj* conformist
**mapagtanggol** *adj* defiant
**mapait** *adj* bitter
**mapalad** *adj* fortunate
**mapamaraan** *adj* systematic
**mapanganib** *adj* risky
**mapanglaw** *adj* gloomy
**mapanira** *adj* harmful
**mapanis** *v* coagulate
**mapaniwalain** *adj* gullible
**mapanuya** *adj* sarcastic
**maparaan** *adj* methodical
**mapatuloy** *v* go on
**mapayapa** *adj* peaceful
**mapekas** *adj* freckled
**mapili** *adj* choosy
**mapilit** *adj* persistent
**mapino** *adv* fine
**mapurol** *adj* blunt, dull
**mapusok** *adj* passionate
**maputik** *adj* muddy
**maputla** *adj* pale
**marahas** *adj* violent
**marahil** *adv* perhaps

**maramdaman** *v* feel
**maramdamin** *adj* emotional
**marami** *adv* much
**marami** *adj* plentiful, many
**maraming asawa** *adj* polygamist
**maraming mani** *adj* nutty
**maraming tao** *adj* crowded
**marangal** *adj* majestic
**marangya** *adj* affluent
**marangya** *v* lavish
**marangya** *n* pomposity
**marikit** *adj* gorgeous
**marilag** *adj* gorgeous
**marinero** *n* sailor
**marka** *n* rate
**marmalada** *n* marmalade
**marmol** *n* marble
**marso** *n* march
**Martes** *n* Tuesday
**martilyo** *n* hammer
**martir** *n* martyr
**marubdob** *adj* devout
**marumi** *adj* dirty, sloppy
**marumihan** *v* contaminate
**marunong** *adj* competent
**marupok** *adj* frail
**mas mababa** *adj* lower
**mas marami** *v* outnumber
**masa** *n* dough
**masabaw** *adj* juicy
**masagana** *adj* abundant
**masagwa** *adj* awful, lousy
**masahe** *n* massage
**masakal** *v* suffocate
**masakit** *adj* painful
**masakitin** *adj* unhealthy
**masalimuot** *adj* intricate
**masama** *adj* bad, evil
**masama ang loob** *adj* spiteful
**masamang pakita** *adv* poorly
**masamang tao** *n* hoodlum
**masanay** *v* acclimatize
**masangsang** *n* stench
**masansang** *adj* fetid
**masarap** *adj* delicious
**masaya** *adj* festive, happy
**masayahin** *adj* cheerful
**masebo** *adj* greasy
**maselan** *adj* delicate
**masid** *v* regard
**masigasig** *adj* eager
**masigla** *adj* dynamic
**masikap** *adj* diligent
**masikip na daan** *n* bottleneck
**masining** *adj* creative
**masining na gawa** *adj* artistic
**masipag** *adj* industrious
**masipsip** *adj* absorbent
**masiyahan** *v* satisfy
**maskara** *n* mask
**maskulado** *adj* corpulent
**mason** *n* mason
**masuburin** *adj* obedient
**masugid** *adj* avid, staunch

**masungit** *adj* grouchy
**masunurin** *adj* submissive
**masusi** *adj* rigid
**masustansya** *adj* nutritious
**masuway** *adj* disobedient
**maswerte** *adj* lucky
**mata** *n* eye
**mataas** *adj* high
**mataas na antas** *adj* classy
**mataba** *adj* chubby, fat
**matabang lupa** *adj* arable
**matadero** *n* butcher
**matagal na** *n* seniority
**matahimik** *adj* silent, still
**matakaw** *n* glutton
**matalas** *adj* deft, sharp
**matalino** *adj* astute, clever
**matalo** *v* outperform
**matalon** *adj* jumpy
**matamis** *n* custard
**matanda** *adj* elderly, old
**matanda na** *adj* senile
**matandang alitan** *n* feud
**matangkad** *adj* tall
**matao** *n* crowd, mob
**matapang** *adj* bold, brave
**matapat** *adj* honest, sincere
**matarik** *adj* steep
**matatag** *adj* constant, steady
**matematika** *n* math
**materyal** *n* material
**materyalismo** *n* materialism
**matibay** *adj* sturdy, hard
**matigas ang ulo** *adj* stubborn
**matind** *adj* dense
**matindi** *adj* acute, intense
**matinding takot** *n* phobia
**matingkad** *adj* vivid
**matinidng epekto** *n* impact
**matinik** *adj* thorny
**matinik na hayop** *n* porcupine
**matipid** *adj* economical
**matipuno** *adj* burly, husky
**matitiis** *adj* tolerable
**matiyaga** *adj* patient
**matrabaho** *adj* cumbersome
**matres** *n* uterus
**matubig** *adj* watery
**matulain** *adj* versed
**matulis** *adj* pointed
**matulis na kuko** *n* claw
**matulog** *v* sleep
**matulungin** *adj* helpful
**matumba** *v* tumble
**matutunaw** *adj* soluble
**matuwain** *adj* jovial
**maulan** *adj* rainy
**maulap** *adj* cloudy, foggy
**maunawain** *adj* broadminded
**maunlad** *adj* progressive
**mausisa** *adj* curious
**may akda** *n* author
**may alam** *adj* aware
**may bahay** *n* housewife

**may bahid** *n* blemish
**may balani** *adj* magnetic
**may balbas** *adj* bearded
**may bigay** *n* donor
**may bisa** *adj* indisputable
**may butas** *n* perforation
**may dyabetes** *adj* diabetic
**may gamit** *adj* useful
**may hangganan** *n* mortality
**may hilig** *adj* interested
**may himig** *adj* melodic
**may hinanakit** *adv* grudgingly
**may isip** *n* maturity
**may kaayusan** *adv* neatly
**may kabuluhan** *adj* sensible
**may kapansanan** *n* handicap
**may kasiraan** *adj* defective
**may kasunduan** *adj* engaged
**may katapusan** *adj* conclusive
**may kaugnayan** *adj* related
**may kinalaman** *adj* relevant
**may kutob** *n* inkling
**may mali** *adj* erroneous
**may nakaabang** *n* provision
**may parusa** *adj* punishable
**may pasubali** *adj* conditional
**may sakit** *adj* ailing, ill
**may sala** *n* culprit
**may sinat** *adj* feverish
**may sumpong** *adj* moody
**may tao** *n* occupant
**may tiwala** *adj* optimistic
**may tubo** *adj* profitable
**mayabang** *adj* arrogant
**mayaman** *adj* rich, wealthy
**may-ari** *n* owner
**mayelo** *adj* frosty
**maym** *v* mime
**Mayo** *n* May
**mayroon** *v* have, may
**medalya** *n* medal
**medida** *n* tape
**medisina** *n* medicine
**medyas** *n* stocking
**mekaniko** *n* mechanic
**mekanismo** *n* mechanism
**meksikano** *adj* Mexican
**melon** *n* cantaloupe
**menor de edad** *adj* minor
**mensahe** *n* message
**mensahero** *n* messenger
**mental** *adj* mental
**menu** *n* menu
**mesa** *n* table
**metal** *n* metal
**metro** *n* meter
**metro** *adj* metric
**mga akala** *n* supposition
**mga dukha** *adj* grassroots
**mga dulo** *n* extremities
**mga kailangan** *n* supplies
**mga kakanin** *n* foodstuff
**mga karayom** *adj* needless
**mga kasunod** *n* antecedents

**mga kinita** *n* proceeds
**mga kostumbre** *n* routine
**mga lalaki** *n* men
**mga larawan** *n* photography
**mga maybahay** *n* wives
**mga nakatatanda** *n* grown-up
**mga nilalaman** *n* contents
**mga pangyayari** *n* scenario
**mga panulat** *n* paperwork
**mga sumusunod** *adv* namely
**mga unang titik** *n* initials
**mikrobyo** *n* bacteria, germ
**mikropono** *n* microphone
**mikrospkopyo** *n* microscope
**milagro** *n* miracle
**milagroso** *adj* miraculous
**militante** *adj* militant
**milokoton** *n* peach
**milya** *n* mile
**milyahe** *n* mileage
**milyon** *n* million
**milyonaryo** *n* millionaire
**minadali** *adv* hastily
**minahan** *n* minefield
**minaliit** *v* belittle
**minasahe** *v* massage
**mineral** *n* mineral
**minero** *n* miner
**minighitis** *n* meningitis
**ministeryo** *n* ministry
**ministro** *n* minister
**ministro** *v* minister
**minorya** *n* minority
**minsan** *adv* once
**minuto** *n* minute
**misa** *n* mass
**misel** *n* missile
**misteryo** *n* mystery
**misteryoso** *adj* mysterious
**misyon** *n* mission
**misyonaryo** *n* missionary
**Miyerkoles** *n* Wednesday
**moda** *n* fashion
**modelo** *n* model
**moderno** *adj* modern
**modyul** *n* module
**molstyahin** *v* molest
**monasteryo** *n* monastery
**monopolyo** *n* monopoly
**monumento** *n* monument
**moralidad** *n* morality
**morge** *n* mortuary
**morpina** *n* morphine
**mortal** *adj* mortal
**motel** *n* motel
**motibo** *n* motive
**motor** *n* motor
**motorsiklo** *n* scooter
**mukha** *n* countenance
**mula** *n* mule
**mula sa** *pre* from
**muling ihalal** *v* reelect
**muling pagkuha** *n* retrieval
**multa** *n* fine

**multahan** *v* fine
**multo** *n* ghost
**multo** *adj* spooky
**mumo** *n* crumb
**mundo** *n* earth, sphere
**munggo** *n* lentil
**mungkahi** *n* suggestion
**munting pisara** *n* slate
**muog** *n* mist
**mura** *adj* cheap
**murang-isipan** *adj* immature
**museyo** *n* museum
**musika** *n* music
**musikero** *n* musician
**muslim** *adj* Muslim
**mustasa** *n* mustard



# N

**na naman** *adv* afresh
**naaayon** *adj* agreeable
**naaayon sa** *n* corollary
**naagnas** *v* decompose
**naagnas** *adj* putrid
**naakit** *v* mesmerize
**naalis** *v* dislodge
**naaninag** *v* reflect
**naantala** *v* delay
**naantala** *adj* stranded
**naayon** *adv* formally
**naayon sa** *pre* concerning
**naayon sa batas** *adj* legitimate
**nababasa** *adj* legible
**nabagabag** *v* dismay
**nabalda** *v* paralyze
**nabalisa** *v* distress
**nabaliw** *v* madden
**nabalot ng pilak** *adj* silverplated
**nabangga** *v* crash, ram
**nabangkarote** *v* bankrupt
**nabibingi** *v* deafen
**nabighani** *v* bewitch
**nabigla** *v* stun
**nabigla** *adv* suddenly
**nabigo** *v* disappoint
**nabigo** *adj* dissatisfied
**nabihag** *n* captivity
**nabili lahat** *n* sellout
**nabingkong** *v* warp
**nabinyagan** *adj* christian
**nabubulok** *v* deteriorate
**nabubulok** *adj* perishable
**nabulok** *v* perish, rot
**nadiskarel** *v* derail
**nadudurog** *adj* shattering
**nadulas** *v* slip
**nag domina** *v* predominate
**nag tubig** *v* precipitate
**nag-aakala** *c* supposing
**nag-aalala** *v* disturb

**nag-aaral** *n* learning
**nagagalit** *adj* furious
**nagalit** *v* anger, upset
**nagalit** *adj* outrageous
**nagamit** *n* consumption
**nagantso** *n* swindle
**nagapi** *v* overpower
**nagawa** *n* achievement
**nag-awat** *adj* arbitrary
**nagbabadya** *adj* alarming
**nagbabadya** *v* loom
**nagbabanta** *adj* impending
**nagbalat-kayo** *v* camouflage
**nagbanggaan** *v* clash
**nagbanta** *v* threaten
**nagbibintang** *v* allege
**nagbiro** *adv* jokingly
**nagbitiw** *v* resign
**nagbunga** *adj* fruitful
**nagbunyi** *adj* jubilant
**nagbutas** *v* bore
**nagdalo** *n* attendant
**nagdurusa** *v* suffer from
**nagespiya** *v* spy
**naghihiganti** *adj* malevolent
**naghihingalo** *adj* dying
**naghikab** *v* yawn
**naghimagsik** *adj* revolting
**naghiwalay** *v* split up
**nagiba** *v* cave in
**nag-iingay** *adv* noisily
**nag-iisa** *adj* alone, single
**nagkagulo** *v* conflict, riot
**nagkahalaga** *v* amount to
**nagkahiwalay** *v* drift apart
**nagkakagulo** *adj* conflicting
**nagkamali** *v* err, mess up
**nagkamali** *n* mistake
**nagkasakit** *v* afflict
**nagkataon** *adj* coincidental
**nagkiskis** *n* friction
**nagkubli** *n* refugee
**naglaho** *v* evaporate
**naglalaman** *v* contain
**naglayas** *n* runway
**naglilihi** *v* conceive
**naglilimbag** *n* publisher
**nagmadali** *v* cram
**nagmamadali** *adv* speedily
**nag-may-ari** *v* own
**nag-may-ari** *adj* suggestive
**nagnakaw** *v* plunder
**nagpadala** *n* sender
**nagpakabaliw** *adv* madly
**nagpakita** *v* appear
**nagpakumbaba** *v* demean
**nag-palit** *v* convert
**nagpapagunita** *v* evoke
**nagpapahiwatig** *adj* implicit
**nagpapanggap** *adj* would-be
**nagpapaupa** *n* lessee
**nagpapautang** *n* creditor
**nagpasya** *n* judgment
**nagrebelde** *v* rebel

**nag-sagutan** *v* blow up
**nagsaliksik** *v* research
**nagsalita** *v* babble
**nagsarili** *n* autonomy
**nagsarili** *adj* independent
**nagsasanay** *n* trainee
**nagsasarili** *adj* autonomous
**nagsaya** *v* revel
**nagsinungaling** *v* lie
**nagsisi** *v* atone, regret
**nagsisisi** *adj* remorseful
**nagsugat** *v* fester
**nagsuka** *v* vomit
**nagsuklay** *v* comb
**nagtaka** *v* wonder
**nagtalo** *v* argue, dispute
**nagtangka** *v* attempt
**nagtapos** *v* graduate
**nagtatag** *n* founder
**nagulantang** *adj* aghast
**nagulat** *v* amaze, surprise
**nagulat** *adj* shocking
**nag-uling** *v* char
**nag-umiyak** *v* cry out
**nag-umpisa** *v* convene
**nagutom** *v* starve
**nag-uulat** *v* report
**nagwag** *adj* triumphant
**nagwagi** *v* succeed
**nagwagi** *adj* successful
**nagwakas** *v* collapse
**nag-wakas** *v* end up
**nagyabang** *v* boast
**nagyeyelo** *adj* freezing
**nahahalintulad** *adj* typical
**nahanap** *v* find
**nahanap** *adj* located
**nahawa** *n* infection
**nahihilig sa** *adj* predisposed
**nahihiya** *adj* shameful
**nahilo** *adj* dazed
**nahinog** *v* ripen
**nahintakutan** *v* daunt
**nahintakutan** *adj* frenetic
**nahiwa-hiwalay** *v* come apart
**nahiya** *adj* ashamed
**nahlata** *v* manifest
**nahuhulog** *v* drop
**nahukay** *v* unearth
**nahulaan** *v* foresee
**nahuli** *v* fall behind
**nahuli** *adv* late
**nahulog** *n* drop, fall down
**naihalo** *adj* mixed-up
**naiinggit** *adj* envious, envy
**naim** *v* affect
**na-inip** *adj* monotonous
**nainis** *adj* irate
**naipit** *n* stalemate
**naipon** *v* accumulate
**na-ipon** *n* buildup
**naipong emosyon** *adj* pent-up
**naisin** *v* intend
**naisin ng matindi** *v* obsess

**naiwan** *n* remainder
**naka tupi** *adj* pleated
**nakaaaliw** *adj* amusing
**naka-awa** *adj* pitiful
**nakabaligtad** *adv* upside-down
**nakabibingi** *adj* deafening
**nakabinbin** *adj* pending
**nakadamit** *v* clothe
**nakahanda** *adj* ready
**nakahihigit** *adj* sublime
**nakahiwalay** *adj* secluded
**nakahukot** *adj* hunched
**nakainis** *adj* offensive
**nakaka aliw** *adj* exhilarating
**nakaka tusok** *adj* stinging
**nakaka-abala** *adj* bothersome
**nakakaakit** *adj* injurious
**nakakaalam** *adj* conscious
**nakakaaliw** *adj* entertaining
**nakakaawa** *adj* pathetic
**nakakabalisa** *adj* distressing
**nakakabawas** *adj* detrimental
**nakakabigla** *adj* stunning
**nakakabigo** *adj* disappointing
**nakakabit** *adj* attached
**nakakabit** *n* attachment
**nakakabwisit** *adj* nagging
**nakakagaan** *adj* extenuating
**nakakagulat** *adj* astonishing
**nakakahawa** *adj* contagious
**nakakahiya** *v* disgrace
**nakakainip** *adj* tedious
**nakaka-inip** *adj* boring
**nakakainis** *adj* annoying
**nakakakanser** *adj* cancerous
**nakakakilabot** *adj* creepy
**nakakakiliti** *adj* ticklish
**nakakalason** *adj* toxic
**nakakalat** *adj* sparse
**nakakaligaya** *adj* enjoyable
**nakakalito** *adj* confusing
**nakakalungkot** *adj* depressing
**nakakandado** *v* lock up
**nakakapa** *adj* palpable
**nakakapag-alala** *adj* worrisome
**nakakapagod** *adj* strenuous
**nakakapagsisi** *adj* regrettable
**nakakapagtaka** *adj* amazing
**nakakapahinga** *adj* relaxing
**nakakasakit** *adj* hurtful
**nakakasilaw** *adj* dazzling
**nakakasira** *adj* damaging
**nakakasugapa** *adj* addictive
**nakakasuya** *adj* disgusting
**nakakatakot** *adj* appalling
**nakakatawa** *adj* humorous
**nakakateawa** *adj* comical
**nakakatwa** *adj* laughable
**nakakulong** *v* jail
**nakalaan** *n* availability
**nakalaan** *adj* vacant
**nakalalason** *adj* poisonous
**nakalap** *n* collection
**nakaligtas** *n* survivor

**nakalililito** *n* maze
**nakalipas** *adj* past
**nakalog** *adj* shaken
**nakalulan** *adv* aboard
**nakalutang** *n* affront
**nakamamangha** *adj* awesome
**nakamamatay** *adj* fatal, lethal
**nakamit** *n* acquisition
**nakapaa** *adj* barefoot
**nakapag-durusa** *adj* agonizing
**nakapagilid** *v* border on
**nakapagod** *adj* gruelling
**nakapagtataka** *adj* mystic
**nakapagtataka** *n* wonder
**nakapahalang** *adj* oblique
**nakapalabas** *pre* without
**nakapaloob** *adj* inlaid
**nakapaloob** *pre* within
**nakapangako** *adj* committed
**nakapilalim** *adj* underlying
**nakapinid** *adj* close, closed
**nakapipilay** *adj* stifling
**nakaraan** *adv* lately
**nakaraan** *adj* previous
**nakaririmarim** *adj* sickening
**nakasabit** *v* cling
**nakasakay** *v* board
**nakasalalay** *n* dependence
**nakasalubong** *v* bump into
**nakasimangot** *v* frown
**nakasisilaw** *n* glare
**nakasulat** *adj* written
**nakatago** *adj* hidden
**nakatakda** *adj* due
**nakatanim** *v* ingrained
**nakatatanda** *n* elder
**nakataya** *n* stake
**nakatigil** *adj* stagnant
**nakatindig** *adj* erect
**nakatira** *adj* inhabit
**nakatira** *v* live
**nakatira** *n* residence
**nakatuon** *n* focus
**nakaugalian** *n* custom
**nakaupo** *adj* seated
**nakaw** *n* loot
**nakawin** *v* steal, snitch
**nakbibighani** *adj* enchanting
**nakikinig** *adj* attentive
**nakikita** *adj* visible, visual
**nakita** *v* see
**nakunan** *n* miscarriage
**nalalapit** *adj* forthcoming
**nalaman** *n* discovery
**nalaman** *v* find out
**naligaw** *adv* adrift, stray
**naligaw** *v* astray
**naligaw** *adj* misguided
**nalililito** *v* confuse
**nalito** *adj* startled
**nalugi** *adj* bankrupt
**nalulula sa barko** *adj* seasick
**nalulunod** *v* drown
**naluma** *adj* outmoded

**nalungkot** *v* sadden
**naluwag** *adj* baggy
**namaga** *v* swell
**namagitan** *n* intercession
**namalantsa** *adj* iron
**namali** *v* mistake
**namaluktot** *v* bend
**namamaga** *adj* sore
**namamahala** *n* coordinator
**namamana** *adj* hereditary
**namamawis** *v* perspire
**namantsahan** *v* blot
**namaril** *n* gunman
**namatay** *v* die out
**namayapa** *adj* deceased
**namimilipit** *v* writhe
**namula** *v* blush
**namumuhi** *v* abhor
**namumuhunan** *n* investor
**namumula** *adj* lurid
**namuno** *v* mastermind
**nana** *n* pus
**nanagimbal** *adj* horrendous
**nanaginip** *v* dream
**nanagip buhay** *n* lifeguard
**nanalo** *v* champion, win
**nananabik** *v* crave, long for
**nananaginip** *v* daydream
**nananaig** *adj* prevalent
**nananakot** *n* terrorist
**nandudurog** *adj* crushing
**nang nararapat** *adv* duly
**nangako** *adj* avowed
**nangako** *v* commit
**nangangapa** *adj* staggering
**nangangaral** *n* preaching
**nanggigitata** *adj* squalid
**nanghahamon** *adj* challenging
**nanghihinguto** *adj* nitpicking
**nanghina** *v* weaken
**nangingibabaw** *adj* towering
**nanginig** *v* tremble, shiver
**nangungupahan** *n* tenant
**nangungutya** *adj* cynic
**nangunguwarta** *v* graft
**nangunguyapit** *adj* scrambled
**nangyari** *v* happen
**naninieahan** *n* inhabitant
**naninilbihan** *n* servant
**naninirahan** *n* settler
**nanloloko** *v* dupe
**nanunubasta** *n* auctioneer
**nanunugod** *adj* aggressive
**na-ospital** *v* hospitalize
**napag-isipan** *n* conception
**napaidlip** *v* doze
**napaka** *adv* very
**napaka halaga** *adj* momentous
**napaka laki** *adj* monumental
**napaka lamig** *adj* icy
**napaka lungkot** *adj* murky
**napaka sakit** *adj* excruciating
**napakadumi** *adj* filthy
**napaka-galing** *adj* superior

N

**napakaganda** *adj* superb
**napakalaki** *adj* gigantic
**napakalamig** *adj* frigid
**napakalayo** *adj* faraway
**napakalubha** *adv* gravely
**napakarami** *adj* innumerable
**napaliligiran** *adj* swamped
**napansin** *v* notice
**napapalooban** *v* encompass
**napapanahon** *adj* opportune
**napasa** *v* bruise
**napatunayan** *adj* proven
**napa-usapan** *adj* deliberate
**napigilan** *adj* subdued
**napilay** *v* maim
**napingkong** *v* dent
**napipilitan** *adj* compelling
**napipinto** *v* lurk
**naputol** *n* nip
**nararapat** *adj* eligible, valid
**nararapat lamang** *v* deserve
**narinig** *v* hear
**naririnig** *adj* audible
**narkotiko** *n* narcotic
**narses** *n* nurse
**nasa** *pre* on
**nasa hilaga** *adj* northern
**nasa hustong isip** *adj* mature
**nasa isip** *adv* mentally
**nasa oras** *adj* prompt
**nasa panahon** *adj* up-to-date
**nasa tropiko** *adj* tropical
**nasagupa** *v* come across
**nasakop** *v* infiltrate
**nasaktan** *v* hurt
**nasalanta** *n* devastation
**nasalanta** *v* wipe out
**nasalubong** *v* run into
**nasangkot** *v* involved
**nasapawan** *v* overshadow
**nasarapan** *adj* ecstatic
**nasasakupan** *n* coverage
**nasira** *v* bog down
**nasira ang ulo** *adj* distraught
**nasirang pangako** *n* breach
**nasiyahan** *adj* elated
**nasugat** *v* wound
**nasunog** *v* burn
**nasunog sa araw** *n* sunburn
**natakot** *adj* frantic
**natakot** *v* frighten, scare
**natalisod** *v* stumble
**natalo** *adj* beaten
**natalo** *v* succumb
**natalo sa desisyon** *v* overrule
**natangay** *v* drift
**natapos** *v* lapse, expire
**natatagong lakas** *adj* potential
**natatanggal** *adj* detachable
**natatangi** *adj* special
**natin** *adj* our
**natira** *n* debris
**natunaw** *v* melt
**natural** *adj* innate

**natuto** *adj* learned
**natutuwa** *adj* glad
**natutuyo** *v* dry
**natuyo** *adj* dry
**naubusan** *v* run out
**na-ulila** *adj* bereaved
**naulit** *n* relapse
**nauna** *pre* ahead
**nauna** *adv* previously
**nauna** *adj* former, prior
**naunahan** *v* outrun
**nautal** *v* stutter
**nauukol** *v* belong
**nauukol sa** *v* pertain
**nauukol sa bahay** *n* household
**nauukol sa laman** *adj* carnal
**nawala** *v* disappear
**nawalan ng dangal** *n* dishonor
**nawalan ng mana** *v* disinherit
**nawalan ng sigla** *v* depress
**nawalang saysay** *v* fall through
**nawasak** *n* wreckage
**nawawala** *adj* missing
**nayon** *n* village, hamlet
**Nederland** *n* Netherlands
**negatibo** *adj* negative
**negosyante** *adj* bourgeois
**nenerbyos** *adj* frenzied
**nerbyos** *n* frenzy
**nerbyos** *adj* nervous
**nerbyosos** *adj* neurotic
**ng** *pre* by, of
**ngalakbay** *n* voyage
**ngala-ngala** *n* palate
**ngayon** *adv* today
**ngayong** *adv* now
**ngipin** *n* tooth
**ngiti** *n* smile
**ngiwi** *n* grimace
**ngumiti** *v* smile
**nguso** *n* nozzle
**nguyain** *v* chew, munch
**ni hindi** *c* nor
**nikotina** *n* nicotine
**nilaga** *n* stew
**nilagdaan** *n* endorsement
**nilalaman** *adj* content
**nilalaman** *n* text
**nilalason** *n* poisoning
**nilamon** *v* eat away
**nilapastangan** *v* abuse
**nilason** *v* poison
**nilaspatangan** *v* rape
**nilikha** *n* creation, creature
**nilito** *v* baffle, startle
**nillinis** *v* cleanse
**niluma** *adj* antiquated
**niluwagan** *v* loosen
**ningas** *v* blaze
**ninuno** *n* ancestor
**nitroheno** *n* nitrogen
**nitso** *n* catacomb
**niyog** *n* coconut
**nobela** *n* novel

N

**nobelista** *n* novelist
**nobya** *n* bride, fiancé
**Nobyembre** *n* November
**nobyo** *n* groom
**noo** *n* forehead
**noong una** *adv* formerly
**normal** *adj* normal
**Norwey** *n* Norway
**nota** *v* note
**notaryo** *n* notary
**nukleyar** *adj* nuclear
**nunal** *n* mole
**nyebe** *v* snow
**nyebe** *n* snow

**o** *c* or
**o kaya** *adv* else
**obispo** *n* bishop
**obligasyon** *adj* compulsory
**obserbatoryo** *n* observatory
**okasyon** *n* occasion
**oksidyen** *n* oxygen
**Oktubre** *n* October
**Olanda** *n* Holland
**olandes** *adj* blond
**Olandes** *adj* Dutch
**oliba** *n* olive
**olimpyada** *n* olympics
**onsa** *n* ounce
**oo** *adv* yes
**opera** *n* opera
**opisyal** *n* officer, office
**opisyal** *adj* official
**opisyal sa hukbo** *n* marshal
**optiko** *n* optician
**opyo** *n* opium
**oras** *n* hour, time
**orasan** *n* clock, time
**oras-oras** *adv* hourly
**organismo** *n* organism
**organista** *n* organist
**orihinal** *adj* original
**orkestra** *n* orchestra
**oso** *n* bear
**oter** *n* otter
**otonyo** *n* autumn

**pa** *c* yet
**paa** *n* foot, feet
**paa ng hayop** *n* hoof, paw
**paakyat** *n* climbing
**paalala** *n* admonition

**paalalahanan** *v* remind
**paalam** *n* farewell
**paalisin** *v* evict, oust
**paamuhin** *v* tame
**paano** *adv* how
**paanyaya** *n* invitation
**paapoy** *n* bonfire
**paapuyan** *n* campfire
**paaralan** *n* school
**paaralin** *v* institute
**paasimin** *v* ferment
**paatras** *adj* backward
**pababa** *adj* downcast
**pabalikin** *v* repatriate
**pabango** *n* perfume
**pabaya** *adj* carefree
**pabayaan** *n* abandonment
**pabayaan** *v* forsake, neglect
**pabibinata** *n* adolescence
**pabilog** *adj* circular
**pabrika** *n* factory
**pabugsu-bugso** *adj* sporadic
**pabula** *n* fable, parable
**pabuya** *n* award, reward
**padala** *n* remittance
**pag - aalam** *n* inquiry
**pag aakala** *n* presupposition
**pag aatang** *n* imposition
**pag alabin** *v* heighten
**pag alay** *n* charity
**pag apura** *n* urgency
**pag asinta** *n* target
**pag bago** *n* deviation
**pag bawi** *n* withdrawal
**pag bayaran** *v* pay back
**pag bibigay** *n* concession
**pag bugbog** *n* scourge
**pag daong** *n* anchor
**pag dating** *n* arrival
**pag dugtong** *n* annexation
**pag galang** *n* tact
**pag gamit** *n* use, usefulness
**pag giba** *n* demolition
**pag gunita** *n* recollection
**pag halal** *n* referendum
**pag hawak** *n* grip
**pag hipo** *n* touch
**pag ihip** *n* puff
**pag init** *n* heating
**pag kagat** *n* sting
**pag labag** *n* infraction
**pag lapastangan** *n* rape
**pag likha** *n* production
**pag lubog** *n* plunge
**pag pawi** *v* obliterate
**pag pigil** *n* interruption
**pag pilipit** *n* twist
**pag piraprasuhin** *v* strip
**pag pisil** *n* grip
**pag rekisa** *n* inspection
**pag sagip** *n* conservation
**pag sagupa** *n* skirmish
**pag sakop** *n* infiltration
**pag sigaw** *n* roar

**pag singit** *n* insertion
**pag sugpo** *n* annihilation
**pag sukat** *n* assessment
**pag talaga** *n* deployment
**pag tangis** *n* wail
**pag tigil** *v* interruption
**pag tingin** *n* care
**pag tubos** *n* redemption
**pag tusok** *n* sting
**pag-aagaw** *n* hijack
**pag-aaklas** *n* uprising
**pag-aalaga** *n* upkeep
**pag-aalala** *n* regards
**pag-aalay** *n* offering
**pagaalinlangan** *n* quandary
**pagaangkat** *n* importation
**pag-aari** *n* ownership
**pag-aari ng ideya** *n* patent
**pag-aawat** *n* mediator
**pag-aayon** *n* adaptation
**pag-agaw** *n* kidnapping
**pag-agos** *n* cascade
**pag-aklas** *n* upheaval
**pag-alala** *n* worry
**pag-alipusta** *n* disdain
**pag-alis** *n* departure
**pagalitan** *v* chide
**pag-alsa** *n* revolt
**pagamutan** *n* hospital
**paganahin** *v* stimulate
**pagandahin** *v* beautify
**pag-angat** *n* promotion
**pag-angkas** *n* hitch
**pag-angkin** *n* claim
**pagano** *adj* pagan
**pag-apoy** *adj* ablaze
**pag-asa** *n* hope, prospect
**pagawaan** *n* workshop
**pagawaan ng alak** *n* winery
**pag-awat** *n* arbitration
**pag-ayaw** *n* dislike
**pag-ayos** *n* renovation
**pagbaba** *n* devaluation
**pagbababadya** *n* loom
**pagbababago** *n* amendment
**pagbababalat-kayo** *n* hypocrisy
**pagbababawal** *n* prohibition
**pagbababawas** *n* subtraction
**pagbababayad** *n* refund
**pagbababaybay** *n* spelling
**pagbagsak** *n* downfall
**pag-bagsak** *n* downturn
**pagbaha** *n* flooding
**pagbahagi** *n* distribution
**pagbalik** *n* return
**pagbalot** *n* wrapping
**pagbanggit** *n* mention
**pagbasa** *n* reading
**pagbati** *n* greetings
**pagbawalan** *v* bar, curtail
**pagbaybay** *n* spell
**pagbibigay lakas** *n* exertion
**pagbibinata** *n* adolescent
**pagbibitin** *n* suspension

**pagbibitiw** *n* resignation
**pagbigyan** *v* cater to
**pagbilang** *n* assessment
**pagbintangan** *v* charge
**pagbubukas** *n* inauguration
**pagbubukid** *n* farming
**pag-bubukid** *n* agriculture
**pagbubuno** *n* wrestling
**pagbubuntis** *n* gestation
**pagbuhos ng ulan** *n* downpour
**pagbukas** *n* opening
**pagbunyag** *adj* exposed
**pagbutihin** *v* develop
**pagdadalaga** *n* teenager
**pagdadalamhati** *n* bereavement
**pagdadalantao** *n* maternity
**pagdagsa** *n* influx
**pagdagundong** *n* rumble
**pagdalaw** *n* visit
**pagdalo** *n* attendance
**pagdaloy sa ugat** *adj* intravenous
**pagdaragdag** *n* addition
**Pagdating** *n* Advent
**pagdikit** *n* fuse
**pagdiriwang** *n* ceremony
**pagdudumi** *n* pollution
**pagdurusa** *n* suffering
**paggalang** *n* courtesy
**pag-galang** *n* reverence
**paggalaw** *n* motion
**paggaling** *n* recovery
**pag-galing** *adj* convalescent
**pag-gamit** *n* usage
**paggamot** *n* treat
**pagganti** *n* reaction
**pagganyakin** *v* motivate
**paggastos** *n* spending
**paggawa** *n* production
**paggawa ng batas** *n* legislation
**paggigiit** *n* insistence
**pag-gising** *n* awakening
**pag-guhit** *n* draw
**paghadlang** *n* interference
**paghahalo** *n* infusion
**paghahambing** *n* metaphor
**paghahanap** *n* manhunt
**paghahanda** *n* preparation
**paghahandog** *n* dedication
**paghaharap** *n* confrontation
**paghahari** *n* reign
**paghahatid** *n* delivery
**paghahati-hati** *n* division
**paghahayag** *n* revelation
**paghalal** *n* poll
**pag-halo-halo** *n* mix-up
**paghamak** *n* contempt
**paghamon** *n* dare
**paghanga** *n* admiration
**paghaplos** *n* caress
**pagharap** *n* presence
**paghawak** *n* grasp
**paghihimagsik** *n* protest
**paghihintay** *n* waiting
**paghihirap** *n* agony

P

**paghihiwalay** *n* parting, split
**pag-himagas** *n* dessert
**paghimas** *n* caress
**paghinalaan** *v* suspect
**paghinga** *n* respiration
**paghirang** *n* appointment
**paghiwalay** *n* isolation
**paghiwalayin** *v* split
**paghuhubad** *n* nudism
**pag-huli** *n* arrest
**pag-iba** *n* deviation
**pag-iba-ibahin** *v* diversify
**pag-ibig** *n* romance
**pagiging ama** *n* fatherhood
**pagiging bihasa** *n* proficiency
**pagiging ina** *n* motherhood
**pagiging negatibo** *n* pessimism
**pagiimbestiga** *n* probing
**pag-iingat** *n* caution
**pag-iisa** *n* solitude
**pag-iisip** *n* sanity
**pag-ikot** *n* rotation, turn
**pag-ikot** *adj* winding
**pag-ilag** *n* yield
**pagindapatin** *v* validate
**pag-inog** *n* orbit
**pagitan** *n* interval
**pag-iwas** *n* avoidance
**pag-iyak** *n* crying
**pagka - inip** *n* boredom
**pagka aba** *n* hail
**pagka antala** *n* holdup
**pagka bahala** *n* tension
**pagka balani** *n* magnetism
**pagka banal** *adj* monastic
**pagka banidosa** *adv* vainly
**pagka bigo** *adj* dejected
**pagka bingi** *n* deafness
**pagka buhya** *n* existence
**pagka bulok** *n* deterioration
**pagka galit** *n* outrage
**pagka hilig** *n* inclination
**pagka hilo** *n* dizziness
**pagka ilado** *n* frostbite
**pagka inip** *n* impatience
**pagka lala** *n* severity
**pagka ligtas** *n* survival
**pagka mahigpit** *n* stern
**pagka mahinahon** *n* serenity
**pagka mahiyain** *n* timidity
**pagka malambot** *n* softness
**pagka malikhain** *n* ingenuity
**pagka matatag** *n* tenacity
**pagka natural** *adj* intrinsic
**pagka salanta** *n* holocaust
**pagka silbi** *n* futility
**pagka strikto** *n* rigor
**pagka takot** *n* shudder
**pagka tali** *n* bondage
**pagka tampalasan** *n* rascal
**pagka tanga** *adj* idiotic
**pagka wala** *n* disappearance
**pagka wasto** *n* precision
**pagka-akit** *n* attraction

**pagka-alinsangan** *n* humidity
**pagkabagal** *n* slow motion
**pagkabaho** *n* stink
**pagka-balanse** *n* equation
**pagkabalisa** *n* anxiety
**pagkabata** *adj* juvenile
**pagkabigla** *n* shock
**pagkabit** *n* connection
**pagkabit-kabitin** *v* thread
**pagkabuhay** *adj* alive
**pagkagalit** *n* loathing
**pagkagulat** *n* panic
**pagkagusto** *n* liking
**pagka-gusto** *n* affinity
**pagkahalata** *adv* obviously
**pagkahalintulad** *n* parallel
**pagkahawig** *n* comparison
**pagkahilig** *adj* prone
**pagkahilig** *n* propensity
**pagkain** *n* meal, food
**pagkaing butil** *n* oatmeal
**pagkaing dagat** *n* seafood
**pagkainis** *n* loathing
**pagkaisahin** *v* unify
**pagkakadikit** *n* tangent
**pagkakagastusan** *n* expense
**pagkakagawa** *n* performance
**pagkakagulo** *n* tumult
**pagkakaiba** *n* distortion, oddity
**pagkaka-iba** *n* assortment
**pagkakaiba-iba** *n* variety
**pagkakaibigan** *n* friendship
**pagkakaisa** *n* solidarity
**pagkaka-isa** *n* alliance
**pagkakakilala** *adv* notably
**pagkakakilanlan** *n* identity
**pagkakalaktaw** *n* omission
**pagkakamali** *n* oversight
**pagkakasangkot** *n* involvement
**pagkakasosyo** *n* partnership
**pagkakasubo** *n* dilemma
**pagkakasundo** *n* accord
**pagkakataon** *n* chance
**pagkakatatag** *n* charter
**pagkakatulad** *n* parity
**pagkakawasak** *n* ravage
**pagkakitid** *adv* narrowly
**pagka-laki** *n* enlargement
**pagkalalaki** *n* virility
**pagkaliban sa** *adj* exceptional
**pagkalimot** *n* amnesia
**pagkalinaw** *adv* plainly
**pagkalito** *n* confusion
**pagkamabisa** *n* effectiveness
**pagkamuhi** *n* hatred
**pagkanditato** *n* candidacy
**pagkansela** *n* cancellation
**pagkaparihaba** *n* rectangle
**pagkaperpekto** *n* perfection
**pagkarumi** *n* contamination
**pagkasabik** *n* eagerness
**pagkasalungat** *adv* opposite
**pagkasapat** *adv* completely
**pagkasira** *n* decadence

**pagkasugapa** *adj* addicted
**pagkasuklam** *n* repulse
**pagkasunod** *n* precedent
**pagkasuya** *n* disgust
**pagkatao** *n* personality
**pagkatapos** *adv* then
**pagkatotoo** *n* realism
**pagkatulala** *n* consternation
**pagkatunaw** *n* condensation
**pagkawala** *n* banishment
**pagkayamot** *n* displeasure
**pagkikita-kita** *n* reunion
**pagkilala** *n* recognition
**pagkit** *n* wax
**pagkuha** *n* subscription
**pagkukulang** *adj* faulty
**pagkukunwari** *n* pretense
**pagkulong** *n* seizure
**pagkumbinsi** *n* persuasion
**pagkumpiska** *n* confiscation
**paglaban** *n* hostility
**paglabas** *n* exodus
**pagladlad** *n* display
**paglaganap** *n* outbreak
**paglagok** *n* gulp
**paglaki** *n* expansion
**paglala** *n* degeneration
**paglalaan** *n* reservation
**paglalabanan** *n* rivalry
**paglalagay** *n* input
**paglalahatla** *n* publication
**paglalaho** *n* eclipse
**paglalakad** *n* hike
**paglalakbay** *n* journey
**paglalangan** *v* trick
**paglalarawan** *n* description
**paglalayag** *n* navigation
**paglamon** *n* glut
**paglangoy** *n* swimming
**paglapastangan** *n* disrespect
**paglapit** *n* approach
**pagliban** *n* absence
**pagliligtas** *n* salvation
**paglilihim** *n* secrecy
**paglilimbag** *n* printing
**paglilitis** *n* trial
**paglinis** *n* purge
**paglipad** *n* flight
**paglipat** *n* transfer
**paglubog** *n* immersion
**paglubog ng araw** *n* sundown
**pagluluksa** *n* mourning
**pagluluto** *n* cooking
**paglupig** *n* conquest
**paglusob** *n* raid
**pagmalupitan** *v* brutalize
**pagmamadali** *n* haste
**pagmamahal** *n* affection
**pagmamatyag** *n* surveillance
**pag-mamay-ari** *n* lordship
**pagmantsa** *n* smear
**pagmasdan** *v* observe
**pagmultuhan** *v* haunt
**pagmumura** *adj* derogatory

**pagnanakaw** *n* heist, theft
**pagnanasa** *n* desire
**pagnasaan** *v* desire
**pagninilay-nilay** *n* meditation
**pagod** *n* exhaustion
**pagod** *adj* tired, weary
**pagong** *n* turtle
**pagopera** *n* incision
**pagpagalit** *n* scolding
**pagpahinga** *n* respite
**pagpalis** *n* shove
**pagpalit** *n* discharge
**pagpalitin** *v* interchange
**pagpalo** *n* smack
**pagpanaw** *n* demise
**pag-panggap** *n* disguise
**pagpanig** *n* discrimination
**pagpanis** *n* coagulation
**pagpansin** *n* observation
**pagpapabaya** *n* negligence
**pagpapadala** *n* money order
**pagpapaganda** *n* improvement
**pagpapahalaga** *n* appreciation
**pagpapahayag** *n* declaration
**pagpapahirap** *n* ordeal
**pagpapahupa** *n* appeasement
**pagpapakalat** *n* dispersal
**pagpapakita** *n* indication
**pagpapalaganap** *n* propaganda
**pagpapalaki** *n* upbringing
**pagpapaliban** *n* postponement
**pagpapalit** *n* transformation
**pagpapalitan** *n* interchange
**pagpapanatili** *n* sustenance
**pagpapanukala** *n* scheme
**pagpapaputok** *n* gunfire
**pagpaparami** *n* reproduction
**pagpapari** *n* priesthood
**pagpapasuko** *n* extradition
**pagpapatala** *n* recruit
**pagpapatalsik** *n* expulsion
**pagpapatama** *n* hit
**pagpapatawad** *n* dispensation
**pagpapatibay** *n* ratification
**pagpapatuloy** *n* resumption
**pagpapatunay** *n* verification
**pagpapaumnahin** *n* apology
**pagparusa** *n* torture
**pagpasok** *n* entrée, entry
**pagpatala** *v* check in
**pagpatay** *n* homicide
**pagpawala** *n* discharge
**pagpayag** *n* consent
**pagpigil** *n* constraint
**pagpili** *n* selection
**pagpilit** *n* coercion
**pagpipigil** *n* restraint
**pagpipilian** *n* option
**pagpipira-piraso** *n* shred
**pagpukaw** *n* provocation
**pagpupulong** *n* meeting
**pagpupunyagi** *n* effort
**pagpuri** *n* commendation
**pagputok** *n* blowout

**pagputol** *n* amputation
**pagsabi** *n* articulation
**pagsabihan** *v* admonish
**pagsabog** *n* blast, explosion
**pag-sagw** *n* abduction
**pagsakop** *n* colonization
**pagsala** *n* strain
**pagsali** *n* participation
**pagsalubong** *n* welcome
**pagsamahin** *v* add
**pagsamantala** *n* exploit
**pagsamba** *n* adoration
**pag-sanga** *n* diversion
**pagsang-ayon** *n* approbation
**pag-sang-ayon** *n* approval
**pagsangkot** *n* implication
**pagsapi** *n* membership
**pagsasalaysay** *n* recital
**pagsasalin** *n* transfusion
**pagsasaling wika** *v* interpret
**pagsasama** *n* fusion
**pagsasama sama** *n* synthesis
**pagsasanay** *n* exercise
**pag-sasara** *n* liquidation
**pagsaya** *adv* joyfully
**pagsigaw** *n* shriek
**pagsikapan** *n* endeavor
**pagsisid** *n* diving
**pagsisigarilyo** *n* smoker
**pagsisikap** *n* application
**pagsisisi** *n* contrition, regret
**pagsugod** *n* aggression
**pag-sugod** *n* assault
**pagsugpo** *n* prevention
**pagsuhol** *n* bribery
**pag-suko** *n* abdication
**pagsulong** *n* progress
**pagsulsi** *n* stitch
**pagsulsol** *n* incitement
**pagsumpa** *n* condemnation
**pagsunod** *n* compliance
**pagsusulit** *n* examination
**pagsusuplada** *n* rebuff
**pagsusuri** *n* analysis
**pag-suway** *n* disobedience
**pagtaas** *n* surge
**pag-taas** *n* ascendancy
**pagtaas ng antas** *n* boost
**pagtadtad** *n* chopper
**pagtagas** *n* leakage
**pagtahimik** *v* repose
**pagtakahan** *v* mystify
**pagtakas** *n* defection
**pagtakip** *n* insulation
**pagtakpan** *v* cover up
**pagtalikod** *adv* back
**pagtalon** *n* leap
**pagtalunan** *n* argument
**pagtanggal** *n* abortion
**pagtanggap** *n* acceptance
**pagtanggi** *n* decline
**pagtangkilik** *n* patronage
**pagtantya** *n* estimation
**pagtapal** *n* plaster

**pagtatae** *n* diarrhea
**pagtatako** *n* discussion
**pagtataksil** *n* infidelity
**pagtatala** *n* recording
**pagtatalaga** *n* ordination
**pagtatalik** *n* sex
**pagtatalo** *n* discord, dispute
**pagtatanghal** *v* exhibit
**pagtatangi** *v* esteem
**pagtatapos** *n* graduation
**pagtawanan** *v* ridicule
**pagtayo** *n* standing
**pagtibayin** *v* ratify
**pagtibok** *n* pulse
**pagtigil** *n* stagnation
**pag-tigil** *n* cease-fire
**pagtindig** *n* standing
**pagtitika** *n* mortification
**pagtitipid** *n* austerity
**pagtitipon** *n* assembly
**pagtitipon-tipon** *n* rally
**pagtitiwala** *n* reliance
**pagtugis** *n* pursuit
**pagtugmain** *v* correlate
**pagtunaw** *n* dissolution
**pagtuon** *n* emphasis
**pagtutol** *n* resistance
**pagtutubos** *n* settlement
**pagtutulungan** *n* collaboration
**pagtuturo** *n* pedagogy
**pagtuya** *n* flattery
**pag-ulan** *n* rainfall
**pagunlad** *n* prosperity
**pag-unlad** *n* evolution
**pag-usapan** *v* discuss
**pag-uugali** *n* behavior
**pag-uugali** *adj* characteristic
**pag-uusap** *n* discussion
**pag-uusisa** *n* curiosity
**pagwagi** *n* victor
**pagwawagi** *n* success
**pagyabang** *adv* proudly
**pahaba** *adj* diabolical
**pahabain** *v* extend, protract
**pahalagahan** *v* merit
**pahalang** *adj* horizontal
**pahamon** *n* challenge
**pahina** *n* page
**pahinain** *v* impair
**pahinga** *n* recess, rest
**pahingahan** *n* camp, patio
**pahingi** *v* beseech
**pahintulot** *n* permission
**pahintulutan** *v* permit
**pahinugin** *v* mellow
**pahiwatig** *n* hint, signal
**paiba-iba** *adj* variable
**pa-ika-ika** *v* limp
**paikliin** *v* abridge
**paiko-ikot** *adj* lingering
**paikutin** *v* whirl, rotate
**pain** *n* bait
**painitin** *v* warm up
**pakainin** *v* feed, nourish

**pakakulong** *n* detention
**pakasalan** *v* marry
**pakawalan** *v* extricate
**pakialaman** *v* encroach
**pakialamero/a** *n* intruder
**pakibagayan** *v* please
**pakikialam** *n* intrusion
**pakikibaka** *n* struggle
**pakikipag-isa** *n* unification
**pakikipagtuos** *n* showdown
**pakikiramay** *n* sympathy
**pakikisama** *n* rapport
**pakikitungo** *n* contact
**pakilala** *n* introduction
**pakinabang** *n* advantage
**pakinisin** *v* smooth
**pakinisin** *adv* smoothly
**pakintabin** *v* polish, shine
**pakiramay** *n* condolences
**pakiramdam** *n* intuition
**pakkipag-alaman** *n* negotiation
**pako** *n* nail, tack, anvil
**pakpak** *n* wing
**paksa** *n* issue, subject
**pakumbaba** *adv* humbly
**pakwan** *n* watermelon
**pakyawan** *adj* wholesale
**pal** *n* combatant
**pala** *n* shovel, spade
**pala away** *adj* troublesome
**pala hubad** *n* nudist
**pala iwas** *adj* evasive
**pala kaibigan** *adj* sociable
**pala utos** *adj* pushy
**palaaway** *adj* belligerent
**pala-away** *adj* quarrelsome
**palaban** *n* fighter
**palabas** *adj* outward
**palabas** *n* way out
**palabasin** *v* let out
**palaboy** *n* bum
**palaboy** *adj* outcast
**palad** *n* palm
**palagay** *n* viewpoint
**palagi** *adv* always
**palagian** *adj* perennial
**palahin** *v* shove
**palaisdaan** *n* pond
**palaisipan** *n* crossword
**palaka** *n* frog, toad
**palakad** *n* process
**palakaibigan** *adj* affable
**palakasin** *v* fortify
**palakihin** *v* amplify
**palakol** *n* ax, hatchet
**palakpakan** *v* applaud
**palakpakan** *n* applause
**palalain** *v* aggravate
**pala-laro** *adj* playful
**palaman** *n* stuffing
**palambutin** *v* soften
**palamigan** *n* freezer
**palamigin** *v* refrigerate
**palamuti** *n* ornament

P

**palamutian** *v* adorn
**palaro** *n* contest
**palaruan** *n* playground
**palasagot** *adj* contentious
**palasalita** *adj* outspoken
**palasong maigsi** *n* dart
**palasyo** *n* mansion
**palatandaan** *n* symptom
**palatuusan** *n* algebra
**pala-utos** *adj* bossy
**palawakin** *v* broaden
**palawit** *n* pendant
**palayain** *v* free
**palayasin** *v* drive away
**palayaw** *n* nickname
**palayok** *n* kettle, pot
**palda** *n* skirt
**palengke** *n* market
**paleta** *n* ingot
**palibot** *n* circuit
**paligid** *n* vicinity
**paligiran** *v* beset, ring
**paligo** *n* bath
**paligoy-ligoy** *adj* garrulous
**paligsahan** *n* competition
**paliguan** *n* bathtub
**palihim** *adv* secretly
**palikpik** *n* fin
**palikuran** *n* bathroom
**palimos** *v* dole out
**paliparan** *n* airfield
**palit** *n* swap
**palitan** *v* alternate
**palito** *n* toothpick
**paliwanag** *n* notation
**palneta** *n* planet
**palo** *n* spanking
**paloob** *adv* inwards
**palooban** *v* enclose
**paltos** *n* blister
**palugit** *n* extension
**palugitan** *v* extend
**paluin** *v* spank, strike
**pamahalaan** *n* government
**pamahid** *n* ointment
**pamahiin** *n* superstition
**pamamaga** *n* inflammation
**pamamahala** *n* regime
**pamamalita** *n* herald
**pamamanday** *n* carpentry
**pamamaraan** *n* strategy
**pamamayani** *n* supremacy
**pamana** *n* legacy
**pamanang lahi** *n* heritage
**pamangkin** *n* nephew
**pamantayan** *n* criterion
**pamasahe** *n* fare
**pamatay-bisa** *n* antidote
**pamatid-uhaw** *n* refreshment
**pamatnubay** *n* guidance
**pamaypay** *n* fan
**pambabastos** *n* harshness
**pambansa** *adj* national
**pambara sa baha** *n* floodgate

P

**pambaril** *n* smoking gun
**pambato** *n* vanguard
**pambayan** *adj* civil
**pambukid** *adj* rustic
**pambura** *n* eraser
**pamigay** *adj* disposable
**pamilihan** *n* mall, market
**pamilya** *n* family
**pamimili** *n* shopping
**pamimirata** *n* piracy
**paminggalan** *n* pantry
**pampadagdag** *n* accelerator
**pampagana** *n* appetizer
**pampaganda** *n* makeup
**pampakapal** *n* padding
**pampalakas** *n* reinforcements
**pampalamuti** *adj* decorative
**pampalasa** *n* seasoning
**pampalito** *n* distraction
**pampasabog** *n* detonator
**pampasabog** *adj* explosive
**pampatulog** *n* sedation
**pampatunaw** *adj* solvent
**pampatuyo** *n* dryer
**pampilipit** *n* twister
**pampook** *adj* local
**pampuno** *n* filling
**pamumuhay** *n* lifestyle
**pamumuno** *n* lead
**pamumuo** *n* formation
**pamunas na papel** *n* napkin
**pamunuan** *v* preside
**pana** *n* bow
**panabikin** *v* excite
**panaderia** *n* bakery
**panadero** *n* baker
**panag-uri** *n* adverb, clause
**panagutan** *v* account for
**panahon** *n* weather, season
**panaklong** *n* parenthesis
**panaksak** *n* dagger
**panali** *n* spur
**panalo** *n* winner
**panambak** *n* landfill
**pananabik** *n* craving
**pananagutan** *n* responsibility
**pananahi** *n* sewing
**pananakaw** *n* burglary
**pananalapi** *adj* financial
**pananalig** *n* creed
**panananakot** *n* terrorism
**panandalian** *adj* fleeting
**pananghalian** *n* lunch
**pananim** *n* crop
**panatiko** *adj* fanatic
**panatilihin** *v* maintain
**panauhin** *n* visitor
**panayam** *n* interview
**pandak** *adj* petite
**pandagat** *adj* marine
**pandama** *n* sense
**pandaraya** *n* trick, hoax
**panday** *n* carpenter
**panday-susi** *n* locksmith

**pandikit** *n* glue, paste
**pandikit na papel** *n* sticker
**pandinig** *n* hearing
**pandiwa** *n* verb
**pandiwari** *n* participle
**pang turok** *n* injection
**pang ahit** *n* razor
**pang akyat** *n* stepladder
**pang anim** *adj* sixth
**pang hakot** *n* trailer
**pang halo** *n* blender
**pang hanap** *n* browser
**pang hatak** *n* trolley
**pang hinging** *n* buzzer
**pang hukay** *n* crowbar
**pang ipit** *n* stapler
**pang isang daan** *adj* hundredth
**pang itaas** *adj* upper
**pang kanluran** *adj* western
**pang labing dalawa** *adj* twelfth
**pang salo** *n* bunker
**pang sampu** *adj* tenth
**pang sangga** *n* armor
**pang ugong** *n* buzzard
**panga** *n* jaw
**pang-aakit** *n* temptation
**pang-aalipin** *n* slavery
**pang-aapi** *n* oppression
**pangako** *n* promise
**pangalagaan** *n* safeguard
**pangalan** *n* name, title
**pangalawa** *n* second
**pangamba** *n* peril
**pangangalaga** *n* commander
**pangangalakal** *n* trade
**pangangalunya** *n* adultery
**pangangaso** *n* hunting
**pangangatawan** *adv* physically
**panganib** *n* hazard, risk
**pang-apat** *adj* fourth
**pangarap** *n* ambition, dream
**pangasiwaan** *v* supervise
**pangatawanan** *v* live up
**pangatlo** *adj* third
**pang-awat** *adj* conciliatory
**pangdalawampu** *adj* twentieth
**pang-dugtong** *n* merger
**panggabi** *adj* nocturnal
**panggagamot** *n* treatment
**pangga-gaya** *n* imitation
**panggap** *n* guise
**panggatong** *n* fuel
**pangginaw** *n* sweater
**panggulo** *n* trouble
**panghalip** *n* pronoun
**pang-halo** *n* mixer
**pangharap** *adj* front
**panghasa** *n* sharpener
**panghihingi** *n* demand
**panghiwa** *n* blade
**panghukay** *n* drill
**panghuli** *adv* lastly
**pang-ihaw** *n* broiler
**pang-iistorbo** *n* harassment

**pangil** *n* fang
**pangiling** *n* abstinence
**pangingikil** *n* extortion
**panginginain** *n* graze
**panginginig** *n* tremor
**pang-init** *n* heater
**Panginoon** *n* God
**pang-ipit** *n* tongs
**pangit** *adj* homely, ugly
**pangitain** *n* mirage
**pangkabit** *adj* riveting
**pangkalahatan** *pro* everything
**pangkalahatan** *adv* overall
**pangkalusugan** *n* fitness
**pangkamay** *n* manual
**pangkapatid** *adj* fraternal
**pangkapit** *n* clamp
**pangkaraniwan** *adj* common
**pangkasal** *adj* bridal
**pangkat** *n* batch
**pangkatawan** *adj* bodily
**pang-kawani** *adj* clerical
**pangkulay** *n* crayon
**pang-labing-isa** *adj* eleventh
**pang-labing-lima** *adj* fifteen
**panglaw** *n* gloom
**pang-lima** *adj* fifth
**panglinis** *n* cleaner
**panglungsod** *adj* civic
**panglutang** *n* buoy
**pangmatagalan** *adj* lasting
**pangngalan** *n* noun
**pangongotong** *n* blackmail
**pang-pito** *adj* seventh
**pangsaksak** *n* plug
**pangsala** *n* screen
**pangsira** *n* destroyer
**pang-siyam** *adj* ninth
**pangsuporta** *n* backing
**pang-ukit** *n* engraving
**pang-ukol** *n* preposition
**pangulo** *n* president
**panguluhan** *n* presidency
**panguna** *adj* main
**pangunahin** *adj* premier
**pangunahin** *n* primacy
**pangungusap** *n* sentence
**pangunguwarta** *n* graft
**pang-uri** *n* adjective
**pang-walo** *adj* eighth
**pangyayari** *n* circumstance
**panig ng ama** *n* paternity
**panigan** *v* discriminate
**panindi** *n* lighter, spark
**panindigan** *v* uphold
**paningin** *n* eyesight
**paninigas** *n* cramp
**paniniil** *n* tyranny
**paniniktik** *n* espionage
**paninirang - puri** *n* calumny
**paninirang puri** *n* slander
**paninisi** *n* reproach
**paniniwala** *n* belief, premise
**panitik** *n* abbreviation

**panlabas** *adv* outdoor
**panlabas** *adj* external
**panlabas na anyo** *adj* exterior
**panlangis** *n* lubrication
**panlilinlang** *n* racketeering
**panlinis** *v* mop
**panloloko** *n* guile, scam
**pan-panahon** *adj* seasonal
**pansala** *n* filter
**pansamantala** *adj* tentative
**pansarili** *n* egoism
**pansin** *n* attention
**pansinin** *adj* mindful
**pansinin** *v* visualize
**pansipsip** *n* straw
**pantalan** *n* harbor, wharf
**pantali** *n* strap
**pantalon** *n* pants, slack
**pantal-pantal** *n* rash
**pantay** *n* balance
**pantay na ilaw** *n* floodlight
**pantayin** *v* flatten
**pantay-pantay** *adj* democratic
**pantulog** *n* nightgown
**panuhin** *n* guest
**panukala** *n* proposition
**panukat** *n* measurement, ruler
**panumbalikin** *v* restore
**panuntunan** *n* guidelines
**panunuri** *n* criticism
**panunurot** *n* hound
**panunuya** *n* mockery
**panusok** *n* thumbtack
**panyo** *n* handkerchief
**papa** *n* pontiff
**papag** *n* bunk bed
**papalabas** *adj* outgoing
**papasok** *n* way in
**papasukin** *v* let in
**papel** *n* paper, tissue
**papel de liha** *n* sandpaper
**papeles** *n* dossier
**papelito** *n* brochure
**papkorn** *n* popcorn
**papuri** *v* commend
**papurihan** *n* compliment
**papusyawin** *v* tarnish
**paputiin** *v* whiten
**paputok** *n* fireworks
**para sa** *pre* for
**paraan** *n* manner, method
**parada** *n* parade
**parakayda** *n* parachute
**parangal** *n* distinction
**parangalan** *v* distinguish
**paratangan** *v* charge
**parating** *adj* incoming
**pareho** *adj* both, same
**pare-pareho** *n* uniform
**pares** *n* pair
**pari** *n* priest, monk
**parihaba** *adj* rectangular
**parinig** *n* innuendo
**parirala** *n* phrase

P

**parke** *n* park
**parmasiya** *n* drugstore
**parmasya** *n* pharmacy
**parmasyotika** *n* pharmacist
**paroko** *n* parish
**parokya** *adj* parochial
**parol** *n* lantern
**parola** *n* beacon
**partisyon** *n* compartment
**paru-paro** *n* butterfly
**parusa** *n* punishment
**parusahan** *v* punish, torture
**pasa** *n* bruise
**pasabugin** *v* detonate
**pasadya** *adj* custom-made
**pasaganain** *v* abound
**pasahan** *n* circulation
**pasahero** *n* passenger
**pasalamat** *adj* thankful
**pasamain** *v* damn
**pasan** *n* burden
**pasanin** *adj* burdensome
**pasaporte** *n* passport
**pasas** *n* raisin
**pasasalamat** *n* gratitude
**pasayahin** *v* cheer
**pasensya** *n* patience
**pasiglahin** *v* encourage
**pasilyo** *n* aisle, hallway
**pasimula** *n* foundation
**pasimuno** *adv* chiefly
**pasimuno** *v* lead
**paskel** *n* placard
**pasko** *n* Christmas
**paso** *n* flowerpot
**pastor** *n* pastor
**pastulan** *n* pasture
**pasukan** *n* entrance
**pasukin** *v* penetrate
**pasulong** *adv* forward
**pasya** *n* resolution
**pasyal** *v* cruise
**pataas** *adv* uphill
**pataasin** *adj* heinous
**pataba** *n* compost
**patabain** *v* fatten
**patag** *adj* flat
**patag na lupa** *n* plateau
**patagilid** *adv* sideways
**patago** *adj* indiscreet
**patahimikin** *v* pacify
**patakaran** *n* policy
**patak-patak** *v* trickle
**patalastas** *n* bulletin
**patalsikin** *v* depose
**patani** *n* green bean
**patapon** *n* castaway
**patas** *n* fairness
**patas** *adv* unfairly
**patatagin** *v* toughen
**patatakip** *n* coverup
**patatas** *n* potato
**patawad** *n* pardon
**patawarin** *v* forgive

**patay** *adj* dead
**patayan** *n* killing
**patayin** *v* kill, slay, die
**patayung-tayungin** *v* stall
**patdin** *v* quench
**patibong** *n* pitfall, trap
**patigasin** *v* harden
**patigilin** *v* interrupt
**pating** *n* shark
**patinig** *n* vowel
**patitiis** *n* tolerance
**patitistis** *n* operation
**patnubayan** *v* guide
**pato** *n* duck
**patotoo** *n* warrant
**patpat** *n* rod
**patriyarka** *n* patriarch
**patrolya** *n* patrol
**patubig** *n* irrigation
**patubigan** *v* irrigate
**patuka** *n* pellet
**patulugin** *v* hypnotize
**patunay** *n* warranty
**patunayan** *v* affirm, vouch for
**patungkol** *n* allusion
**patungkol sa** *v* refer to
**patungkulan** *v* denote
**patungo** *adj* bound for
**patungong** *adv* eastward
**patungong timog** *adj* southern
**patutunguhan** *n* destination
**patuyuin** *v* parch
**pauli-ulit** *n* repetition
**pauna** *n* advance
**pauna** *adj* initial, foretaste
**paunang salita** *n* preface
**paunlarin** *v* civilize
**paupahan** *n* inn
**paupuan** *v* chair
**pausukan** *v* fumigate
**pautangin muli** *v* refinance
**pawalan** *v* release
**pawalang bisa** *v* nullify
**pawalang halaga** *v* veto
**pawalang sala** *v* absolve
**pawalang saysay** *v* refute
**pawis** *n* sweat
**payagan** *v* approve
**payapain** *v* appease
**payaso** *n* clown
**payat** *adj* lean, thin
**payong** *n* umbrella
**payuhan** *v* counsel
**Pebrero** *n* February
**pedal** *n* pedal
**pederal** *adj* federal
**pekas** *n* freckle
**peke** *v* counterfeit
**pekein** *adj* counterfeit
**peklat** *n* scar
**pelikula** *n* movie
**pelus** *n* velvet
**pendyulum** *n* pendulum
**penggwin** *n* penguin

**peninsula** *n* peninsula
**pensyon** *n* pension
**pera** *n* currency
**peras** *n* pear
**peregrino** *n* pilgrim
**perlas** *n* pearl
**perpekto** *adj* perfect
**peste** *n* pest, plague
**pestehin** *v* pester
**petrolyo** *n* petroleum
**pidbak** *n* feedback
**pigain** *v* squeeze, wring
**pigil na pigil** *adj* uptight
**pigilan** *v* hinder, deter
**pigilin** *v* quell, repress
**pila** *n* queue
**pilak** *n* silver
**pilay** *adj* cripple, lame
**pilay** *n* limp
**pilay** *v* sprain
**pilayin** *v* cripple
**pildora** *n* pill
**pili** *n* choice
**piliin** *v* select, pick
**pilik-mata** *n* eyelash
**pilipitin** *v* twist
**pilit na pumasok** *v* break in
**pilitin** *v* coerce, force
**pilosopo** *n* philosopher
**pilospiya** *n* philosophy
**piloto** *n* pilot
**piluka** *n* hairpiece

**pilyo** *adj* naughty
**pinaalam** *v* notify
**pinaasim** *n* cider
**pinagalitan** *v* scold
**pinagana** *n* activation
**pinag-aralan** *n* degree
**pinagmulan** *n* ancestry
**pinagmulan** *v* originate
**pinagpalitan** *n* precursor
**pinagtapat** *v* match
**pinahalagahan** *v* cherish
**pinahayag** *adv* expressly
**pinahina** *v* water down
**pina-igsi** *n* contraction
**pinaka kaunti** *n* minimum
**pinaka marami** *adj* maximum
**pinaka mataas** *adj* archaic
**pinaka puno** *adj* principal
**pinakahuli** *adj* latest
**pinakamahusay** *adj* best
**pinako sa krus** *n* crucifixion
**pinala marami** *adj* utmost
**pinalabas sa laro** *v* strike out
**pinalamig** *adj* ice-cold
**pinalayas** *v* displace
**pinalo** *v* smack
**pinamudmod** *v* disseminate
**pinamumunuan** *adj* leading
**pinamunuan** *adj* leaded
**pinanganak** *adj* born
**pinanggalingan** *n* source
**pinapawisan** *v* sweat

**pinasan** *v* burden
**pinatigas** *adj* petrified
**pinatungkulan** *n* addressee
**pinatungkulan** *adj* null
**pinawalang-bisa** *v* disregard
**pingkong** *n* dent
**pinili** *v* opt for
**pinilipit** *adj* twisted
**pinilit** *adv* forcibly
**pinilit** *v* oblige
**pininid** *v* close
**pinirito** *adj* fried
**pinisa** *n* compression
**pinisilin** *n* penicillin
**Pinland** *n* Finland
**pinsala** *n* injury
**pinsalain** *v* harm
**pinsan** *n* cousin
**pintagono** *n* pentagon
**pintahan** *v* paint
**pintig ng puso** *n* heartbeat
**pinto** *n* door, pint
**pinto sa likod** *n* backdoor
**pintor** *n* painter
**pintura** *n* paint
**pinugutan** *v* behead
**pinukpok** *v* bludgeon
**pinuno** *n* chief, head
**pinya** *n* pineapple
**pipa** *n* pipe
**pipi** *adj* mute
**pipino** *n* cucumber
**piramida** *n* pyramid
**pira-piraso** *adv* asunder
**pira-piraso** *n* crumb, rubble
**pira-pirasuhin** *v* shred
**piraso** *n* chunk, fragment, piece
**pirasuhin** *v* rip apart
**pirata** *n* pirate
**piring** *n* blindfold
**piringan** *v* blindfold
**pirma** *n* sign, signature
**pisain** *v* compress, squash
**pisara** *n* blackboard
**pisil** *v* grip
**pisngi** *n* cheek
**pista** *n* holiday
**pistola** *n* pistol
**pitak** *n* column
**pitaka** *n* wallet
**pitasin** *v* pluck
**pito** *adj* seven
**pitsa** *n* chip
**pitsel** *n* jug
**pitumpo** *adj* seventy
**planggana** *n* basin
**plano** *n* diagram
**plantsa** *n* iron
**plastik** *n* plastic
**platito** *n* saucer
**plato** *n* plate
**plays** *n* pliers
**plorera** *n* vase
**pluma** *n* pen

**pluta** *n* flute
**plutonyum** *n* plutonium
**pngkalahatan** *adj* comprehensive
**Poland** *n* Poland
**polder** *n* folder
**polyito** *n* pamphlet
**pondo** *n* budget, funds
**pondohan** *v* fund
**poot** *n* wrath
**pormula** *n* formula
**porselana** *n* porcelain
**porsyento** *adv* percent
**portalesa** *n* bulwark
**portugal** *n* Portugal
**Portuges** *adj* Portuguese
**posas** *n* handcuffs
**poskard** *n* postcard
**posporo** *n* phosphorus
**poste** *n* post
**potograpiya** *v* photograph
**ppaninda** *n* stock
**praktikal** *adj* practical
**prangka** *n* candor
**prangka** *adj* candid
**prangkisa** *n* franchise
**Pransya** *n* France
**Pransya** *adj* French
**prayle** *n* friar
**premyo** *n* prize
**preno** *n* brake
**preso** *n* prisoner
**pribado** *n* privacy
**pribilehyo** *n* privilege
**prinsesa** *n* princess
**prinșipe** *n* prince
**prismo** *n* prism
**prito** *n* fries
**probinsya** *n* province
**problemado** *adj* problematic
**produkto** *n* by-product
**programa** *n* program
**programer** *n* programmer
**propesor** *n* professor
**propesyon** *n* profession
**propesyonal** *adj* professional
**proporsyon** *n* ratio
**prosteyt** *n* prostate
**proyekto** *n* project
**prusisyon** *n* procession
**prutas** *n* fruit
**prutas na mapula** *n* strawberry
**prutina** *n* protein
**pugad** *n* nest
**pugante** *n* fugitive
**pugita** *n* octopus
**pugo** *n* quail
**pugon** *n* oven, stove
**pugutan** *v* decapitate
**puhunan** *n* capital
**pukawin** *v* arouse, stir up
**pukpukin** *v* pound
**pukyutan** *n* pollen
**pula** *adj* red
**pulagada** *n* inch

P

**pulang bato** *n* ruby
**pulbo** *n* powder
**pulbos** *n* prowler
**pulbura** *n* gunpowder
**pulbusin** *v* pulverize
**pulgas** *n* flea
**pulikat** *n* spasm
**pulis** *n* cop, police
**pulitika** *n* politics
**pulitiko** *n* politician
**pulmonya** *n* pneumonia
**pulong** *n* session
**pulot** *n* syrup
**pulot-gata** *n* honeymoon
**pulot-pukyutan** *n* honey
**pulpito** *n* pulpit
**pulsera** *n* bracelet
**pulubi** *n* beggar
**pulutin** *v* pick up
**pulutong** *n* array, group
**puma** *n* panther
**pumaibabaw** *v* stand out
**pumailalim** *v* go under
**pumapayag** *adj* willing
**pumarito** *v* come forward
**pumasok** *v* enter, go in
**pumila** *v* line up
**pumula** *v* redden
**pumusta** *v* bet
**pumutok** *v* rupture
**puna** *n* remark
**punahin** *v* remark
**punasan** *v* wipe
**punda** *n* pillowcase
**pungus** *n* fungus
**punitin** *v* rip, tear
**punla** *n* seed
**puno** *n* tree
**puno ng** *n* ringleader
**puno ng buhay** *adj* vibrant
**puno ng kamay** *n* wrist
**puno ng kusinero** *n* chef
**punong-puno** *adv* fully
**puntod** *n* grave
**punuin** *v* fill
**punuing muli** *v* refill
**punung-puno** *adj* replete
**punyas** *n* cuff
**purga** *adj* laxative
**purgatoryo** *n* purgatory
**puri** *n* reputation
**purihin** *v* comment, praise
**purok** *n* district
**pusa** *n* cat
**pusit** *n* squid
**puso** *n* heart
**pusod** *n* belly button
**pusta** *n* bet
**pustiso** *n* dentures
**putakti** *n* wasp
**putbol** *n* football
**puti** *adj* white
**puti ng itlog** *n* egg white
**putik** *n* clay, mud

**putikan** *n* bog
**putok** *n* rupture
**putok ng baril** *n* gunshot
**putol-putulin** *v* mutilate
**putulan** *v* trim
**putulin** *v* amputate, prune
**puwet** *n* butt
**pwesto** *n* booth
**pyador** *n* guarantor
**pyanista** *n* pianist
**pyano** *n* piano
**pyansa** *n* bail
**pyansahan** *v* bail out

# R



**rabanos** *n* radish
**rabis** *n* rabies
**radar** *n* radar
**radyesyon** *n* radiation
**radyo** *n* radio
**radyos** *n* radius
**raket** *n* rocket
**raketa** *n* racket
**ranggo** *n* rank
**rantso** *n* ranch
**rasista** *adj* racist
**rasyon** *n* ration
**rasyonan** *v* ration
**rayo-ekis** *n* X-ray
**rayos ng tunog** *n* ultrasound
**rayuma** *n* rheumatism
**rebelde** *n* rebel
**red teyp** *n* red tape
**regalo** *n* gift
**regla** *n* menstruation
**rehyon** *n* region
**rekisahin** *v* inspect
**relihiyon** *n* religion
**relo** *n* watch
**relohero** *n* watchmaker
**renda** *n* bridle, rein
**rendahan** *v* rein
**repolyo** *n* cabbage
**reptila** *n* reptile
**republika** *n* republic
**reputasyon** *n* prestige
**reserba** *adj* spare
**reseta** *n* prescription
**resibo** *n* invoice, receipt
**restorante** *n* restaurant
**resulta** *n* result
**resulta ng ginawa** *n* output
**retirido** *n* retirement
**retiro** *v* retire
**reyna** *n* queen
**riles** *n* track, rail
**riles ng tren** *n* railroad
**ripa** *n* raffle
**ritmo** *n* rhythm

**rmapa** *n* ramp
**rosaryo** *n* rosary
**rosas** *adj* pink
**rurok** *n* peak, heyday
**Ruso** *n* Russia

# S

**sa** *pre* at, in, to
**sa buong mundo** *adj* worldwide
**sa dakong loob** *adj* inward
**sa gilid ng baybay** *n* coastline
**sa gilid ng burol** *n* hillside
**sa gitna** *n* midair
**sa gitna ng** *pre* among
**sa halip** *adv* instead
**sa halip na** *n* lieu
**sa harapan** *n* foreground
**sa hinaharap** *adv* hereafter
**sa ibabaw ng** *pre* upon
**sa ibang bayan** *adv* abroad
**sa ilalim** *adj* underground
**sa ilalim** *pre* underneath
**sa isang banda** *adv* partly
**sa itaas** *pre* above
**sa iyo** *pro* yours
**sa kabila** *pre* behind
**sa kabila ng** *pre* amid
**sa kabila ng** *adv* regardless
**sa kabilang ibayo** *adv* beyond
**sa kabuuan** *adv* virtually
**sa kalayuan** *adv* farther
**sa kanya** *pro* hers, his
**sa kasalukuyan** *adj* present
**sa labas** *adv* outdoors
**sa loob** *adv* indoor
**sa loob** *adj* inside
**sa malas** *adv* apparently
**sa may pinto** *n* doorstep
**sa ngalan** *adv* behalf (on)
**sa ngayon** *adv* currently
**sa pagitan** *pre* between
**sa paligid** *pre* around
**sa paligid** *adj* outer
**sa pamamagitan** *pre* through
**sa panahon** *pre* during
**sa pangkalahatan** *adj* outright
**sa pangyayari** *adv* incidentally
**sa paningin** *n* view
**sa pilitan** *adj* obligatory
**sa salita** *adv* verbally
**sa simula** *n* inception
**sa simula** *adv* initially
**sa taas ng burol** *n* hilltop
**sa umpisa** *n* onset
**saan** *adv* where
**saan man** *c* wherever
**Sabado** *n* Saturday
**sabaw** *n* broth, soup
**sabay** *adj* simultaneous

**sabihin** *v* say, tell
**sabik sa pag-uwi** *adj* homesick
**sabi-sabi** *n* hearsay
**sabitan** *n* hanger
**sabotahe** *n* sabotage
**sabsaban** *n* manger
**sabungan** *n* cockpit
**sadyang ginawa** *adj* built-in
**sagabal** *n* deterrence
**sagana** *adj* bustling
**sagarin** *v* minimize
**sagasaan** *v* run over
**sagayon** *adv* alright
**saging** *n* banana
**sagip** *n* rescue
**sagipin** *v* salvage
**sagisag** *n* emblem
**sagot** *n* answer, reply
**sagutin** *v* answer, reply
**sagwan** *n* oar
**sahig** *n* floor
**sahod** *n* income
**sakalin** *v* choke, smother
**sakit** *n* disease, illness
**sakit ng tiyan** *n* colic
**sakit ng ulo** *n* headache
**sakit sa baga** *n* tuberculosis
**sakit sa dugo** *n* leukemia
**saklaw** *n* sanction
**saklawan** *v* sanction
**saklawin** *v* occupy
**sako** *n* sack
**sakong** *n* heel
**sakramento** *n* sacrament
**saksak** *n* stab
**saksakan** *n* switch
**saksakin** *v* stab, stagger
**saksakyan** *v* shuttle
**saksi** *n* testimony
**saktan** *v* inflict
**sakupin** *v* dominate
**salaan** *n* strainer
**salad** *n* salad
**salagubang** *n* beetle
**salagubang** *n* cricket
**salain** *v* drain, filter, distill
**salamangka** *n* magic
**salamangkero** *n* magician
**salamat** *n* thanks
**salamin** *n* glass, mirror
**salansan** *n* stack, pile
**salapi** *n* cash
**salarin** *adj* criminal
**sala-salabat** *v* criss-cross
**salat** *adj* deprived
**salaula** *n* slob
**salawahan** *adj* volatile
**salawikain** *n* slogan
**saligang-batas** *n* constitution
**saliksik** *n* research
**salin** *n* version
**saling lahi** *n* generation
**salin-wika** *n* interpreter
**salipawpaw** *n* airplane

**salita** *n* word
**saliwa** *adj* awkward
**salmon** *n* salmon
**salon** *n* saloon
**salsa** *n* sauce
**salubong** *n* encounter
**salubungin** *v* meet
**salungat** *adj* dissonant
**salungatin** *v* oppose
**salungguhitan** *v* underline
**salu-salo** *n* gathering
**sama ng loob** *n* grudge
**samabahin** *v* venerate
**samahan** *v* accompany
**samahan** *n* association
**samakatuwid** *v* boil down to
**samakatuwid** *adv* therefore
**samakatwid** *adv* thus
**samantala** *adv* meantime
**samantalahin** *v* exploit
**samba** *n* worship
**sambahin** *v* glorify
**sampal** *n* slap
**sampalataya** *n* faith
**sampalin** *v* slap
**sampu** *adj* ten
**sana** *adv* hopefully
**sanay** *adj* habitual
**sanayin** *v* coach, train
**sanaysay** *n* statement
**sandalan** *n* leaning
**sandali** *n* moment
**sandalyas** *n* sandal
**sandata** *n* armaments
**sanga** *n* branch, stem
**sangay ng militar** *n* infantry
**sang-ayon** *adj* favorable
**sanggano** *n* gangster
**sanggol** *n* baby, infant
**sanggunian** *n* reference
**sangkap** *n* ingredient
**sanglaan** *n* pawnbroker
**sanhi** *n* factor
**sankatauhan** *n* mankind
**sanlibong gramo** *n* milligram
**sanlibong metro** *n* millimeter
**sanlibutan** *n* humankind
**sansinukob** *n* universe
**santo** *n* saint
**santo papa** *n* Pope
**sapa** *n* creek, stream
**sapad** *n* flat
**sapagkat** *c* because
**sapagkat** *pre* since
**sapat** *adj* ample, enough
**sapat lamang** *adj* marginal
**sapatos** *n* footwear
**sapatos pang yelo** *v* ice skate
**sapawan ang iba** *v* overstep
**sapilitan** *adj* mandatory
**sapin sa napilayan** *n* splint
**sapot** *n* cobweb
**sapot ng gagamba** *n* spiderweb
**sarado** *n* closure

**saranggola** *n* kite
**sardinas** *n* sardine
**sareyd** *n* charade
**sarhento** *n* sergeant
**sarili** *adj* personal
**sariling akda** *n* copyright
**sariling pananaw** *n* standpoint
**sari-sari** *adj* various
**sariwa** *adj* fresh
**sariwain** *v* freshen
**sariwang gulay** *adj* lush
**sarten** *n* saucepan
**sasakyan** *n* cab, vehicle
**sastre** *n* tailor
**satananiko** *adj* satanic
**sawa na** *adj* fed up
**sawata** *n* control
**sawatahin** *v* eradicate
**sawatain** *v* control
**sawi** *adj* doomed
**saya** *n* cheers
**sayaw** *n* dance
**sayawan** *n* dancing
**seda** *n* silk
**seguridad** *n* security
**seguro** *n* insurance
**sekretarya** *n* secretary
**sekto** *n* sect
**sekundarya** *adj* secondary
**selos** *n* jealousy
**seloso** *adj* jealous
**selyado** *adj* hermetic
**selyo** *n* postage, stamp
**sementeryo** *n* graveyard
**semento** *n* cement
**semestre** *n* semester
**semilya** *n* sperm
**seminaryo** *n* seminary
**senado** *n* senate
**senador** *n* senator
**sensilyo** *n* coin
**sensitibo** *adj* sensitive
**sensus** *n* census
**senswal** *adj* sensual
**sentensya** *n* conviction
**sentensyahan** *v* convict
**sentimental** *adj* sentimental
**sentimetro** *n* centimeter
**sentimo** *n* cent, penny
**sentimyento** *n* sentiment
**senyasan** *v* beckon
**sepilyo** *n* brush
**seramika** *n* ceramic
**serbedor** *n* waiter
**serbedora** *n* barmaid
**serbesa** *n* beer
**serbidora** *n* stewardess
**serbisyo** *v* service
**seremonya** *n* rite
**seresa** *n* cherry
**sermon** *n* sermon
**sero** *n* zero
**sertipiko** *n* certificate
**serye** *n* series

**Setyembre** *n* September
**sibat** *n* arrow, spear
**sibilisasyon** *n* civilization
**sibuyas** *n* onion
**siga** *adj* bully
**sigarilyo** *n* cigarette
**sigasig** *n* enthusiasm
**sigaw** *v* scream, shout
**sigawan** *n* shouting
**sigla** *n* ardor, zeal
**sigurado** *n* guarantee
**siguruhin** *v* guarantee
**sigwa** *n* tempest
**sikayatri** *n* psychiatry
**sikipan** *v* tighten
**siklista** *n* cyclist
**siko** *n* elbow
**sikolohiya** *n* psychology
**sila** *pro* they
**silangan** *n* east, orient
**silanganan** *adj* eastern
**silawin** *v* dazzle
**silbi** *n* service
**sili** *n* pepper
**silid** *n* room
**silid kainan** *n* dining room
**silid para sa alak** *n* cellar
**silid sa barko** *n* cabin
**silid tanggapan** *n* living room
**silid tulugan** *n* bedroom
**silid-aralan** *n* classroom
**silindro** *n* cylinder
**silipin** *v* peep, sneak
**silis** *n* spice
**siluin** *v* snare
**silungan** *n* sanctuary
**silya** *n* chair
**silyang di gulong** *n* wheelchair
**silyon** *n* armchair
**simbahan** *n* church
**simbolo** *n* symbol
**simboryo** *n* dome
**simbuyo** *n* urge
**simoy ng hangin** *n* breeze
**simple** *adj* simple
**simula** *adj* preliminary
**simula ng** *c* since
**simula noon** *adv* since then
**simulan** *v* begin, start, spearhead
**simulan** *n* beginning
**sina una** *adj* primitive
**sinadya** *adv* knowingly
**sinag** *n* gleam, ray
**sinag** *v* glow
**sinakop** *v* colonize
**sinaktan** *v* injure
**sinalansan** *v* stack
**sinalanta** *adj* infested
**sinapupunan** *n* womb
**sinara** *v* shut off
**sinasabi** *adj* telling
**sindihan** *v* ignite, spark off
**sinehan** *n* cinema
**singaw** *n* steam

**singhal** *v* growl
**singhutin** *v* sniff
**singilin ng labis** *v* overcharge
**singilin ng sobra** *v* rip off
**singit** *n* groin
**singkamas** *n* parsnip
**singkaw** *n* yoke
**singko** *n* nickel
**singsing** *n* ring
**sinigurado** *v* reassure
**sinigwelas** *n* plum
**sinimulan** *v* launch, start
**sining** *n* artwork, painting
**sinipi** *n* quotation
**sinira** *v* ruin, debunk
**sino** *pro* who
**sinok** *n* hiccup
**sinopla** *v* rebuff
**sinta** *adj* darling
**sintas** *n* shoelace
**sinturon** *n* belt
**sinubasta** *v* auction
**sinugod** *v* assault
**sinulid** *n* thread, yarn
**sinuman** *pro* anyone
**sinundan** *v* precede
**sinungaling** *adj* liar
**sinusundan** *adj* preceding
**sinuway** *v* defy
**sipain** *v* kick
**siper** *n* zipper
**sipi** *n* duplication
**sipi ng ginana** *n* payslip
**sipiin** *v* copy, duplicate
**sipiin** *n* copy
**sipilis** *n* syphilis
**sipit** *n* pincers
**sipol** *n* whistle
**sipon** *n* mucus
**sipsipin** *v* absorb, suck
**sira** *n* flaw, damage
**sira ang ulo** *n* psychopath
**siraan** *v* denigrate
**siraang puri** *v* discredit
**sirain** *v* destroy, pillage
**sirena** *n* mermaid
**sirko** *n* circus
**siruhano** *n* surgeon
**sirum** *n* serum
**sisi** *n* blame, remorse
**sisihin** *v* blame
**sisiw** *n* chick
**sistema** *n* system
**siwang** *n* backlash
**siya** *pro* he
**siya ng kabayo** *n* saddle
**siya nga** *adv* indeed
**siyam** *adj* nine
**siyamnapu** *adj* ninety
**siyang tunay** *adv* surely
**skirp** *n* script
**sobra** *n* surplus
**sobrang bigat** *adj* overweight
**sobre** *n* envelope

**sobyet** *adj* soviet
**solohin** *v* monopolize
**solusyon** *n* solution
**sona** *n* zone
**soolohiya** *n* zoology
**sopa** *n* couch, sofa
**sorbetes** *n* ice cream
**soriso** *n* sausage
**sosyalismo** *n* socialism
**spa** *n* spa
**spark piag** *n* spark plug
**stilo** *n* style
**stilo** *adv* sternly
**strikto** *adj* strict
**subalit** *c* although, but
**subasta** *n* auction
**subukan** *v* try
**subukin** *v* test
**sugal** *n* game
**sugapa** *n* addiction
**sugapa sa alak** *adj* alcoholic
**sugat** *n* wound
**sugo** *n* envoy
**sugpo** *n* prawn
**sugurin** *v* attack, assail
**suha** *n* grapefruit
**suhol** *n* bribe
**suhulan** *v* bribe, corrupt
**suka** *n* vinegar
**sukat** *n* dimension, size
**sukat ng bigat** *n* scruples
**sukatan** *n* parameters
**sukatin** *v* measure
**sukdulan** *adj* extreme
**sukdulang init** *n* heatwave
**suklay** *n* comb
**suko** *n* surrender
**sulat** *n* letter, mail
**sulat kamay** *n* autograph
**sulatan** *n* desk, mail
**sulatin** *n* journal
**sulayap** *n* glimpse
**sulda** *v* solder
**suldahin** *v* weld
**suliranin** *n* problem
**sulo** *n* torch
**sulsihan** *v* darn
**sulsulan** *v* incite
**sulyap** *n* glance
**suma** *n* sum
**sumabog** *v* burst into, erupt, explode
**sumagana** *v* flourish
**sumaglit** *v* drop in
**sumailalim** *v* undergo
**sumakay** *v* embark, ride
**sumaksi** *v* testify
**sumalanta** *adj* disastrous
**sumali** *v* participate
**sumalungat** *adj* dissident
**sumalungat** *v* dissuade
**sumandal** *v* lean
**sumandali** *adv* shortly
**sumang-ayon** *v* conform

**sumaya** *v* enjoy
**sumbong** *n* grievance
**sumbrero** *n* hat
**sumibol** *v* bloom
**sumigaw** *n* scream, shriek
**sumilong** *v* shelter
**suminag** *v* gleam
**sumingit** *v* squeeze in
**sumipol** *v* whistle
**sumisid** *v* dive
**sumpa** *n* oath, pledge
**sumpong** *n* tantrum, fit
**sumuka** *v* throw up
**sumuko** *v* surrender
**sumulong** *v* progress
**sumulyap** *v* glimpse
**sumumpa** *v* pledge, vow
**sumunod** *v* comply
**sundalo** *n* soldier
**sundan** *v* follow, track
**sundin** *n* obedience
**sundin** *v* obey
**sungay** *n* horn
**sungot** *n* whiskers
**sunod sa uso** *adj* trendy
**sunod-sunod** *n* chronology
**sunog** *n* burn, fire
**suntok** *v* clench
**suntukin** *v* punch
**sunugin** *v* cremate
**suot** *n* wear
**suplada** *n* snub
**suporta** *n* backup, bracket
**suportahan** *v* cushion
**suriin** *v* analyze
**susi** *n* key
**suso** *n* snail
**suson** *n* layer
**suspindihin** *v* suspend
**suwapang** *adj* greedy
**suwayin** *v* disobey
**suyuin** *v* coax
**Sweden** *n* Sweden
**sweldo** *n* salary, wage
**swerte** *n* luck
**Swiso** *adj* Swiss
**Switserland** *n* Switzerland
**sya** *adj* her
**sya** *pro* herself, she
**syensa** *n* science

# T

**taagahanga** *n* admirer
**taakpan sa araw** *n* sunblock
**taas** *n* height
**taba** *n* fat
**tabako** *n* tobacco
**tabing** *n* screen, shield
**tabing dagat** *adj* seaside

**tabingi** *adj* crooked
**tabla** *n* board, lumber
**tabla** *adj* deadlock
**tablang nakasabit** *n* scaffolding
**tablang talunan** *n* springboard
**tableta** *n* tablet
**tadhana** *n* destiny, doom
**tadtarin** *v* chop, mince
**tag gutom** *n* famine
**taga - awat** *n* arbiter
**taga alalay** *n* supporter
**taga balita** *n* informer
**taga bilang** *v* counter
**taga Eyuropa** *adj* European
**taga hatol ng laro** *n* umpire
**taga hilaga** *adj* northerner
**taga kalinga** *n* patron
**taga kanluran** *adj* westerner
**taga labas** *n* outsider
**taga lupa** *adj* terrestrial
**taga nayon** *n* villager
**taga Norwey** *adj* Norwegian
**taga pamahala** *n* custodian
**taga pastol** *n* shepherd
**taga patnubay** *n* guide
**taga Pinland** *adj* Finnish
**taga Poland** *adj* Polish
**taga Rusya** *adj* Russian
**taga sanay** *n* trainer
**taga Seweden** *adj* Sweedish
**taga silangan** *n* easterner
**taga syudad** *adj* urban
**taga tadtad** *n* butchery
**taga tatak** *n* marksman
**taga tuklas** *n* scout
**taga turo** *n* coach
**taga tustos** *n* supplier
**taga ulat** *n* informant
**taga-Britanya** *adj* British
**tagag-likha** *n* maker
**taga-hanga** *n* fan
**tagahatid** *n* usher
**tagain** *v* hack
**tagal** *n* duration
**tagalinis** *n* janitor, maiden
**Tagapag likha** *n* creator
**tagapag mana** *n* heir
**tagapag-alaga** *n* caretaker
**tagapagdala** *n* bearer
**tagapag-gigay** *n* contributor
**tagapag-ligtas** *n* Messiah
**tagapagsalita** *n* rector
**tagapag-sulda** *n* welder
**tagapakinig** *n* listener
**tagapamagitan** *n* referee
**tagapamahala** *n* curator
**tagapamalita** *n* announcer
**tagapangaral** *n* preacher
**tagapangasiwa** *n* manager
**tagapangisiwa** *n* butler
**tagapa-ulat** *n* reporter
**tagapayo** *n* adviser
**tag-araw** *n* summer
**tagas** *n* leak

**tagasanay** *n* coach
**tagasunod** *n* follower
**tagasuri** *n* censorship
**taga-tanggap** *n* admittance
**taga-tuos** *n* accountant
**taga-usig** *n* prosecutor
**taghoy** *n* howl
**tagihawat** *n* pimple
**tagiliran** *n* flank
**taglamig** *n* winter
**tagpi** *v* patch
**tagpian** *v* mend, patch
**tagpuan** *n* date
**tag-tuyot** *n* drought
**taguan** *n* storage
**tagumpay** *n* triumph
**tahanan** *n* home
**tahasan** *adv* frankly
**tahiin** *v* darn
**tahimik** *adj* calm, quiet
**tahol** *n* bark
**taimtim** *n* sincerity
**tainga** *n* ear
**takadang oras** *n* curfew
**takal ng gamoth** *n* dosage
**takas** *n* defect
**takbuhan** *n* stampede
**takdaan** *v* schedule
**takdang araw** *n* deadline
**takdang panahon** *n* term
**takdang-arakin** *n* homework
**takigrapiya** *n* shorthand
**takilya** *n* box office
**takip** *n* cover, lid
**takip silim** *n* nightfall
**takot** *adj* afraid
**takot** *n* fear, fright
**takpan** *v* cover
**takpan ang bahagi** *v* overlap
**taksil** *adj* unfaithful
**taktak** *n* waterfall
**taktika** *n* ploy
**takutin** *v* horrify, terrify
**talaan** *n* recruitment
**talaarawan** *n* memoirs
**talaba** *n* shellfish
**talababa** *n* footnote
**talamak** *adj* chronic
**talambuhay** *n* biography
**talasalitaan** *n* dictionary
**talasan** *v* sharpen
**talastas** *n* broadcast
**talata** *n* paragraph
**talatakdaan** *n* schedule
**talbog** *n* bounce
**tali** *n* leash, string
**talikod** *adj* rear
**talino** *n* talent, wit
**talo** *n* defeat
**talon** *n* jump
**talsatasan** *n* communication
**talukap ng mata** *n* eyelid
**talukbong** *n* hood
**talulot** *n* petal

**talumpati** *n* speech
**talunan** *n* failure, loser
**talunin** *v* defeat, beat
**taluntunin** *n* trail
**tama** *adj* correct, proper, right
**tama lamang** *adj* reasonable
**tamad** *adj* insolent, lazy
**tamang ayos** *n* decorum
**tamang bilang** *adj* considerable
**tamang-tama** *adj* exact
**tambak** *n* pile
**tambakna trabaho** *n* backlog
**tambangan** *v* ambush, block
**tambo** *n* reed
**tambol** *n* drum
**tambutso** *n* muffler
**tamilmil** *v* nibble
**tampalasan** *adj* harsh
**tampipi** *n* briefcase
**tanaw** *n* visibility
**tanawin** *n* outlook
**tanda** *n* tag
**tandaan** *v* trace, mark
**tandang** *n* cock, rooster
**tanga** *adj* clumsy, moron
**tanggalin** *v* detach, lay off
**tanggapan** *n* admission
**tanggapin** *v* accept, admit
**tanggi** *n* refusal
**tanggihan** *v* decline
**tanghal** *n* exhibition
**tanghali** *n* noon
**tanging karapatan** *n* prerogative
**tangkain** *n* attempt
**tangke** *n* tank
**tangke ng tubig** *n* cistern
**tangkilik** *adj* dependent
**tangkilikin** *v* patronize
**tanikala** *n* chain
**tanim** *n* plant
**taniman** *n* orchard
**taniman ng ubas** *n* vineyard
**tanong** *n* question
**tanso** *n* bronze, copper
**tantya** *n* appraisal
**tantyahin** *v* estimate
**tanungin** *v* ask, question
**tao** *n* person
**taon** *n* year
**taong baliw** *n* madman
**taong naglalakad** *n* pedestrian
**taong nakakainis** *n* nuisance
**taong walang hiya** *n* scoundrel
**taon-taon** *adj* annual
**taos puso** *adj* heartfelt
**taostado** *n* toast
**tapag silbi** *n* barman
**tapag-salita** *n* speaker
**tapakan** *v* trample
**tapalan** *v* plaster
**tapangan** *v* hearten
**tapat** *adv* earnestly
**tapat** *adj* frank, faithful
**tapete** *n* carpet, rug

**tapik** *n* pat, tap
**tapon** *n* cork
**tapos** *n* lapse
**tapunan** *v* throw
**tapusin** *v* finish, wrap up
**tarangkahan** *n* gate
**tarheta** *n* card
**tartar** *n* tartar
**tasa** *n* cup, mug
**tatag** *n* poise
**tatak** *v* seal
**tatak** *n* brand
**tatak ng daliri** *n* fingerprint
**tatak ng postal** *n* postmark
**tatakan** *n* seal
**tatakan** *v* stamp
**tatlo** *adj* three
**tatlong bahagi** *n* trimester
**tatluhan** *adj* triple
**tatlumpo** *adj* thirty
**tatsulok** *n* triangle
**tauhan** *n* crew
**taun-taon** *adv* yearly
**tau-tauhan** *n* puppet
**tawa** *n* laugh, laughter
**tawad** *n* bid, plea
**tawag** *n* call
**tawagan** *v* phone
**tawagin** *v* call, summon
**tawagin ulit** *v* recall
**tawang nakikiliti** *v* giggle
**tawaran** *v* bid
**tawiran** *n* ferry
**tayo** *pro* ourselves, us
**tayroyd** *n* thyroid
**teatro** *n* theater
**teheras** *n* berth
**teklado** *n* keyboard
**teknikal** *adj* technical
**tekniko** *n* technician
**teknolohiya** *n* technology
**tela** *n* cloth, fabric
**telebisyon** *n* television
**telegrama** *n* telegram
**telepono** *n* telephone
**teleskopyo** *n* telescope
**tema** *n* theme
**temeperatura** *n* temperature
**tenis** *n* tennis
**teorya** *n* theory
**terible** *adj* terrible
**teritoryo** *n* territory
**terminolohiya** *n* terminology
**termometro** *n* thermometer
**terno** *n* suit
**testamento** *n* testament
**testigo** *n* eyewitness
**teyp rekorder** *n* tape recorder
**tianpay** *n* bun
**tibi** *adj* constipated
**tibok** *n* throb
**tiga timog** *n* southerner
**tigang** *adj* barren
**tigasan** *v* stiffen

**tigdas** *n* measles
**tigil** *n* stop
**tigil putukan** *n* truce
**tigilan** *v* hold back
**tigre** *n* tiger
**tiisin** *v* endure
**tikling** *n* crane
**tiklupin** *v* fold
**tiktik** *n* detective
**tila** *n* looks
**tila** *v* seem
**tila** *adv* somewhat
**tila gatas** *adj* milky
**timba** *n* bucket, pail
**timbangan** *n* scale
**timbangin** *v* weigh
**timbre** *n* doorbell
**timog** *n* south
**timog - silangan** *n* southeast
**timon** *n* helm
**tinadtad** *n* chop
**tinaga** *v* bludgeon
**tinaggihan** *v* refuse
**tinago** *v* store
**tinamaan** *v* hit
**tinanggap** *n* intake
**tinapay** *n* bread
**tindahan** *n* store
**tindahan ng aklat** *n* bookstore
**tindera** *n* seller
**tindig** *n* pose
**tingga** *n* platinum
**tingin** *n* look
**tingkayad** *n* tiptoe
**tingnan** *v* look at
**tingnan muli** *v* go over
**tinidor** *n* fork
**tinig** *n* voice
**tinigil** *v* stop by
**tinik** *n* thorn
**tiniwalag** *n* dismissal
**tinta** *n* ink
**tinulungan** *v* aid
**tinusta** *v* toast
**tinyente** *n* lieutenant
**tipak** *n* block
**tipirin** *adv* sparingly
**tipunin** *v* assemble
**tira** *n* leftovers, scrap
**tirahan** *v* scrap
**tirante** *n* suspenders
**tirintas** *n* braid
**tisa** *n* chalk
**tisis** *n* thesis
**tistisin** *v* operate
**tiwala** *n* credibility
**tiya** *n* aunt
**tiyak** *adj* certain, sure
**tiyak na tiyak** *adv* undoubtedly
**tiyakin** *v* ascertain
**tiyan** *n* stomach
**tiyo** *n* uncle
**tolda** *n* tent
**tonelada** *n* ton

**tonika** *n* tonic
**tono** *n* tone, tune
**tonsil** *n* tonsil
**tore** *n* tower
**torero** *n* bull fighter
**torneyo** *n* tournament
**torta** *n* omelette
**tostrador** *n* toaster
**totoo** *adv* really
**trabahador** *n* worker
**trabaho** *n* job, work
**tradisyonal** *adj* classic
**trahedya** *n* tragedy
**trak** *n* tractor, truck
**trak na panghila** *n* tow truck
**trangkaso** *n* flu
**trapiko** *n* traffic
**trapiko** *v* traffic
**traydor** *n* traitor
**tren** *n* train
**tribo** *n* tribe
**trompeta** *n* trumpet
**trono** *n* throne
**tropa** *n* troop
**tropeyo** *n* trophy
**tropiko** *n* tropic
**tsaa** *n* tea
**tsaleko** *n* vest
**tsart** *n* chart
**tsek** *n* check
**tseke** *n* paycheck
**tsimenea** *n* fireplace
**tsimeneya** *n* chimney
**tsinelas** *n* slipper
**tsismis** *n* gossip
**tsismosa** *adj* nosy
**tsokolate** *n* chocolate
**tsunami** *n* tidal wave
**tsuper** *n* chauffeur
**tuamakas** *v* escape
**tubero** *n* plumber
**tubig** *n* fluid, water
**tubo** *n* gain, profit
**tubong bayan** *n* hometown
**tugunin** *v* correspond
**tuhod** *n* knee
**tuka** *n* beak, peck
**tukain** *v* peck
**tuklasin** *v* explore
**tuksuhin** *v* tempt
**tuktok** *n* crest, summit
**tula** *n* poem, poetry
**tulad** *pre* like
**tulad ng** *c* as
**tularan** *n* format
**tulay** *n* bridge
**tuldok** *n* period, dot
**tuli** *n* circumcision
**tuliin** *v* circumcise
**tulo** *n* drip
**tulog** *adj* asleep
**tulog** *n* sleep
**tulong** *n* aid, help
**tulong-tulong** *n* coordination

T

**tuloy-tuloy** *adj* continuous
**tulungan** *v* assist, help
**tuluyan** *n* continuity
**tumaas** *v* move up, rise
**tumaas o bumaba** *v* fluctuate
**tumagal** *v* outlast
**tumagas** *v* leak
**tumaghoy** *v* howl
**tumahimik** *v* silence
**tumahol** *v* bark
**tumakas** *v* defect, flee
**tumakas** *n* deserter
**tumakbong mabilis** *v* dash
**tumalbog** *v* bounce
**tumalbog** *adj* reflexive
**tumalikod** *v* rear
**tumalon** *v* jump, leap
**tumambak** *v* pile up
**tumangis** *v* cry
**tumango** *v* nod
**tumaob** *v* capsize
**tumatagos** *n* piercing
**tumatawa** *v* chuckle
**tumatawag** *n* calling
**tumawa** *v* laugh
**tumayo** *v* get up, stand up
**tumbukin** *v* drive at
**tumibok** *v* pulsate
**tumigil** *v* shut up, stop
**tumili** *v* screech
**tumindig** *v* erect, arise
**tumingin** *v* look
**tumingin sandali** *v* glance
**tumira** *v* reside, dwell
**tumitibok** *v* throb
**tumitig** *v* gaze, stare
**tumitira** *v* lodge
**tumiwalag** *v* secede
**tumiwarik** *v* overturn
**tumog** *n* sound
**tumor** *n* tumor
**tumubo** *v* grow up
**tumulo** *v* drip
**tumuloy** *v* come in
**tumungga** *v* guzzle
**tumunog** *v* sound
**tuna** *n* tuna
**tunawin** *v* dissolve
**tunawin** *n* thaw
**tunay** *adj* genuine, real
**tunay na lalaki** *adj* virile
**tunay na tunay** *adj* undeniable
**tungkod** *n* cane, staff
**tungkol sa ina** *adj* maternal
**tungkol sa mata** *adj* optical
**tungkulin** *n* capacity
**tungo sa** *pre* towards
**tunog** *n* dial tone
**tunog ng ahas** *v* hiss
**tupa** *n* lamb, sheep
**tupi** *n* crease, pleat
**turismo** *n* tourism
**turista** *n* tourist
**turko** *adj* Turk

**Turkya** *n* Turkey
**turnilyo** *n* screw
**turnilyuhin** *v* screw
**turo** *n* advice
**turuan** *v* educate
**tuso** *adj* shrewd
**tusukin** *v* pierce, prick
**tuta** *n* puppy
**tutuli** *n* earwax
**tuusin** *v* compute
**tuwa** *n* cheers
**tuwalya** *n* towel
**tuwid** *adj* straight
**tuwing ika-apat** *adj* quarterly
**tuyain** *v* deride, mock
**tuyo** *adj* dried
**tuyong damo** *n* hay
**tuyot** *adj* arid
**tyan** *n* tummy
**tyani** *n* tweezers
**tyun ap** *v* tune up
**ubas** *n* grape

**ubasan** *n* grapevine
**ubo** *n* cough
**ubod** *n* bud, pulp
**ubusin** *v* deplete
**ugali** *n* character, trait
**ugaling bata** *adj* childish
**ugat** *n* artery, vein
**ugong** *n* buzz
**uhaw** *adj* thirsty
**uking** *n* cinder
**ukol sa** *pre* about, regarding
**ukol sa** *adj* akin
**ukol sa bukid** *adj* rural
**ukol sa puso** *n* angina
**ukol sa puso** *adj* cardiac
**ukol sa tubig** *n* artisan
**ukol sa utak** *adj* cerebral
**ulan** *n* rain
**ulang** *n* lobster
**ulap** *n* cloud
**ulap na hamog** *n* fog
**ulat** *n* report
**ulat ng oras** *n* timetable
**ulila** *n* orphan
**uling** *n* coal, ore
**uliran** *adj* ideal
**ulit** *adv* anew
**ulit** *n* recurrence
**ulitin** *adv* again

**ulitin** *v* repeat
**ulol** *v* fool
**ulol** *adj* silly
**ulser** *n* ulcer
**ululin** *adj* fool
**umaambon** *v* drizzle
**umaan** *v* pass
**umaasa** *v* expect
**umaasa** *adj* hopeful
**umaayon** *adj* consistent
**umabante** *v* pull ahead
**umaga** *n* morning
**umagos** *v* flow
**umakyat** *v* ascend, go up
**umalis** *v* depart, vacate
**umangal** *v* complain
**umani** *v* harvest
**umapaw** *v* exude
**umapila** *v* appeal
**umasa** *v* lean on
**umasa sa** *v* rely on
**umasim** *v* curdle
**umatras** *v* move back
**umawit** *v* sing
**umayaw** *v* quit
**umayon** *v* adapt
**umayon** *adj* compliant
**umayos** *v* behave
**umbok** *n* hump
**umihi** *v* urinate
**umilag** *v* shirk, shun
**uminom** *v* drink
**umiral** *v* prevail
**umistambay** *v* hang around
**umiwas** *adj* preventive
**umiyak** *v* cry, weep
**umpisa** *v* commence
**umpisahan** *v* initiate
**umubo** *v* cough
**umuga** *v* sway
**umugong** *v* buzz
**umulan** *v* rain
**umulit** *v* recur
**umungol** *v* moan
**umunlad** *v* prosper
**umupo** *v* sit
**umurong** *v* shrink
**umusbong** *v* sprout
**umusok** *v* smoke
**umutang** *v* owe
**umuuga** *v* wobble
**umuupa** *n* lessor
**umuupo** *n* sitting
**umuutal** *v* slur
**una** *adj* first
**una sa lahat** *adj* foremost
**una sa lahat** *adv* primarily
**unahan** *v* overtake
**unan** *n* pillow
**unang labas** *n* debut
**unang palapag** *n* ground floor
**unang plano** *v* premeditate
**unano** *n* midget
**unawaan** *n* treaty

**unawain** *v* understand
**unggoy** *n* ape
**ungol** *n* moan
**unit-unti** *adv* piecemeal
**unlapi** *n* prefix
**unos** *n* cyclone
**unti-unti** *adj* gradual
**unwain** *v* comprehend
**unyon** *n* union
**uod** *n* worm
**upa** *n* lease, rent
**upahan** *v* employ, hire
**upos** *n* stub
**upuan** *n* seat, stool
**uri** *adj* kind
**uri** *n* species, type
**uri ng damo** *n* hashish
**uri ng mani** *n* walnut
**uri ng materyal** *n* specimen
**uri ng pagluluto** *n* steak
**urong-sulong** *adj* adamant
**usa** *n* deer
**usapin** *n* issue
**usigin** *v* prosecute
**uso** *n* fad, trend
**usok** *n* fumes
**utak** *n* brain, marrow
**utak sa buto** *n* bone marrow
**utang** *n* consignment
**utong** *n* nipple
**utos** *n* precept, order
**utusan** *v* command
**uwak** *n* crow
**uwiang pasyente** *n* outpatient

**wagi** *n* victory
**wakas** *n* collapse, end
**wakas** *adj* ultimate
**wakasan** *v* end
**wala** *v* empty, nothing
**wala** *pre* none
**wala** *pro* no one
**wala ninuman** *pro* nobody
**wala sa panahon** *adj* untimely
**walang sahig** *adj* groundless
**walang alambre** *adj* wireless
**walang anak** *adj* childless
**walang asal** *v* misbehave
**walang awa** *adj* merciless
**walang bahala** *n* carelessness
**walang basehan** *adj* baseless
**walang bayad** *adj* complimentary
**walang buhay** *adj* lifeless
**walang dahilan** *adj* inexcusable
**walang dangal** *adj* dishonorable
**walang desisyon** *adj* indecisive
**walang Diyos** *adj* godless
**walang emosyon** *adj* impersonal

U

W

**walang galang** *n* brat
**walang galang** *adj* impolite
**walang gana** *adj* disinterested
**walang ginagawa** *adj* idle
**walang gulugod** *adj* spineless
**walang halaga** *adj* petty
**walang hanggan** *adj* endless
**walang hiya** *adj* shameless
**walang hugis** *adj* amorphous
**walang humpay** *adv* nonstop
**walang ingat** *adj* careless
**walang isip** *adj* irrational
**walang kahulugan** *n* nonsense
**walang kakayanan** *n* disability
**walang karanasan** *adj* inexplicable
**walang kasiyahan** *adj* insatiable
**walang katapatan** *n* insincerity
**walang katapusan** *adj* infinite
**walang katiyakan** *n* insecurity
**walang kawad** *adj* cordless
**walang kinalaman** *adj* unrelated
**walang koryente** *n* blackout
**walang laban** *adj* defenseless
**walang lakas** *adj* powerless
**walang laman** *adj* empty
**walang lasa** *adj* tasteless
**walang laylayan** *adj* seamless
**walang malay** *adj* unconscious
**walang manggas** *adj* sleeveless
**walang masabi** *adj* speechless
**walang metal** *adj* unleaded
**walang moralidad** *n* immorality
**walang oras** *adj* timeless
**walang pag-asa** *adj* desperate
**walang pag-iimbot** *adj* unassuming
**walang pagkaka-isa** *n* disunity
**walang pagod** *adj* tireless
**walang pagsisisi** *adj* blameless
**walang pahintulot** *n* disapproval
**walang pakay** *adj* aimless
**walang paniwala** *n* agnostic
**walang pera** *adj* penniless
**walang proteksyon** *adj* unprotected
**walang punla** *adj* seedless
**walang puso** *adj* heartless
**walang sandata** *adj* unarmed
**walang saysay** *adj* pointless
**walang silbi** *v* atrophy
**walang silbi** *n* disadvantage
**walang silbi** *adj* useless
**walang sira** *adj* flawless
**walang tahanan** *adj* homeless
**walang takot** *adj* intrepid
**walang tibay** *adj* unstable
**walang tigil** *adj* relentless
**walang tiwala** *n* distrust
**walang trabaho** *adj* jobless
**walang ulap** *adj* cloudless
**walanga kabuluhan** *adj* senseless
**walang-bisa** *n* annulment
**walanghiya** *adj* disgraceful
**walang-kabuluhan** *n* farce
**walang-laman** *adj* void
**walis** *n* broom

**walo** *adj* eight
**walrus** *n* walrus
**walumpu** *adj* eighty
**wasakin** *v* raze, wreck
**wasto** *adj* precise
**wat** *n* watt
**wealang halaga** *adj* meaningless
**websayt** *n* web site
**welga** *n* strike, walkout
**wika** *n* language
**winakasan** *v* break off
**wisikin** *v* wiggle
**wlang hanggan** *adj* indefinite

**yakap** *n* embrace
**yakapin** *v* embrace
**yanig** *n* jolt
**yaon** *adj* those
**yapak** *n* footstep
**yapakan** *v* tread
**yapusin** *v* cuddle
**yarda** *n* yard
**yari sa kahoy** *adj* wooden
**yari sa kamay** *adj* handmade
**yate** *n* yacht
**yaya** *n* babysitter
**yelo** *n* frost, ice
**yelo sa dagat** *n* iceberg
**yema** *n* yolk
**yero** *n* zinc
**yodo** *n* iodine
**yugto** *n* chapter
**yumanig** *v* jolt
**yumuko** *v* bend

# Word to Word® Bilingual Dictionary Series

**Language - Item Code - Pages**
**ISBN #**

**Albanian - 500X - 306 pgs**
ISBN - 978-0-933146-49-5

**Amharic - 820X - 362 pgs**
ISBN - 978-0-933146-59-4

**Arabic - 650X - 378 pgs**
ISBN - 978-0-933146-41-9

**Bengali - 700X - 372 pgs**
ISBN - 978-0-933146-30-3

**Burmese - 705X - 310 pgs**
ISBN - 978-0-933146-50-1

**Cambodian - 710X - 376 pgs**
ISBN - 978-0-933146-40-2

**Chinese - 715X - 340 pgs**
ISBN - 978-0-933146-22-8

**Farsi - 660X - 328 pgs**
ISBN - 978-0-933146-33-4

**French - 530X - 320 pgs**
ISBN - 978-0-933146-36-5

**German - 535X - 352 pgs**
ISBN - 978-0-933146-93-8

**Gujarati - 720X - 334 pgs**
ISBN - 978-0-933146-98-3

**Haitian-Creole - 545X - 322 pgs**
ISBN - 978-0-933146-23-5

**Hebrew - 665X - 316 pgs**
ISBN - 978-0-933146-58-7

**Hindi - 725X - 362 pgs**
ISBN - 978-0-933146-31-0

**Hmong - 728X - 294 pgs**
ISBN - 978-0-933146-31-0

**Italian - 555X - 362 pgs**
ISBN - 978-0-933146-51-8

All languages are two-way:
English-Language / Language-English.
More languages in planning and production.

**Japanese - 730X - 372 pgs**
ISBN - 978-0-933146-42-6

**Korean - 735X - 344 pgs**
ISBN - 978-0-933146-97-6

**Lao - 740X - 319 pgs**
ISBN - 978-0-933146-54-9

**Pashto - 760X - 348 pgs**
ISBN - 978-0-933146-34-1

**Polish - 575X - 358 pgs**
ISBN - 978-0-933146-64-8

**Portuguese - 580X - 362 pgs**
ISBN - 978-0-933146-94-5

**Punjabi - 765X - 358 pgs**
ISBN - 978-0-933146-32-7

**Romanian - 585X - 354 pgs**
ISBN - 978-0-933146-91-4

**Russian - 590X - 298 pgs**
ISBN - 978-0-933146-92-1

**Somali - 830X - 320 pgs**
ISBN- 978-0-933146-52-5

**Spanish - 600X - 346 pgs**
ISBN - 978-0-933146-99-0

**Swahili - 835X - 308 pgs**
ISBN - 978-0-933146-55-6

**Tagalog - 770X - 332 pgs**
ISBN - 978-0-933146-37-2

**Thai - 780X - 354 pgs**
ISBN - 978-0-933146-35-8

**Turkish - 615X - 348 pgs**
ISBN - 978-0-933146-95-2

**Ukrainian - 620X - 337 pgs**
ISBN - 978-0-933146-25-9

**Urdu - 790X - 360 pgs**
ISBN - 978-0-933146-39-6

**Vietnamese - 795X - 324 pgs**
ISBN - 978-0-933146-96-9

## Order Information

To order our Word to Word® Bilingual Dictionaries or any other products from Bilingual Dictionaries, Inc., please contact us at (951) 296-2445 or visit us at **www.BilingualDictionaries.com**. Visit our website to download our current Catalog/Order Form, view our products, and find information regarding Bilingual Dictionaries, Inc.

PO Box 1154 • Murrieta, CA 92562 • Tel: (951) 296-2445 • Fax: (951) 461-3092
www.BilingualDictionaries.com

## Special Dedication & Thanks

Bilingual Dicitonaries, Inc. would like to thank all the teachers from various districts accross the country for their useful input and great suggestions in creating a Word to Word® standard. We encourage all students and teachers using our bilingual learning materials to give us feedback. Please send your questions or comments via email to support@bilingualdictionaries.com.